Goethe and Anna Amalia:

A Forbidden Love?

Goethe and Anna Amalia:

A Forbidden Love?

Ettore Ghibellino

Translation: Dan Farrelly

Carysfort Press

A Carysfort Press Book in association with Peter Lang

Goethe and Anna Amalia: A Forbidden Love?
by Ettore Ghibellino

Translated from the German by Dan Farrelly

Original title: *J.W. Goethe und Anna Amalia: Eine verbotene Liebe*
A.J. Denkena Verlag, Weimar

First published in Ireland in 2007 as a paperback original by
Carysfort Press, 58 Woodfield, Scholarstown Road,
Dublin 16, Ireland
ISBN 978-1-78997-121-7

Typeset by Carysfort Press
Cover design by Alan Bennis

This book is published with the financial assistance of
The Arts Council (An Chomhairle Ealaíon), Dublin, Ireland

Carysfort Press acknowledges the financial assistance of
Ireland Literature Exchange (Translation Fund), Dublin, Ireland.
www.irelandliterature.com
info@irelandliterature.com

For Ilse Nagelschmidt

DF

Contents

Illustrations

Nos 1, 3-15, 17-20, 22-26, 28-33, 35, 37, 39, 40 by courtesy of Klassik Stiftung Weimar

Front Cover: by Bennis Design, using nos 18 and 19

Translator's Preface

Ettore Ghibellino's *J.W. Goethe and Anna Amalia: Eine Verbotene Liebe* first attracted my interest as a book which contains, I think, a revolutionary hypothesis. The accepted opinion, namely, that Goethe's platonic lover during the first decade of his life in Weimar was Charlotte von Stein, one of Anna Amalia's ladies-in-waiting, is challenged in this book by the hypothesis that Goethe's beloved was not Charlotte von Stein but the Dowager Duchess Anna Amalia herself. Naturally, this hypothesis which Ghibellino has set out to prove has caused consternation in some quarters. Since the publication of Goethe's letters to Frau von Stein, scholars have generally accepted that Charlotte was the woman who inspired him to write much of his post-1775 love poetry and, in particular, the plays *Iphigenie auf Tauris* and *Torquato Tasso*. One of the main reasons given for his 'escape' to Italy in 1786 has been that he could no longer bear being kept at arm's length by Charlotte, a married woman, and it has often been thought that, in his late thirties, he had his first full sexual experiences in Rome in the arms of an Italian widow.

Ghibellino claims that Charlotte von Stein was presented as Goethe's (platonic) lover as part of a highly effective cover-up – designed, at first, by Goethe and Anna Amalia to protect their relationship from public view, and then by the Ducal family to protect its precarious position as a tiny Duchy at a time when Prussia and Austria strove to swallow up small, vulnerable principalities. The personal danger to both Goethe and Anna Amalia from a relationship which was not acceptable to the ruling European families was all too evident from the experience, in 1773, of the Queen of Denmark and her lover. When it was discovered that the Queen had given birth to a child fathered by her middle-class lover, the Queen was sent into exile and her lover was executed!

The *need* for a cover-up was apparent. The *fact* that there was, indeed, an official cover-up is suggested by the disappearance of all the documents from Weimar archives which could throw any light on the relationship between Goethe and Anna Amalia. When in 1827 the Grand Duke Carl August deputed Chancellor von Müller to put Anna Amalia's papers and letters in order and to catalogue them, von Müller did this and showed the result to Goethe. Today there is no trace of the papers and letters. Not even the catalogue is to be found. Goethe's own bequest was completely in the control of the Ducal family and shows clear traces of censorship.

One of the fascinating aspects of Ghibellino's book is his thesis that many of the thousand letters that Goethe wrote to 'Charlotte von Stein' could not have been meant for her at all – for a variety of reasons. One of the most convincing of these reasons is that the addressee would, in some cases, need to have had considerable knowledge of Italian and Latin. These languages were not at all part of Charlotte's education, whereas Anna Amalia had a thorough grounding in both of them. Ghibellino maintains that the loyal lady-in-waiting had become a conduit for letters which Goethe could not have addressed directly to the Dowager Duchess for fear of their love being discovered.

Ghibellino offers much more. Many questions arise from his interpretations of *Tasso*, *Römische Elegien*, *Wilhelm Meister*, the *West-östlicher Divan*, and *Trilogie der Leidenschaft*. Future studies will be dedicated to each of the problems he raises, and further serious research is being carried out to show that his hypothesis clarifies issues which heretofore have either not been clarified or not even identified. Documents unearthed in archives outside of Weimar have given strong indications that Goethe and Anna Amalia had a love relationship which they tried to conceal. Further archives – also outside of Weimar's control – are being examined for more evidence to support the hypothesis.

A central claim of Ghibellino's thesis is that Goethe's creative writing also functions as autobiography. *Dichtung und Wahrheit* (Goethe's autobiographical work written between 1811 and 1831) covers the years from his birth in Frankfurt am Main (1749) until the year of his arrival in Weimar in 1775. While he continued, after 1813, to write autobiographically about his Italian Journey – he was in Italy 1786-1788 – and about his time with Duke Carl August's army in France around 1792, it has to be noted that these were periods he spent *outside* Weimar. There are no such autobiographical writings about his first Weimar period from November 1775 until his departure for Italy in September 1786. Ghibellino explains this by reference to the extreme danger that might result from an open description of his personal circumstances in Weimar. An important clue to the understanding of Goethe's solution to this problem is his famous statement that all of his writings are fragments of an extensive confession. Ghibellino sees in this a hint – to be followed up – that for these years Goethe's creative works are the substitute for open autobiographical writing, so that, for instance, the poems, the plays (*Iphigenie* and *Tasso*) and the *Wilhelm Meister* novels tell the story of his life in Weimar.

Naturally, this contention will require further examination and discussion. It is not Ghibellino's aim to replace literary criticism and analysis with a study of the biographical elements included in the works, but this latter study is not invalidated by the fact that the works are literary. In other areas of research in which the sources of biographical detail are sparse – as is the case, for instance, with some mediaeval poets – scholars are confident that they can glean biographical (and social) information from the works of lyrical poets. This is also the experience of some art historians, who combine artistic analysis of paintings with a study of what the paintings yield up about the life and times of the painter. The term 'biographical fallacy' is to be handled with care.

Readers who are convinced by the evidence supporting Ghibellino's hypothesis will see in it the discovery of one of the very great love stories in European history – to rank, for instance, with that of Dante and Beatrice, and Petrarch and Laura.

Alongside my role as translator I have, with the author's consent, performed a modest editorial function. I trust that in this I have done the book no harm. My thanks are due to Ettore Ghibellino for his expansive generosity and willingness to help and advise. I admire his dedication to ferreting out the truth through his probing questions. The careful and thorough research evinced in the thirty-five pages of Ghibellino's endnotes should earn his book an important place in the modern world of Goethe scholarship.[1]

My thanks are due to Ilse Nagelschmidt, who first drew my attention to the existence of Ghibellino's book and who has been an inspiration every step of the way; to Lorraine Byrne Bodley for her many useful comments and suggestions regarding the translation itself; to Éimear O'Connor and Mary McAuliffe for advice on matters

[1] One editorial note: the flawed language of the French quotations is not the responsibility of any living person, but is a reflection of the language as it was spoken and written at court in Germany around 1800.

of art history and literary history; to Lilian Chambers of Carysfort Press for her eagle-eyed scrutiny of the manuscript; to Eamonn Jordan of Carysfort Press for his unflagging moral support; to Barbara Brown for the endless hours she spent, with great care and expertise, poring over the bibliography and the forest of scholarly endnotes; to Sheila Kreyszig for corrections of the manuscript and for useful suggestions regarding style and formatting.

Special thanks are due to my wife, Una, for her moral support and for the interest she takes in all I do. At times she is a miracle of tolerance. My daughters, Noreen and Ciara, and my son, Mark, give me – perhaps without realizing it – continual encouragement.

My thanks are due, finally, to the Ireland Literature Exchange for supporting Carysfort Press in commissioning this translation.

A last word: any errors which, despite the generous help I have received from various quarters, may still have crept into the manuscript, are my own, just as the entire translation, for good or ill, is also my own.

Dan Farrelly, Dublin, March 2007

1 | Introduction

Once error lies like a foundation under the ground
It will be built on, and never be seen in the light of day.
Xenien (c. 1796), 165

...in the sciences the most absolute freedom is necessary, for here we are not working for today and tomorrow but for a progressive series of ages beyond our grasp. But even if error gets the upper hand in science, there will still remain a minority favouring truth, and if truth withdraws into the mind of one single man, that does not matter. This one man will work away silently, in obscurity, and a time will come when people will ask about him and his convictions or when, in a more generally enlightened age, these views can dare to re-emerge.
Wilhelm Meisters Wanderjahre [Journeyman's Years] (1829), III, 14

Innumerable works deal with the life of the poet Johann Wolfgang Goethe, attempting to interpret, explain, and understand his unique literary works. But more than 170 years after his death, and despite an undiminishingly intense preoccupation with his life and work, many noticeable contradictions remain. Why did Goethe remain in Weimar in 1775, and why, at the age of only twenty-six, was he appointed minister in the face of vigorous opposition? Why did he not marry and why instead did he choose to enter into an indefinable liaison with the married Frau von Stein? In 1786, why did he rush off to Italy and wait for weeks in the port of Venice? On his return from Italy, why did he take Christiane Vulpius for a lover, although he did not treat her as a social equal; and why did he not marry her for nearly two decades, even though his son thereby grew up as a bastard? In his writings, why does the theme of a forbidden love for a highly placed, unattainable woman constantly recur? Why does Goethe's love poetry give witness to the profoundest feeling of love for 'a unique one', although he is supposed to have had only superficial relationships with many women?

These and other contradictions can be explained if we suppose that Goethe loved the Duchess Anna Amalia and remained true to her until the end of his life. Since this love was forbidden, it had to be concealed. But the lovers were still able to communicate their tragic love story to the world. They had to do it in code, which must be the reason why for most of his life Goethe had recourse to 'the enigmatic, to ciphers, hermetic formulas, masks, disguises, and encoding'.[1]

Since this book [the German original] first appeared, the question has often been asked: 'Why did no one until now know about Goethe's love relationship with Anna Amalia?'[2] The main reason for this is that in the Duchy of Sachsen-Weimar-Eisenach it was treated as a state secret. From 1786 onwards, all the Dukes used every means at their disposal to suppress all documents referring to Goethe's secret love for the Princess Anna Amalia. The basis of Goethe research was subject to the massive influence of the family of Sachsen-Weimar-Eisenach. The Dukes could manipulate the archives however they wished. It was known amongst researchers that 'the Weimar archive ... had more seals and locks than any other' (1858).[3] Researchers knew exactly where crucial documents were kept: 'Much and perhaps the most important [material] is not in the archive at all, but in the private library of the Grand Duke' (1857).[4] Even when crucial documents were not in the Grand Duke's possession, there were ways and means of preventing their publication. This is evidenced by the case of the heiress of Carl Ludwig von Knebel, Goethe's close friend. When selling manuscripts contained in Knebel's bequest in 1864, she warned the agent entrusted with the transaction to examine the contents most thoroughly and search for utterances which could compromise the family von Sachsen-Weimar-Eisenach, since 'her whole livelihood would be endangered for the slightest thing that might come to light'. When he married Luise Rudorff (1798) Knebel adopted her illegitimate son (1796), a child of Carl August. The 'diary from the "eventful year 1798"' is missing down to this day.[5]

All but a few of Anna Amalia's letters to Goethe and to her son Carl August are considered lost. When Carl August entrusted Anna Amalia's letters and papers to Chancellor von Müller, requiring him to look through and catalogue them, von Müller reported with enthusiasm that these would throw 'a glorious light on the character of Goethe and the Duchess!'[6] When shown the first results of von Müller's work, Goethe wrote to him on 24 July 1828:

> It is a great joy to me to know that this work, which has to be carried out with insight and loyalty as well as caution and taste, is in your

> hands. In this way very special documents will be rescued; [they are] priceless, not from a political but from a human point of view, because only these papers will give a proper insight into the way things were at the time.

These papers have disappeared without trace. When what was left of Anna Amalia's letters was, from 1872, carefully sifted through, the ruling Grand Duke insisted on a two-fold right: to correct and to supervise in the case of any publication – which, however, was not to come about.[7]

Until now it has been impossible to explain why Goethe's grandchildren, for more than half a century and for no apparent reason, refused access to his bequest to researchers, writers, and publishers, most of them ardent admirers of Goethe. 'They have been warned, scolded, spurned because they did not open the way to the temple's treasures.'[8] From childhood onwards Goethe's heirs were tied to the family Sachsen-Weimar-Eisenach. They were treated generously and shown good-will. In response the Ducal family expected that documents in the bequest which could have revealed his forbidden love for Anna Amalia would not become public. The sale negotiations in 1884 between Goethe's grandson Walther Wolfgang (1818-1885) and the German Reich regarding the sale of Goethe's bequest show, for example, that the reigning Grand Duke took it for granted that he had wide-ranging claims over the bequest. He made it a condition of the sale

> that nothing of it will ever be published without my express knowledge and permission. If this [directive] is not observed I would use every means in my power – including Emperor and Empress – to prevent the transaction with the Reich.[9]

In the end, Walther Wolfgang bequeathed his grandfather's literary and family archive to the reigning Grand Duchess Sophie. The day he died, 16 April 1885, the Grand Duke wrote in his diary: 'I command that all important rooms be sealed.' Well-informed archivists knew what happened next:

> The Princess [Sophie] acted immediately: without hesitation she had the valuable papers, which, in the meantime had been shamefully covered in dust, brought to her in baskets and boxes ... First she herself, protected from the dust by long gloves, sat for days and paged through the uniquely valuable inheritance, in admiration, astonishment, and horror here and there in her prudish way, and tried to alter or even blot out anything against the Church, anything erotic or anything sexual.[10]

She actually cleansed Goethe's bequest as had already happened with Anna Amalia's papers. In 1998 a document surfaced which was among those deliberately suppressed. An anonymous vendor offered the Goethe National Museum, through the Hamburg art dealer le Claire, a drawing of Goethe's (ill. 15), which shows an encoding of Anna Amalia's initials. This invites the obvious question whether the anonymous vendor owns any further revealing documents belonging to Goethe and Anna Amalia.

It is true that the Sachsen-Weimar-Eisenach family played the role of patron and promoter of Goethe research by setting up the Goethe Archive in 1885; in the same year it encouraged the formation of a Goethe Society, of which it became patron; in 1886 it made Goethe's house accessible to the public as a National Museum and in 1887 commissioned a comprehensive edition of Goethe's works. At the same time they distorted Goethe's and Anna Amalia's biographies by suppressing, holding back, and manipulating crucial documents. A three-volume cleansed selection of Goethe's letters to Frau von Stein – in other words, to Anna Amalia – appeared between 1848 and 1851, at a time when there was no longer anyone alive who could have critically appraised Goethe's pretended 'love relationship' with Frau von Stein during the period 1775 to 1786. These letters contained deliberate references to Frau von Stein's personal and family sphere, so that anyone who – with permission or otherwise – saw the letters would not realize that Anna Amalia was Goethe's lover. Apart from the suppression and cleansing of documents, it was the camouflage achieved by these little additions that made the cover-up supplied by Frau von Stein virtually impenetrable. In 1874 a completely uncritical two-volume biography of Frau von Stein appeared showing her as Goethe's friend. Once this error became the foundation stone of Goethe scholarship, from around 1885 the cleansed Goethe bequest was made more and more available under the supervision of cultural officials who were loyal to the monarchy.

Critical observers suspected that the foundations of Goethe scholarship were laid in sand, a result

> of the secrecy and of the whole way Goethe's letters and writings, his life and his memory were handled. There was no lack of intentional concealment, distortion of the truth, arbitrary changes and omissions and the like.[11]

But after the epoch-making transition from the monarchy to the Republic in 1918, the fundamentals of Goethe scholarship were no longer seriously questioned. This is explained largely by the continuity of personnel in culture administration and of researchers – both groups mostly loyal to the monarchy. But Goethe's biography remained full of mysteries and obvious contradictions. The fact that important documents of both Anna Amalia and Goethe were longer to be found in the archives – for instance, the official correspondence between them during Goethe's first decade in Weimar – should have attracted attention. It was known that Chancellor von Müller had drawn up a detailed catalogue of Anna Amalia's letters and documents. There was never any inquiry as to why this is no longer extant.[12]

At the same time there is no lack of contemporary sources which mention the love between Goethe and Anna Amalia. However, until now they have not been analysed. Of great value here are the letters of the wife of Count Johann Eustach Görtz, who was tutor to the Princes in Weimar from 1762 to 1775 and from 1778 was a Prussian diplomat with the rank of Minister. Fortunately, these letters were kept in the far-off Donzdorf near Göppingen, otherwise it is likely that they would have been suppressed like those of Goethe and Anna Amalia. In a letter of 12 October 1782, for example, Countess Görtz writes to her husband:

> Frau von Stein continues to play the role assigned to her as best she can. Nearly every evening in her house she eats potatoes with Goethe and the Duchess [Anna Amalia]. Her husband turns a blind eye to all of this.

Excerpts from these letters, which were written in French and show Goethe and Anna Amalia as secret lovers and Frau von Stein as a cover for her, were included in contemporaries' reports about Goethe. Passages from these letters appear here for the first time in English translations from the French.13 There are also other sources which point to a deception and which have not been evaluated. An example of this is found in the frequently cited memoirs of Countess Henriette von Egloffstein which only became accessible with the end of the monarchy in 1919. Here we read sentences like:

> In the meantime one must admire the skill with which this woman [Frau von Stein] was able to carry off her artificial game, so that even in later years she was considered to be Goethe's lover.

Since the available biographies of Goethe and of Anna Amalia were not questioned, these and other sources received no attention.

2 | The State Secret

Bid me not speak, bid me be silent
For my secret is imposed on me
My deepest inner self I'd show to you
But fate will not allow it.

When the time is right the light of day
Will banish night, which must be illuminated;
The hard rock will open its bosom
And not begrudge the earth its deeply hidden springs.

All find peace in the arms of a friend,
There the breast can give vent to its grief;
But my lips, now sealed because of a vow,
Will open only if the gods allow.
Mignon, *Wilhelm Meisters Lehrjahre* [Apprenticeship Years] (1790), V, 16

If strength and an open courageous character graces the man
Deep secrecy perhaps becomes him still more.
Reticence, you conqueror of cities! Princess of the peoples!
Precious goddess, who leads me securely through life,
What fate is mine! In fun the muse, like Amor,
The villain, opens my closed lips.
Römische Elegien (1790), XX

The poet, scientist, and statesman Johann Wolfgang von Goethe (1749-1832) was forced, until the end of his life, to keep a secret about the woman for whom he had undying love. Without knowledge of this secret an essential part of his work cannot be understood and his greatness as a truly loving poet can only be glimpsed. When at the end of *Torquato Tasso* (1780-1790) it becomes clear that the hero has a forbidden love for the Princess and not the lady-in-waiting of the same name whom they hide behind, we read:

> When something quite unexpected happens,
> When we gaze upon something monstrous,
> Our mind stops still a while,
> We have nothing to compare it with.

Late in life Goethe said, referring to the secret:

> The true history of the first decade of my Weimar years I could only present in the guise of a fable or a fairytale; the actual fact is something the world would never credit. ... I would hurt a lot of people, perhaps do some good, but only for a few, and do myself no justice ... the world may know what I have become and what I have achieved; what it was like in detail is to remain my secret alone.[14]

The Minister Goethe was obliged to keep silence. He could only hint at the secret, which he entrusted to his poetic writings: 'To you, hexameter, to you, pentameter, let it be entrusted', as he wrote in his *Römische Elegien* (1788-1790) regarding his 'deep secret'.

Goethe's autobiography *Dichtung und Wahrheit* ends with his departure for Weimar at the age of twenty-six. Individual autobiographical works each reflect only a part of his later life. Communication of the full course of his life was to be entrusted to both parts of his *Wilhelm Meister* novel, if only in an encoded form. There are only two works at which Goethe worked for nearly his whole life: *Faust* (c. 1772-1831), and *Wilhelm Meister* (1777-1829). In a conversation with his literary assistant Johann Peter Eckermann (1792-1854) on 25 December 1825 Goethe gave an indication about how his novel was to be interpreted:

> Beneath the seeming trivialities of *Wilhelm Meister* there is something higher, and it is only a question of having eyes, knowledge of the world, and a sufficient overview to become aware of the large picture within the small. For others, life as it is described is enough.

Only when one looks with 'eyes, knowledge of the world and an overview' can one find in the novel the proper representation of Goethe's life.

Previous accounts of Goethe's life in the first ten years of his life in Weimar are unconvincing in one essential point: his alleged love for Charlotte Albine Ernestine[15] von Stein, née Schardt (1742-1827). The love relationship with her is supposed to have begun shortly after his arrival in Weimar in November 1775 and to have lasted until 1789. Only the letters of Goethe to 'Frau von Stein' are extant. In the *Mitteilungen über Goethe* (1841) by Friedrich Wilhelm Riemer (1774-1845) – an attempt to give a living picture of the poet and statesman by someone who was Goethe's close collaborator for more than three decades– Frau von Stein is only mentioned in a footnote.[16] Not once does Goethe glorify the name of Frau von Stein in his writing. Only in the publication of Goethe's letters to 'Frau von Stein' in three volumes from 1848-1851 – letters which were in reality written to the Duchess Anna Amalia (1739-1807) – were details of the alleged love relationship with the lady-in-waiting made public. Since then it has been the subject of much discussion, moving between the 'worthlessness' of Frau von Stein' and her being Goethe's 'most beautiful creation', between 'wretchedness and an ideal image'. The writer Friedrich Martin von Bodenstedt (1819-1892) wanted, with the verses 'Blessed be the lofty bond/That gave birth to such glorious things',[17] to write off as superfluous the constantly recurring discussion of whether the relationship was an erotic one. Even today there are still attempts to define the alleged love relationship[18] – a sign that it is not convincing.

There is mention of a 'strange relationship',[19] 'one of the most mysterious love relationships in world literature',[20] 'this chimera of a relationship',[21] 'this half-real, half-love-affair',[22] or of 'one of the most contradictory phenomena of German literary history'.[23] 'To find out the truth is a wish, a dream', writes one biographer.[24] A recent attempt to describe the relationship between the two ends with the sad conclusion: ' ... one cannot help getting the impression that writing made him [Goethe] happier than the actual presence of Frau von Stein.'[25] A biographer writes about the personality of Frau von Stein: 'Taking all visible elements together one ends up with a kind of double being.'[26]

Already in Goethe's life-time many were puzzled by 'this strange relationship of Goethe to the Chief Equerry's wife'.[27] About a year after the death of Frau von Stein, Henriette von Egloffstein (1773-1864) wrote:

> The character of this woman [Frau von Stein] belonged indisputably to the noblest. Her mind, although I never thought it particularly significant, helped her to navigate past the many rocks of court life ... It is undeniable that Frau von Stein, with the best will in the world, had to possess a great deal of cunning and worldly wisdom; otherwise it would have been impossible to retain, until the end of her long career, a position which brought her, without the slightest interruption, so close to Duchess Luise and Goethe that only death could dissolve this deep relationship over which, even now as I write this, there is an impenetrable veil. Only Goethe is in a position to lift it, and he will hardly find a way to do it. As a result, even next generations will not come to any clearer judgement of something that remained a mystery to the great man's contemporaries. But,

> however this may be: what lies under the veil cannot be anything unworthy.[28]

Frau von Stein deviates quite crassly from the glorious poetic image that Goethe draws of his beloved. Even if taking into account the most positive reports about her, the seven-times mother remains immeasurably far from the ideal image drawn by Goethe. She can be represented as a cool and prudent woman, as interesting, but not beautiful, and as having an average education. But Goethe sings of something resembling a goddess, a highly cultured, very beautiful, rich, and in every respect outstanding woman. Poets like to represent reality in an idealized form, but Goethe never tires of showing that his beloved is a real woman, that he cannot find the words to celebrate her appropriately. In a letter to 'Frau von Stein' on 20 March 1782 we read:

> O best one, all my life I have had an ideal wish about how I want to be loved. I have in vain sought fulfillment always in a crazed dream, but now that the world becomes daily clearer to me, I find it finally in you in such a way that I can never lose it.'

On 17 June 1784 he writes to the same: 'In you I have a yard-stick for all women, even for all human beings; through your love a yard-stick for all of fate.' These comparisons do not fit Frau von Stein, the married lady-in-waiting, because through them Goethe raises the beloved into the highest spheres. Significantly, an alignment of Frau von Stein with famous female figures of poetry like Dante's Beatrice and Petrarch's Laura did not happen; she remains in the background, a contradictory figure surrounded by mystery. That Goethe presented the figure exactly as she was for him is seen in Tasso's confession (ll. 1092 ff.):

> Whatever resounds in my poetry
> I owe it all to one alone
> There is no vague mental image
> Hovering before my eyes
> Appearing sometimes in brilliant light
> Before my soul, and sometimes then withdrawing.
> I have seen it with my eyes,
> The paragon of every virtue, of all beauty.
> What is created with this as model
> Will remain.

And a few verses later (ll. 1105ff.):

> And what has greater right
> To survive for centuries and quietly
> Continue its work

Than the secret of a noble love
Entrusted modestly to a lovely song?

Tasso mentions the 'secret of a noble love', Goethe's monument to his beloved. With Frau von Stein there was, as such, no secret. Everything seemed to be completely out in the open. Precisely this is where what Goethe refers to as 'eyes, knowledge of the world, and overview' is to be applied, especially since Frau von Stein and Anna Amalia play prominent roles in Goethe's life. There are many indications that Goethe and Anna Amalia wanted the secret soon to be revealed. For Goethe the revelation of the secret of his life was of fundamental importance. His life is not a 'to some extent messed up life', as Johanna Schopenhauer (1766-1838), a profound admirer of Goethe, judged it to be.[29] In his old age Goethe was considered to be a 'stiff, cold person who did not at all seem to bear any relationship to his poetic works'.[30] What is at stake here is the truth about Goethe's whole work, since this cannot be properly interpreted without Anna Amalia as the beloved who is intimately bound up with him for his whole life. 'The more fiery and more convincing his words sound, the more they are a product of poetry', writes one biographer in relation to the letters to 'Frau von Stein'.[31] The love letters, which in the opinion of some are the 'most loving of all that were ever written',[32] were therefore to be seen as mere products of Goethe's imagination. Was Goethe then to be seen as 'incapable of great love and real loyalty'?[33] But, in Goethe's own words, what is presented in the foreground as life will not satisfy the 'genuine reader', who will have to look for a deeper meaning. With the uncovering of the Weimar state secret Goethe can be seen as a genuinely loving poet whose poetry has the mark of truth. Poetry is 'that which nature alone bestows,/Something that remains out of reach of all effort and striving,/Something that neither Gold,/Nor sword, nor cleverness, nor perseverance/Can force to happen.' (*Tasso* ll. 234ff.) Goethe is not unworthy of this high calling; he always wove only his own life in his writings, but he had to do it in code. During his whole life he could not swerve from the principle, 'to transform into an image, a poem, that which gave me joy or pain and thereby to have closure ... And so everything of mine that has become known is really nothing but fragments of a great confession'.[34] Goethe never used the word 'poetry' [Dichtung] in the sense of something freely invented. 'Truth is the body', according to Riemer, 'poetry is only the garment, the frame which limits and surrounds the real picture.'[35]

Goethe's leads are to be taken seriously. They point to the secret of his life. When asked by his long-time collaborator Friedrich Kräuter (1790-1856) to write something about the brilliant years of Duchess Anna Amalia during his first decade in Weimar, the aged Goethe replied: ‘I wouldn’t know how to describe this time. I would have to do it in the form of a fairytale, in which Amalia, the all-powerful fairy, enlivens and creates everything.’[36] From 1775 onwards, until his death, Goethe worked at writing this fairytale, and it is a question of finding the key to it, so that the ‘whole inner depths’ of a truly loving poet can become abundantly clear: ‘In due course the sun will drive away/The dark night, and it must be lit up.’

3 | Anna Amalia and Charlotte von Stein

> I will follow you, even if to the underworld.
>
> Charlotte von Stein, *Dido* (1795)

> Goethe keeps on talking about perfect love, and poor Frau von Stein, none so dumb as she, puts up with the public gossip – as well as what Goethe broadcasts – and the bad moods of his woman [Anna Amalia]. So you can see nothing has changed.
>
> *Countess Görtz to her husband,* 11 June 1780.

Goethe arrived in Weimar on 7 November 1775. Its population of around 6,000 was experiencing a change of government. Anna Amalia was handing over to her son Carl August (1757-1828), who, on 3 September was declared by Emperor Joseph II (1741-1790) to have reached his majority. Anna Amalia now bears the title of Dowager Duchess, which would not incline one to think of a beautiful 36-year-old woman who had a hunger for life. 'She is small of stature', said an unknown observer around this time,

> has a good appearance, a spiritual expression, a Brunswick nose, beautiful hands and feet; she walks lightly but majestically, speaks very beautifully, but quickly, and has in her whole attitude much that is pleasant and winning.[37]

An event at the end of 1775, in which Goethe and Carl August participated, gives an insight into the relationship between the Duchess Anna Amalia and her lady-in-waiting Frau von Stein. A participant reported:

> Suddenly the door opened and, behold, the old Duchess came in with the Chief Equerry's wife, an excellent, good, beautiful Frau von Stein. Both carried two old swords from the armoury, a yard longer than myself, and dubbed us knights. We remained sitting at table, and the

> ladies walked around us and poured champagne for us. After the meal we played blind man's buff. We kissed the Equerry's wife, who was standing beside the Duchess. In what other court does such a thing happen?[38]

Anna Amalia is indeed involved in the game, but she is shielded by the lady-in-waiting from anything that would be an abuse of etiquette, for the one who is kissed is Frau von Stein.

The duchy of Sachsen-Weimar-Eisenach was, because of divisions by inheritance, made up of separated states comprising a population of about 100,000.[39] In 1741, Ernst August I (1688-1748) –named 'The Tyrant' – had, in addition to the duchy of Weimar, inherited the duchy of Eisenach, as well as Jena and Allstedt. When he died he was survived by several daughters from two marriages, and the sickly eleven-year-old Crown Prince Ernst August Constantin (1737-1758). The country was deeply in debt. At first the Crown Prince was under the tutelage of the Duke of Gotha, who cherished the hope that, if the Crown Prince died childless, the duchy would fall to him. Thus the Prince was kept 'like a State prisoner under strict surveillance'.

> The poor orphan was subjected to the most unworthy treatment ... with a view to the complete destruction of his health – which was in any case unstable – or at least to the weakening of his mental strength, so that he could be declared incapable of governing.[40]

In December 1755, at the instigation of the Duke of Coburg, the Emperor in Vienna declared that he had reached his majority. Three months later Ernst August Constantin was in Brunswick looking for a bride. In March 1756 the marriage with Princess Anna Amalia took place. When the young duchess moved with her suite from Brunswick to Weimar, one of the chamber maids mocked: 'Is the gate being closed with a carrot?'[41] The ducal pair was 'a young couple enjoying life'; they 'resided in Schloss Belvedere, and played like children in the square at the front of it'.[42] In 1757 Anna Amalia gave birth to the Crown Prince, Carl August. By 1758 her husband had died. Anna Amalia was pregnant again at the time of his death, and in the same year her second child, Friedrich Ferdinand Constantin (1758-1793), was born.

Through the birth of her sons the hopes of the neighbouring Princes of Gotha and Coburg that the duchy might fall to them were dashed. Thanks to a secret will of her husband, Anna Amalia was to become the sole guardian of Carl August and Regent of the Duchy of Sachsen-Weimar-Eisenach.[43] Only after tough exchanges with the Viennese chancery of Emperor Francis I (1708-1765) – a man who himself lived in the shadow of his wife, Empress Maria Theresia (1717-

1780) – could Anna Amalia become sole Regent. Previously there had been talk of a shared guardianship between Anna Amalia and King Frederick V of Denmark. Then the Elector of Saxony, Frederick August II, was to be co-guardian and co-Regent. This latter was the prince who left governing to his corrupt minister, Henry Count of Brühl (1700-1763), who used his position for personal enrichment. After all the wheels were set in motion in Weimar against this solution, Anna Amalia took over her nineteen-year Regency on 30 August 1759. Her father was to be co-Regent until she herself reached her majority at the age of twenty-one. A few months after taking office, she sacked the powerful Minister, Count Heinrich von Bünau (1697-1762), so that the business of government was now in her hands. As Regent she distinguished herself by her clever manoeuvring in times of war. During the last phase of the Seven Years War (1756-1763) which resulted in the territorial status of 1756 remaining unchanged, Anna Amalia was able to negotiate cleverly with her uncle Frederick II (1712-1786), King of Prussia, and the Emperor's party. She had to supply troops for both powers, and at the same time she unofficially declared a general amnesty for deserters on both sides.[44]

Anna Amalia's sixteen-year-long period of government was marked by the spirit of enlightened absolutism. This was a form of rule in which there was no separation of powers and no chartered fundamental rights. The ruler, though not subject to any control, at least saw himself as the first servant of his people. Anna Amalia's reign was distinguished by the strict and disciplined way she had consolidated finances and by the development of the infrastructures of the Duchy. At the end of her reign she had created the conditions required to promote science and art in Weimar, to the extent that Anna Amalia's Court of Muses made history. In 1763 Anna Amalia had already drawn the writer and teacher Johann C.A. Musäus (1735-1787) into her circle. Musäus's employment as Pastor in Eisenach foundered because of the bitter opposition of the local peasants, who thought him unsuitable because he had danced at a festival.[45] He wrote poems of homage for Anna Amalia's birthdays, for example, on 24 October 1771, with the prelude 'Die Stufen des Menschlichen Alters'. The final verse was as follows:

> Sublime, full of humanity and mildness
> Is the noble lady of our village.
> Who can see the image of the Princess
> And find his heart lukewarm?
> The guardian angel must always be around her.
> It never leaves good Princes' side.

> Every single day she lives
> Is a festival for all the land.

Later Musäus often played roles in the amateur theatre. It was reported of him: 'The childlike, good, cheerful, and original Musäus was uncommonly successful in the low comic roles, for which he was admirably suited because of his drole exterior.'[46]

In 1772 Anna Amalia engaged the already famous writer Christoph Martin Wieland (1733-1813) as Prince's tutor. News of this spread throughout the whole of Germany. Carl Ludwig von Knebel (1744-1834), was engaged in 1774 as tutor to Anna Amalia's second son. While he was still a Prussian soldier (since 1765), he wrote that Wieland was the 'first German writer who, as such, made the breakthrough to becoming a courtier no matter how small the court.[47] Before gaining this position, Wieland had often travelled from Erfurt to Weimar, where he

> paid homage, with complete enthusiasm, to the beautiful Regent, who was thirty-four at the time. When I drove back to Erfurt in this frame of mind on one occasion, while in the carriage I sketched out the plan for a birthday scene 'Aurora', in which I could say the sweetest things to the Duchess.[48]

Engaging Wieland was of great importance, for it was a time in which the theatre was looked on as a place where people behaved immorally. In 1773 Wieland wrote about Anna Amalia, who after [the duchy] had recovered from the devastating effects of the Seven Years War, was attempting to set up a theatre in Weimar: 'And so Weimar enjoyed an advantage that no other town in Germany could boast of: a German theatre which everyone could visit three times a week without having to pay.'[49] In the same year, on the occasion of Anna Amalia's birthday, the drama *Merope* by Friedrich Wilhelm Gotter (1746-1797) was performed. Previously Gotter had been with Goethe in Wetzlar as a probationer at the Imperial Chamber Court (1693-1806) and had become friends with him.[50] Anna Amalia even had the seven-year-old Carl August play a role in the theatre. He is supposed to have acted 'without the slightest embarrassment, with appropriately expressed feeling and a good memory'.[51] Even later Carl August repeatedly took on roles as an actor in the theatre financed by himself and his mother.[52]

Anna Amalia set great store by a first-rate education for her children: 'A properly formative education of her princely sons', Goethe said in 1813, 'was the main concern of a tender mother, who herself was extremely cultured.'[53] When Anna Amalia brought the theatre company of Heinrich Gottfried Koch (1703-1775) to Weimar (1768-

1771), Christian Felix Weiße (1726-1804) was writing pleasing Singspiels based on French models, to which Adam Hiller (1728-1804) wrote nice popular melodies. Weiße dedicated to Anna Amalia, as protector of the German muses, what was probably his most important operetta, *The Hunt*.[54] At the premiere in Weimar it was accompanied by a poetic expression of thanks. On 4 February 1770 Weiße wrote about Anna Amalia as 'a Princess whose outstanding qualities of mind and heart bring happiness to her people, evoke the admiration of strangers, and are an adornment of the century'.[55] Under the influence of the popular Weiße-Hiller singspiels Goethe wrote texts like *Claudine Von Villa Bella* (dating from 1774), *Jery and Bately* (1779), or *Lila* (dating from 1776).[56] Goethe knew Koch's theatre company from his student days in Leipzig (1765-1768). The company also gave the first performance of his *Götz von Berlichingen* in Berlin in 1774. When Anna Amalia succeeded in engaging the Seyler Theatre Company for Weimar (1771-1774), this was 'an extremely fortunate coup. The Seyler company was the best theatre company in Germany at that time'.[57] After handing over the reins of government to Carl August, Anna Amalia's intention was to devote herself especially to the development of an amateur theatre. Shortly after his arrival in Weimar, on behalf of Anna Amalia, Goethe offered a post to the famous singer and actress, Corona Schröter (1751-1799), which she accepted in 1776. For scenery and costume design in the amateur theatre (1775-1784) Adam Friedrich Oeser (1717-1799), the Leipzig painter, sculptor, and art theoretician, worked alongside Georg Melchior Kraus (1737-1806), who was employed in Weimar since October 1775.[58] As early as 1755, shortly before Anna Amalia's marriage, Oeser had painted a portrait of her bridegroom on horseback. From 1767 until 1774 he was consulted as artist and advisor for the building of the house of Minister Jakob Friedrich von Fritsch (1731-1814). In 1774 Anna Amalia occupied this house when the town residence was burned down. From this time on it was called Wittumspalais and was to be occupied by the Princess until her death (ill. 12).[59]

One of the ladies-in-waiting of Anna Amalia was Charlotte von Stein. Her father, Johann Wilhelm Christian von Schardt (c. 1711-1790), had already served under 'the tyrant' Ernst August I, after whose death he was the tutor of of Anna Amalia's future husband. Schardt's need for pompous representation and his passion for collecting objects of art brought him close to insolvency, which was warded off only by using up nearly the whole of his wife's dowry. This money had been allocated to the education of the children. When in 1755 Ernst August Constantin began his reign and it was time to reward his tutors, von Schardt was rather pointedly given only 275 Taler, while his colleague was given 20,000.[60] Anna Amalia considered him a spendthrift who lived beyond his means, and she abruptly forced him into retirement. He seems to have imposed himself on those around him as a self-styled humanist and art connoisseur. He was seen as 'a court marshall who had justifiably been withdrawn from active life'. This was the view expressed (in February 1776) by Siegmund von Seckendorff (1744-1785), who, with ambitions to be a musician and writer, was engaged at the Weimar court as a chamberlain.[61] A pedantic theology student as well as a father whose qualities were supposedly misunderstood were the educators of the von Schardt children, who felt that they had had an unhappy childhood. The basic education that Charlotte von Stein received consisted of reading, writing, arithmetic, Bible study, and singing, along with domestic work. After this she had instruction in French, dancing, piano, and conversation.[62] In 1758 Charlotte had become Anna Amalia's lady-in-waiting.[63] The Princess 'had the goodness to choose her as a 'Hoffräulein'.[64] She remained Anna Amalia's lady-in-waiting until the Duchess died; 'this was formally the 'main profession' she practised until the death of her mistress (Anna Amalia) in 1807.[65] Only the copy of a no longer extant self-portrait dated 1787 gives an impression of Charlotte von Stein's appearance (ill. 24);[66] apart from that there are only a few silhouettes and a few unclear drawings of her in her old age.[67] 'With regard to the appearance of Charlotte von Stein it is no longer possible to reach any clarity', says one biographer.[68] Given the number of painters working in Weimar it would have been enough to express a wish for a portrait to be done. The Duchess Luise (1757-1830) even had a portrait of herself painted by the famous Johann F.A. Tischbein (1750-1812), only to give it to her friend, Charlotte von Stein, as a present. Charlotte von Stein writes in a letter to one of her sons: 'The portrait of the Duchess now adorns my cabinet, but the extremely ornate frame kills the rest of my furnishings stone dead.'[69] Nor did Frau von Stein have a bust of herself made. The court sculptor Gottlieb Martin Klauer (1742-1801), whom Anna Amalia brought from Rudostadt to Weimar in 1774, would have done it at a moment's notice, since he had already done one of another of Anna Amalia's ladies-in-waiting, Luise von Göchhausen.[70] Apart from a self-portrait showing her in half profile and made with the help of two mirrors, Frau von Stein did not want images of herself to be made. A small medallion (ill. 25), dating from around 1785, shows Frau von Stein in exactly the same pose as in the self-portrait.[71] Goethe's 'soul-mate' was to be seen only in profile.

After the strict rearing in her parents' house, Charlotte had, as lady-in-waiting, access to the brilliant court of Anna Amalia with its manifold festivals and entertainments. A smile from the Princess was enough to bring happiness to a lady-in-waiting. In 1764 the 21-year-old married Josias von Stein (1735-1793), who during Anna Amalia's reign was promoted to Equerry and was at the same time lord of the manor on his Kochberg property. Under Carl August, von Stein was promoted to Chief Equerry and was responsible for around 130 draft- and saddle horses, the coach park and the stud in Allstedt.[72] For the impecunious daughter of von Schardt it was a good match. Josias von Stein was a good-looking man as well as a good dancer and rider. 'He doesn't drink, he doesn't gamble, and he has a practical turn of mind. He treats his wife well, trusts her, and respects her.'[73] After the marriage Frau von Stein seems to have become especially close to Anna Amalia.[74] She gave birth to seven children, of whom only three boys survived infancy. Goethe was later to take an interest in the education of her youngest son, Gottlob Friedrich Constantin von Stein (1772-1844), called Fritz. In 1762 the Duchess Anna Amalia granted a scholarship to a brother of Frau von Stein so that he could study law. All three of Charlotte's brothers entered into state service in Weimar and were promoted by Anna Amalia. In 1773 Anna Amalia gave the father the honorary title of 'Excellency' and an order; although old Schardt still had no concrete function, he was satisfied with the honour. The Baltic writer, Sophie Becker (1754-1789), wrote in her diary on 2 March 1785 while on a visit to Weimar:

> Old Schardt also paid a visit, and as soon as he came in [into the salon of Countess Bernstorff] Goethe ran off. The old man scares off anyone with brains. He's an obsolete court flunkey who lives for the smile of his ruler.[75]

Schiller judged: '... in this family [von Schardt] the women are clever and the men as dumb as can be.'[76]

In the years of transition between reigns, Frau von Stein performed important services for her mistress Anna Amalia. Caroline, Countess Görtz (1749-1809), reports in a letter to her husband on 29 December 1774: ' ... Stein is becoming more and more the favourite of the Duchess [Anna Amalia] ... soon she will have put all the others in the shade.'[77] On 24 April 1775 she writes again to her husband: 'Stein continues to be on the best footing with the Duchess [Anna Amalia] ... she is becoming a writer; I am told she has written quite nice verses.'[78] After 'long, patient wooing'[79] she became a close friend of Carl August's wife, Duchess Luise, and a good friend of both of her ladies-in-waiting.[80] As a result Anna Amalia's loyal, devoted lady-in-waiting became part of the inner circle of her daughter-in-law Luise. The second task was more difficult: that of the secret concerning Goethe.

4| Beginnings

> *Maman* [Anna Amalia] is one in heart and mind with the genius *par excellence* [Goethe] and malicious tongues are saying that, despite her cool attitude towards him in public, he is missing almost every evening at mealtime.
>
> Gräfin Görtz to her husband, 14 March 1778

> God, to whom I have always remained true, has richly blessed me in secret, for my fate is completely hidden from human beings; they can neither see nor hear anything of it.
>
> Goethe to Lavater, 8 October 1779

In 1785 Goethe lost his nerve when he heard about the necklace affair in Paris. In the *Tag- und Jahresheften* (1817-1830) entry for 1789 he reports:

> ... in the year 1785 the necklace story made an incredible impression on me. In the abyss of immorality in town, court, and state that was revealed here I had ghostly visions of what would be the most dire consequences. For a considerable time I could not rid myself of these visions, with the result that I behaved so strangely that friends confessed to me that my behaviour seemed like that of a madman.

Through the trial that followed Goethe seemed convinced that the 'axe was being laid to the root of kingship'.[81] 'We know', said Riemer, 'that the infamous necklace affair terrified our poet like the head of the Gorgon'.[82] Here the question arises whether Goethe overreacted at the news because he feared for the political stability of France or whether he had other reasons.

In the necklace affair, Countess de la Motte (1756-1791), a lover of Cardinal Rohan (1734-1803), a Prince of the Church who had fallen out of favour at court, pretended to him that he could win back the favour of Queen Marie-Antoinette (1755-1793) if he helped her as guarantor to acquire a fantastic necklace consisting of 647 diamonds. The cardinal was taken in by this swindle which was made plausible by, among other things, forged letters and a meeting with the 'Queen' in the Venus Grove of Versailles. In reality Rohan met with an actress, a certain Nicole Leguay d'Oliva (1761-1789), who looked like the Queen. He ordered the necklace for the Queen and, on 1 February 1785, handed it over to her supposed valet, who passed it on to the swindler, La Motte. When the payments by the Queen failed to eventuate, the swindle was discovered. From the middle of August 1785 arrests were made. News of the necklace affair spread like wildfire throughout Europe. The trial took place in May 1786. The outcome was that Cardinal Rohan was banned to a monastery and required to pay off the debts to the jewellers out of Church funds.[83] The affair aroused the antipathy of the French population and in hindsight was looked on as a beacon for the French Revolution. The fact that the jewellers could suspect that the Queen had used underhand means to purchase the necklace was enough totally to discredit Marie Antoinette, who was already seen as irresponsible. In a conversation with Eckermann on 15 February 1831 Goethe said:

> The event immediately precedes the French Revolution and is, in a certain sense, its foundation. The Queen, so intimately involved in the unfortunate necklace affair, lost her dignity, even the respect due to her, and so, in the opinion of the people, the status that would have made her unassailable. Hatred does no harm to anyone, but contempt brings about a person's fall.

The reason why Goethe, who himself had railed against the gods in the poem 'Prometheus' (1774) – 'I know nothing more wretched under the sun than you, gods' – seemed to his friends to react like a madman to the necklace affair is at first not clear, especially since the dramatic consequences for the royal family at the time could not be foreseen. Goethe's reaction makes sense if one assumes that a comparable affair was taking place in Weimar, which, if it were to become known, would have resulted in the most dire consequences for himself and for the ducal family. The affair in Weimar was Goethe's love for the Duchess Anna Amalia. This love relationship was not allowed to be known, since for a middle-class man, even one who in 1782 became a member of the lower nobility of the Empire, a liaison with a princess was not permissible. If the lovers had publicly ignored this prohibition Anna Amalia would have exposed the tiny principality to serious sanctions, from which her son, Carl August, as ruling Duke, would be the first to suffer. At the head of the principalities of the Holy Roman Empire (c. 962 and 1806) there were only a few families belonging to the higher nobility, and these only allowed marriages within their own ranks. To make the forbidden love relationship with Anna Amalia possible, Charlotte von Stein was put forward as Goethe's lover. Goethe's reaction to the necklace affair mirrored his fear of the consequences if his secret were to be discovered. This state secret, a more serious equivalent of the necklace affair, was so brilliantly managed that it was maintained for over two hundred years. The love between Anna Amalia and Goethe is evident as early as 1776. 'I am enjoying very good times with the Dowager Duchess', Goethe writes on 14 February 1776 to Johanna Fahlmer (1744-1821), 'we're carrying on with all kinds of tricks and nonsense'. Outwardly their love is protected by the pretence that Charlotte von Stein is Goethe's platonic lover. To make this odd liaison believable a meeting in Ilmenau was arranged. At the beginning of August 1776 Charlotte von Stein was returning from a stay at the spa in Pyrmont and made a detour via Ilmenau to see Goethe, who was there on official business. The Duke was also in Ilmenau with his courtiers and with at least some of his forty personal servants, including two Moors,[84] and with his collaborators and other companions – like the painter Kraus, for instance. Charlotte von Stein arrived in Ilmenau in the evening of 5 August 1776. Goethe spent a part of 6 August with his 'beloved' and with her visited the nearby Hermann's Cave. For anyone who did not already know, it was now clear that something was going on between Goethe and Charlotte von Stein. Goethe wrote of this meeting to Gottfried von Herder (1744-1803), who had met Charlotte in Pyrmont and who was soon called to the highest ecclesiastical dignity in Weimar on Goethe's recommendation: 'I have the angel Stein again ... for a whole day my eye did not leave hers.'

In a letter of 8 August 1776 to 'Frau von Stein' referring to the day they shared on 6 August 1776, a different picture emerges: 'Dear angel, I have been working on my Falcon. My Giovanna will have a lot of Lili in her, but you will allow me to put in a few drops of your being – just enough for colouring.' So, some drops of the lady he is writing to are necessary, because 'a lot' of Lili Schoenemann (1758-1817), Goethe's earlier fiancée in Frankfurt (1775), is not enough to make up the substance he requires. The indication in the letter of 8 August that he is working on the 'Falcon', a piece which he will soon put aside again, is revealing. The title and the characters in the piece point to the novella of Boccaccio (1313-1375), *The Falcon* (Decameron V, 9).[85] Boccaccio's story deals with a young nobleman, Federigo, who uses up his fortune in courting the rich noble lady Giovanna. But it is only when he is completely impoverished that he succeeds in conquering the widow Giovanna through his noble disposition. All that is left of the fragment 'The Falcon' is a few words on a page of note paper, including: 'Still tremble! Shake! To be caught ... ', 'Am I not driven to her, do I not kiss her hand, her glove, the hem of her garment!'

Goethe, who soon after his arrival in Weimar was confronted with the necessity of deception, describes in the fragment what he feels: the trembling, the shaking that overcomes him at the thought of being surprised with his beloved. He could not have kept his secret if he had developed this piece, in which a beautiful, rich widow played the main part. The fragment is enough to show that Giovanna is a Princess, since only a Princess had the hem of her garment kissed. Subjects had to bow down to do this and thereby expressed their submission. At court balls and before performances in the theatre the gentry were allowed to kiss the coat of the Duchess Anna Amalia.[86] To kiss the coat of Anna Amalia's lady-in-waiting, Frau von Stein, would have been a presumptuous breach of protocol. Her official duty was to entertain the Princess she served and to look after her well-being. She was worlds apart from the rank of Princess. Anna Amalia's official title was: 'Widowed Duchess of Saxony, Jülich, Cleve and Berg, also Engern and Westphalia, born Duchess of Brunswick and Lüneburg, Landgravine in Thüringen, Margravine of Meissen, princely Countess of Henneberg, Countess of the Mark and Ravensberg, Frau of Ravenstein etc. Coins with her image as ruling Duchess were struck.[87] In a covered gondola big enough to accommodate musicians Anna Amalia had herself propelled over the artificially constructed lakes (ill. 13). Her walks were official events. Her former page remembers:

> The Duchess was accustomed, on Sundays and Feast Days, to go for a walk in the Esplanade after dinner. The time was divulged to the nobility and they came in their numbers and sat down on the benches lining the Esplanade and waited. The Regent usually appeared in taffeta and with the whole court; the Chief Marshall led the way and a page carried her train ... Behind these followed the lower court servants; these consisted of runners, court officials, and a dwarf ... Also many people of property and citizens hurried to the Esplanade, because otherwise they seldom had occasion to have such a close look at their Princess.[88]

The introductory formula with which the Princess promulgated laws gives a clear indication of the all-powerful nature of her rank: 'By the grace of God We Anna Amalia ... command each and every one of our Prelates, Counts, and Gentlemen, those of knightly and noble rank, officials, lawyers, mayors and councillors in towns, mayors, judges, deputy mayors, as also all subjects in general ...'[89] Goethe was not preoccupied, therefore, on 6 August, with Frau von Stein but with the Princess Anna Amalia.

In the letter of 8 August 1776 a poem for 'Frau von Stein' is included:

> Oh what you have been to me
> And I to you!

No, I despair of the truth
No longer
When you are there
I feel I should not love you
And when you are not
I feel I love you so, so dearly.

The truth of the situation no longer makes him despair. For love of Anna Amalia he is prepared to be deceitful. In the same letter he says with reference to Frau von Stein's presence in the cave: 'It is like in a spirit world, it is also for me like in a spirit world. A feeling without feeling.' At the end of the letter Goethe writes: 'Your relationship to me is holy, strange ... it is not visible to human eyes.' These lines cannot refer to Frau von Stein for in Ilmenau everyone had seen her with him. After the time in the Hermannstein cave with Frau von Stein on 6 August 1776 Goethe cut a capital S into the rock face. The S is meant to stand for the sun (☉), supposedly the symbol for Frau von Stein. In his diaries Goethe referred to his closest friends at the Weimar Court with symbols drawn from the planetary system. Anna Amalia was the moon (☾), Frau von Stein the sun (☉).[90] At the beginning of the biography of his early years, *Dichtung und Wahrheit* (1811-1831), Goethe describes the transition of his affection from Charlotte Kestner (1753-1828) to Maximiliane Brentano (1756-1793) – his models for the epistolary Werther novel (1774) – in the following words:

> It is a very pleasant feeling when a new passion begins to stir in us before the old one has completely faded. You are happy to see, opposite the setting sun, the rising of the moon and you enjoy the double brilliance of both heavenly bodies.

According to this, when Goethe has found the great love of his life, he has to apply both symbols, sun and moon, to her. Goethe dedicated a description of sun and moon to the Duchess Anna Amalia. In a letter from Switzerland to 'Frau von Stein' he reports on 24 October, Anna Amalia's fortieth birthday, a sublime experience:

> On the 24 October at the Vallée de Joux ... we [Goethe and Carl August] went by horse up the mountain and, in climbing, had the most glorious view over the Lake of Geneva, the Savoy and Wallis mountain ranges. Behind us we could make out Lausanne and through a light mist the area around Geneva. Directly opposite we saw Mont Blanc towering above all the mountains of Faucigny. It was a brilliant sunset, too much for the human eye. The moon came up, almost full, and we climbed higher. Through fir forests we climbed up the Jura and saw the lake in the scented air and the reflection of the moon on the water. It became ever brighter.

They celebrated Anna Amalia's birthday even in Switzerland. Carl August reports in a letter of 28 October: 'We celebrated your birthday, dearest Mother, in a wonderful valley; yes, we celebrated it well.' Anna Amalia's birthdays are a key to unlock the Weimar state secret. In general, birthdays were of enormous importance in the life of the court. The birthdays of the Princes were celebrated with great pomp. Since 1764 in Weimar there were poems dedicated to the Princes as well as descriptions of the celebrations, in which the whole court took part and subjects expressed their 'most devoted congratulations'.[91] Goethe and Anna Amalia always mark one another's birthday. For Goethe's birthday on 28 August 1781 Anna Amalia arranged a performance of the shadow-play *The Birth of Minerva*:

> ... from the book of fate, Minerva ... proclaimed the 28 August the happy day on which one of the wisest and best men was born into the world. Then a winged genius (spirit) bearing Goethe's name floated down from the clouds onto the stage, Minerva placed a garland on this name and dedicated to him Apollo's golden lyre and the wreaths of flowers of the Muses. Then Iphigenie and Faust appeared as fire transparencies in the clouds. The whole play was designed to do nothing other than to honour Goethe.[92]

His birthday was celebrated even when he was absent from Weimar. For example, while he was in Italy it was celebrated in Weimar with a garden festival, illuminations, and fireworks, and a report of it was sent to him.[93]

The journey to Switzerland had begun on 12 September 1779 and lasted several months. On 4 November 1779 Anna Amalia wrote to Goethe's friend, Councillor of War, Johann Heinrich Merck (1741-1791):

> I can't thank you enough, dear Merck, for the trouble you take to render the dreary evenings bearable [through acquiring copper engravings and suchlike things for her], especially this year, when I am so alone. The news I get from the travellers often makes my head spin. It is painful to hear of nothing but glorious things and not to get near them except through a dim telescope.[94]

There was even a rumour that Anna Amalia would travel to Switzerland to join the little party,[95] which had suddenly changed its travel plans and was heading for Switzerland instead of going to Frankfurt and the Rhine area.[96] In a letter to 'Charlotte von Stein' on 1 January 1780 from Darmstadt, where they were making a detour on the return journey, Goethe's attitude is unmistakable [ill. 23]: 'I like this Princess Charlotte, | : the cursed name is pursuing me everywhere : | but I have nothing to do with her. I like looking at her, and that's what princesses are there for.' Goethe can hardly have written this letter to Charlotte, for it is impossible that he would say the name of his adored one was cursed. 'His Charlotte' was supposed to be a kind of goddess for him. Here Goethe even uses musical repeat signs (| : ... : |), so that the text between these signs is meant to be read twice: ' the cursed name is pursuing me everywhere'. The fact that this name is doubly cursed for him becomes intelligible if one assumes that Goethe is writing to Anna Amalia and that Frau von Stein did not see the letter. This statement is one of many in Goethe's letters to 'Frau von Stein' that let us see through the attempted cover-up.

The Swiss journey was to be an educational triumph. In the diary entry for 17 January 1780 we read: 'Everyone is very happy with Carl August. They are praising us. The journey is a great success, an heroic poem!' It took great effort to deal with the young Duke – who was virtually all-powerful in his Duchy – to prevent him from becoming a violent, unjust ruler. An incident that took place in the house of Johann Justin Bertuch (1747-1822) – a publisher and writer, amongst other things, who, beginning in 1775 made a translation of Cervantes's (1547-1616) novel *Don Quixote* (1605-1615) - shows that worries concerning the young Duke were quite justified. When Bertuch brought his wife Caroline (1750-1810) into his house for the first time, he had a visit from the Duke and Goethe:

> The Duke began by saying that he had heard that Bertuch set up his house in a devilishly philistine way, had had a fine looking night commode made and was carrying on with great luxury. So he would have to see what this was about. Straight away his eye fell on a pair of mirrors which he was about to smash with his sword, but he took heed when Bertuch said he would have them replaced, at the Duke's expense, by ones of equal value. He desisted and said that the mirrors should stay for the sake of Frau Bertuch so that she could look at herself in them. Then the Duke examined Bertuch's writing desk, found a novel by Göchhausen which he proceeded to demolish by tearing and burning out pages, sprinkling tobacco in the book, and sent the lot to Fräulein von Göchhausen sealed in Bertuch's name. Finally he hacked and stabbed at the new wallpaper because it [he considered it] was devilishly philistine to paper over the bare walls ... Bertuch held back his annoyance but some days later fell seriously ill. When the doctor spoke of danger of death the Duke came at midnight as if to apologize, and Goethe left the room in tears, pressing the hand of the deeply insulted woman and said to her it was a very hard beginning.'[97]

There are other reports about the behaviour of Princes. Some, of no political importance, stand out. It was reported of Prince Joseph of Hildburghausen that in the Privy Council he had a very sharp dagger to hand which he threw at the councillors if a suggestion displeased him. The Count of Bayreuth is said to have had a hunter's lad shot dead for daring to contradict him, and Prince Hyazinth of Nassau-Siegen had a peasant executed to demonstrate to his subjects that power over life and death was in his hands.[98]

Carl August's father-in-law, Count Louis IX, was not interested in government business. He preferred to occupy himself with the military or with his mistress, 'who was not impartial to drink', bathed naked in village ponds, and then called out to the peasants: 'N'ai-je pas le C.[ul] plus beau que vos visages' [Don't I have an arse that's prettier than your faces?] He was continually having soldiers painted in all conceivable kinds of uniforms and he composed march music. In a letter of 18 September 1780 Merck reports to Carl August about his father-in-law:

> Two band masters are required to attend, with their subordinates, from 8 in the morning until 4 in the afternoon when the warming pan is brought, to put notes to the marches the Count composes. With two fingers he plays the marches on the piano and then they have to be written down and often also tried out immediately. He has brought it to the point where in one day he composed up to 300 marches and at present he has on paper 52,365 marches of his making. The number of painted soldiers is unbelievable.

5 | Rise and Fall of a State Minister

> I am settling into this world without deviating by a hair's breadth from the kind of existence that sustains me inwardly and makes me happy.
>
> Goethe to Merck, 14 November 1781

> The news won't be at all so new for you. You will have been amazed by the dismissal of Kalb, and not less by the news of Goethe's elevation to the nobility. The love affair [Liebschaften] of the latter with his miserable old jade [Anna Amalia] is still quite alive. The influence which this clique exerts over the Duke and Duchess is greater than ever.
>
> Countess Giannini to the Countess Görtz, 12 August 1782

In the summer of 1781 Merck brought excitement to his circle of friends in Frankfurt. Goethe's mother Catharina Elisabeth (1731-1808) writes to her son on 17 June 1781 about what Merck has said:

> ... in any case you [Goethe's mother] should try to get him back here; the dreadful climate there is surely not good for him. He has fulfilled his essential role. The Duke is now as he ought to be. The rest of the muck can be done by someone else. Goethe is too good for that etc.

Goethe answers his mother on 11 August 1781:

> Merck and others misjudge my situation quite badly. They only see the sacrifices I make, not what I gain, and they cannot comprehend that I am becoming daily richer by daily giving so much. You remember the last days I was with you before coming here [Weimar]. Under circumstances like those I was certain to be destroyed. The disproportion between the narrow, slow-moving middle-class circle and the breadth and speed of my nature would have driven me mad ... How much better it was to see myself put in a situation for which I was in no way prepared ... where, left to myself and my fate, I went

> through so many trials which many hundreds of people may not need, but which were of the utmost importance for me.

Advised by Anna Amalia, Goethe took on many state duties so as to gain, from the vantage point of an important post, valuable experience which would stand him in good stead as a writer. In a letter of 8 March 1781 to 'Frau von Stein' Goethe describes the role played by Anna Amalia:

> Since I am always making parables, I said to myself yesterday that you are to me what an Imperial Commission is to the princes of the empire. You teach my heart, which is everywhere in debt, to act more economically and to find its happiness in a pure relationship of income and expense.

Anna Amalia used all her powers to help the poet to develop under ideal conditions, and so Goethe writes to 'Frau von Stein' (12 March 1781): 'I humbly implore you, finish your work, make a good man of me.'

For Goethe to become the most influential minister was a hard battle. Soon after the beginning of Carl August's reign various parties had formed around the young Duke in a struggle for power in the duchy: beside the conservatives who wanted continuity under Carl August there was the Prince's tutor Count Johann Eustach von Schlitz, named Görtz (1737-1821). Görtz had gained ever more influence over Carl August, who had been entrusted to him when he was just five years old. According to Görtz, only the nobility should have ruling functions.[99] Middle-class people should not have crucial roles. Those who already had them – two of the three members of the Privy Council – should be dismissed. As the day of Carl August's enthronement approached Anna Amalia became increasingly convinced that Count Görtz was 'ambitious, restless, and an intriguer.'[100] In a fit of temper, she would like to have had him shamed and driven out.[101] Görtz, who as an educator had inflexible moral attitudes,[102] did not shy away from intrigues against Anna Amalia in order to acquire important posts for himself under Carl August's government. For example, in 1772 Görtz planned, behind Anna Amalia's back, a coup d'état with the collaboration of the Gotha Minister Silvius von Franckenberg (1728-1815).[103] The idea was that, as early as his seventeenth birthday in 1774, Carl August should be enthroned by the Emperor as ruling Duke. Since, according to Görtz Anna Amalia did not act 'through divine inspiration she had to be taught by human means!' Anna Amalia would have to be shown 'that there was nothing else for her to do except to declare her son's majority as quickly as possible. In this way she would secure for herself an indisputable right to his gratitude and enjoy in peace the fruits of her work as regent.'[104] The nearer the day of Carl August's enthronement approached, the more Anna Amalia's influence diminished. Görtz reckoned with the open enmity of Anna Amalia. On 12 October 1775 he reported to his wife, for example, that in 1771 the Duchess had 'already hated him as much as now'.[105] Surprisingly, on 9 December 1773, Anna Amalia, upset, suggested to First Minister von Fritsch that Carl August be declared of age on his seventeenth birthday:

> In a word, I am tired of the life I am now forced to lead; I am not political enough to be able always to hide my indignation from those who deserve it. I can see that it brings me nothing, and so I have decided to rid myself of the regency.

Minister von Fritsch, whom Görtz considered to be his worst enemy,[106] persuaded Anna Amalia to give up this idea. To this end he organized a cavalier's journey for the Princes which was to bring them to Paris.[107] Before his reign began Carl August wrote to her on 16 March 1775 how pleased he and Count Görtz were that she did not intend to withdraw to her widow's residence in Allstedt, as laid down in the marriage contract, but to remain in Weimar. Conversely it followed that Carl August as Duke could require her to withdraw to her widow's residence. In that case Anna Amalia could only avoid banishment to the country by remarrying.

With Goethe's arrival in Weimar, however, the young Duke lost interest in Görtz and Goethe became his best friend. In a letter to Merck on 22 January 1776, Goethe writes:

> I am now caught up in all court and political doings and will hardly ever be able to get away. My position is advantageous enough and the duchies of Weimar and Eisenach are always an arena for gauging how one is suited to a role in the world.

The conservative faction would for a long time reject the young genius, so that without Anna Amalia Goethe could not have survived in Weimar. Conversely, Anna Amalia would not have remained in Weimar without Goethe, for she would have had to look on helplessly as her son, surrounded by flatterers, was exposed more and more to corruption. Since Anna Amalia was not known as Goethe's beloved, people were time and again puzzled that Carl August held on to Goethe: 'For court circles and Weimar society it was as surprising as it was for later observers that the Duke took Goethe as his ally and vice versa, and no one could make any sense of it.'[108] Anna Amalia, on the other hand, was even likened to a Meissen rococo figurine, and her guiding hand was completely unappreciated:

> More than previously it now became clear how adaptable Anna Amalia could be and how much ingenuousness was to be found in this Meissen rococo figurine that held court in the Wittumspalais. Enticed by the great magician Goethe, her curiosity for life dared to emerge. It is as if, in relaxed society, she wanted to regain a part of the youthful happiness she had missed out on.[109]

Only a few lines from 'Frau von Stein' to Goethe in the first Weimar decade are extant. Amongst these, according to a very early witness,[110] there is a letter which Goethe included in his play *Die Geschwister* (1776):

> The world becomes dear to me again – I had made myself so free of it – dear to me again through you. My heart reproaches me; I feel that I have torture in store for you and me. Six months ago I was so ready to die, but that is no longer so.

These lines apply exactly to Anna Amalia's situation, but not to that of Frau von Stein, the course of whose life remained essentially unchanged. On the other hand the Duchess had to hand over the reins of government to her immature son and had already, at the end of 1773, with reference to this change, written to Minister von Fritsch: ' ... I'm tired of living'. In the poem 'An den Mond' (c. 1777) – in his diaries Goethe assigned the moon symbol (☾) to Anna Amalia – the beloved is to close herself off from the world 'without hatred': 'Blessed the one who can, without hatred, close herself off from the world, clasp a man to her bosom and enjoy with him ...' In Anna Amalia's letter of 9 December 1773 to Minister von Fritsch, she writes:

> ... eyes are now only on the rising sun [Carl August]; I am not jealous of it; I am content to have made my subjects happy. Perhaps they had not, for a long time, experienced happiness like that under my regency. This is my whole reward and I consider myself very lucky ... I repeat that I want nothing more than to be freed of the regency and the guardianship.[111]

In Goethe's official testimonial to the Princess (1807), he writes: 'The calm awareness that she had carried out the duty required of her accompanied her to a quiet, private life of her choosing.' Thus Anna Amalia withdraws from the world without hatred. The last strophe of the poem 'An den Mond' reads (final version):

> Which, not known by men
> Or not realized by them
> Passes through the labyrinth of the breast
> In the night.

What is not known or realized is that Goethe has to keep secret the identity of his beloved. What Goethe grasps, what gives his breast material for his love poetry, must pass through a labyrinth. In the breast of the poet a veil is spread around his adored Anna Amalia. For the uninitiated there is no identifiable person behind his love poetry. She is veiled in the darkness of night until Anna Amalia becomes known as the woman in Goethe's life. They show only in code that they belong together – in creative writing, in paintings, and also in hints. In 1779, for example, the secret lovers have two busts made in profile as pendants: Goethe looks to the right and Anna Amalia to the left (ill. 4 and 5). On 8 October Goethe writes to his friend Johann Caspar Lavater (1741-1801): 'My God, to whom I have always remained faithful, has rewarded me richly in secret, for my fate is completely hidden from men; they can see and hear nothing of it.' On 1 September 1780 Knebel writes to Lavater:

> He [Goethe] will undoubtedly be misunderstood and he himself seems to live with it. Beauty which is visible only under a mask attracts him all the more. He himself is a wonderful mixture – or a double nature made up of hero and actor. But the former is in the ascendancy.'[112]

Knebel must have collaborated energetically on improving the external presentation of the tragic-comedy with Frau von Stein. On 15 December 1778 Goethe writes in his diary: 'With Knebel about the crooked ways of society. He told me what my situation looked like from the outside. He was right in saying: from the outside.' With his friend Knebel, who was also close to Anna Amalia and to Charlotte von Stein and of whose secrecy he could be absolutely sure,[113] Goethe repeatedly discusses his difficult situation, for example, on 30 April 1785: 'How good it is to discuss one's situation confidentially with friends.'[114]

If the lovers, of unequal rank, had revealed their love it would not have been possible for them to exercise a decisive influence over the Duke and thus to have a controlling effect on the fate of the land. Goethe's most important task was to ensure that out of the overburdened 18-year-old Duke a fine ruler of his people would emerge. Carl August was not yet familiar with the workings of the state and its legalities; his marriage to Luise was unhappy from the beginning, since she proved to be distant and closed. Goethe made this judgement about Luise in a letter to 'Frau von Stein' on 12 April 1782: 'I feel deep pity for the poor Duchess. I don't see any cure for this ill. If she could find an object which would attract her heart to it, there would be, with luck, perhaps some prospect for her.' It is true that Luise was nice and capable of attracting and keeping a man, 'it's just that, if I may say so, with her it always remains a bud ... One cannot be more pleasant than the Duchess is, even if she is comfortable with people only for moments.' Goethe made the following judgement about Carl August in a letter to 'Frau von Stein' – and so in reality to the Duke's mother – on 11 March 1781:

> I am now no longer surprised that princes are so mad, dumb, and foolish. Rarely do they have such talents as the Duke [Carl August], rarely are they surrounded by such intelligent, good people and friends as he is, and yet his progress is not in proportion, and the child and the fish-tail peep out when you are not expecting it. I have also noticed what is the worst thing about him. However impassioned he is about what is good and right, he is less at home there than with what is improper. It is amazing how sensible he can be, what insights he has and how much he knows, and yet when he wants to indulge himself he has to do something stupid, even if it is just the crushing of wax candles.

The Duchess Luise sometimes made Goethe, as Carl August's closest friend, responsible for his discontent and constant unfaithfulness. In the judgement of a biographer: ' ... under pressure of circumstances sometimes the Princess fell into a bad humour with regard to Goethe, which was slow to dissipate.'[115]

After his strict upbringing the exuberant young Duke wanted to let off steam. Since Goethe himself was a young man of 26 he could still go along with him. He wrote to Lavater on 6 March 1776: 'Rest assured – I have now set sail on the waves of the world – completely determined to discover, to win, to do battle, to founder, or to blow myself up sky-high.' The genius years at the beginning of Carl August's reign meant unruly feasting, wild horse-riding, long walks, climbing tours in the mountains, nights of drinking, ice-skating, fencing, and all the while everything was caricatured, mocked, and joked about. 'The trend in those days to live outdoors, to spend time and to find enjoyment there, is well known', Goethe commented in his old age.[116] The Duke especially liked to shock the middle-classes by dressing up in the clothes of Goethe's Werther, hero of the novel: a blue jacket, yellow knee hose, and a round grey hat.

> In those days everyone had to go around in a Werther jacket, which the Duke also wore, and if someone could not obtain one the Duke had one made for him. The only exception for the Duke was Wieland, who was too old for this fancy-dressing.[117]

On 6 March 1776, Frau von Stein writes to her friend, the doctor Johann Georg von Zimmermann (1728-1795), about Goethe:

> I myself would wish he would give up something of his wildness which makes people here unjustly see him in a bad light. It is nothing more than that he hunts, rides at breakneck speed, cracks a big whip – all in the company of the Duke. Certainly this is not his own bent, but for a while he has to do it to win over the Duke and then establish something good.[118]

The morose Chamberlain von Seckendorff, who was jealous of the middle-class upstart, reports in a letter of 5 February 1776:

> Every day is distinguished by new, extraordinary pleasures without the slightest regard for what people say, for, according to the view of his advisors, which he follows all too closely, there is no propriety in the world, nor should there be. According to their view, all the rules currently in force stem only from human whims, and the head of the state is in a position to abolish them.[119]

Subjects held Goethe, the stranger, responsible for all that was negative in the behaviour of the young Duke. All over Germany there was talk of the genius climate in Weimar. The poet Friedrich Klopstock (1724-1803) prophesied a violent death for Goethe.[120] Only thanks to Anna Amalia's experience as regent was Goethe able to negotiate the political rocks and to develop and secure his position at court. It is due to her influence that Carl August finally took seriously his duties as father of the country. Knebel wrote about Carl August in a letter to Lavater on 1 September 1780: ' ... keep in mind that Goethe has given him two thirds of his existence!' In his old age Wieland said to Chancellor Friedrich von Müller (1779-1849) that Goethe gave 'unbelievable service to our Duke in the first years of his reign. With what self-denial and enormous sacrifice he [Goethe] devoted himself to him, how much that was noble and great that slumbered in the young Prince was developed and brought to light by him.'[121] In Eckermann's *Gespräche mit Goethe*, 23 October 1828, Goethe said about Carl August, who had died some months previously: 'He was like a fine wine but still fermenting mightily. He didn't know what to do with his energies and we often came close to breaking our necks. But the Duke soon worked his way through this Sturm und Drang period to salutary clarity ... so that it became a joy to live and work with him.'

Goethe's meteoric rise was met with envy and his genius with rage and hatred.[122] Goethe was seen as a stranger and intruder. His being middle-class caused annoyance.[123] In mid-December 1778, for example, Minister Goethe wrote in his diary: 'I am not suited to this world. When you leave your house you are walking in nothing but muck.' By the middle of 1776 he was Privy Councillor of Legation with the considerable salary of 1,200 taler, which at last made him financially independent of his parents in Frankfurt. As a Minister without portfolio he was a member with a vote in the highest government body, the Privy Council, which advised the Duke and prepared his decisions. The decisive factor in his appointment was Anna Amalia, for she used her whole influence as former regent to work in his favour. After Carl August failed to persuade Minister von Fritsch not to resign over Goethe's appointment,[124] Anna Amalia succeeded, writing to him in a letter of 13 May 1776:

> The reasons you give have deeply troubled me. They are not worthy of a man of your intellectual calibre and experience of the world. You are prejudiced against Goethe, whom you perhaps know only from untrue reports or whom you judge from a false perspective. You know how dear my son's reputation is to me and how hard I have worked, and am still working, to have him surrounded by men of integrity. If I thought Goethe was one of those creeping creatures for whom nothing is more sacred than their own interests and who only act out of ambition, I would be the first to oppose him. I don't want to speak to you about his talents or his genius. I speak of his morality. His religion is that of a true and good Christian; it teaches him to love his neighbour and to try and make him happy. And surely that is the first and main intention of our Creator! But let us leave Goethe aside and speak of you. Go into yourself, my friend! ... You say that people everywhere would criticize my son if he took Goethe into the Council. But won't people everywhere also criticize you if you leave the service of my son for such a paltry reason? Make Goethe's acquaintance, try to get to know the man himself! You know that I look carefully at my people before I judge them and that experience has taught me much about judging character ... Believe a friend who is devoted to you with gratitude and affection! ... Again, go into yourself![125]

While Anna Amalia was writing these lines she was writing the score for Goethe's Singspiel *Erwin und Elmire* for a performance on 24 May 1776 in the amateur theatre. In 1775/76 Heinsius did the painting 'Anna Amalia as Composer' (ill. 2). The Princess is depicted half-size seated at the piano holding a roll of music in her hand. At the same time Anna Amalia commissioned Kraus to do a painting of 'Goethe in Love' (ill. 3),[126] in which the beloved is to be seen only as a silhouette and is unknown until now.[127]

The letter made a deep impression on Minister von Fritsch. The 'tried and trusted servant of the state ... no longer trusted his own judgement.'[128] Because Anna Amalia says in her letter that her son asked for her to intercede, it seems as if the 18-year-old Carl August had been the sole driving force in the appointment. According to critical Goethe biographers: 'Yet the singleness of purpose of the young Duke in pursuing the formal appointment of Goethe as Minister in Weimar remains astounding.'[129] Anna Amalia writes at the beginning of the letter to von Fritsch: 'I entreat you to listen to a friend who only wants the best!' Then: 'My son the Duke has manifested his confidence in me and shown me the correspondence that has taken place between you.' In reality, Anna Amalia had returned, without Carl August realizing it, to the centre of political power again through Goethe. The letters of Anna Amalia to her son would indirectly give information about this, but they were suppressed: 'Also later efforts, undertaken from different directions, have failed to track them down.'[130] One single letter, of 28 July 1795, is extant, in which Anna Amalia complains to Carl August about a visitor in her residence in Tiefurt who subsequently in Weimar gave vent to criticism of alleged statements by Herder:

> You can easily imagine, dear son, how annoying I must find this thing – that someone has no respect for my house and tries to spread slander and gossip about those I have received into my circle. I wanted to report all this to you, dear son, to have you informed of the truth. I would like all such vile, small-minded, dirty gossip could be brought to light as such. ... Goodbye, I love you with all my heart.[131]

Only in 1786, when Goethe told the Duke about his secret did Carl August understand that his mother was Goethe's beloved from the beginning and that they had constantly consulted one another about the way to behave.

His appointment as Minister made it possible for Goethe to show that his leading position in the Duchy was due to his ability. On 22 June 1776 Wieland wrote to Lavater: 'He [Goethe] is now Privy Councillor and has a seat in the ministry of our Duke – he is favourite minister, factotum, and bears the sins of the world. He will do a lot of good, hinder a lot of evil, and that will have to console us, if it is possible, for the fact that as poet he is lost to the world for many years. Goethe doesn't do anything by halves. Now that he has entered on this career he won't rest until he reaches his goal; he will be as great as a minister as he was as a poet.'[132] In the Privy Council Goethe became acquainted with the whole range of administrative and political decisions required for ruling and administering the duchy. During his first decade in Weimar about 23,000 cases, in 750 formal sittings, were dealt with.[133] Goethe was present at more than 500 of these sittings. In a letter of 22 February 1786 to Lavater, Carl August said of his Minister Goethe: 'His existence is one of the most industrious, most moral, and best that have endured over a period of thirty years.' In 1783 the poet and statesman was required, though it was not within the competence of the Privy Council, to decide whether an infanticide should be executed, a tragedy like the one depicted in the first part of Goethe's *Faust* (from 1772). After a long struggle with himself Goethe officially decided that, in line with the prevailing law of the Empire (1532),[134] it was 'more advisable to retain the death penalty', whereupon the 26-year-old Duke signed the sentence of death.[135] Gradually Goethe was given, along with his activity in the Privy Council, further leading functions in the Mines Commission (1777), the War Commission (1779), and in the Road Building Department (1779). In June 1782 the Minister was made head of the Chamber for Finance, and in 1784 direction of the Ilmenau Tax Commission was added.

Silver and copper were meant to be produced in Ilmenau from the old mine, which had been closed. Carl August, who had great hopes of quick wealth, pushed forward energetically with the project. The letters of Anna Amalia to Goethe's mother show that she was au fait with Goethe's stays and work in Ilmenau. On 13 July 1781, for example, she writes to her friend in Frankfurt: 'I can also tell you that the much beloved son Wolf is healthy and well, that he has been in Ilmenau on business, has made all kinds of little excursions as well and has returned happy and healthy.'[136] On 22 February, Anna Amalia writes to her again: 'Your son has gone to Ilmenau on mining business. They want to look for silver mines and so make Weimar rich. May God bless the work!'[137] Planning and making the old mine functional, with Goethe doing the paper work, took much energy; mountains of reports document the undertaking that was pursued without success for four decades.[138]

Looking back, in an entry in 1794 in his *Tag- und Jahreshefte* (1817-1830), Goethe said about the reason for the failure of this undertaking: 'We had plagued ourselves for several years with mining in Ilmenau; to risk such an important undertaking in isolation was only excusable in young, active, and over-enthusiastic people. In the context of a big mining organization it could have been fruitfully developed; but with limited means, with foreign though capable managers sometimes brought in from outside, while we could get a clear picture, the execution was nevertheless neither circumspect nor energetic enough, and the work, especially given unexpected natural features, was more than once inclined to falter.'[139] As director of road-building, Goethe was in charge of all the roads linking the 285 localities in the duchy with one another. The same with town paving. Goethe's job was the maintenance, improvement, and new construction of streets and roads, which on the whole were in very bad condition.[140] Two of the oldest and most important trading routes went through the Duchy of Sachsen-Weimar. The law governing these roads – relating to escort, escort privileges, taxes on foreign armies, toll and suchlike – dated back to the Middle Ages. With his colleague Jean Antoine Joseph de Castrop (1731-1785)[141] Goethe was continually travelling to inspect roads and pushed on with the building of the main roads between Weimar and Erfurt and Weimar and Jena.

> The road to Jena before it was made into a main road was in a condition that was normal for roads in the duchy: no stone base, drivable in the summer, in the autumn and spring full of marshy spots, crossed by streams flowing down onto the roads from neighbouring hills, and in the winter often so impassable that horse and carriage sometimes suffered damage.[142]

As in the sphere of collecting taxes and in his work as director of the War Commission, Goethe's first task was to counteract the laziness, the dull routine, and corruption in the civil service as well as to achieve order and economy. When Goethe noticed around 1782 that the economies achieved by hard work were thoughtlessly squandered by Carl August, he revised his thinking with a view to making the most of his budget.[143] As Minister of War Goethe had a plethora of duties to perform. He had to learn to cope with desertion and the oppressive poverty of the soldiers. About every three years a recruiting of soldiers had to be carried out for the whole duchy. He worked energetically at the reduction of the miniature army, the kernel of which, the army, was reduced from 532 men to 248.[144] He increased the life of uniforms by having the worn-out uniforms recycled.[145]

Alongside work in government and administration – Goethe galloped through the duchy on a white horse that answered to the name of Poesie – the poet made the main contribution to the blossoming of the Weimar amateur theatre (1775-1784) which was directed by himself and Anna Amalia. In Weimar, after the residence was burnt down in 1774, performances were in the redoubt house on the Esplanade that was otherwise meant to be used for masked balls and other feasts and was managed by the court huntsman, building contractor and post-master Anton Georg Hauptmann (1735-1803).[146] As required, a stage was erected and dismantled again.[147] Later, Goethe, who must have had enough of Hauptmann's 'brothel management',[148] pressed on with plans and sketches to have a theatre built, and for this Anna Amalia made a plot of land available opposite the Wittumspalais (ill. 12).[149] Outside the town, in Anna Amalia's Ettersburg residence in the forest, there was a stage which was enlarged in 1777. In good weather there were open-air performances. With the change of Anna Amalia's summer residence from Ettersburg to Tiefurt in 1781 there were also performances in the park there.

Despite his manifold duties as Minister Goethe wrote many small plays for the amateur theatre; he did further work on *Iphigenie*, *Tasso*, *Egmont*, and *Wilhelm Meister*, and he wrote many poems, among them pearls of world poetry, such as the ballads 'Der Erlkönig', 'Der Fischer', and 'Der Sänger'.

When, after eight years, enthusiasm for the amateur theatre had died down, in 1784 the theatre company of Joseph Bellomo (1754-1833) was engaged. At the beginning of 1791 this company moved on, and the decision was made to set up a standing court theatre with professional actors. Artistic direction of the theatre was entrusted to Goethe. In about a quarter of a century he was to stage up to 650 plays.[150] In this, Goethe could fall back on his 8-year experience in directing the amateur theatre, having played more than twenty roles as dancer, actor, and in pantomime; he had experience of several stages which already had very good technical equipment.[151] Goethe was also familiar with matters concerning scenery and costume. His colleague, the painter Kraus, gained the reputation for being one of the best costume designers of his time.[152]

Karl August Böttiger (1760-1835) wrote:

> One of the happiest periods was the time when the Duchess, who still retained some of the glamour of her regency and now wanted to enjoy her leisure, lived in Ettersburg. Living like gypsies. Torch-lit comedy in the forest.[153]

In the beautiful summer nights Anna Amalia had the area around the residence lit up and she invited guests for music, dance and fireworks.[154] There was a report about a ball given by Anna Amalia in the forest residence in Ettersburg in 1777. Nearly 200 couples were present, mainly young people from neighbouring localities.

> Before the Duchess came out of the residence accompanied by nobility, the local people were given wine and beer as refreshments ... Duchess Amalia took her place in front of the residence, sitting with older ladies and men who had no wish to dance, among them the wife of Councillor von Fritsch, the Chamberlain von Lyncker, von Goethe and others. In front of where the Duchess was sitting a hole had been dug in the courtyard about fifteen yards in diameter and shallow at the sides. This hole was filled with water ... The dancing began with a Polonaise in which the dancers wheeled around the courtyard in different movements and then suddenly went through the middle of the hole. Of course the young women resisted going into the water but were forcefully dragged into it by the sturdy peasant lads. After this, despite the clothes being wet and soiled, the dancing was more orderly and continued late into the night, when everyone gradually started to leave.[155]

At the beginning of 1778 Countess Görtz reports to her husband: '*Maman* [Anna Amalia] is becoming younger every day' and '*Maman* danced like a mad young thing'.[156] And on 26 April 1778 she writes: 'Yesterday's news is a holiday excursion to Jena to see a student comedy. The Dowager Duchess went there with her dear friend Goethe.'[157]

An unnamed traveller says of a masked ball:

> The Duchess [Anna Amalia] looked superb *en domino* [in her costume] and shone also with her finery and jewels. She is a beautiful dancer, light on her feet, and dignified ... she danced with everyone who approached her and stayed until three in the morning when all the dancing was nearly over.

The same person reports about another masked ball: 'The Duchess [Anna Amalia] was *en reine grecque* [masked as a Greek queen], a superb mask which, like everything, became her very well.'[158]

Anna Amalia took an interest in everything that concerned Goethe. She invited his friend Merck, who before his Weimar years had given him important stimulus and support, to accompany her in her trip to Frankfurt and the Rhine area (1778). Merck writes to Wieland on 1 August 1778:

> I found the Duchess [Anna Amalia] from beginning to end the same in herself and with me. The best part is, as with her son, the great healthy mind. One can be in agreement with her precisely in matters in which one most wants to agree – for instance, about you and about Goethe ... It disturbed me that, apart from the Duchess, no one had a good word to say about Goethe, and God knows he can't have deserved that of them. He is not malicious, but he doesn't do what people want – who can?[159]

Anna Amalia invited Merck to come to Weimar (1779), corresponded with him, valued him as a connoisseur of art, and commissioned him as her agent to make art purchases for her. From a letter of Wieland to Merck of 8 January 1781 it is clear how very much at home Goethe was in the Wittumspalais. He was completely relaxed there. Wieland was visiting Anna Amalia and was showing her a manuscript of Merck's when Goethe came in and asked what they were reading. He then took the manuscript and read from it out loud. It turned into

> a regular academic lecture, and the result was that Goethe, after consultation on different points and arguments pro and contra, got a large quill from the Duchess's writing table and drew a line through the preface as thick as your arm.'[160]

The spacious garden of the Wittumspalais (ill. 10 and 12) consisted of two parts which were separated by the town wall. Since 1776 Anna

Amalia had leased the strip of land behind the town wall (torn down in 1793) which she could have access to from her courtyard. She had a tower which was part of the town fortification turned into a pavillion and commissioned Oeser to decorate it with Chinese landscapes. [161]A water-colour painting by Anna Amalia shows the English garden (ill. 10), in which without being disturbed or observed she could receive any visitor. Passing mentions continually point to Goethe's closeness to Anna Amalia. Luise von Göchhausen reports to Merck on 26 April 1780 that Wieland had been sent a manuscript on loan 'with the express stipulation not to let it out of his hands. The Duchess [Anna Amalia] and Goethe have ... read it'.[162]

In a conversation with Eckermann on 7 October 1827 Goethe makes it very clear that he had loved the resident of the Wittumspalais. In the conversation they are dealing with the question of magnetic attraction between people:

> I remember a case from my first years here, when I had very soon fallen passionately in love again. I had been away on a rather long journey and had been back a few days but because of court business which preoccupied me until late at night I was always prevented from visiting my beloved. Also, our affection had already attracted people's attention, and so I was avoiding going there in daylight so as not to add to the talk.

However, on the fourth or fifth evening Goethe went to her house, but noticed that some ladies were visiting. Later all the lights were out, but he still roamed around the town and hoped that on the basis of his strong longing for her she too would come out and meet him. At this point in the narrative suddenly Anna Amalia's Wittumspalais is mentioned:

> Meanwhile I had gone down the Esplanade as far as the little house inhabited by Schiller in later years, when I suddenly decided to turn around and go back to the [Wittums] palace and from there down a little street to the right. I had hardly gone a hundred steps in this direction when I saw a female figure coming towards me which looked exactly like the woman I was longing for ... We passed very close by one another so that our arms made contact. I stopped and looked around. So did she. 'Is that you', she said, and I recognized her dear voice. 'At last', I said, and was happy to the point of tears ... I accompanied her to her door and into her house. She went ahead of me up the dark stairs. She was holding my hand and to a certain extent pulling me after her. My happiness was indescribable.

With regard to his appointment as Permanent Privy Councillor in 1779 Goethe writes in a letter to 'Frau von Stein' of 7 September 1779: ' ... it seems miraculous to me that at the age of thirty, as if in a dream, I reach the highest honour available to a citizen in Germany.' In 1782 came the patent of nobility which now made him presentable at court. The Duchess Luise now accepted Goethe's invitations to dine with him 'because he belongs to the nobility'.[163] For the young Duchess it was 'repugnant', according to a 19th century biographer 'that a young man of the middle classes [Goethe], no matter how gifted, should be so very closely associated with the Duke [Carl August]'.[164] In contrast to Anna Amalia, Luise was an arch defender of the barriers establishing social division. When Charlotte von Lengefeld (1766-1826) married the middle-class poet Friedrich Schiller, Luise told the bride that she deeply regretted it.[165] Goethe owed to Anna Amalia the patent of nobility issued by Emperor Joseph II. In a letter of 18 February 1781 to 'Frau von Stein' he writes to his beloved, referring to her in the third person: 'Yesterday the Dowager Duchess spoke at length about the fact that the Duke needed to and wanted to have me raised to the nobility. I just gave my opinion very simply.' Besides that, Goethe attained the degree of Master in the Freemasons' Lodge, Anna Amalia zu den drei Rosen (founded in 1764), to which he was admitted in 1780.[166] The leading people in Weimar were members of the Anna Amalia lodge, among them Carl August, von Fritsch, Musäus, Kraus, Wieland and Bertuch. Herder, too, had been a Freemason in Riga, but did not enter the lodge in Weimar. The secret society of Freemasons has mediaeval precursors and in its modern form is known to have been in Scotland since 1688. Lodge members from all social classes go through a training system with the different grades: apprentice, journeyman, and master.[167] But around 1740 there is already evidence of attempts to include further grades above that of master. Just at the time that Goethe became a Freemason there was a raging quarrel whether the Anna Amalia Lodge should follow the 'strict observance', according to which there are three grades higher than the master: the Scottish grade, the noviceship, and, finally, as the last grade, the inner order. Before the final grade it was necessary to swear an oath of unconditional obedience to an unknown superior.[168] In Weimar they decided against the 'strict observance' system. The work of the Anna Amalia lodge was at a standstill from 1782 and resumed around 1808 in the traditional framework of three grades.[169] Historically the phenomenon of secret societies is to be explained by the fact that in the 18th century there was a development in the social and economic conditions, while the political order stood still on the more primitive monarchical level.[170]

In the summer of 1782 Goethe was given the presidency of the Chamber of Finance. In fact, the year 1782 represents the climax of Goethe's career as a statesman, since, after Carl August, he was by far the most important man in the Duchy; and yet on 26 February 1782 he writes to Knebel: 'So much for the brilliant shell of our existence. The inner part belongs to the old, except that with the continual change one part gets worse and the other better.' The need to be deceptive with regard to his forbidden love became ever more problematic for Goethe and often put him into a mood of depression. Even for the statesman there was not just the brilliant side, for Goethe had too many portfolios. In addition, Carl August's foreign policy had him preoccupied with the idea of a union of princes as a third power beside Prussia and Austria, something which only came about through Napoleon Bonaparte (1769-1821) with his Confederation of the Rhine, at first made up of sixteen German principalities.

The problem of deceit preoccupied Goethe more and more. During his Harz journey in the winter of 1777 he writes in his diary on 8 December: 'Lied throughout the afternoon'. On the journey he assumed the identity of an artist, was called Weber, came from Gotha, and was travelling on family business. The next day he writes: 'In my disguise I daily see how easy it is to be a rogue and what advantages an assumed identity gives you over the powerless self-centredness of people.' Later Goethe will deal thoroughly with the problem of lies and deception in *Der Großkophta* and in *Wilhelm Meister*. On the one hand Goethe is in love and this love is most beautifully reciprocated, and on the other hand he is forced daily to deny this love:

> The infinite gods gave their favourites everything,
> Gave all the infinite joys
> All the infinite pain.

In the letter to Countess August zu Stolberg (1753-1835) of 17 July 1777 which contain these lines, clarification is given: 'Thus I sang recently, in a glorious moon-lit night as I climbed out of the river that flows through the meadows in front of my garden. And daily that proves true of my situation.' As early as 13 June 1777 Wieland complained, in a letter to Merck, that Goethe was closed: '... instead of the all-enlivening warmth that used to radiate from him there is a political frost around him. He is always good and does no harm, but he doesn't communicate any more.[171] On 13 May 1780 Goethe makes the entry in his diary: 'No one sees the burdens I bear for myself and others. What is best is the deep silence in which I encounter the world, and grow, and gain what they can't take from me with fire or sword.' But Goethe's inner and outer burdens in maintaining the cover-up increased from year to year. In a letter to 'Frau von Stein' of 18 February 1782 he writes:

> I have a deep-seated worry, a mood that plagues me and has for a long time caused me alarm. You must let me tell you, you must comfort me. I feel pain as I anticipate the next moment in which I see you again. You must forgive me. It's to do with thoughts which arise out of my love, ghosts which are dreadful for me and which only you can dispel.

People around him who could not know that he was worried about his forbidden love attributed his visibly increasing malaise to his performance of so many duties. For example, Wieland wrote, in a letter to Merck of 5 January 1784:

> [Goethe] suffers only too visibly, in body and soul, from the oppressive burden he has taken on for our benefit. It sometimes pains me to see how he puts a brave face on it and lets the affliction gnaw away at his insides like a worm.[172]

Goethe was aware that he had to reduce the burden of his work as state Minister and to liberate his love relationship out of the nerve-wracking state of a nocturnal love. In the meantime, his love for Anna Amalia has him tied to Weimar. On 23 November 1783 he writes to 'Frau von Stein': ... if it were not for you I would have shaken everything off long ago.' On 24 August 1784 he writes to 'Frau von Stein':

> It's certain I would have gone far, far away,
> To the furthest reaches of the world,
> Had not the mighty stars
> Linked my destiny to yours,
> So that only now I know myself in you.
> My poems, strivings, my hopes and my desires
> Are all for you and what you are.

Probably the situation would have remained like this for a long time if Goethe had not been forced by external circumstances to take flight. That Goethe had made detailed plans for them to leave for America is clear from the *Wilhelm Meister* novel, but the project foundered. Thirty years later Goethe admitted to the art collector Sulpiz Boisserée (1783-1854), in a conversation on 2 August 1815: 'What would have come of it if thirty years ago I had gone to America with a few friends and had heard nothing of Kant etc?'[173] But the hope that emigration to America could succeed gave the lovers, for a long time, the strength they needed to maintain the cover-up. For instance, when the lovers, in the life they shared – limited to night-time – read travel adventures, they imagined a happy future for them together. In a letter to 'Frau von Stein' of 5 December 1783 Goethe writes: 'Come soon, beloved, so that I can enjoy the best part of my life. Let's read some Pagé.' In 1782 the travel adventures of Vicomte de Pagès (1748-1793) *Voyages autour du monde* had been published. In his letters to 'Frau von Stein' Goethe had also spoken of fleeing by himself. He wanted to impress on Anna Amalia how important it was that they flee together. On 8 July 1781 he writes from Ilmenau:

> I long for you without admitting it to myself. My mind is becoming narrow and finds no pleasure in anything. Sometimes worry takes over, another time discouragement, and an evil spirit misuses my absence from you, paints for me the most burdensome side of my condition and advises me to rescue myself by fleeing; but soon I feel that a glance, a word from you can dispel all these mists ... We are indeed married, that is: joined by a bond which promises love and joy and results in suffering, worry, and wretchedness.

6 | Flight to Italy: 'Oh, What an Error!'

> There are, in fact, few people who have an imagination which grasps the truth about the real; instead, they like to be in strange countries and circumstances of which they have no understanding and which their imagination can concoct for them. And then there are others who cling to the real and, because they are altogether lacking in poetry, make demands on it which are too narrow.
>
> Goethe's *Conversations with Eckermann*, 25 December 1825

> [Baron von Goethe] still has the same influence over the husband [Carl August] and the wife [Luise] and over Frau von Stein, who as previously still plays the role allotted to her as well as she can. She eats potatoes almost every evening in her house with Goethe and the Duchess [Anna Amalia]. Her husband completely ignores it all.
>
> Gräfin Görtz to her husband, 12 October 1782

In 1785, Goethe undertook his first journey with Knebel to the West Bohemian health resort Karlsbad. The journey was repeated the following year, but the poet did not return this time to Weimar but fled on 3 September 1786 in great haste to Italy. Goethe did not turn his back on Germany because he could no longer bear life at court or because official business threatened to destroy his artistic talent. His departure from Karlsbad was a flight dictated by politics of State. In a letter to Carl August of 20 January 1787 Goethe unmistakably calls his journey to Italy a 'flight' (Flucht). Shortly before, in a letter to 'Frau von Stein' of 23 December 1786, he also refers to it as a 'fall' (Sturz). In *Tasso* he will write (ll. 2701 ff.):

> My soles are burning
> On this marble floor; my mind
> Will find no rest until the dust
> Of the open road surrounds me in my haste.

On 17 August 1786 the Prussian King Friedrich II died. His first official act, in 1740, had been a military attack on Austrian Silesia,. which he described as a rendez-vous with fame. He did this under the pretext that he was unwilling to accept the Austrian accession to the throne of a woman, through which, in 1740, the Arch-Duchess Maria Theresia of Austria came to power. In Goethe's satire *Die Vögel* (1780) Prussia is represented as an eagle: 'Black, with a crown on its head, it makes its beak wide open, sticks out a red tongue, and shows a pair of claws which are ever willing ... No one feels comfortable who looks at it.' During the Bavarian War of Succession (1778/79), as Minister for War, Goethe advised Carl August voluntarily to provide troops for the Prussians, because otherwise they would, with a show of naked force take away useful, married, and settled people (letter of 9 February 1779). Appointed Minister for War on 5 January 1779, Goethe tried to keep King Friedrich II at bay. As early as January he wrote in his diary: 'We only have a few more moves and then it is checkmate for us. A courier to the king. Days of grace in the meantime.' Friedrich II threatened to occupy the tiny Duchy. The Privy Council decreed forbidding all discussion of the war in the inns of the Duchy for fear of giving a pretext for an intervention.[174] As an old man, Goethe spoke of a kind of conspiracy against Prussia at a time when there was fear of the supremacy of Friedrich II.[175] The heir to the throne, Friedrich Wilhelm II (1744-1797), was still less predictable. Before coming to Weimar as tutor to the prince (1774) Knebel had long served in his army and judged him as being of dull and indifferent mind.[176] His favouritism and preoccupation with mistresses was to bring Prussia to the brink of bankruptcy.

The fact that Carl August was no longer working for the creation of an independent Union of Princes as a third power in Germany alongside Prussia and Austria and (1785) joined the union dominated by Prussia was not enough to make him a friend of Prussia. During the change of throne in Prussia it was not possible to depend on conditions as they had been in the previous political regime. Only Prussia and Austria stood firm as opposite political poles. In diplomatic circles the rumour was circulating that the new Prussian king wanted to convert to Catholicism with a view to being eligible to become Holy Roman Emperor, a title which since 1438 had, almost without exception, belonged to the Habsburgs.[177] Precisely at this time something unexpected happened in Weimar: someone knew about Goethe's secret, about his forbidden love for the Princess Anna Amalia, and anonymously let it be known.

Goethe's letters from Italy to Carl August report, in code, about the search for and discovery of the person who divulged the secret

(Verräter). In this time of political uncertainty knowledge of the secret by an unknown third party was highly dangerous. Goethe feared that the Prussians would intervene and could even use his forbidden love with a Duchess as a pretext to annex the Duchy. On 3 September 1786 Goethe drew the logical conclusions from the 'discovery' and took flight from Karlsbad to Italy under the name of Johann Philip Möller. On 2 September Goethe writes to the Duke:

> I just ask you not to let anyone notice that I am away. All colleagues and subordinates and others in my circle expect me back one week to another and it is good that it should remain so and that I, during my absence, be seen as someone expected back.

Frau von Stein's son Fritz, who lived in Goethe's house, reports: 'Because he was constantly expected back I stayed in his house for nearly six months.'[178] Because the 'traitor' was not known, everyone was, as much as possible, to be kept in ignorance of Goethe's whereabouts.

In Goethe's letter to Carl August of 18 September 1786 from Verona foreign policy is mentioned: 'Sometimes I would like to know what is happening in Berlin and how the new master is behaving, what news you have, and what role you yourself are playing.' Further: 'The newspapers tell me somewhat late all the exciting events in the world. Görtz in the Hague; the governor and the patriots armed; the new King has sided with [the Duke of] Orange! What will come of that?' Decisive here is the name Görtz, Goethe's and Anna Amalia's embittered enemy from earlier days. This is the key to the understanding of Goethe's flight. Since 1778 Count Görtz was in Prussian employ and had now been sent by the new King as extraordinary ambassador to the Hague.[179] Previously Görtz had been active in Weimar: in 1762, at the age of 25, he was engaged by the Duchess Anna Amalia as tutor to her sons. Before his pupil Carl August took over the reins of government Count Görtz was involved in intrigue behind Anna Amalia's back and planned a coup to oust the Duchess before Carl August's eighteenth birthday.[180] After this Görtz followed another plan. In a letter to von Fritsch shortly after the changeover of government on 3 September 1775 Anna Amalia expressed her serious concern that 'Görtz's whole plan would be put into operation'.[181] Görtz's plan was the immediate change of personnel occupying the key positions in government and administration, something that von Dalberg (1744-1817), the Electoral governor in Erfurt, mentions in a letter to Anna Amalia on 12 July 1775: ' ... he [Görtz] is doing an injustice in advising his Highness the Duke to use his accession to power to make changes [affecting government].[182] 'A little earlier, in a letter of 9 July 1775, von Dalberg exhorted Görtz to more moderation:

> Why immediate changes? Noises are being made everywhere that Carl August is not on good terms with his mother, and more than once I heard it with my own ears: he [Carl August] is in the wrong, for his mother ran a good administration. What would be so wrong if Carl August were to make no changes in the first months. I must admit that I never had the impression that the work of the Duchess's Privy Council was bad or that the Council was so laughable that an immediate reform was urgently needed – which would really be an insult to his mother ... I beg you, stay calm. Everything will be all right.[183]

Anna Amalia dismissed Görtz demonstratively two months before Carl August reached his majority.

In a letter of 2 July 1775 to Minister von Fritsch she writes: 'The business with Görtz is completely finished', and then on 4 July 1775 she required of Minister von Fritsch to water down two flowery expressions of gratitude in the decree of dismissal, because she was 'convinced that he [Görtz] had fundamentally spoiled my son'.[184] Görtz still held to his plan to change the personnel in all key positions in the Duchy before the beginning of Carl August's reign, but Wieland, who was privy to the plan, revealed it, and all the details, to Anna Amalia. In a letter of Dalberg to Görtz on 17 August 1775 we read:

> If Wieland said to the Duke that I had commissioned him to oppose Franckenberg, then he is lying. If he is the one who divulged Carl August's plan to the Duchess, a plan which had been revealed to him in confidence, and you are sure of it, I will despise him forever.[185]

On 17 September 1775 Countess Görtz reports to her husband:

> The governor [Dalberg] told me he received him [Wieland] with coolness. I had the impression that Wieland wanted to apologize to him, but he avoided it ... The Duchess assured the governor that she had quite independently decided to act against you (Görtz's dismissal in July).[186]

After being installed as ruler on 3 September 1775, the 18-year-old Carl August made no move to implement any sort of plan. Anna Amalia's counter plans seem to have been effective. Carl August generously enhanced the arrangements for his tutor and appointed him on 30 October 1775 as chief private tutor to his wife Luise, who had chosen him – a vain attempt to set up something in rivalry with the widow's court of her mother-in-law, Anna Amalia. Böttiger reported: 'Only Görtz stayed with the ruling Duchess. Otherwise the

Dowager Duchess drew all to herself.'[187] Count Görtz's star was waning. On 7 October 1775 his wife wrote to him:

> I am certain that the governor will try everything to bring you closer to the Duchess [Anna Amalia], but I am afraid he won't succeed. My friend, you are too trusting, you have been betrayed ... I wish we were not staying here any longer.[188]

Goethe's arrival in Weimar brought Count Görtz down from his ambitious plans, and the meteoric rise of the foreign genius finally deprived him of the reigning Duke's favour which he had won through his thirteen years of work as tutor. In a letter to his wife on 2 April 1776 Görtz refers to Goethe as the 'cause of our torments'.[189] It was above all Görtz who, shortly after Goethe's arrival in Weimar, spread inflammatory rumours about the behaviour of the *Sturm und Drang* geniuses at the Weimar court causing grave concern. Such rumours moved Klopstock, for example, to write a fatherly letter of warning to Goethe (8 May 1776), which Goethe rejected in annoyance (21 May 1776): 'Dear Klopstock, spare us such letters in future', which led to a rift between the poets. Wieland, who from 1772, together with Görtz, had taken over the education of the Princes and for a short time had flirted with his ambitious plans, but now in the meantime completely on Anna Amalia's and Goethe's side, wrote about Görtz in a letter to his friend Merck on 5 July 1776:

> Let the shabby fellows gossip. Count Görtz is now also making preparations to travel in your direction and to Mainz and Mannheim to instigate all kinds of things there against Goethe and me. The miserable wretch! But no more about this scum. Come and see for yourself what we are doing. You won't regret it.[190]

On 24 July 1776 he writes again: 'Görtz is smearing us everywhere with muck.'[191]

In 1776 Görtz, in bitter disappointment, handed in his request to be relieved of his duties in Weimar and was looking around for a new post.[192] Two audiences with King Friedrich II in the spring of 1776 were at first unproductive.[193]

For Anna Amalia the appointment of Goethe was a liberating step. It enabled her to avoid a situation which was rife in most princely courts in Germany: namely, that power was in the hands of corrupt Ministers and such as had ambitions only for their own personal enrichment. Above all, her plan, along with Goethe, to build up a Court of Muses (Musenhof), was no longer endangered. Goethe invented the word 'gegörzt' for acting with political ambition,[194] since on the eve of the Bavarian War of Succession (1778/9) Count Görtz, through the intervention of his brother – a Prussian general – was entrusted by Friedrich II with an important diplomatic task. Friedrich II had met Count Görtz as tutor to the Prince in Anna Amalia's sphere of influence in 1763 and 1771. Shortly before this last meeting his brother had left a post in the Danish army to take up a post in the Prussian army.[195] In the Bavarian War of Succession – also known as the potato war because apart from small skirmishes nothing happened but theft – Friedrich II tried with all diplomatic means to prevent large areas of Bavaria being taken over by Austria. The Bavarian Wittelsbach line had died out. The heir, Elector Karl Theodor von der Pfalz (1724-1799), a man of the world and an art-lover, wanted to avoid conflict and entered a contract with Emperor Joseph II: for money payments and for titles of nobility for his illegitimate children he would hand over large parts of Bavaria to the Emperor. The task of the Count Görtz as a private citizen of neutral Weimar was, in Zweibrücken, to persuade the nephew and heir of the Elector to speak out loudly against his foolish uncle for selling his birthright for a mess of potage.[196] Carl August and Goethe inclined more towards the Emperor's side than to Prussia. Friedrich II wrote to his brother on 3 March 1778:

> The gentlemen in Saxony are being difficult. The Princes of the Empire are vacillating reeds. They have no energy, no sense of honour. I had to urge the Prince of Zweibrücken on. Left to himself he would have accepted shame like his uncle, the Elector of the Pfalz. I know what a wretched lot these Princes of the Empire are, and I have no intention of becoming their Don Quixote. If Austria is allowed illegally to acquire despotic rights over Germany we'll be putting weapons into their hands for use against ourselves ... I consider war is inevitable.[197]

Since Count Görtz informed Duke Carl August about the diplomatic mission only afterwards, the result was a rift between the two. In a letter of 19 March 1778 which was drafted by Goethe, Carl August writes to Görtz in very bad humour:

> At a time when the great powers in the German Empire are at loggerheads, my situation and my duty leave me no course but quietly to await the outcome of the crisis, and – since there is nothing to be gained for me and mine, but something to lose – to follow, if necessary, one party or the other, even if unhappily. These ideas, which you have nourished and so often thought acceptable, have to seem ambiguous to the public because of the step you have taken. After such a close relationship with me, declaring your loyalty to me, you go out as a member of my court and without my knowledge carry out crucial public negotiations for one party. I could only wish that you would have considered in what a strange light I must appear to those who believe, or don't believe that I had prior

> knowledge of this. They will be astonished either at the behaviour of my people towards me or at my stance in Germany's present critical situation ... But be assured that my regard for you remains unshakable.[198]

Goethe and Anna Amalia dictated this letter to the immature Carl August who was just twenty years old. The letter, carefully formulated, reproaches Count Görtz, who has been looking for a post for over a year, with disloyalty – in the narrower sense to Saxony-Weimar and in the broader sense to the Emperor in Vienna. For Görtz, who was receiving a generous pension paid by Carl August, only one hope was left: the prospects extended to him by Friedrich II. Görtz answers Carl August on 5 April 1778 and defends himself against the charges:

> The displeasure which your Highness shows concerning the steps I have taken is extremely painful to me ... nor do I dare to attempt to justify myself ... for the present, only these few words in my defence. The King's commission came quite unexpectedly and without any initiative on my part. It was the King's own initiative. My own brother, whom I dearly love, and whose well-being depends on the King, brought it to me. Your Highness had variously said in writing and by word of mouth that you considered me quite free. I can furthermore assure you that nothing in the whole commission would give a basis for one or other of the great courts to think there was anything disadvantageous in it for them. ... This – to be able to contribute to the preservation and peace of Germany – doubled my zeal. ... I am not capable of deliberately doing wrong ... forgive me if I have been so unfortunate as to have displeased you and let [me] enjoy your favour again.[199]

In the archives of Count Rechberg in Donsdorf there is a letter of Countess Görtz to her husband in Zweibrücken on 14 March 1778.[200] In it there is explicit mention of the forbidden liaison between Goethe and Anna Amalia. For Countess Görtz this is an exceptional situation. She has to watch how in Weimar there are attempts to deprive her husband of his pension and to do serious damage to his reputation. In this context she refers to the secret liaison between Goethe and Anna Amalia. Logically Görtz should proceed against Anna Amalia, for she is the one who through Goethe and Carl August wants to have her revenge against Count Görtz:

> *Maman* [Anna Amalia] is one in heart and mind with the *génie par excellence* and malicious tongues are saying that despite her distant attitude towards him in public he is missing from supper almost every evening ...
>
> People have found ways and means of making him [the Duke] enraged with you because you left here without taking him into your

> confidence. No doubt the liaison between Maman and Goethe is behind it. They are united in their attempt to do you a disservice.[201]

A few days later Countess Görtz writes to her husband: 'My sole fear is a letter from Goethe which the Duke will only put his signature to.'[202] The Görtz family, the great losers in Goethe's becoming Carl August's intimate friend, were soon liberated from the 'Weimar hell', for King Friedrich II, satisfied with the conduct of the diplomatic mission, appointed Count Görtz a Prussian Minister of State on 6 April 1778. The Duke of Zweibrücken would soon say that he requested the protection of Friedrich II and that he would never agree to the contract with the Elector. Friedrich II answered him: 'Your letter gives me great satisfaction. Your agreement [to the contract] would mutilate Bavaria without any hope of restoration. You would have everything to lose by it and nothing to gain.'[203] For Görtz the appointment as Prussian Minister did not lead to a final break with Weimar. On the contrary, the guilt of a secret liaison between the Princess Anna Amalia and the middle-class Goethe would have been a serious weapon for Görtz, especially in the hands of a Friedrich II. Overnight, from being a loser Count Görtz had become an outstanding winner. From the tiny Duchy of Weimar he moved as Minister to Prussia, one of the great European powers. Relieved, he wrote from Zweibrücken to Carl August (who did not answer him) on 10 April 1778 in mocking overtones:

> His Majesty has commanded me to come to Berlin as State Minister and Grand Maître de la Garderobe. I would only be happy to accept this position if your most gracious Highness would agree to restore me to your favour and goodwill and would be assured of my most devoted loyalty to your Highness.[204]

In May 1778, the Prince of the Empire, Carl August, travelled to Berlin with his Minister Goethe for exploratory political talks. On 17 May 1778, at a working meal for high-ranking figures in the Palace Unter den Linden, Görtz was also present. Graf Lehndorff makes a note of it in his diary:

> He [Carl August] seems to be a handsome young man, though there is something unfriendly about his face. With him is Goethe, the famous author of 'Werther' and 'Götz von Berlichingen', whom the Duke has made his Privy Councillor. Goethe controls him now after ousting the previous tutor, Count Görtz, who has just now entered our service.[205]

Goethe was both fearful of and disgusted by the slippery floor of Berlin diplomacy. Even before entering the gates of Berlin, Goethe wrote to 'Frau von Stein' on 14 May 1778: 'The great play with people, and the gods play with the great.' Summarizing his first and last journey to Berlin, he wrote in a letter to 'Frau von Stein' on 19 May: 'This much I can say: the higher the society the more loathsome the farce.'

Relations between Count Görtz and Weimar were not severed. His wife, a von Üchtritz of Gotha by birth, occasionally came to Weimar and was received at court. The letters she wrote to her husband continually make explicit reference to the forbidden love between Goethe and Anna Amalia. The couple saw through the cover-up and spoke about it disparagingly. Countess Görtz writes to her husband on 11 June 1780: 'Goethe keeps on talking about perfect love, and poor Frau von Stein, none so dumb as she, puts up with the public's as well as Goethe's gossip, and the bad moods of his woman [Anna Amalia]. So you can see nothing has changed.'[206] On 24 December she reports to her husband: More than ever Frau von Stein is putting on a public show with her friend [Goethe]. In the end, things are much the same as we left them.'[207] Countess Görtz was in contact with ladies at the Weimar court who kept her informed of the news, including the forbidden love between Goethe and Anna Amalia. The Chief [female] Tutor of Duchess Luise, Countess Wilhelmine Giannini (c.1719-1784), also saw through the cover-up. She reports to Countess Görtz on 29 August 1781: ' ... the last named [Anna Amalia] has just performed yet another act of folly. Yesterday in Tiefurt she celebrated Goethe's birthday with a shadow play comedy and a small fire-works display. How do you like that?'[208] In a letter of 12 August 1782 to Countess Görtz, Countess Giannini mentions the dismissal of August von Kalb (1747-1814), President of the Chamber of Finance, and directly afterwards the forbidden liaison:

> Our news won't be really new to you, though you will be amazed that von Kalb has been dismissed, and not less amazed that Goethe has been raised to the ranks of the nobility. The love affair of the latter with his miserable jade [Anna Amalia] is still very much alive. The power that this clique has over the Duke and Duchess is greater than ever. My illness and resulting absence has made it possible for them to gain a lot of ground. It would make you vomit, but I am not worried. If they take it too far I know where to go and where I will be received with open arms.[209]

Countess Giannini wanted to go to Berlin if Goethe and Anna Amalia were to act too wildly. Goethe was appointed as successor to the frivolous von Kalb, who had not only proved himself incompetent but had also incurred enormous debts. But only a few people knew this, and from the outside it looked as if Minister Goethe could not acquire enough offices for himself. People around von Kalb tried in vain to create a scandal out of the dismissal.[210]

From Weimar, in a letter of 11/12 October 1782 Countess Görtz reports candidly to her husband:

> I spent the day yesterday at court ... Baron Goethe greeted me very heartily and, showing great interest, asked me for news about you. He continued the conversation until I was called upon to play. Frau von Stein smothered me with her affection. [12 October] Regarding Baron von Goethe: he had become very nice and chatty and has assumed the style of a cavalier. He still has the same influence over the husband [Carl August] and the wife [Luise] and over Frau von Stein, who as previously still plays the role allotted to her as well as she can. She eats potatoes almost every evening in her house with Goethe and the Duchess [Anna Amalia]. Her husband completely ignores it all. He has filled out and has become fat, and he remains as lacking in taste and as false as ever.[211]

It would seem that the Chief Equerry Josias von Stein knew of the deceit by which his wife was made out to be Goethe's lover. Since he was in fact not being deceived, he was easily able to accept the display required by Anna Amalia. In addition, he gave court gossip reason to think he was involved in a liaison with the lady-in-waiting von Waldner.[212] The mention precisely of potatoes as the evening meal is a reference to the difference in rank between Goethe and Anna Amalia. Friedrich II forced his peasants, from 1756, to cultivate the prolific potato plant, which had come from Central America to Europe in 1493. As late as the 19th century Prussian aristocrats in some areas considered themselves too sophisticated to eat potatoes like the peasants. When Countess Görtz writes to her husband in Berlin that Goethe and Anna Amalia ate potatoes every evening, she is saying that the Princess Anna Amalia was mixing with something beneath her, namely, the upstart Goethe, whose grandfather Friedrich Georg Goethe (1657-1730) was a tailor and whose grandmother Cornelia, née Walther (1668-1754), was an inn-keeper.

It was therefore Görtz whom Goethe had in mind when he feared a Prussian conspiracy after the change of sovereign. He thought it possible that Görtz was just waiting for the change to make political capital out of the Weimar state secret – with a view to ingratiating himself with the new King Friedrich Wilhelm II. Friedrich Wilhelm had already shown the bad side of his character in his dealings with Anna Amalia's younger sister, Elisabeth Christine Ulrike von Braunschweig (1746-1840), betrothed to him in 1765. The Prussian heir to the throne had several lovers even after his marriage and was quite open about his relationships with them. His wife followed his example. King Friedrich II judged the situation – which concerned the daughter of his beloved sister Philippine Charlotte – as follows:

> The husband, young and dissolute, given over to loose living, was untrue to his wife on a daily basis. The Princess, whose beauty was still blossoming, felt grossly insulted because of the scant notice paid to her charms. Her vivacity and the good opinion she had of herself led her to seek revenge for the wrong done to her. She soon gave herself over to a life hardly less dissolute than that of her husband. The result was catastrophic and soon became public.[213]

Here the unbelievable cynicism of Friedrich II is revealed. His ostentatious rejection of the unscrupulous power politics attributed to Machiavelli (1469-1527) was only meant to cover up his own lack of scruples in political and human affairs. It is not conceivable that a head of State, so perfectly aware of the situation, could not have come to the aid of his politically inexperienced niece. It was unanimously agreed that blame for the marriage scandal was to be laid at the door of Elisabeth Christine Ulrike; the divorce took place in 1769 and the 22-year-old was banished and virtually imprisoned in Stettin, where she lived for another seventy-two years. King Friedrich II must have been satisfied for some reason or other with the outcome of the marital conflict. Perhaps the name of his niece reminded him of his wife Elisabeth Christine (1715-1797), also a Princess of Braunschweig, whom he had to marry in 1733. When he acceded to the throne (1740) he banished her without ever having touched her.[214]

After more than ten years of deception Goethe's and Anna Amalia's nerves were long since raw. Towards the end of 1785 Anna Amalia's easy-going younger son caused a diplomatic incident by his reprehensible behaviour towards King Friedrich II. For this reason Anna Amalia, as Dowager Duchess, wrote several letters of apology to her uncle, for example, on 9 October 1785: 'It would make me extremely happy if I could flatter myself that Your Majesty would continue to show me and my sons the honour of your favour.' Carl August even asked for a personal audience with the Prussian king to apologize for the behaviour of his brother. The audience was graciously granted to him.[215] Since the spring of 1786 the death of the ailing King Friedrich II was imminent, and precisely at this time a 'traitor' let it be known that he knew the state secret about Goethe and Anna Amalia. What could be more feasible than to suspect the intriguer Görtz, who had seen through the deception with Frau von Stein? Goethe and Anna Amalia thought that Görtz wanted to revenge himself on them, probably with the aim of extinguishing the tiny duchy. With the new King anything could happen. The sculptor Johann Gottfried Schadow (1764-1850) said about his regime: 'There was extreme dissoluteness in the court. Everyone got drunk on champagne, gobbled up the greatest delicacies and gave free rein to every passion. The whole of Potsdam was a bawdy house.'[216]

When Goethe revealed the secret to Duke Carl August in Karlsbad, he immediately took a sounding of the situation in Berlin. Carl August writes to Görtz on 18 September 1786: 'Our new King seems to want to win general respect and confidence through doing good and through moderation. How easily he will achieve this, given the excellent qualities of his heart.'[217] The Prussian diplomat Johann Friedrich von Stein, Carl August's informant in Berlin, reports from Potsdam on 6 October 1786: 'To the scrutinizing eye there is no activity which would give even an initial clue to the execution of well thought-out plans.'[218] Carl August writes to Minister von Franckenberg in Gotha on 16 October 1786: 'Despite all opposition the King is remaining true to the political system.'[219] At the very latest when the new Prussian King expressed his confidence in Carl August and called him to Berlin to entrust him with a sensitive diplomatic mission in Mainz, it became clear that there was no threat of danger from the new King. On 13 November 1786 Carl August writes to Görtz: 'I can report to you very briefly, my dear Count, that, following the King's orders, I am leaving here the day after tomorrow and travelling via Dessau to Berlin. Everything I hear from there fills me with joy.'[220] To judge from this, Görtz had not tried to exploit his knowledge about the forbidden love between Goethe and Anna Amalia. Instead, Carl August will from now on be helpful to him and involve him in his political dealings. In a letter of 15 January 1787 he even allayed Görtz's fears about the new King's inconstant goodwill:

> I can certainly assure you that the King is not dissatisfied with you, but that he certainly is aware of and values your services. ... You have glowing prospects if you stay in the service you are in and where excellent men are needed.[221]

In 1788 Carl August even transferred his voting rights to Görtz at the Reichstag in Regensburg.[222]

Goethe soon realized that he and Anna Amalia had overreacted. Their severe security measures had also made it nearly impossible to prove that there was a secret liaison. In the *Römische Elegien* (1788-1790) Goethe will choose the image of a scarecrow for the unfounded fear of a Prussian intervention. He has the beloved say (Elegy XVI):

> O what an error took hold of you!
> It was only a scarecrow that chased you away.
> Industriously we sewed the patches together from old clothes and reeds.
> Industriously I helped with it, bent on harming myself.

On 28 September the poet had arrived in Venice, a city with a large port from which ships sailed out into all parts of the world. If he had really only wanted to reach Rome as quickly as possible he would not have made a detour of about two hundred kilometres, travelling via Venice and staying there for a whole week as well. Goethe's letter to Carl August from Verona on 18 September sounds as if he would never come back again:

> It could come about that I would have to ask something of you using another name. If you receive a letter in my handwriting, even signed with an unknown name, please grant the request it contains.

Originally Goethe did not know where the journey would take him. In *Tasso* we read (ll. 2238 ff.):

> Where am I to guide my steps
> To flee from the nauseous things around me,
> To avoid the abyss that lies before me?

If developments had made it advisable not to return to Germany again, Goethe would have boarded a ship in Venice and tried his luck in America. But since his fears proved to be unfounded he could set about giving meaning to a journey born of necessity. Above all he had to clarify his future relationship with Anna Amalia and find out who had betrayed their secret. He had also long been convinced that an educational journey would contribute enormously to his cultural development and to the ennobling of his faculties.

As early as 1775 he wanted to set out for Rome when the coach which was to bring him to Weimar did not arrive. On 3 November he writes from Rome to the Duke with the request: ' ... so let me finish well what has begun well and what seems to have heaven's blessing.' In the letter from Rome on 20 January 1787 Goethe thanks the Duke for allowing him to stay in Italy until the identity of the 'traitor' has been established and his future relationship with Anna Amalia clarified: 'How grateful I am to you that you accommodate me so kindly, give me your helping hand, and reassure me regarding my flight, my continued absence, and my return.' The stay in Italy, which has since been declared a trip for study and work, was approved by Carl August, but its length was not defined. In a letter to Merck of 25 February 1787 Anna Amalia describes Goethe's way of life in Rome:

> This much I can tell you: he is very well and feels at home there. He has almost no other company than that of the young Tischbein. There are few people, and there will be few people, who will see and study Rome the way he does.[223]

Looking back, Goethe said about his stay in Italy: 'In the course of the past two years I had constantly observed, collected, thought, and tried to develop every one of my talents.'[224]

In a letter to Carl August on 23 October 1787, after more than a year of his stay in Italy, he talks about Anna Amalia. Goethe chooses the 23 October as a coding for the actual theme. Since 24 October is Anna Amalia's birthday, her son Carl August knows, without further indications, that she is the person in question. Goethe is clearly embarrassed, because he, at thirty-eight years of age, is talking to the thirty-year-old Carl August about his forty-eight-year-old mother: 'Much as I am used to communicating with you and have no real enjoyment without wanting to share it with you, I am still somewhat embarrassed now when I take up my pen to write to you.' What follows is a reference to the volcanic origin of the Alban mountains near Rome: 'And we live here as if on burnt out volcanoes on the battlefields and encampments of the previous age.' Goethe's stormy passion for Anna Amalia is therefore supposed to be burnt out.

> I feel only too well in this foreign country that I am older. All relationships are formed more slowly and more loosely; I have lived my best days with you and yours, and that's where my heart and mind are, although the ruins of a world are in the other pan of the scales.

After his return from Italy Goethe will write in the *Römische Elegien* (1788-1790) in reference to his first decade in Weimar, his flight and his return (XV, l. 43f.):

> Here you saw a world come into being,
> Then you saw a world lying in ruins,
> Then from the ruins a new, almost greater world came into being.

The letter of 23 October 1787 also deals with the 'traitor'. Goethe uses as a code a reference to the Second Silesian War (1744/45), also started by Prussia as a war of aggression. He noticed a trough at the edge of Lake Nemi in Rome. In the course of their attempt to invade southern Italy, an attempt which was thwarted at the battle of Velletri in 1744, the Austrians had used this trough to water their horses. Then we read: 'I immediately remembered what you once wrote to me about your part in the battle of Velletri.' Since Carl August was born in 1757, thirteen years after the battle of Velletri, and could have had no involvement in it, the war of aggression referred to here could only be meant in a transferred sense. With this comparison Goethe confirms that he has received and understood news about the 'betrayer' of his secret. He continues: 'I was tempted to cut a sliver out of the trough and so send you a military relic fit for a compatriot.' With this he intimates to Carl August that with regard to the 'traitor' there is as yet no all-clear signal. In the next letter of 17 November 1787 the relic is given a special mention: 'You have received two letters from me ... one contains news of a military relic from the area.' But only when the 'traitor' is found will he report that he has the 'relic'. In the letter of 7 December 1787 Goethe is referring to Prussia as a 'half enemy country', even though Carl August entered the Prussian army with the rank of a Major General on 25 September 1787. In the meantime, on 24 August 1787 Turkey had declared war against Russia. Austria was an ally of Russia, and Prussia, England and Holland formed a defensive alliance with Turkey. Carl August participated, on Prussia's side, in the alliance's negotiations at the Hague. [225]

In a letter to Duke Carl August of 29 December 1787, between the lines Goethe makes fun of the surveillance he is under in Rome: ' ... If you sometimes have anything important to write to me you can do so without worrying. I have never seen any trace of a letter being opened.' Goethe appears here to be quite naïve, but in reality he is lulling the spies for the Church state or for Austria into a false sense of security.[226] The Austrian ambassador to Rome, Count Cardinal Herzan, for example, reported to Vienna on 3 March 1787:

> Herr Goethe has been staying here for the last two months: he sought to remain incognito and so changed his name to Müller. His letters come to him addressed under this name. ... he has travelled to Naples with this person [the painter Tischbein]. I have ordered my secretary, whose integrity I can rely on, to make closer contact with them on [Goethe's] return so as to keep a watchful eye on his doings and possible secret intentions.[227]

It is very probable that Goethe's companion residing with him, the painter Johann Heinrich Wilhelm Tischbein (1751-1829), spied on him for the Church State[228] – the very man who painted the most famous portrait of the poet, 'Goethe in der Campagna die Roma' (ill. 16). Tischbein was at first described by Goethe very favourably: 'My very good friend ... where could I have got a better guide?' (*Italienische Reise,* 7 November 1786). But then, on 2 October 1787: 'He is not so genuine, so natural, so open as his letters. I can only describe his character by word of mouth.'[229] Only when Tischbein returned to Germany and was in contact with Anna Amalia, who was often in his company during her stay in Italy, did Goethe overcome his anger and come a bit closer to him.

Since Goethe took into account that he might be spied upon, on 10 January 1787 he sent his friends in Weimar a cut stone with the request that they use it in future to seal his letters. 'Frau von Stein' received an extra one. On 17 February 1787 he tells her: 'I am burning your letters immediately, though I don't want to. But thy will be done.' At the same time her letters always seem to be formulated in code. In a letter of 8 June 1784 from Eisenach he writes: 'Your dear letters have arrived. I am so used to your presence that they seemed cold, and I had first to accustom myself again to giving what you write the meaning which words from your lips have.' Goethe knew, therefore, that his letters could, without authority, be opened at any time, but his correspondence was so encoded that he had no need to be particularly worried. For really important communications there were more secure channels, as can be seen from the entry of 16 February 1788: 'The Prussian courier brought me a letter some time ago from our Duke ... Since he could write without restraint he described for me the whole political situation, his own situation etc.' The Duke reports in a letter to his mother Anna Amalia on 11 January 1788: 'I wrote a twelve-page letter to Goethe [and sent it] through a courier who was going to Rome.' This letter from Carl August, which is no longer extant, was of crucial importance for Goethe, who answers on 25 January 1788 that he considered the day he received the twelve-page letter 'the most joyful he had spent in Rome'. The 'traitor' had finally been discovered, and so it was possible for Goethe to return to Weimar without feeling insecure.

Hidden behind insignificant personal questions, an inquiry was made by Carl August and Anna Amalia in Weimar to find out the 'traitor'. At first Goethe suspected his servant and secretary Philipp Friedrich Seidel (1755-1820) who had accompanied him from Frankfurt to Weimar. In a letter to Carl August on 7 December 1787 he writes:

> Just a word about your household affairs ...I would like you to have Schmidt examine Seidel. Have him examined, examine him yourself on your return. If I am not deceiving myself, you won't find anyone equal to him in this class of people.

In the foreground, the issue was only one of promoting Seidel to Treasury Commissioner. For an ordinary procedure of this kind such a careful examination by several persons would not have been necessary, least of all by the Duke himself. With 'examination' is meant a criminal investigation with a view to unmasking the 'traitor'. Further, Goethe compiled a list of the names of all persons who, theoretically, could know about the secret. In a letter to the Duke on 15 December 1787 he writes: 'I am planning another exercise: I am arranging to have heroic subjects drawn as I want them ... Frau von Stein can give you more details, or at least the list of subjects.'

With the twelve-page letter from Carl August Goethe now knew the identity of the 'traitor', for in his answer of 25 January 1788 he writes:

'The greatest worry I have at home is Fritz. He is coming to an age where nature begins to stir and the rest of his life can so easily be corrupted. Please keep an eye on him.' The fourteen-year-old Fritz, the youngest son of Frau von Stein, had, it seems, been the 'traitor', the Fritz whose education Goethe had taken in hand since the boy was seven and who as an eleven-year-old lived in the house of the poet and Minister with the five servants. The boy spent the best years of his childhood with Goethe and was the 'general favourite of the educated circles in the town.'[230] Young Fritz was constantly in Goethe's company, went with him on journeys, took dictation of letters – also to 'Frau von Stein'. Bills, cash-books, and other things went through his hands. He learnt all kinds of things, including writing in various types of script.[231] In a letter of 19 January 1788 to 'Frau von Stein', directly before he received the twelve-page letter from Carl August, Goethe was already writing: 'My greetings to Fritz. His eyes worry me.' But there was never any mention that Fritz had an eye problem. What Goethe means is that being around him Fritz could have seen too much. In compiling a list of 'heroic subjects' for Carl August and so going through all the persons he had dealings with in Weimar to see whether, theoretically, they could have known the secret, Goethe must have been especially suspicious of Fritz. In the summer of 1786 he had already opened a sealed letter to 'Frau von Stein'. This is clear from a postscript to a letter to 'Frau von Stein' of 6 July 1786: 'Since Fritz has opened the letter again I can add another word for you.' What was in the first instance seen as pardonable misbehaviour appeared now in another light: Fritz had spied on Goethe. After arriving back from his Italian journey under a full moon, the first thing Goethe did was to have Fritz come to him at six o'clock in the morning. Fritz told his brother Carl: '[I was] so glad to see him again that I couldn't say a word to him.'[232] This speechlessness was a result of his bad conscience, for he had, by his anonymous admission that he knew the secret, separated the lovers and aroused fears of Prussian military sanctions. Later Goethe dealt with the 'betrayal' in his autobiographical novel *Wilhelm Meisters Wanderjahre*, which he began to dictate immediately after the death of Anna Amalia in 1807. In this novel the hero is enticed into a trap by a boy named Fitz, there is 'suddenly ... a shot ... and at the same time two hidden iron gratings closed'. The hero, however, is immediately freed, so, as with Fritz's 'betrayal', it was only a false alarm. The name Fitz is derived from Fritz as a pet-name for Friedrich.[233] Also the title 'Where is the Traitor Hiding? (Wo steckt der Verräter?) in the first version of the novel (1821), which in the second version (1829) was changed into 'Who is the Traitor' (Wer ist der Verräter?) points in the direction of betrayal. Later in the novel

Goethe will show how the 'traitor' let them know that he is privy to their secret.

Fritz could not have anticipated what consequences his anonymous admission would have, but his motives are understandable. For the boy, Goethe and Anna Amalia had done something monstrous to his mother by pretending, with a view to deceiving the public, that she was Goethe's platonic lover. If Fritz chose for his coat of arms the inscription 'Strive for the Truth', which was also to be on his gravestone, this is linked with the reasons which justify his action. Although Goethe's relationship to his former charge remained cool after his return from Italy,[234] he had already, in a letter of 9 February 1788, directed his friend Seidel to take Fritz under his wing: 'Now I have something to say to you about Fritz. Think about whether you have time, leisure, and the wish to look after Fritz and to him give some instruction.' What follows is Goethe's notion of training Fritz in bookkeeping to prepare him for a career as a Weimar official. His 'betrayal' was never really forgiven and the youthful prank was to cast a shadow over his whole life. Fritz became a page and in 1793 a Treasury assessor with a yearly salary of 300 Thaler. He studied in Jena, Hamburg, and London. After that Carl August surprisingly wanted to send him as an unsalaried clerk into the backwater of Silesia. Fritz himself never fully trusted Goethe or Duke Carl August and so he preferred an unpaid post in Breslau to service in Weimar – from which he resigned in 1797. On several occasions negotiations with Carl August for his return ended unsuccessfully, with Frau von Stein trying to persuade Goethe to intercede for her favourite son. When Fritz decided in 1801 to return to service in Weimar, both Goethe and the court gave him the cold shoulder. This was a heavy blow for Frau von Stein. Far away from Weimar, Fritz von Stein was to founder, both privately and professionally.[235] When his former pupil was engaged in 1803, later married and became a father, Goethe did not congratulate him.[236]

7 | Italy: 'The Turning Point'

> That you are sick, sick because of me, pains me beyond expression. Forgive me. I myself am wrestling with death and life, and no tongue can say what I was feeling. This crash has brought me back to myself. My love! My love! ... In life and death I am yours.'
>
> Goethe's letter to 'Frau von Stein', 23 December 1786

> The main aim of my journey was to heal the physical and moral ills that tortured me in Germany and finally made me useless; the other aim was to quench the thirst for true art. The first aim was fairly successful, the second completely.
>
> Goethe's letter to Carl August, 25 January 1788

Looking back on his twenty-two-month stay in Italy Goethe refers to it as the turning point in his life. After more than a decade of passionate love for Anna Amalia he was suddenly separated from her once he had revealed their secret to Duke Carl August in Karlsbad. In the *Italienische Reise* [Italian Journey (1816-) Goethe gives a full description of this sojourn. He wrote the first of three parts (Karlsbad until his arrival in Rome), once with references to his beloved 'Frau von Stein' and another time without them. The one with references to the beloved, the *Tagebuch für 'Frau von Stein'* of 1786, was first published in 1886 as part of Goethe's bequest.[237] A letter of Frau von Stein to Knebel on 30 October 1816 has never ceased to cause astonishment:[238]

> I hear Goethe's *Italienische Reisen* being praised by my friends outside Weimar. But he has never showed them to me. Sometimes he sends me part of a good dish from his table, but he doesn't honour me with any higher nourishment.

Goethe's *Italienische Reise* was published in 1816, and Frau von Stein, for whom it was allegedly written, did not even receive a present of it.

A critical examination of Goethe's *Italienische Reise* shows that it was really Anna Amalia who received the description of his journeys. It is striking that several entries include inscriptions only in Latin. On 21 September 1786 he writes about one of these: 'The whole of it, especially the end, is a glorious text for later discussions.' On 26 September there is a Latin inscription without a translation, on 1 October the Italian and Latin text of an oratorio, on 7 October an Italian sentence. Frau von Stein could not understand these texts since she could not read these languages and was always dependent on translations.[239] Anna Amalia could read both Latin and Italian. While Anna Amalia was reigning Duchess, pupils from the Gymnasium recited 'learned things' in Latin in honour of her birthday.[240] When her regency came to an end Anna Amalia studied systematically to deepen her knowledge of languages.[241] It is inconceivable that Goethe would send his beloved texts she could not understand, especially since he asked her in his letter of 18 September 1786 not to show the texts to a third party, introducing the diary with the words: 'But don't say anything to anyone about what you receive. For the time being it is for you alone.' On 14 October 1786 he writes from Venice: 'My diary is finished ... But keep it to yourself, as I have only written it for you.' This request was also taken seriously, for in the letter of 6 January 1787 he concludes: 'Do what you wish with my diary when it arrives. Let anyone enjoy it who wants to; my veto derives from the uncertain days. May they never come again.'

The obvious discrepancy with the language accomplishments of the supposed receiver is to be found also in other letters of Goethe to 'Frau von Stein'. On 14 November 1781, for example, he writes: 'My dearest, send me the skull, the drawing of it, the Latin text, and an assurance of your love.' It is obvious that the beloved was immersed in studies of anatomy and was reading a book in Latin on the subject, and so it could not have been Frau von Stein. In a letter to 'Frau von Stein' on 19 November 1784 he writes: 'I am bringing with me the Latin Spinoza in which everything is much clearer and more beautiful.' That does not sound as if he is going to be continually doing translations for the beloved.

That Goethe was not writing to Frau von Stein but to Anna Amalia is clearly evidenced by the letter of 12 December 1781. Goethe had received an Italian translation of his novel *Die Leiden des Jungen Werther* (1774) by Michele Salom from Padua. He was not satisfied with the quality of the translation and writes to 'Frau von Stein' (ill. 23):

> ... his translation is almost entirely a paraphrase; but the glowing expression of pain and joy which inwardly never cease to consume one another has totally disappeared and so the reader doesn't know what the fellow wants ... You must see it and judge for yourself.

For this, excellent knowledge of the Italian language would be necessary. Only Anna Amalia had this knowledge. She had been receiving instruction in Italian since the middle of the 1760s and wrote translations from Italian into French and German and later from German into Italian.[242] On 23 October 1765, in a letter to her Minister von Fritsch, Anna Amalia refers to herself as a 'novice' in the Italian language,[243] but at the point where Goethe wants to have her examine the *Werther* translation Anna Amalia is engaged in translating the fairytale *Amor and Psyche* of Apuleius (c.125-161 AD) from Italian into German. It was published in her *Tiefurter Journal*, an edition of eleven handwritten copies (1781-1784). From 1775 she had lessons in Italian from Christian Joseph Jagemann (1735-1804) whom she had engaged as her librarian. Jagemann was one of the most proficient Italian experts in Germany. He had lived as a monk in Florence and was then appointed as Director of the Catholic Gymnasium in Erfurt. On the occasion of his appointment [in Weimar] he converted to Protestantism. He became known for his Italian grammar book and for a comprehensive Italian dictionary. When the loyal Jagemann asked Anna Amalia for a pension so that he could withdraw from the world again, the Princess made him change his mind with a letter written in Italian:

> If your philosophy makes you decide to lead a solitary life, I am in agreement, and you are right. What can today's world offer a man who can think the way you do and has merited so much ... Whatever about that, my friendship will follow you even into hell.[244]

Jagemann stayed with his Princess, of whom Böttiger wrote in 1791:

> This noble Princess dedicates her muse entirely to the sciences and arts. Nothing is foreign to her, nothing lies outside her orbit; but the Italian language – into which she translates our classical writers and sends them to her friends in Rome and Naples after she has read them to Councillor Jagemann for his approval – along with music and painting is her favourite preoccupation.[245]

Anna Amalia built up the most comprehensive Italian library of any German Princess in the 18th century.[246] When Goethe wrote from Naples on 25 May 1787 to 'Frau von Stein', 'I am glad you are reading so much about Italy; you will become much more acquainted with things Italian', this did not apply to Frau von Stein, who was not particularly interested in Italy. In a letter to Charlotte von Lengefeld on 12 January 1788 Frau von Stein laughs at the Italy fever that has broken out since Goethe's journey to the south: 'Everyone here wants to go to Italy; I say everyone, but that is not quite true. I myself like my house and home, and anyone who is not contented at home will not be contented anywhere else.'[247] In a letter to her friend Knebel on 21 March 1787 the allegedly sorrowing Frau von Stein wrote with a mocking overtone: 'Naples has fished Goethe away from us.'[248]

Since the beginning of his flight to Italy Goethe had written an entry every day in his *Tagebuch für 'Frau von Stein*. On the 23 and 24 October, the birthday of Anna Amalia, there is for the first time a gap of two days. On 25 October he assures 'Frau von Stein': 'I have thought of you so much these two days that I would at least like to put something on paper.' In this diary entry there is an omission – which is not the case with the general version of the *Italienische Reise* – recording the conversation with a Count Cesare, a travelling companion. The Count is interested in the fact that Goethe is a Protestant and he asks him whether in this religion it was possible 'to live on good terms with a pretty girl without exactly being married to her'. Goethe said it was, because the Protestant 'priests are prudent people who take no notice of such small matters'. In an addendum to the subject of Anna Amalia's birthday Goethe refers to the reason for his flight: he lived 'on good terms' with a pretty Protestant girl, Anna Amalia, but was not allowed to marry her.

On 26 October Goethe mentions, not without a mocking tone, Frau von Stein's Kochberg property:

> When I saw the poor peasants, here too, laboriously turning over the stones, I thought of your [dein] Kochberg and said with tears burning inside me: 'when will I be celebrating a beautiful evening in Kochberg with her [ihr] again? I tell you [dir], my love, if only they didn't have the advantage of the climate here!'

The poet plays with the words 'dein', 'ihr', 'dir', and gives the impression that he is speaking of two persons. Anna Amalia could easily travel incognito the thirty-five kilometres to Kochberg to meet secretly with Goethe on the property of her lady-in-waiting without fear of being disturbed. For example, when in the autumn of 1776 Frau von Stein was having English lessons from Goethe's friend Jakob Michael Reinhold Lenz (1751-1792), Anna Amalia stayed there for several days.[249] This would explain why Goethe was often in Kochberg when Frau von Stein was not there. When she was there, the poet would mostly come in company with friends[250] so that he could be seen to be with his 'beloved'. On 24 December 1780 Countess Görtz, who saw through the deception, reported to her husband about such arrangements that Frau von Stein was 'putting on a public show with Goethe'.[251] But Goethe never felt at home in Kochberg. On 27 August 1779 the poet wrote in his diary: 'In the afternoon to Kochberg. Simple and good life there. The first time I felt at ease there, but I still can't like the place or the area.' Frau von Stein's spacious accommodation was at the disposal of the lovers Goethe and Anna Amalia for their secret meetings; similarly in Weimar, as is clear from the letter of Countess Görtz to her husband on 12 October 1782: 'Frau von Stein ... as previously still plays the role allotted to her as well as she can. She eats potatoes almost every evening in her house with Goethe and the Duchess [Anna Amalia].'[252]

On 27 October 1786 Goethe writes from Terni:

> Again sitting in a cave ... I direct my prayer to you, my dear guardian angel. Only now do I feel how spoilt I am. To live ten years with you, to be loved by you, and now to be in a foreign country. I knew it would be like this, and only the most extreme necessity could force me to make the decision. Let us have no other thought than that of ending our lives together. I have climbed Spoleto and was on the aqueduct, which is also a bridge from one mountain to the other. The ten arches, built with bricks, fill the valley and are standing there so quietly for centuries, and water is still spouting up everywhere in Spoleto.

There is a drawing of Goethe's linked to this description of the aqueduct in Spoleto; it is a water-colour from 1806 depicting an aqueduct in a mountainous landscape and formed out of the letters AMALIE (ill. 28). Anna Amalia was for Goethe the bridge to a way of life which made possible the development of his genius. She makes links, but more than that, she brings water – which for Thales of Miletus (c.625-c.547 BC), one of the seven wise men of antiquity, was the origin of all things, the fundamental condition of all life.

On 13 December 1786 Goethe writes: 'I am gradually recovering here from my salto mortale'. He is trying to achieve clarity about his future with Anna Amalia. In this respect his journey to Sicily will be decisive. The only letter from Sicily that Goethe did not burn he gave as a present, on 16 February 1818, to his friend Carl Friedrich Zelter (1758-1832) with the words:

> ... so I am sending you an age-old page which I could not burn when I consigned to the fire all my papers relating to Sicily and Naples. It is such a beautiful passage written at the turning point of the whole adventure and sheds some light backwards and forewards.

In this letter of 18 April from Palermo Goethe seems relieved, since he now knew what the future of his love for Anna Amalia was to be:

> My love, another word of farewell from Palermo. ... Farewell, most beloved, my heart is with you, and now that distance and absence have, as it were, purged away all that was stagnating between us, the beautiful flame of love, fidelity, and remembrance is again burning and shining merrily in my heart.

On 1 March 1818 Zelter answers (and Frau von Stein was still alive): 'Your note from Palermo gives me unspeakable joy. Who, then, is the blessed creature for whom this spring day dawns?' Goethe gave no reply.[253] In a letter of 18 April 1787 he writes of departure and farewell in the deeper sense: the renunciation [Entsagung] motif is found for the first time. In his *Italienische Reise* which he is working on from 1813, he writes under the entry Palermo 13 April 1787: 'Italy without Sicily leaves no image in the mind: only here is the key to everything.' The key to the understanding of the second half of Goethe's life is to be sought in Sicily, because that is where he makes the decision to renounce the physical aspect of his love for Anna Amalia. After more than a decade of deception the inspiration to renounce this love amounts for Goethe to a liberation from an oppressive burden. Renunciation means a transformation of his love for Anna Amalia. Later, she herself, in the first of her *Fünf Briefe über Italien*, written in the 1790s,[254] gives an important insight into her understanding of love:

> And so with Roman women one must not look for any tender love or ethical feeling that curbs and ennobles the sensual drives. They are also not capable of the friendship which, for others, still remains after the fires of passion have been quenched.

Ethical feeling curbs and ennobles the sensual drives, but, even without sensual passion, for her and Goethe there remains a special kind of friendship. The journey to Sicily brought the liberating decision. The conflict that Goethe experienced is reflected in *Tasso* and *Nausikaa*.

Tasso was the only work which Goethe wanted to bring with him to work on in Sicily: 'I'm taking Tasso, and only Tasso, with me, and I hope he will be finished and bring you joy.'[255] But in Sicily the Nausicaa material from the *Odyssee* (VI, ll. 13ff.) of Homer (eighth century BC) proved a strong attraction. In this story, the ship-wrecked, godlike Odysseus meets Nausicaa, the daughter of the King of the Phaeacians. She is as beautiful as a goddess, but Odysseus cannot become her husband because he is married to Penelope and wants to return home to her. Goethe, during the crossing from Naples to Palermo, consumed only bread and wine for several days, supposedly because of sea-sickness (entry of 30 March 1787). He did the same on the return journey from Messina to Naples (entry of 13 May 1787). In a letter of Tischbein to Goethe after 10 July 1787, which the poet quotes in his *Italienische Reise* (1813-) because it would recapture the mood at the time, Tischbein reports that Goethe's Sicilian companion told him how 'you [Goethe], despite the money you paid, fasted, partly because you were not feeling well and partly because you had decided to, and nearly starved.' In the light of this it seems that Goethe saw his journey to Sicily as a kind of pilgrimage. On this highly classical soil, with a copy of Homer in his hand, the 'Greek' Goethe was looking for an oracle from the gods about his future relationship to his Princess Anna Amalia. Sicily was for him an oracle sanctuary. On 2 April he is still reporting: 'The plan for my drama [*Tasso*] flourished during these days in the belly of the whale.' But on 16 April he writes in Palermo that he is continually pondering the plan for *Nausikaa*. According to the diary entry of 8 May at Messina, on the beach he is still thinking about the plan for *Nausikaa*. From memory he adds to the entry, in 1814, three pages which give information about the planned structure of *Nausikaa*, which he wants to treat as a tragedy: Nausikaa is wooed by many suitors but only feels attracted to Odysseus, the nameless, unusual stranger. Her love for him is enkindled, and the wonderful Nausikaa 'irrevocably compromises herself in the eyes of her countrymen'. But Odysseus tells Nausikaa that he is already married and that he must leave her, so she finds her death in the sea. 'There was nothing in this composition that I could not paint from my own personal experiences.' Goethe reports further in 1814 that he spent nearly the whole of his stay in Sicily dreaming of Nausikaa:

> Following my praiseworthy or unpraiseworthy habit, I wrote down little or nothing about it, but worked through most of it in my mind, down to the last detail; but there it lay, dislodged by subsequent distractions, so that at present I can only recall a fleeting memory of it.

Goethe's idea is that from the very beginning there was no hope for the love between Nausikaa and Odysseus. After the liberating decision in favour of renunciation he gave up the development of *Nausikaa* and worked on *Tasso* instead.

The *Nausikaa* manuscript was written on the same paper as a drawing which Goethe completed in 1787 in Sicily and which shows a rock formation in the sea (ill. 15). The drawing was attributed to Goethe because of the characteristic strokes and because of the paper used.[256] There can be no doubt that Goethe is the author of the drawing when one sees in it the link with Anna Amalia. The rocks form two arches through which there is a view of the horizon. The line of the sea-level makes two letters 'A' out of the arches. 'A A' is Anna Amalia's seal. In her coat of arms there are two golden 'A's on a blue background. When she was the reigning Duchess, coins were struck bearing the initials AADS, standing for Anna Amalia Duchesse Saxoniae.[257] In 1779, shortly before Anna Amalia set out in a festive procession from the Wittumspalais for her forest residence in Ettersburg, Goethe, who had chosen the decoration which was to be at the head of the procession, reported to 'Frau von Stein': 'Here I am sending you a double 'A'. I would like to have something to give you every hour of the day.'[258] In his letters Wieland spoke of her 'Highness AA', for instance in a letter to Merck on 1 August 1779.[259] Suddenly her librarian Jagemann comes up with the novel idea of publishing an Italian weekly newspaper in Weimar. It was to report not just about Italy but also about other countries, including Germany. From the beginning of 1787 until the middle of 1789 Jagemann published *La Gazzetta di Weimar* from Anna Amalia's Wittumspalais. In this way Anna Amalia could stay close to her lover, at least in her thoughts.

Since the 'traitor' had not yet been identified, Goethe writes on 5 January 1788: 'Towards Easter I feel that things are coming to a head. I don't know what will happen.' But some days later, when he received the twelve-page letter from Duke Carl August, he replied on 25 January 1788 that he had at last got the all-clear with regard to the 'traitor', since Fritz von Stein presented no danger. Now Anna Amalia had to be convinced that the Sicilian oracle was right: that in future they had to be renunciants. When Anna Amalia had recovered from fear of a Prussian intervention and had dealt with the pain of Goethe's flight, she still believed in their future as secret lovers. She offers, even as late as 1787, to travel to him in Italy. In the meantime Goethe was convinced of the need for renunciation. In a letter of 17 November 1787 to the Duke he writes: 'And now a word about your mother's journey, which weighs heavily on my heart. She was intending to come here this year.' Goethe strongly advised against this journey in the autumn: 'I have been in this country for over a year and know what is in store for distinguished travellers. I know how difficult it is for strangers to combine to some extent enjoyment, accommodation, and propriety.' Towards the end of his report of October 1787 in the *Italienische Reise* Goethe refers to the fact that some who have been 'left behind' are planning, to set out for Italy to 'enjoy the same happiness', and among them Anna Amalia:

> Of course, in the intellectual and art-loving circle of our Duchess Amalia it was customary to see Italy as the New Jerusalem of all really cultured people and to cherish in heart and mind, as only Mignon could express it, an intense longing to be there.

This mention of Mignon in connection with Anna Amalia is already an indication of who is meant by the mysterious female figure in the autobiographical novel *Wilhelm Meister*. Goethe puts into her mouth a series of beautiful songs, like the song about the pain of the beloved caused by separation (*Lehrjahre* IV, 11):

> Only those who know longing
> Know what I suffer!
> Alone and separated
> From every joy
> I search the firmament
> On every side
> Oh, he who loves and knows me
> Is far away
> I am dizzy, there is a fire
> Inside me
> Only those who know longing
> Know what I suffer!

Again in 1788 Anna Amalia wants to travel to Italy and hopes that Goethe will stay with her there. On 25 January 1788 Goethe writes to the Duke: 'You wish me to expect your mother on a visit to Italy. I will speak openly about it.

> ... The main aim of my journey was to heal the physical and moral ills that tortured me in Germany and finally made me useless; the other aim was to quench the thirst for true art. The first aim was fairly successful, the second completely. Since I was living quite freely, doing exactly what I wanted, I could not blame circumstances, compulsion, or relationships.

Here Goethe refuses also the second opportunity of staying in Italy with Anna Amalia and gives as the reason that he can no longer bear the deception about his love. 'If you require me to stay here to serve your mother' Goethe will do it gladly, but it doesn't suit him, 'because every day I feel less inclined to do anything by halves'. After this Carl August recalls Goethe to Weimar. On 17 March 1788 Goethe answers 'with a joyful: I'll come! ... the best way for me to thank you must be through unconditional honesty.'

By rejecting the possibility of staying in Italy and serving as Court Chamberlain to Anna Amalia during her sojourn, he makes it clear that a resumption of their earlier nocturnal love was impossible for him. But for a long time Anna Amalia still cherished the hope that Goethe would agree to the plan and, together with her, spend an unforgettable time against the backdrop of Italy. In a letter to Merck of 6 January 1788 in which Anna Amalia speaks of her 'adventurous plan' of travelling to Italy, she says: 'Goethe will return at Easter, but that is not yet certain.'[260] With the decision to complete his *Tasso* Goethe reached the turning point of his life, for the secret lovers become the renunciants, 'Die Entsagenden', which is the subtitle of *Wilhelm Meisters Wanderjahre.* Only by renouncing the physical aspect of his love for Anna Amalia can Goethe return to Weimar. For this reason the ageing Goethe says to Kanzler von Müller on 30 May 1814: 'Since I crossed the Ponte Molle [the northern bridge of the Tiber in Rome] on my way home I have not had one purely happy day.'

It was not easy for the lovers to keep to their decision to renounce their love. On 31 October 1788 Goethe writes from Weimar to Anna Amalia, who has recently been living in Rome: 'Why did I come back!' and almost simultaneously Anna Amalia writes in a letter of 5 November 1788: 'A propos, you are expected here; oh, do come!' However, after more than ten years Goethe no longer wanted to keep up a love relationship only made possible by constant deception. Renunciation remained the main melody of Goethe's future love poetry, as for example in the poem 'Nähe des Geliebten':

> I think of you when the shimmering sun is reflected on the sea;
> I think of you when the moonlight ripples on the spring waters.
> I see you when the dust rises in the distance on the road.
> When deep at night the wanderer trembles on the narrow path.
> I hear you when with muffled roaring the wave rises.
> I listen in the hushed clearing when all is silent.
> I am with you, no matter how far away you are; you are close to me.
> The sun sets, soon the stars will shine for me. If only you were here.

Anna Amalia accepted renunciation as a solution, as she shows in Tischbein's painting 'Anna Amalia in Pompeii at the tomb of the Priestess Mammia' of 1789 (ill. 17) which she later gave as a present to Goethe.[261] This painting is a pendant to the painting 'Goethe in the Campagna of Rome', likewise by Tischbein, 1786/87 (ill. 16), and shows Anna Amalia's attitude: she and Goethe are facing one another if the paintings are correspondingly hung beside one another. While Goethe is resting on an overturned and broken obelisk, Anna Amalia is seated on an exedra, a half-round stone bench, which is at the same time the tomb of an ancient priestess. In this way she can ingeniously be linked to the Priestess Iphigenie, who can be seen in relief behind Goethe.[262] In his play *Iphigenie auf Tauris* the young Goethe identified himself with the hero Orestes who is pursued by the Furies and is wandering around in a half-crazed state. His sister, the Priestess Iphigenie, saves him from the destruction that threatens him, and comforts him. With the choice of this material Goethe was best able to express Anna Amalia's role in transforming him from the *Stürmer und Dränger* with no direction – who, like the hero of his Werther novel, was on the brink of the abyss – into the unique classical poet. In the painting 'Anna Amalia in Pompeii' the Princess does not only refer to herself as Goethe's Iphigenie. Now that their love has to be purged of the necessity of deception, she wants to dedicate her life, like a Priestess, to something higher: Goethe's poetic genius. Anna Amalia had an imitation of the half-round stone bench in the painting placed at the entrance to the park in Weimar opposite the house of Frau von Stein.

Anna Amalia had agreed to the renunciation of physical love for Goethe. Even between 1775 and 1786 the lovers had to deny themselves, because they could not allow their happiness to be seen. But now they even have to renounce the hidden happiness of a fulfilled love. Goethe is no longer prepared to carry on the deception because in this way Anna Amalia can never become his wife. On 21 February 1787 he says:

> I cling to you with every fibre of my being. It is terrible the way memories often tear me apart. Oh, dear Lotte, you don't know what violence I have done myself and am still doing myself. The thought of not possessing you galls and consumes me, no matter what I call it and no matter which way I look at it. No matter what forms I give to my love for you, it always, always – forgive me for saying to you yet again what has so long lain dormant and silent.'

In *Tasso* the poet Goethe uses the formulation: 'Allowed is what you like' (l. 994), to which the Princess replies:

> Cognate hearts meet
> And share the enjoyment of the beautiful world:
> But allowed is what is fitting' (l.1006).

This is the continual conflict between the lovers. Anna Amalia submitted herself to the monarchical system, which forbade her as Princess to enter an official relationship with anyone under her rank, even if he were the greatest poet. Goethe, on the other hand, would have wished above all to break away and to marry Anna Amalia in America. During his stay on the highly classical soil of Sicily, Goethe found the solution he needed to the dilemma that, on the one hand, he had found the love of his life, and, on the other hand, was no longer prepared to keep up the deception: the solution was the renunciation of his sensual love for Anna Amalia, which becomes the turning point in his life.

Against this backdrop, a purely fortuitous approach from Christiane Vulpius (1765-1816) to the resigned Goethe is unthinkable. Goethe came back to Weimar after a sojourn of twenty-two months in Italy. His great love, Anna Amalia, is making preparations for a journey to Italy which will likewise last twenty-two months, beginning on 15 August 1788. Traditionally it is believed that Goethe became acquainted with Christiane on 12 July and immediately fell in love. The exact circumstances of this meeting remain obscure. [263] Christiane is supposed to have lived unnoticed with Goethe, for months, in his garden house. How they could manage that will 'always remain the secret of the two lovers'.[264] That Goethe would have started a love affair with another woman before Anna Amalia's departure suggests that Carl August made it an essential condition of his remaining in Weimar. The Duke also spent a lot of time with him immediately after his arrival[265] in order to reconcile Goethe's future position in Weimar with his own interests. Carl August demanded that he adopt a way of life to guarantee that what had now become a state secret be maintained as such in the future. Court gossip was saying at first that Goethe would be Anna Amalia's travelling companion in Italy. The sister-in-law of Anna Amalia's chamberlain Friedrich Hildebrand von Einsiedel (1750-1828), Emilie, said somewhat spitefully:

> ... the old affection for Goethe is not the only reason [for Anna Amalia's desire to travel]. ... her charms of ten years ago had not the power to bind him where only very moderate beauties competed with her, and now she thinks she can succeed in Rome where ideals of beauty surround him, and Goethe surely knows how to perform ['singen'] in Rome. But not so the poverina Duchessa!!!'[266]

Sophie von Schardt (1755-1819), Frau von Stein's sister-in-law, reports in a letter of 19 June 1788: 'Friend Goethe came back late in the evening yesterday; they say that the Dowager Duchess [Anna Amalia] will move heaven and earth to make him accompany her back to Italy.'[267] The lady-in-waiting von Wedel (1750-1815) reported to Countess Görtz on 23 June 1788: '... old maman [Anna Amalia] seems to be in a bad mood since this time [of Goethe's arrival on 18 June]. I think she hoped Goethe would go back with her, but apparently he doesn't want to.'[268] Deliberate misinformation was used as a reliable instrument in the Duchy. On a diplomatic mission for the Prussian King, for example, Carl August wrote from Berlin to Knebel asking him to spread a lie about his whereabouts:

> It is not possible for me to arrive in Jena on the 10th, so go to Weimar and tell everybody that instead of finding me in Augsburg you found a letter in which I told you I had gone to Paris and did not know when I would be returning. Should my brother-in-law [Christian v. Hessen-Darmstadt be with you, tell him to reinforce this lie and spread it. My wife knows about it all, but in public you must pretend you are bringing her a letter from me.[269]

Only on the day after Anna Amalia's departure for Italy did the Prussian Major General Carl August go off to his garrison in

Aschersleben[270] – after the liaison between Goethe and the Princess Anna Amalia had been dissolved to his satisfaction and thus the danger to his position of power – and later to the monarchy as a form of state – had been averted. Goethe was still the subject of gossip as being Anna Amalia's travel companion, first in the winter of 1788/89 and then in the summer of 1789.[271] This, as was clear to everyone, he did not like.

An account in the memoirs of Countess Henrietta von Egloffstein, who, despite her integrity, was until now not taken seriously,[272] throws further light on the plans forged for Goethe's return to Weimar. Henrietta's brother had been appointed to a post in Weimar. She visited him in the autumn of 1787 and wanted to remain in Weimar for the winter. Approximately a year before, one of her governesses wrote about Henrietta that she had a very promising future, 'since both in body and mind she was way ahead of her years ... so that this thirteen-year-old girl was considered perfect in, and admired for, her development. Whoever sees her is enchanted by her'.[273]

In her memoirs, Frau von Egloffstein writes that suddenly 'Frau von Stein's secret plan came to light: to marry [verbinden] her to Goethe, who was far away from Weimar'. The Countess, who was very conscious of social standing, writes with regard to the liaison between Goethe and Christiane: 'I was deeply annoyed with Frau von Stein that the idea would ever occur to her of linking me with Goethe.'[274] When Henrietta's mother heard of the plan of marriage with Goethe, she decided – she had her own marriage plans for her daughter – to remove Henrietta from Weimar without delay:

> although ice and snow had made the roads completely impassable and the weather was extremely cold ... despite the notions and pleas of all our friends, who seriously advised against a trip to Franconia in the harsh season ... at the end of February 1788 I had to say goodbye to the paradise of my youth and its dear inhabitants.[275]

Although many in Weimar sought the hand of the beautiful Countess,[276] Henrietta was rushed away from Weimar when the plan to marry her to Goethe was forged. Her mother knew, therefore, that the driving forces behind the move were so powerful that it seemed advisable to leave the Duchy without delay. From this it is clear that in Weimar they were searching for a wife for Goethe.

Another circumstance indicates who made the choice of Henrietta. Anna Amalia, after she had had Henrietta trained in singing, invited her to sing for her. Henrietta reports in her memoirs:

> I can see the lovely green room bathed in the intimate half-light ... with moving expression which seemed to come from the heart, the

> verse was repeated: 'to preserve this heart, oh, I cannot, I cannot' – and the last note had hardly subsided when I felt myself clasped in the arms of the Duchess. – ... she assured me she had never seen nor heard anything more harmonious than the words of the song and my figure, from which, in humble posture, the plaintive tones emanated as from a nightingale.[277]

Since Carl August had made it a condition of Goethe's return that he take a wife, Anna Amalia attempted to find the one who in her view was the most suitable. Interestingly, in the winter of 1801/02 Goethe chose Henrietta as his partner when, for the first and last time, he organized a *Cour d'amour* in his house in imitation of the minnesingers.

In 1841, Riemer, whose wife was a close friend of Christiane, energetically challenged the idea that a wife was sought for Goethe before his return home from Italy:

> The report about the way Goethe became acquainted with, and afterwards lived with, this woman [Christiane] was probably based on female gossip. It was malicious and false. Goethe did not get to know this girl straight after his return from Italy; still less is it true that his friends brought her to him. He met her while he was walking in the park and she handed him a petition for her father.[278]

But Christiane could not have done this because her father had already died two years previously.[279] This clumsy attempt of Riemer to create a myth was not refuted by the contradiction. Instead, 'father' was replaced by 'brother'. Since that time, Christiane is supposed to have become acquainted with Goethe when, walking in the park, she handed him a petition on behalf of her brother. Böttiger reports in his book *Literarische Zustände und Zeitgenossen*, whose reliability is vouched for by modern research,[280] that there was another woman picked out for Goethe:

> Goethe wanted to marry a certain Fräulein von Voß, who is now Frau von Staff in Eisenach. But she preferred Staff. Out of spite against Frau von Stein (who had morally sucked him dry and filled him with the distrust that today gives him a jaundiced view of people), he had recourse to Dame Vulpia.[281]

After Fräulein von Egloffstein had to flee from the Duchy to avoid marriage with Goethe, the choice fell on Fräulein Amalie Friederike von Voß, who already knew Goethe. On 21 January 1782 Goethe, dressed as a magician, had danced with her and wrote on 23 November 1782 to 'Frau von Stein': 'You are going to Vosses today and I would also like to come.' On 23 July 1784 the young woman, along with her mother, was a guest in Goethe's garden.[282] But above all Carl

August was acquainted with Amalie Friederike. This becomes clear where Carl von Lyncker (1767-1843), Anna Amalia's page, writes:

> Every week or fortnight there were masked balls, always attended by the gentry and the nobility ... The celebrations were always crowded and lively. ... The Duke, usually wearing a winter coat, danced mainly waltzes and almost without exception with the oldest Fräulein von Voß, who was slender and tall, and whose graceful movements earned her the name of 'Grace Voß'.[283]

But Amalie Friederike married the Forester Christian Friedrich August von Staff, who, in 1815, rose to the position of Master of the Hunt.[284] In the Fourier book there was an entry on 6 July 1788 shortly after the wedding: 'the new married couple, the page von Staff together with his wife, were presented to Their Highnesses and were invited to eat at table with them.'[285] Goethe and Anna Amalia were also present. Amalie Friederike cherished her time with Goethe and Carl August. On 1 November 1800 she wrote to Goethe: 'Remember a distant friend who prizes as the happiest moments in her youth those she spent as your guest at the round table ... Though these happy days are now long past they are often fresh in my memory.'[286] Contrary to what Böttiger reports, it is likely that not Fräulein von Voß but Goethe himself was against the union, because a woman from the higher echelons of society did not fit in with his plan for renunciation.

What Goethe had in mind for a companion was a woman like Clärchen in his play *Egmont* (1788), which he had just completed. In this play Goethe confronted his readers with a strange heroine. The Prince and freedom fighter Egmont chooses Clärchen, a simple and honest girl of the people. For Egmont she is not a partner of equal rank, and he does not love her. He can only offer her his friendship. She accepts this. She loves him and at the end of the play she becomes a heroine and finally a goddess of victory.[287] Indirectly, Goethe, who in Weimar was identified with Egmont,[288] was showing through the Clärchen figure what kind of woman he wanted at his side after renouncing the physical aspect of his love for Anna Amalia. With an openness that was rare for him, Goethe writes about this figure in a letter to 'Frau von Stein' from Italy on 3 November 1787:

> I don't quite understand what you are saying about Klärchen and am waiting for your next letter. I can see that you don't allow for a nuance between the harlot and the goddess. But since I have made her relationship to Egmont exclusive; since I have made her to be more in love with the perfection of her lover, made her ecstatic in the enjoyment of the incomprehensible rather than in sensuality; since she relates to her lover with the most intense feeling of the eternity of love, and is finally glorified in his mind through the dream that

> transfigures her, I don't quite know where to place this middle nuance. But I do understand that for the dramatic requirements of the stage the different shades I have enumerated above are perhaps too discrete and unconnected or are linked by hints which are too subtle. Perhaps a second reading would help. Perhaps your next letter will add something.[289]

Faced with the offer of marrying Fräulein von Egloffstein or Fräulein von Voß on his return to Weimar, Goethe is explaining to 'Frau von Stein' that what is missing for her is a fine distinction,[290] a nuance which exists between harlot and goddess. The nuance that Goethe has in mind is that of a woman who sees her beloved man as perfect and is ecstatic because of the incomprehensible fact that he belongs to her. This description fits Christiane Vulpius perfectly. As a simple woman of the people, she looks up to Goethe as to a godlike figure. She was the daughter of a low-ranking Weimar official and grew up in penurious circumstances. Christiane had been taught to write adequately and she helped considerably to support her family. She was employed making artificial flowers in a workshop owned by Caroline Bertuch (from 1778). A letter of Goethe's to Fritz Jacobi (1743-1819) of 9 September 1788 makes it clear that Christiane was a discarded mistress of Carl August.[291] Jacobi had inquired of Goethe if he knew a good young secretary, to which Goethe replied recommending Christiane's brother Christian August Vulpius (1762-1827), but admitting:

> I took him on some years ago. In my absence he was without any support and went, as I mentioned, to Nürnberg. Of course, I can't say that I know him very well. I took an interest in him without observing him. I gave him some support without scrutinizing him.

'Interest ... without observing' and 'support without scrutinizing' are formulae characterizing the court regime of favouritism; they suggest a directive on the part of Duke Carl August who granted support to his mistresses where possible.

Carl August was a 'sexually very active Prince' according to a benign interpretation;[292] elsewhere, more clearly, there is mention of 'erotic excesses'.[293] Carl August had affairs with innumerable women and girls. He visited brothels, where he contracted sexual diseases. Girls from all social echelons in the Duchy had to be protected from the Duke's snares.[294] Carl August had had dozens of illegitimate children with village girls. They were known in Weimar by the fact that the Duke used the 'Du' form with his sons but the 'Er' form for others.[295] On his cavalier's journey to Paris the seventeen-year-old Carl August – after his engagement with Princess Luise von Hessen-Darmstadt in Karlsruhe – was introduced to physical love in Epernay near Paris by a certain Jeannette Brossard, for which she received for decades a yearly pension of 500 francs.[296] A few days before his marriage in Karlsruhe Carl August took his pleasure with three women. Countess Görtz tells her husband about it in a letter of 11 September 1775: 'Yesterday he [Carl August] stayed with the Werther girl until one [a.m.], drank punch, sang and exchanged kisses with [the girls] Bechtolsheim and Kauffberg; it was a test of who could kiss better.'[297] For a harlot in the Hague who had infected Carl August with gonorrhoea he instructs his collaborator: 'Look for a girl called Enkchen to whom I owe my warm piss. Tell her that I am cured and that I hope the same for her, and assure her of my affection.'[298] Even in other countries people laughed about Carl August's sexual excesses, for instance, in the journal *Moniteur* which expressed its suspicion that the reason why there were so many French emigrants in the small Duchy was the interest the ruler of the land had taken in beautiful French girls.[299]

After his return from Italy it was only in the foreground that Goethe wanted a replacement for his goddess Anna Amalia, whom he regarded as the love of his life. Renunciation was only to exclude the physical aspect of his love for Anna Amalia but otherwise to ennoble it by raising it to the highest spiritual realms. Faithful unto death, the truly loving poet wanted no Henrietta von Egloffstein, no Amalie Friederike von Voß, but rather the under-privileged Christiane Vulpius. He must have already seen her in the little town of Weimar before his departure for Italy, at the very latest in the summer of 1786 when he inspected the artificial flowers workshop where she had been working since 1782.[300]

Her father, Johann Friedrich Vulpius, was one of the many badly paid minor officials in Weimar. He worked for many years without receiving a wage. In 1782, after a hearing in the Privy Council, he had to give up his job because of administrative irregularities. So as not entirely to drop Johann Friedrich Vulpius, a man who had served in the administration for thirty-two years, Goethe found him employment in road building. This was all accompanied by Christiane's stubborn petitioning.[301] Now, for his return to Weimar, Goethe chose Christiane Vulpius as his mate. In *Wilhelm Meisters Lehrjahre* (1796) the hero is forced to leave his beloved. He reflects on this (VIII, 7):

> It is disturbing always to be searching, but much more disturbing to have found and then to be forced to part company. What other enquiries am I to make in the wide world, what else am I to look for? What region, what town keeps a treasure equal to this one? Am I to travel, only ever to find what is inferior?

Time and again the link between Klärchen and Christiane has been seen. Caroline Herder (1750-1809) wrote a letter to her husband in Italy on 8 March 1789: ' ... he has the young Vulpius as his Klärchen and often has her visit him etc.'[302] By planning to have children with Christiane – on 25 December 1789 August Vulpius (1789-1830) was born – his renunciation became final. Both Anna Amalia and Christiane Vulpius were unequal in rank with Goethe, the one too high and the other too low. This is exactly the situation in his *Egmont*, where the poet

> [weaves in] the gentle hint of an agreement between her [Margaret of Parma] and Egmont ... [that one could call] the theme of forbidden love of a subject for a monarch.[303]

Klärchen, who could expect friendship but not love from Egmont, leads the conversation around to the Regent of the Netherlands, Margaret of Parma, by saying about her (III, Klärchens Wohnung):

> **Klärchen**: She has the mind of a man. As a woman she is different from the likes of us seamstresses and cooks. She is big, courageous, determined
> **Egmont:** Her upper lip has hair, and sometimes she has an attack of gout. A true Amazon!
> **Klärchen:** A majestic woman! I'd be afraid to approach her.

Here Klärchen is expressing the missing nuance between harlot and goddess, namely, 'seamstresses and cooks'. Later in the play, when Egmont is condemned to death, he says (V, Gefängnis):

> Is the justice of a King in which you trusted all your life, is friendship with the Regent, which was (you can admit it to yourself) almost love, have they now, like a brilliant sunset, suddenly disappeared and abandoned you on the dark path?

In *Dichtung und Wahrheit* (1811-1831) Goethe will say about his *Egmont* that in it the hero [won] the silent affection of a Princess and the clearly expressed affection of a girl of nature (Book 20).

When in 1789 Goethe left the distinguished house am Frauenplan to move into one on the other side of the town wall, it was not for reasons of space,[304] because the western half of one of the biggest houses in Weimar was still spacious enough. In reality Goethe had to move to avoid a public scandal when Christiane Vulpius, whom he did not intend to marry, became pregnant at the beginning of 1789. Even after the move the outraged Duchess Luise had Goethe informed that 'she found it strange that he let his child [August Vulpius] be carried around every day under her nose'.[305] He wrote to Anna Amalia on 14

December 1789: 'On your return Your Highness will find me in new lodgings.'

According to one tradition, during his sojourn in Silesia in 1790 Goethe had made a marriage proposal to the 21-year-old Henriette von Lüttwitz.[306] This seems to be true, insofar as the offer was in fact made, but it originated from Duke Carl August. Carl August, who did not understand Goethe's renunciation, would have tried to press Goethe to a union in keeping with his social standing. Not being officially allowed to contradict his ruler, Goethe said nothing about his alleged proposal. Thirty years later, as can be shown, Carl August made another marriage proposal in Goethe's name, without telling him, this time to Ulrike von Levetzow (1804-1899).

Not until 1792 did Carl August think it was feasible for Goethe to move back to the house am Frauenplan. Karoline Jagemann (1777-1848), Carl August's concubine, wrote about this in her memoirs:

> He [Goethe] was the first and only person who dared, without fear, to show contempt for public opinion, and people found this all the more offensive as they saw in it an abuse of the privilege of friendship often shown to him by the Duke.[307]

Shortly after Anna Amalia's death in April 1807 Goethe characterized his recently wedded wife Christiane in conversation with acquaintances:

> First I have to tell you that my wife has not read one line of all my works. She cannot live in the world of the intellect. She is made for keeping house. In this regard she relieves me of all worries; this is her domain, her kingdom. In addition, she loves dressing up, she loves parties and going to the theatre. She is not without a certain level of culture which she has achieved in my company and by going to the theatre.[308]

The forty-year-old Goethe did not know at first how to handle his relationship with Christiane. He only knew that he wanted to remain faithful to Anna Amalia all his life. He did not try to interest Christiane in his intellectual work, which, with the Duchess, he might have managed. From this point of view we can understand the reproach made by Karoline Jagemann, the outstanding actress and opera singer who knew Christiane when they were children: 'Goethe gave no thought to raising his partner to a higher level at a time when she was capable of it; instead, he left her to her lower instincts.'[309] Goethe's mother said, after she became acquainted with Christiane in Frankfurt: 'You can thank God! Such a lovely, glorious, unspoilt creature is seldom to be found.' [310] Christiane was never a hostess in Goethe's house. She was not even allowed to be present at social gatherings. Until their marriage in 1806 she was, as a rule, invisible for Goethe's circle. Goethe always addressed Christiane as 'dear child' and she called him 'dear Privy Councillor' [Geheimrat].[311] Schiller, who from 1794 onwards was frequently a guest in Goethe's house, completely passes over her[312] – which is what the man of the house wanted. The literary critic Garlieb Helwig Merkel (1769-1850), in a letter of 1801 to Böttiger, spoke of 'the old bachelor'.[313] To be able to work on his writing, to which his love for Anna Amalia was central, he had to flee the presence of Christiane. He writes to Schiller on 9 December 1797 that he 'can only work in absolute isolation and that the well-springs of my poetry are diverted not only by conversation, but also even by the presence in the house of beloved and valued persons'. In his renunciation, Goethe is not able to immortalize Anna Amalia in his writings when Christiane and August are nearby, and so he has to remove himself from them. Frau von Stein, in a letter to Charlotte Schiller on 13 June 1798, makes the sarcastic comment about Goethe's sojourns in Jena: ' ... his domestic situation here must drive the poetry out of him'.[314]

Goethe gave Christiane everything she could want. She learnt dancing, made expensive trips to the spa in the summer, entertained a wide circle of friends, and made frequent visits to the theatre. Known officially as 'Goethe's Housekeeper', she did keep house and warded off from him anything that was unpleasant. Thanks to Christiane, Privy Councillor von Goethe, who was in every way attractive to women, was shielded from any really serious overtures from women. In such circumstances as these he was able to live the life of renunciation.

> The marriage was a contented one. Neither disturbed the other. To Goethe it was important to show respect for his wife, also in public, and to avow his affection for her. I often saw her on his arm as they walked along. There was a proud expression of contentment on her face, and she always had respect for her husband that bordered on fear.[315]

There was one thing on which Christiane, though showered with attentions and privileges and loving Goethe deeply – even to the point of idolatry – had no claim: his heart. For Goethe still loved Anna Amalia now as he had loved her before. There was no room for anyone beside his Princess. And if Christiane worked at her refinement as Goethe would have wanted and became one of the most interesting women in Weimar, very aware of being the wife of this unique poet, even she could not compete with the unknown woman to whom Goethe's heart belonged.

Goethe will on several occasions burn letters and other documents relating to Christiane.[316] What has survived shows an obviously warm, affectionate tone. In his writings Goethe will pass over the death of his 'dear little wife', much to the bewilderment of his biographers.[317] In the entry in T*ag- und Jahreshefte* (1817-1830) for 1816, the year of Christiane's death, Goethe only mentions the deceased Empress of Austria. This news had put him in a state of mind that 'has never left me'. In this way Goethe makes it clear to posterity that the life he shared with Christiane, dictated by practical necessity, was only his private life and concerned neither his writing nor the woman of his heart celebrated in it. Against this backdrop it is possible to understand the poem written on 6 June 1816, the day of Christiane's death. Both the 'sun' and the 'loss' refer with irrefutable logic to Anna Amalia, to whom he turns when faced with the decease of Christiane:

> In vain you try, o sun,
> To shine through the dark clouds!
> The whole value of my life
> Is to weep for her loss.

In a conversation with the Weimar Princes' tutor Frédéric Soret (1795-1865) on 5 March 1830, Goethe assesses the women he has loved during his life:

> She [Lili, his fiancée in Frankfurt, 1775] was in fact the first one that I truly and deeply loved. I can also say that she was the last one; for all small affections which I experienced in the rest of my life were, when compared with this first one, only light and superficial.

The formulation 'I can also say' [auch kann ich sagen] might suggest that there is something he cannot say, namely, that in Anna Amalia he had found his undying love. In a conversation with Chancellor von Müller on 8 June 1821 Goethe said Anna Amalia was 'the most lovable, superb and indefinable person'.[318] So he is not allowed to *define* Anna Amalia, to give precise explanations. He can only glorify her through the veil of his writing. The conversation then led naturally to the subject of *Die Wahlverwandtschaften* and *Wilhelm Meisters Wanderjahre*. In addition, Lili was the deepest and truest of the minor affections. With Anna Amalia the 'genius of geniuses'[319] could speak to the beloved on an *equal* footing.

Goethe's renunciation was difficult. Several statements testify that after his return from Italy he was felt to be an unhappy man. Outwardly he adopted a closed, taciturn, and stiff attitude, precisely in the context of Weimar court society. This was met with resentment,[320] but these people were partly to blame for his renunciation. On 5 July 1791 Friedrich Munter (1761-1830) noted in his diary: 'I visited

Goethe, too, and found him much more friendly than usual, though still cold, as he is towards everyone. He is a very unhappy man. He must be continually unhappy in himself.'[321] This attitude is strikingly illustrated in a portrait of Goethe painted in 1795 (ill. 26) by his close friend and collaborator Johann Heinrich Meyer (1760-1832).[322] Frau von Stein speaks of an 'extinguished star' in a letter to her son Fritz on 10 July 1793. Countess von Egloffstein found the poet in the years 1795- 1797 'abrupt, taciturn, with a bourgeois stiffness, cold as an ice-floe in his attitude, and more off-putting than attractive'.[323] The young writer Jean Paul (1763-1825) wrote on 18 June 1796: '[Charlotte von Kalb] painted him, as everyone did, as very cold about everybody and everything on earth ... every word was ice'.[324]

For Anna Amalia, too, renunciation was to be painful for the rest of her life. A painting from 1795 shows Anna Amalia in the melancholy mood of these years (ill. 27). In her *Gedenkblättern* the almost blind and impoverished Charlotte von Kalb (1761-1843) wrote about Anna Amalia, whom, like Goethe and Wieland, she called Olympia:

> When she encountered beauty in the course of a reading or in music her appreciation was often shown by tears ... Thus she was often surrounded by noble minds who presented to their Princess the most beautiful and the best of their inspired works. This celebration, this phenomenon was worthy of mankind; [it was] humanity in the manifestation of its most heartfelt generosity. In such surroundings simplicity, too, is capable of understanding and can give its response; and, something that is rare in social intercourse, in this circle there was more love than admiration. There was no shining, no sparkling, so seeking after fine phrases, no arguing: the rich well-springs of life flowed without restraint.[325]

Caroline von Herder made a similar judgement in her memoirs:

> The most beautiful social evenings were to be had in her [Anna Amalia's] house, where she gathered the most gifted men around her. Concerts, readings from old and new poets, especially the Greeks and Italians, or from Shakespeare, Lessing, Goethe, Wieland, Einsiedel, Knebel, Herder amongst others; or conversations about art, literature, and politics provided material for entertaining conversation. While the outcome of political world events was uncertain, intelligent men could make their comments, give expression to their views, hopes, and fears about the great happenings of the age, no matter how much their views were at variance with one another. In all this, the kindly Duchess represented urbanity and humanity. Equally pleasant were the social occasions at her summer residences, in the early years in Ettersburg, and later in Tiefurt.[326]

During the time that Anna Amalia and Goethe were not working together in Weimar on her idea of the Court of the Muses things had become quiet there again. Only after Anna Amalia's return did Goethe establish the Friday Society in her Wittumspalais as a forum for scientists and artists, and in September 1791 the poet, as president, made the inaugural speech. Monthly, and with the reigning Duke and Duchess in attendance, gatherings were held for lectures and discussions. Böttiger[327] reports about the first session that Goethe had begun with a paper on the colour prism:

> He demonstrated the main ideas on a blackboard – on which he had already drawn the figure – so clearly that a child could have understood it. Goethe is just as good as an incisive demonstrator at the blackboard as he is as poet, actor, and opera director, science researcher and writer. He declared himself in this small circle point-blank as an opponent of Newton's [Newton, 1643-1727] colour theory, which has been completely overturned by his experiments.

Then Herder spoke about 'the real immortality for future generations'; this was followed by Privy Councillor and Keeper of the Archives Voigt, who used an archive document from the year 1167 to report on the brilliant Emperor Friedrich Barbarossa (1122-1190). The botany professor Bartsch gave a lecture which, beginning with the nautilus and with a snail from the sand of the sea that is only clearly visible under the microscope, dealt with the evolution of the earth 'before it was abandoned by the ocean'. The scientist Johann Georg Lenz (1748-1832) gave an introduction into the world of intestinal worms 'which he had himself extracted from the intestines of many animals and dissected ... It had in the meantime become late, and since it was now close to 9 o'clock, some of the lectures, for example that of Councillor of Legation Bertuch who wanted to talk to us about Japanese and Chinese tints of colour, had to be postponed until the next session.

The university of Jena (founded 1548) became, thanks to Goethe's influence in the sphere of culture and science, one of the leading universities in Germany.[328] 'No other university had such a liberal administration, and so the teachers and students who came here were precisely the ones who loved protesting.'[329] Caroline Herder reports that after Goethe was appointed president of the treasury board 'he [strove], through economies and retrenchments, to establish a fund for extraordinary expenses, especially for the University of Jena.'[330] In the small town of Jena there were, for a time, the most important scholars and the most promising talents of the epoch, for example, Fichte, Schelling, Hegel, Humboldt, Thibaut, Brentano, Tieck, Voß, Schiller, Novalis, and the towering Hölderlin. Jena owed its extraordinary power of attraction above all to Goethe and Anna

Amalia with their programme of educating through art and science. A favourite turn of phrase of Goethe was: 'It is really only a question of lifting it.'[331] The opening lines of the poem 'Das Göttliche', dedicated by Goethe to Anna Amalia and printed in her *Tiefurter Journal* in 1783, are as follows: 'Let man be noble, helpful and good' [Edel sei der Mensch,/Hilfreich und gut]. Anna Amalia commented in her simple *Betrachtungen über Kultur*:

> It is not easy to achieve true culture ... When mind and heart with inner strength unite like sisters, and reason and understanding exist harmoniously together, the result is real culture which elevates the person and comes closer to the image of God.[332]

That with renunciation the time of their physical love had finally come to an end is expressed in encoded form. Goethe, who until the time of his death will erect literary memorials to his beloved, marks this final transition with a description of the *Igeler Säule* in Trier, a 23-metre-high sandstone pillar monument with reliefs, from around AD 250. Goethe was passing this monument on the way to the campaign of the first Coalition army against revolutionary France on 23 August 1792 and again on the return towards the end of October 1792. Goethe joined Carl August's regiment, which had advanced in the Champagne region. During the Valmy bombardment the French revolutionary army fired up to 20,000 shells on 20 September 1792 and brought about the retreat of the Coalition army. The retreat ended in an unbelievable catastrophe. Goethe was in mortal danger several times. 22,000 Prussian soldiers alone were killed.[333]

On 22 October 1792, Goethe, who had only just escaped death, stood in front of the *Igeler Säule* in Trier, but only on 24 October 1792, on Anna Amalia's birthday, will he have found time to write up his notes. According to a legend, the monument is associated with St Helen (c.250-329), the mother of Emperor Constantine I (c.272-337) who put the Church of the catacombs on an equal legal footing with the ancient religions (313), and that is the only reason the monument was not destroyed as heathen. Goethe made a thorough examination of the structure of the pillar, of the individual reliefs and the inscription, and was the first to give them an 'essentially correct' interpretation.[334] The monument portrays the life of the Secundiner, a draper's family, and ties in their existence with motifs from Roman mythology about 'a transition into a better life, into immortality'.[335] In Goethe's *Kampagne in Frankreich* (1822), written from the perspective of 1792, he says, after a detailed study of the monument:

> And so, preoccupied with such reflections, it was my earnest desire to celebrate privately the birthday of our honoured Duchess Amalia, to

> recall her life, her noble activity and beneficence. From this came, in a quite natural way, the stimulus to dedicate to her in my thoughts a similar obelisk and to decorate all its areas with the individual events of her life and her virtues.

The word 'recall' [zurückrufen] and the circumstance that he wants to erect a monument [Grabmal] to her, would have been an anachronism in 1792, when the Princess was still alive.[336] However, the monument is not seen in relation to the person of Anna Amalia, but rather to their forbidden love, which now only exists on the higher level of renunciation and has 'died' on the physical level. Goethe, who worked for better research on and conservation of the ancient monument, dedicates his interpretation of the *Igeler Säule* to Anna Amalia by using it to commemorate her birthday.

Anna Amalia herself found ways of expressing, in encoded form, her love for Goethe. In a water colour ascribed to Kraus at least some important details were painted by Anna Amalia. She also did other pictures in collaboration with Kraus [her drawing instructor][337] and sometimes included Goethe.[338] The prize picture of the Weimar Court of the Muses,[339] from around 1795, the water colour *Abendunterhaltung bei Anna Amalia* (ill. 20), encodes her forbidden love. In this painting Goethe is largely obscured by Anna Amalia's chamberlain von Einsiedel. His back and the back of his head are visible. Since this picture is the only contemporary depiction of the famous social life in Anna Amalia's house, the question arises as to why the famous Goethe did not feature clearly. On the right-hand edge of the picture is Herder holding in his hand a page that shows the profile of a young man. Herder is looking upwards with a gaze and facial expression suggesting that he, as a cleric, is turning to God. A book lies open in front of Goethe. In an unusual way Goethe has laid a finger on it. Following the direction the finger is pointing, one can see that it points above Anna Amalia's brush to the page with the profile of the young man in Herder's hand. This image is meant to portray Goethe himself, so that his face can in fact be seen in the painting. The way Herder is sitting resting his left arm with the hand hanging down loosely and the right arm stretched out and holding a page with the profile of a person recognizable on it, down to the two buttons on the cuff of the left arm, bears close similarity to the picture *Der Verliebte Goethe* commissioned by Anna Amalia and painted by Kraus in 1775/76. This picture shows Goethe sitting in the same posture as Herder's, except that he is looking at the profile of a lady and is not transfigured and looking up to heaven. With the picture painted around the same time – *Anna Amalia als Komponistin* (1775/76) – Anna Amalia is pointing to herself as the unknown lady in the silhouette that Goethe is holding in his hands (ill. 2). Through using the same pose for Herder in the water colour *Abendunterhaltung bei Anna Amalia* she is creating a new reference to herself.

After Anna Amalia met Goethe's mother in 1778 in Frankfurt she commissioned a copy of the oil-painting *Der Verliebte Goethe* to give it to her friend [Goethe's mother] in 1779. She also gave Goethe's mother a large silhouette of herself, and in a letter of 21 April 1779 she answered a question relating to this: 'You would like to know, dear mother, who made my silhouette. It is your son who drew it for the most part.'[340] In 1795, when the glowing passion had been transformed into a special kind of friendship, the Churchman Herder, pictured on the water colour *Abendunterhaltung bei Anna Amalia*, seems to be asking for pardon for the forbidden love and one of the most unbelievable deceptions in history. The reason for the deception is also encoded in the water colour. Emilia Gore (1760-1826) is sitting opposite Anna Amalia, but her face is not to be seen. Carl August adored 'the beautiful Emilia' the very first time he met her in Pyrmont in 1785. 'Good luck with your new acquaintance, the lovely English woman', Goethe wrote on 15 August 1785, 'if luck is the word for being launched again into a dangerous sea'. After the Gore family had settled in Weimar in 1791 Emilia became Duke Carl August's beloved for a long time.[341]

It can be assumed that Anna Amalia encoded the forbidden love in several water colour paintings. Possibly they were more obvious, for many were suppressed. In a letter of 17 February 1821 Goethe reports that there were several such depictions

> which stemmed from evening entertainments in Anna Amalia's house, in which a highly cultured circle gathered and each in his own way entertained himself and others. While some played cards, others music, we – your Highness, the Englishman Gore, his eldest daughter and I busied ourselves with different kinds of sketches; Councillor Kraus observed the gathering with a painter's eye and occasionally made nice pictures, some of which we still have.

8 | *Tasso*: ‘A Dangerous Undertaking’

> To anticipate what noble souls feel
> Is a most desirable and worthy profession.
> ‘Vermächtnis’ (1829)

> And what has greater right
> To last and to continue its quiet influence
> Than the secret of a noble love
> Entrusted modestly to a lovely song?
> *Tasso* (1790) ll.1105ff.

In *Torquato Tasso* (1780-1790) the poet loves a Princess, but this love is forbidden. To protect it, a lady-in-waiting is put forward as the beloved of the poet. To prevent the context being easily recognized as autobiographical, Goethe hides it, with all the means at his disposal, in a psychological drama with a very sparse plot. In a conversation with Chancellor von Müller on 23 March 1823 about the success of *Tasso* there is the ironic statement: ‘Everything that happens in it is purely inward, so I was always afraid that outwardly it would not become clear.’ In the autumn of 1780 Goethe began work on *Tasso* after the idea for it came to him on the way to Erfurt. By 1781 he had a first version, which is no longer extant. This is the one that Goethe re-worked, starting in 1788. Towards the end of his stay in Italy he wrote on 1 February 1788: ‘“Tasso” has to be revised. What I have is leading nowhere. I can’t complete it like this, nor can I throw it all away.’ In March 1788 he tells the Duke: ‘ ...My endeavours to complete it come, strangely enough, at the end of my sojourn in Italy, and I couldn’t wish it to be otherwise.’ At this point the poet knew how he wanted to portray the past, because he understood how to shape his future relationship with Anna Amalia.

In *Tasso* Goethe looks back on his first decade in Weimar and works on it 'with indecent [unerlaubt] care', as he formulates it in a letter to Herder on 10 August 1789. Carl August was afraid that developing the material would be a threat to the state secret. On 1 October 1788 Goethe tries to allay his fears:

> ... I am hoping to get on top of the 'Tasso' material. It is one of the strangest situations I have been in, since I have to grapple not only with the difficulty of the subject but also with your prejudice. The more I work at it the more I hope to succeed.

So Goethe promises a masterpiece of disguise, for only those who know his secret are to be in a position to understand *Tasso*, and the Duke is soon satisfied. On 6 April 1789 Goethe writes to him: 'Your wife tells me that she enjoyed the first scenes of Tasso. This fulfils my specially cherished wish in this dangerous undertaking.' In a letter of 3 August 1789 Carl August writes to his mother Anna Amalia, who is in Italy: '"Tasso" is finished. A great masterpiece. I am curious to know how you like it.' It was not a matter of writing the play to flatter the Duke and the court.[342] The difficulty consisted in expressing the context of the secret in such a way that the biographical basis was not immediately obvious. That is why Goethe refers to *Tasso* as a 'dangerous undertaking'. Because he succeeded in this, Carl August, who in everything to do with the secret always advised extreme caution, calls it a great work of art [grosses Kunststück].

Since as a result of the deceptions Goethe's real biography was not known, there is a 'chaos of opinions and counter-opinions' amongst interpreters of *Tasso*.[343] Thorough observers concede that they encounter barriers when interpreting the play. 'We have to admit that questions remain.'[344] It was always suspected that there was a biographical background to the piece. The Princess was mainly thought to be Frau von Stein and sometimes the reigning Duchess Luise.[345] The memoirs of early years of Henriette von Egloffstein point to Luise:

> Those who had exact knowledge of early events at court maintained that from his arrival in Weimar Goethe was gripped by the most violent passion for the young Princess and found himself in the same position between her and Frau von Stein as his Tasso.[346]

According to this, in critical court circles Goethe's liaison with Frau von Stein was seen as a veil behind which a Princess was hidden. The editor of Henriette's memoirs of her youth, also a von Egloffstein and therefore from a family that for a hundred years had served in the highest positions in the Duchy of Sachsen-Weimar-Eisenach, published them in 1919 directly after the fall of the monarchy. The editor adds to Henriette's comparison between Goethe and Tasso: 'I will have to leave it to the reader to test the validity of this view of the relationship of Frau von Stein to Goethe by referring to Goethe scholarship.'[347] This mocking challenge shows that for the family of the von Egloffsteins the indefinable liaison of Goethe with Frau von Stein was understood to be a deception. The rumour that in his first ten years in Weimar Goethe had a liaison with the Duchess Luise, along with the suppression of documents, played a decisive role in preserving and deepening the state secret. Critical people at court who knew Charlotte von Stein and did not accept that she was Goethe's lover were distracted by the rumours about Luise from knowing the truth of the matter. It was a delicate subject, for it meant that the liaison had taken place at a time when the Duchess Luise gave birth to the heir of the throne (1783), so that such a suspicion would call into question the legitimacy of the ruling authority in the Duchy.

Charlotte von Kalb, too, held the view that in *Tasso* the Duchess Luise was portrayed as the Princess and Frau von Stein as her lady-in-waiting. In a letter to her husband Carolina Herder writes: 'Dear Kalb takes 'Tasso' to refer too literally to Goethe, the Duchess, the Duke, and Stein ['die Steinin'].[348] The biography of the cool, closed Luise, who pedantically insisted on her princely rights as an expression of a supposedly higher level of human existence, gave no basis for relating Goethe's works, or numerous references to his life's secret, directly to her. It was said amongst servants: 'Even those whose loyalty she was sure of often felt uncomfortable in her presence.' 'She was not able to relate easily to people.'[349] When Chancellor von Müller showed Goethe the obituary notice he had written for the Duchess Luise, Goethe commented (18 February 1830): 'The Princess should not be shown in too liberal a light. She insisted strongly on her rights. Her social condescension was more a function of her rank.'[350] Directly following this is the further comment to von Müller about the burning of all his collected letters up until 1786 when he left for Italy. Here Goethe is saying that because of a pathological preoccupation with rank he was forced to flee to Italy, since the Princess Anna Amalia was too 'high' for him.

Precisely the rumour of a liaison between Goethe and Luise, who despised her mother-in-law Anna Amalia – not least for associating with the middle-class – helped to prevent people from knowing that a Princess was Goethe's beloved and the muse of his unique love poetry. In a letter to her brother shortly after Anna Amalia's death on 10 April 1807 Luise's animosity is apparent: 'It is a good piece [Goethe's obituary *Zum Feyerlichen Andenken der Durchlauchtigsten Fürstin und Frau Anna Amalia*] and one is somewhat astonished to realize that even after her death she [Anna Amalia] still enjoys the privilege already accorded to her in her life-time: namely, that of a good reputation.'[351] This shows that, for Luise, Anna Amalia had not deserved a good reputation. Similarly a biographer judges: 'The death of her mother-in-law [Anna Amalia], who was never close to her in the thirty-two years of their life together, meant a change, not a gap.[352]

Goethe gave many hints for the correct interpretation of his *Tasso*. On 19 April 1781 in a letter to 'Frau von Stein' he writes: 'since you want to assimilate all that Tasso says, I have written to you so much today that I can't write anymore'. On 20 August 1781 Goethe writes: 'While writing on Tasso I have been adoring you. My whole soul is with you.' Half a century later, in a letter of 10 January 1829, the poet claims: 'In my "Tasso" I have transfused my heart's blood, perhaps more than I should have.' Since Anna Amalia's role in Goethe's life was not visible, the love story in *Tasso* was neglected in favour of the court motif. In the twentieth century the existence of the poet and his relationship to society occupied centre stage. These are important aspects, but they should not be allowed to supplant the essence of Goethe's play, for *Tasso* is an autobiographical play in which he sings of his love for the Princess Anna Amalia. This work becomes a milestone in the development of German lyrical language:

> 'Tasso' gives us Goethe's language at its most perfect. These iambics have taught Schiller iambics and have given Schlegel the language in which he, as it were, changed Shakespeare into a German poet.[353]

Tasso treats of the love of a poet to a unique lover (ll. 1092ff.):

> Whatever resounds in my song
> I owe it all *to one, to one* alone.
>
> And what has greater claim
> To last for centuries, quietly at work,
> Than the secret of a noble love
> Entrusted humbly to a charming song?

Tasso does not deal with 'fairytales'. The Princess stresses (ll. 276ff.): 'He does not want to heap one fairytale on another/Which entertain, then/Deceiving, like loose words die away.' Countess Leonore Sanvitale, the Princess's friend whose role corresponds to that of a lady-in-waiting, also points out that Tasso is singing of only one lady (ll. 183f.): ' ... he glorifies/One single image in all his rhymes'. Goethe's *Tasso* deals with the love which the poet cherishes in secret: ' ... my heart [is] secretly [im stillen] consecrated to you' (l. 911).

Richard Wagner (1813-1883) made the telling judgement that *Tasso* is a play, the whole point of which is the relationship between

Tasso and the Princess. In a letter to the writer Mathilde Wesendonck (1828-1902) of 15 April 1859, Wagner writes:

> I took up 'Tasso' today and read it quickly from beginning to end. ... How Goethe could write that!– Who is in the right here? Who is in the wrong? ... Finally only our heart finds out who suffers the most, and a voice also tells us this is the one who has the deepest vision. But the master [Meisterin] of suffering is clearly the Princess. For anyone with profound insight there is only one contrast here: that between Tasso and the Princess: Tasso and Antonio are less of a contrast, and their conflict is of less interest to deeper minds. If we look beyond the play [über das Stück hinaus] all we have left is the Princess and Tasso.[354]

Anna Amalia has clearly drawn attention to herself as the direct model for the Princess in *Tasso*. One can begin with the water colour *Besuch der Villa D'Este* of 1789 (ill. 14). Goethe sent a part of his *Tasso* to Italy so that Anna Amalia could read it there. In a letter to her on 17 April 1789 he writes: 'Herder will have presented to your Highness some scenes from Tasso. The main thing is how they are read in Rome. Goethe then points to Sorrento, the birthplace of Tasso, as a suitable place for a reading. But Anna Amalia has a better plan which leads to Tivoli and the Villa D'Este. In antiquity Tivoli was called 'Tibur' and, as early as 1776, Anna Amalia compared Tibur with Tiefurt, where her second son still lived at the time.[355] On 20 December 1788 Anna Amalia's lady-in-waiting, Luise von Göchhausen, writes to Wieland that Herder had already been in Tivoli. This journey seems to have been well prepared. In a letter of 23 May 1789 the swiss painter Angelica Kauffmann (1741-1807), who was living in Rome, writes to Goethe: 'Two weeks ago I was in respectable company in Tivoli, in the Villa D'Este. Among the big cypress trees Herder read to us the part of Tasso you sent.'[356] In a letter to Angelica Kaufmann of 7 September 1789 Anna Amalia speaks of this sojourn which she captured in *Besuch der Villa D'Este*: 'Goethe will send you his "Tasso"; perhaps you have it already. When you read it think of the little place in the Villa D'Este. That's where one should enjoy it!'[357] Hippolytus of Este, the builder of the famous Villa with its terraced park and manifold fountains, is mentioned in *Tasso* (l. 69). A descendant of the Italian house of Este was Guelph IV (died 1101), the founder of the Guelph dynasty. In their turn, the Guelphs founded the Duchy of Braunschweig-Lüneburg (1235), to which Anna Amalia belonged;[358] and so the blood of Este flowed in the veins of Anna Amalia, the Princess who belonged to the Guelphs of Braunschweig. In the second of the *Fünf Briefe über Italien* Anna Amalia writes: 'I went first to the Villa D'Este which is most gloriously situated and is a striking proof of the great and noble mentality of this race.

Goethe's treatment of the biography of the historical Tasso does not correspond to real life. No person clearly reflects an historical one, and the friendship between both the Leonores is pure invention.[359] According to the first biography by Giambattista Manso (1619-1634), Princess Leonore of Este was the lover of Tasso, but in the second biography, by Pierantonio Serassi (1785), which Goethe acquired in Italy, it had been established that there was no relationship between them.[360] The central theme of *Tasso*, therefore, his love for the Princess, was not an historical fact in Tasso's life.[361] It was Goethe's invention that Tasso could safely sing of his adored Princess because her lady-in-waiting had the same name, which left open the question of whom he had in mind. Goethe needed this passage to indicate the role played by Frau von Stein in hiding the Weimar state secret from the eyes of his contemporaries who were familiar with Tasso and his writings as part of the basic education of the time.[362] In the play, Tasso means the Princess Leonore, but he only uses the name Leonore by itself, so that for the public the lady-in-waiting Leonore Sanvitale can be meant. The deception through Frau von Stein, who let her name be used to protect Anna Amalia from the public, is expressed by Goethe's use of the older biographical tradition going back to Manso (ll. 197ff.):

> **Princess:** And when he gives his object a name
> He calls it Leonore.
> **Leonore:** It is your name, as it is mine.
> I would resent it if it were another.
> I rejoice to see he hides his feeling for you
> In this double meaning.
> I am content when with the lovely sound
> Of this name he thinks of me as well.

That Leonore Sanvitale is happy that the poet also thinks of her reminds us of what Frau von Stein said in relation to Goethe: 'I consider myself lucky that I am able to listen to his golden words.'[363] Tasso's life was the basis Goethe had long sought after to erect a loving monument to his beloved. In a conversation with Eckermann of 6 May 1827 he says:

> I had the life of Tasso, I had my own life, and by throwing together two such strange figures with their peculiarities, the image of Tasso came to me ... the rest – the court, the life, the love relationships were in Weimar the same as in Ferrara, and I can with justification say of my work: it is bone of my bone and flesh of my flesh.

But since the Ferrara presented in *Tasso* in not at all historical, the only historical foundation for the forbidden love for a Princess is Weimar. Hence Goethe is saying clearly that in Weimar a poet secretly loves a Princess, and that to protect this love from the public eye a lady-in-waiting is put forward as his lover.

The action of the play *Tasso* takes place not in Ferrara but rather in the nearby Court of Muses, Belriguardo, a parallel to the Court of Muses of Anna Amalia, which likewise existed separately from the court of the reigning Duke.[364] In 1797, Carl August's clever and power-conscious concubine, Karoline Jagemann, made the comparison between Anna Amalia's Tiefurt and Ferrara: 'Artists and scholars, interesting women and odd personalities who came to Weimar felt drawn by this activity as Tasso was to the court of Este.'[365] In Tiefurt, on 23 August 1781, the first version of *Tasso*, which was later destroyed, had its first reading. The action takes place in one day. The first and last scene give the impression that they began with spring and ended with autumn. The lovers have two dialogues which make up a sixth of the verses of the play, one at the beginning and the other at the end. These are crucial. The rest fills out the details to form a complete picture. Right at the beginning of the first dialogue between the Princess and Tasso we can see his undying love for the Princess (ll. 750ff.):

> **Tasso:** My footsteps follow you uncertainly,
> O Princess, and thoughts that have
> No measure and no order
> Are stirring in my soul.
>
> ...
>
> But when I cast a glance towards you and hear,
> When listening hard, a word from your lips,
> Then a new day dawns around me,
> And all my chains then fall away.

Tasso is an inexperienced youth (l. 813), the young friend of the Princess (844). The feelings of the young poet are indescribable when he sees his adored lady (ll. 2798ff.):

> If I heard her voice my breast was
> Penetrated by an inexpressible feeling.
> If I looked at her the bright light of day
> Was dull for me; irresistibly I was drawn to her,
> Her eyes, her mouth. My knees felt weak
> And all my strength of mind was needed
> For me to stand up straight and not
> Fall down at her feet.

Tasso met Princess Leonore of Este, the sister of the Duke of Ferrara, Alfonse II, after the Princess had recovered from a serious illness. After taking over the government while her son was still a minor, Anna Amalia writes in *Meine Gedanken* (c. 1772): '... in the years where everything is normally blossoming, for me there was mist and darkness.' Two months after Anna Amalia was freed from the burden of regency in the Duchy Goethe arrived in Weimar (November 1775). The Princess is delighted (ll. 860ff.):

> For the first time I left my sick room,
> Supported by my women.
> Then along came Lucretia full of joy for living
> And leading you by the hand.
>
> You were the first I met in my new life.
> You were new to me and unknown.
> I hoped great things for you and me
> And up until now this hope has not deceived us.

With the image of the younger sister Lucretia, who is only given an isolated mention in *Tasso* and who has no relevance to the action of the play, Goethe makes a daring reference to the biographical background of his play. The historical Princess Eleonore d'Este (1537-1581) had two sisters, one of whom was called Lucretia. Goethe was able to use this because it calls up an association with Lucretia Borgia (1480-1519), Pope Alexander Borgia's notorious daughter, who, in her third marriage, came as Princess to the court of Ferrara. Anna Amalia's own younger sister, Elisabeth Christine Ulrike, was the unfortunate young woman who, because of her excesses, was divorced from the Prussian Crown Prince and banished at the age of twenty-two. In *Tasso* it is Lucretia who comes to Leonora holding Tasso by the hand. She is the personification of the warning about what happens to a woman who, like Elisabeth Christine Ulrike, in the eyes of the public does not behave in accordance with traditionally accepted moral and ethical norms. Until now Anna Amalia and Goethe had managed to live in secrecy the love that was not acceptable within the monarchical social system, so the Princess can say:

> I hoped great things for you and me
> And up until now this hope has not deceived us.

If the lovely, unsullied happiness is linked to Lucretia's presence at court – 'For since the day she left no one was able to replace the pure joy you had' (ll. 895ff.) – Goethe is alluding to the ploy used to maintain the smoke-screen. In *Tasso* the catastrophe, the separation of the lovers, is prepared by Lucretia's departure. The mutual happiness of Goethe and Anna Amalia could only be sustained as long as they heeded the warning embodied in Lucretia and no one discovered their secret. But in the play, Tasso himself, blinded by the hope of finally being able to make an open declaration of his love for the Princess, goes so far as to divulge their secret. All that he achieved by this was their definitive separation.

The Princess had a special plan for the handsome young man: the poet should link up with the statesman. To express his two contrasting roles in Weimar, that of the poet and that of the Minister of State, Goethe adds the figure of Antonio to that of Tasso. He has the Princess say to Tasso (ll. 956ff.): 'You have to be united! I flatter myself that I can quickly bring this about. But don't resist as you usually do!' Tasso is open to the Princess's plan (ll. 1159): 'I am hers, hers to educate and form.' The Princess is certain her plan will succeed (ll. 1686f.): 'I urged the young man on; he gave everything;/How beautifully, how warmly he surrendered himself totally to me!' Leonore Sanvitale agrees to the plan (ll. 10707ff.):

> And if they knew what was good for them
> They would be united in friendship.
> Then they would be like one man and would go
> Through life with power, happiness, and joy.'

Now both persons have to find one another. Tasso will say to the statesman (ll. 1266ff.):

> O take me, noble man, to your bosom
> Initiate me, so hasty and inexperienced
> Into a moderate way of living.

Tasso explains why this union should take place (ll. 1277ff.):

> The Princess hopes for it, she wants it – Eleonore,
> She wants to lead me to you, you to me. O let us now fulfil her wish!
> Let us go before the goddess, united,
> To offer her our service, our very selves,
> To serve her, united, as worthily as possible.

Against this backdrop Goethe's remarks to 'Frau von Stein' can be seen as ironic, for example, where he writes in a letter of 17 December 1782: 'I am really made to be a private individual and cannot understand how fate has wanted to patch me into State administration and a princely family.'

The portrayal of the Princess becomes a song of praise to Anna Amalia. Leonore Sanvitale says about the Princess (ll. 59f.): 'A noble person attracts noble people/And knows how to keep them, as you do.' This is above all a reference to the Weimar Court of the Muses. In line 107 the Princess says she has a command of ancient languages. Anna Amalia has a command of Latin and ancient Greek. Duchess Luise is the only other one of whom we know that Herder taught her the fundamentals of Latin.[366] The Princess says of herself furthermore (ll. 116ff.):

> I am happy, when clever men are speaking,
> That I can understand their meaning.
> Whether a judgement of a man
> Of days gone by, and of the value of his deeds;
> Or whether there is discussion of a science
> Which, developed through experience,
> Is useful to mankind and elevates it:
> No matter where the noble conversation leads
> I like to follow. I follow it with ease.

Anna Amalia liked to gather scholars around her. In Goethe's official obituary *Zum Feyerlichen Andenken der Durchlauchtigsten Fürstin und Frau Anna Amalia* (1807) he says about her quiet private life which [from 1775] she gladly chose, that

> she felt happy surrounded by art and science as well as by the natural beauty of her country residence. She was at home in the company of intellectual people and enjoyed making connections of this kind, maintaining them, and making them fruitful. There is no name of consequence originating from Weimar that did not at one time or another have contact with her circle.

In Jena, Anna Amalia was not only remembered for improving the professors' salaries during the time of her regency.[367] It is clear from the academic memorial speech in 1807 that she took pains to attract first-class professors;[368] she showed 'admirable strength of character and constancy in her benevolent promotion of them, and, when necessary, she protected and defended them.' When the theologian Ernst Jakob Danovius (1741-1782) was accused of heresy

> she fearlessly defended this intelligent theologian against the accusations of his ill-disposed colleagues, and declared on this occasion quite rightly that without freedom in doctrine and opinion in the universities there could be no science and scholarship, and even the most talented could produce nothing of importance ... We know how Anna Amalia liked to be in the company of professors either to learn from hearing the scholars speak about the sciences or to get their advice.[369]

When Carl August found in Anna Amalia's bequest that a pearl bracelet was missing, it turned out that the Princess had sold it to enable Herder, one of the leading theologians of his time, to go to a spa on a health cure.[370]

The Princess, as Tasso's muse, has inspired him to create his songs. Without her he cannot write. Tasso explains to Leonore Sanvitale the consequences of being separated from his beloved (ll. 2251ff.):

> And if all of that were now lost?
> If you saw a friend you once thought rich
> And suddenly found he was a beggar?
> You are right. I am no longer myself,
> And yet I am myself as much as I ever was.
> It seems to be a riddle, and yet it isn't one.
> The quiet moon, that gives you joy by night,
> With its irresistible light draws to it your eye, your mind,
> By day drifts on, a pale unnoticed cloud.
> I have been overcome by the brilliance of day,
> You know me, I don't know myself at all.

The poet who loses his muse is a beggar. Outwardly he remains the same, but inwardly he is robbed of his treasure. The point where this can happen is the one in which Tasso is 'overcome by the brilliance of day', in other words: his night love has been discovered. When the poet wants to leave for Rome, the Princess reproaches him (ll. 3179f.): ... You are throwing away, resentfully, all that you possess.' She does not want to admit that he can only remain if they openly confess their love (ll. 3212ff.):

> I find no counsel in my heart
> And find no comfort for you and – us.
> My eye looks around to see if a god
> Could offer us aid, could show me
> A healing herb, a potion
> That would bring peace to your mind, peace to us!
> The truest word that lips can speak,
> The most beautiful healing remedy,
> Now has no effect.
> I have to leave you, but my heart cannot do it.

The reason why Tasso cannot continue living as before is that he has involved himself in something that is destroying him as a poet, because he can only sing of his beloved from behind a veil of deception. But since he cannot free himself of her, he is prepared to destroy himself (ll. 2222ff.): 'So I cannot repent, even if my life's destiny were gone forever – I gave myself to her and happily followed/The sign that led to my destruction.' Tasso's condition becomes worse and worse (ll. 3254ff.):

> Is it confusion that makes me follow you?
> Is it madness? Is it an inspired mind
> That only now has grasped the highest, purest truth?

Yes, it is the feeling which alone
Can make me happy on this earth,
Which alone could make me feel so wretched
When I resisted it and tried to ban
It from my heart. I thought to fight
This passion, I struggled
With my deepest self, rashly
Destroyed my very self to which
You completely belong.

The poet not only has to veil his love because of the laws of a monarchical class-society, to which the Princess says with resignation (ll. 1670f.): 'O that we no longer know how to follow the pure, quiet signals given by the heart!' Even the link with Antonio is impossible, just as Goethe, too, is in danger of becoming just a Minister of State and neglecting his poetry, for he cannot do justice to both sets of demands. At the zenith of his career as a Minister Goethe confesses in a letter to 'Frau von Stein' on 4 June 1782:

> How much better it would be for me if, separated from the political struggles, I could, close to you, my dearest, turn my mind to the sciences and arts for which I was born. Adieu. Love me, for I am yours.

On 10 August 1782, shortly before he received the title of nobility arranged for him by Anna Amalia, the poet writes: 'Really I was born to be a poet.' The Princess finally has to realize that her plan to unite Tasso and Antonio has failed: 'Just look at them: face, voice, gaze, walk! At odds with one another in everything.' Leonore Sanvitale insists (ll. 1704ff.): 'They are two men who are enemies for the very reason that nature did not make them into one.' Now the poet wants to separate himself from the statesman to be a poet and in this way to carry out his god-given duty (ll. 2339ff.):

Tasso: And if I am wrong about him [Antonio], I'm glad I'm wrong!
I think of him as my worst enemy
And would be inconsolable if I now
Had to think more kindly of him ...
No, from now on I have to think of this man
As the object of my deepest hatred.
Nothing can deprive me of the pleasure
Of thinking worse and worse of him.

His poetry is at stake (ll. 2324ff.):

[it is that] which nature alone can give
Which all effort and striving cannot achieve,
Something that neither gold nor sword
Nor brains nor perseverance can bring about.

Tasso has given his poem to Duke Alfonse, but now he wants it back to refine it in Rome. Goethe could either be the complete statesman or the complete poet, though after his first ten years in Weimar he no longer believed he could achieve much as a statesman without having the reins of government in his hands. Shortly before his flight to Italy he writes to 'Frau von Stein' on 10 July 1786: 'I always say that whoever wants to work in administration without being the ruler is either a philistine, a rogue, or a fool.' On 17 March 1788 he now writes: 'I can say that after a year and a half of isolation I have found myself; but as what? – an artist!' Only at the Court of Muses in Weimar did he find the conditions he needed for living as a poet. Working full-time as a poet was still unusual, and Goethe's poetic work was seen as a secondary activity. The historical Tasso in Ferrara was an exception. Klopstock, because he was supported by the King of Denmark, could devote himself primarily to his writing, but as a rule poets were always busy with other activities: they were educators of princes, house tutors, or librarians. Now, after detailed consultations between Carl August and Anna Amalia,[371] Goethe was in a position, if not to devote himself entirely to poetry, to shift the balance in favour of his writing. He is now first and foremost poet and researcher and his secondary activity is state service, largely in cultural administration. Tasso speaks to the Duke of his unbridled urge to research and to write:

> It is in vain to resist this urge
> Which alternates within me day and night.
> If I am not to think or write
> Life is no longer life for me.
> Just try to forbid the silkworm to spin
> Even though his spinning brings him closer to death.
> He weaves the precious web
> From within himself and does not cease
> Until he has enclosed himself in his coffin.

The second problem is Tasso's relationship to the Princess. There is a solution. Goethe knows the 'healing herb', the potion that would bring peace to Tasso's mind and 'peace – to us!' which the Princess searches for in vain (ll. 3216ff.). Goethe's stage direction reads (after l. 3283): 'He falls into her arms in a tight embrace.' Tasso does this in front of all the others in the play, who, according to a stage direction, 'have for a while been visible in the background'. By grasping the only possibility he sees for continuing to live at court, namely, an open declaration of his love for the Princess, he thereby loses her, because she is not prepared to permit this. She pushes him away and hurries off. The secret of their love has, however, become known to the Duke, who sees to their separation. Antonio will then say (ll. 3290ff.):

When something quite unexpected happens,
When we look on something monstrous,
Our minds stand still a while,
We have nothing to compare it with.

Before Tasso answers Antonio, the stage direction says: 'after a long pause'. This underlines the importance of Antonio's statement. There is no historical model with which Goethe's fate can be compared. A unique poet is forced to conceal the true identity of his beloved and thus hinder the interpretation of his works which glorify her. Tasso himself looks in vain for historical antecedents (ll. 342ff.):

Is there no other example in history?
Does no other noble man occur to me
Who suffered more than I ever suffered
So that I can understand myself through the comparison?

His despair is expressed in lines 3409ff.:

Then all is lost? ...
Is no talent left? ...
Is all my strength wiped out? ...
Have I become nothing,
Completely nothing?
No, it is all there! And I am nothing!
I am estranged from myself, and she is estranged from me.

The stage direction for the last scene reads: 'Antonio comes to him and takes him by the hand.' Tasso says to Antonio (ll. 3434f.): 'You stand firm and quiet, I seem like a wave in a storm.' Antonio is the rock, Tasso the wave (ll. 3442ff.): 'This wave reflected the sun so beautifully, the stars rested on this breast which moved so gently.' In his hour of need the poet has a support (ll. 3446ff.):

In this danger I no longer know myself,
And no longer am ashamed to admit it.
The rudder is broken, the ship is cracking
On all sides. The ground bursts open under my feet!
I hold on to you with both arms!
Like this the sailor clutches the rock
On which he was supposed to perish.

The poet clutches onto Antonio, who has taken him by the hand. Anna Amalia has, therefore, rightly seen that Goethe, to go through life with 'power, happiness, and joy', had to follow her advice and achieve the status of a statesman, even if for a long time it looked as if it would destroy him as a poet. Goethe's primary function is now that of a poet. His secondary function is that of a statesman of the highest rank in the Duchy. On this solid basis he can lament his suffering as a lover in a spirit of renunciation (ll. 3432f.): 'And if man falls silent in his pain,/A god gave me the gift to say how I suffer.' These lines reflect Goethe's work programme for the future and show how serious he is about renunciation. He will lay an incomparable number of works at Anna Amalia's feet. He will have to encode them, but he leaves behind enough clues so that some day these treasures of world literature will be understood to refer directly to his beloved Anna Amalia. Weimar took leave of its dead Poet Prince on 27 March 1832 with a performance of *Tasso*. The whole audience was dressed in mourning attire.

9 | Anna Amalia: An Outstanding Woman

> Whatever can be heard in my song
> I owe it all to one, and one alone!
> No vague elusive image
> Floats before my mind
> Approaching in all brilliance
> And then withdrawing from my soul.
> With my own eyes I have seen it,
> The archetype of virtue, beauty.
> The work this model has inspired will endure.
> *Tasso* (1790), ll. 1092ff.

> He is no lover who does not hold
> The faults of his beloved for virtues.
> *Maximen und Reflexionen.* From the bequest

Where there is talk of Anna Amalia there is no lack of superlatives, although she always tried to stay in the background. Her teacher, the Abbot Johann F. Jerusalem (1709-1789), characterized the fifteen-year-old Princess in these words (1754): 'And so she will probably never be known by everyone, for she will hide her good deeds; but she will be infinitely treasured by those who have the good fortune to be close to her.'[372]

In a letter to Merck in August 1778, Wieland writes that Anna Amalia is 'one of the most endearing and glorious mixtures of human being, woman, and Princess that has ever been known on this earth.'[373] Her page writes in his memoirs: 'A peculiar loveliness played around her well-formed, gently closed mouth, and everyone to whom she opened it in friendliness was overjoyed.'[374] About her external appearance we read: 'In her dress she was always elegantly modern, though always without exaggeration. She had a delicate build; she was not tall, but everyone saw in her the Princess, and showed her reverence.'[375] Goethe's mother, Catharina Elisabeth, could hardly give adequate expression to her enthusiasm after she had received Anna Amalia in Frankfurt in the summer of 1778:

> ... Great and Best Princess! In my life I have enjoyed many a good thing, have passed through many happy years, but when compared with 1778 they will all have to yield – in truth, I have known great and noble souls ... But to become acquainted with an Amalia!!! God! God! This is no babble, no chat or false gush of feeling, but such a true feeling that tears come into my eyes.

Henriette von Egloffstein reports:

> She [Anna Amalia] spoke little, praised and reproached only with her eyes, and yet she electrified everyone who was lucky enough to be allowed to approach her ... The Princess lived quietly like a philosopher, without concerning herself with the bustle of the outside world, and yet she had such an enlivening effect on the minds of others that they seemed greedy for her praise. At the same time, no talent was unnoticed by her; she gave everyone support or encouragement.[376]

Johanna Schopenhauer said in a letter to her son on 13 April 1807:

> ... she had beautiful, large, flashing eyes that saw into your heart ... There was something indescribably kind and friendly in her whole being ... She was the bond that held together the better people here [in Weimar]. While she ruled for her son until he became of age, she changed Weimar from being a wretched village into what it is now.[377]

Anna Amalia's page recalled:

> Every one of us pages was glad to wait on the Wednesday table of the Dowager Duchess, to which only one or two of the nobility but always several of the so-called literary, artistic types were invited. Goethe, Wieland, and Herder regularly got into lively arguments. The result was a conversation which was interesting in itself, but was often so loud that the Duchess, insisting on moderation, sometimes had to end the meal earlier than would otherwise have been the case.[378]

Even long after her death, Anna Amalia was called 'one of the most appealing figures of all times and countries ... a phenomenon in which, to an unusual extent, genuine and most noble womanliness was paired with manly vigour and determination.'[379] Anna Amalia is seen as

> one of the purest instances of womankind in our history. ... Wherever noble people have dedicated themselves to the cultivation of the arts and sciences, this Princess may stand before them as an example to be followed.[380]

Johanna Schopenhauer began a biography of Anna Amalia in 1817 –for the 'guardian angel of all that is good and beautiful'.[381] Apart from what is mentioned in a letter to her publisher we know nothing more.[382] The Princely family could hardly have allowed this clever woman access to the private papers of Anna Amalia without endangering the state secret concerning Goethe and Anna Amalia. When Carl August entrusted Anna Amalia's letters to Chancellor von Müller, the latter wrote to Henriette von Egloffstein on 19 May 1828:

> The Archduke yesterday entrusted me with the letters of his mother [Anna Amalia] and his own early correspondence with Goethe, Herder, Wieland etc, to go through them and put them in order. This gives me unspeakable enjoyment! What treasures and what glorious light they throw on the character of Goethe and the Duchess! My enjoyment would be greater if I could share it with someone, namely, yourself and Line [Henriette's daughter].[383]

In talking to Chancellor von Müller, Goethe said the amount of correspondence was enormous: 'How industrious the Dowager Duchess was, how much she wrote is unbelievable.'[384] Yet the amount of her correspondence that Carl August's successor in government made accessible to the public does not throw any 'glorious light ... on the character of Goethe and the Duchess'. Goethe, to whom Chancellor von Müller presented the first results of his browsing and cataloguing of Anna Amalia's letters, wrote to him on 24 July 1828:

> It is a great joy to me to know that this business is in your hands, since it is to be treated with insight and loyalty as well as with caution and taste. In this way unusual documents will be saved; they are invaluable not from a political angle but from a human point of view, because only these papers can give a clear picture of the way things were at the time.

In 1781 Anna Amalia moved her Court of Muses to the country residence in Tiefurt, which is much closer to Weimar than the forest residence Ettersburg. Tiefurt became a centre for art and science in the middle of a beautiful park. 'Early in the morning the Duchess was to be seen there [in Tiefurt] in simple attire, her beautiful hair rolled up under a plain straw hat, feeding her hens and pigeons.'[385]

For her summer sojourns she drastically reduced the number of her court attendants and took with her only her lady-in-waiting Luise von Göchhausen and two servants. Guests were put up in a 'small, nicely appointed lodging in a well-kept farmhouse' in the village very close nearby. Wieland was a frequent guest in Tiefurt.[386] These were ideal conditions for the Princess to receive a guest in secret with little danger of it being known. A letter of Anna Amalia to Merck on 4

August 1781 shows how Goethe's presence in Tiefurt was taken for granted:

> The bas-relief delivered to me by post yesterday gave me no end of joy. It is an excellent copy. The whole piece is beautiful. *Il nudo*, as the Italians say, *è tanto dolce e soave per inginocciarsi* [is so sweet and gentle that you want to kneel down before it]. Goethe was with me when it arrived. He was wide-eyed. He certainly didn't dislike it![387]

A letter from Luise von Göchhausen to Knebel shows that Goethe lived in Tiefurt:

> O Knebel, get on the first available horse and delight us by appearing here some nice evening. This is for the Duchess, Goethe, and myself our dearest wish, when, in this dear, dear temple, we see the sun go down or the moon rise in its quiet glory. ... The Duchess [Anna Amalia] will hold a little celebration for you taken from a forest-and-water drama by Goethe, called *Die Fischerin*.[388]

Goethe and Anna Amalia worked together in shaping the garden and residence in Tiefurt. Anna Amalia's secretary Johann August Ludecus (1742-1801) informs Knebel on 5 June 1782: 'The Duchess has introduced some features in Tiefurt ... a grotto on the other side of the Ilm, just opposite the hermitage, looks very well. Goethe made an inscription for it.'[389] Goethe planned the entrance to the garden. Anna Amalia writes to Knebel on 8 November 1782: 'I want to send you a plan Goethe has had made for me for the entrance to the garden.'[390] On 25 November 1782 Ludecus writes to Knebel:

> The Dowager Duchess is having the garden in Tiefurt extended up to the balcony and now the wall from the house to the garden is being broken down and made broader towards the garden. This idea comes from Goethe.[391]

In Anna Amalia's account books Goethe's signature is to be found not only in connection with the amateur theatre but also with the park in Tiefurt. On 3 July 1782 Goethe wrote receipts: 'Two carolin for a monument erected in Tiefurt with inscription and garden seat ... Goethe'.[392] Knebel's diary entry for 22 July 1784 implies that Goethe stayed overnight with Anna Amalia in Tiefurt:

> At mid-day I drove to Tiefurt with Einsiedel [Anna Amalia's chamberlain] ... We spent the afternoon ... I read something to them, and towards evening Goethe arrived. We had supper and I walked back with Einsiedel.[393]

Anna Amalia closely observed the friends of Goethe who in 1779 arrived in his wake and, apart from Herder, did not stay. There was, for example, the strong-willed Johann Christoph Kaufmann (1753-1795), an apothecary from Winterthur, who visited Goethe in the autumn of 1776 and in the following winter 1776/1777. He rode into Weimar on a white horse with free-flowing mane. Chest bared to the navel, Kaufmann spoke in oracles and preached a return to nature. His motto was: 'You can achieve what you want to.'[394] Through his gaze and laying-on of hands Kaufmann was successful in curing the sick. Partly for this reason he seems to have been convinced he had a missionary calling.[395]

> Kaufmann seemed to be the genius who could achieve all he wanted, but he soon found out here that he could not dislodge Goethe from the Duke's favour and himself easily become the cock of the walk.[396]

When he was about to move on a few weeks later, Kaufmann's next task was in Dessau. The pedagogue Johann B. Basedow (1724-1790) founded an educational establishment 'Philanthropin' [love of mankind] based on principles like learning through play, multi-religious education, physical development, education for happiness, and usefulness to the community. Kaufmann wanted to 'improve ... [this establishment] or smash it'.[397] Anna Amalia wrote to Merck on 28 December 1778:

> Dear Merck, I have always been writing to you in my thoughts; but since wise mother nature did not endow me with such a nose bone as she gave to the lucky Kaufmann, by virtue of which he can achieve everything he wants, I have had to content myself with wanting only what I can achieve.[398]

In April 1776 the talented writer Lenz, who had caused a stir with his unpolished writing, came to Weimar. In a letter to Herder on 28 August 1775, on Goethe's birthday, Lenz described himself as the 'stinking breath of the people who could never dare to enter the lofty realms of the great'.[399] In Wieland's judgement 'he only has half of a poet in him and has little talent to be anything completely'.[400] Frau von Stein's view is expressed in a letter to Zimmermann on 10 May 1776: 'Lenz, Goethe's friend, is here, but he is no Goethe.'[401] In Weimar they envisaged finding him a position as a reader at social gatherings. Lavater, too, tried to influence the Duchess Luise to help in this.[402] But Lenz only wanted to be a writer, with a leading role in the Duchy (like his friend Goethe, who was a Minister), although he had only an unfinished course of theology studies to recommend him. In a letter to Goethe in July 1776 Lenz describes his absurd notion of Weimar as an exhibition town for French businessmen and large trade concerns: 'You are here in the heart of Germany ... to get France to agree is a special problem. There is no nation in the world more difficult to deal with ... whether the Duke would for this reason make contracts with the other Saxon courts, especially with Electoral Saxony, is not my concern.'[403] But Weimar was not on any trade route and had very bad roads, something which was soon going to be an ongoing task for Goethe as director of road building. Lenz approached Carl August with ideas for a complete military reform in the tiny Duchy, involving the formation of a brave Amazon corps comprised of noble harlots.[404] Alongside this he busied himself with plans to restructure the French army with the basic idea of using them at the same time as farmers. In Weimar he was looking for patrons who would present his plans to the French government or even to the French King.[405]

Along with his role as court jester Lenz immediately fell madly in love, in Weimar, with – Anna Amalia. Here another young poet lay at the feet of the highly cultured Princess. At the end of April 1776 Lenz writes to his colleague Gotter, a poet in Gotha:

> Should you have a copy of the *Barber of Seville* I would be much obliged if you would kindly lend it to me for a week. The Dowager Duchess is very much in love with it and I have promised to translate it for her so that we can perform it here.[406]

Of the few poems written by Lenz in Weimar two of the longer ones refer to Anna Amalia. The first relates to Anna Amalia's composition of Goethe's *Erwin und Elmire*, which was performed on 24 May 1776 and constitutes a literary account of Goethe's love relationship with Lili [Schönemann]. With the title 'Auf die Musik zu Erwin und Elmire' – ['set to music by Her Highness, the widowed Duchess of Weimar and Eisenach'] Lenz has 'an Erwin of today appear for the second time and fly into the arms of the 'real Elmire'. The poem closes with the lines: 'Yes, Your Highness, you conjure up for us Elmire in every wilderness .../And so you lead us from there more blissfully and readily into Elysium.'[407]

In the second poem, which begins with the line 'When Amalia of late travelled to her Prince' Lenz has the highest deity, Zeus, order the Sun God to make a glorious firework display for Anna Amalia, who is on her way to Tiefurt. When this does not happen as he wishes it, Zeus is angry and will in future see to it himself personally: 'In future when the Duchess travels here from Tibur/ He wants to make the fireworks himself.'[408] When recently in Krakau the manuscript of Lenz's fragmentary story *Die Fee Urganda* was studied, the decoding of two figures was found in the margin: Pandolfo stands for Knebel and Queen Miranda for the Duchess Anna Amalia.[409] In this story the fairy Urganda must 'for the first time in her life' find that 'even half-goddesses are not above humiliation', that a mortal is more beautiful – here Queen Miranda (Anna Amalia). Lenz continues, in the fragment, to glorify Anna Amalia as the 'wonderful Miranda who can do everything', as the 'perfect Miranda'.[410] Since in the story the name of Anna Amalia is encoded, we have here not flattery but Lenz's own genuine feelings.

In a letter in the autumn of 1776 Lenz makes it clear that he has undying love for a woman in Weimar, and it is very likely that he means Anna Amalia. The addressee of this letter was probably Goethe, her secret lover:

> My dear brother! I find myself in a cruel quandary. The question is whether I am allowed to be in love. It became so strong in my heart this morning ... I asked myself is it not vanity, selfishness, or even something worse that has kindled this unholy fire in your heart ... God, the thought in which I found all the comfort in my life – this unique thought is sin. To do something for her – you know it was the only thing that bound me to this life. ... But I am firmly resolved to take to the grave with me this holy whim not to exchange her for any other creature – say what you like about it. She cannot and, I hope, will not lose her worth. It is well for me if she never loves me ... What is her value for me? – Everything. There is no value left for me if I stop loving her. My existence is in vain. What I did was for her – she alone is and can be the reliable judge of my actions – and whoever understands my relationship to her.[411]

The next of Lenz's extant letters is a birthday greeting and a present for Anna Amalia for the 24 October 1776:

> Since my Muse has once and for all stubbornly remained silent on the occasion of birthdays and name days I have tried to celebrate Your Highness's birthday at least with a representation of the rock in front of which you stood, lost in admiration, during your stay in Kochberg. Should this Sisyphus labour even succeed in recalling for Your Highness how the rock looks in its natural surroundings it would be of infinite value to me ... [412]

From the few surviving pieces of evidence from Lenz's stay in Weimar it is clear that he was in love with Anna Amalia.

Wieland was worried by the behaviour of Goethe's friends, which threatened to worsen his already difficult position as favourite not only with the staid state administration but also with the court circles who were proud of their noble status. At the end of June 1776, Friedrich Maximilian Klinger (1752-1831) had also hurried to Weimar to visit his *Sturm und Drang* colleagues. Klinger had given up his law studies in Giessen in the fifth semester. Through Goethe's mediation he had been taken on by a friend who was a law scholar.[413] Klinger said of himself around this time that he 'had no goal or purpose'. 'I run around in infinite confusion and flee hither and yon from myself, the most dreadful [of all creatures].'[414]

In his writings we find heroes who always go around with a pistol pointed at their heads. Lenz and Klinger, as main representatives of the *Sturm und Drang* movement, were caught up in a confusion of intentions, wishes, and hopes which blinded them to what was actually achievable. Wieland reports to Merck:

> Lenz went to Eremum [in Berka] a week ago, where he is probably eating grasshoppers and animals in the wild and either writing a new drama or planning a project to improve the world, which for some time now has been his pet task. Unfortunately, Klinger has come, too! He is a good fellow but he bores us and depresses Goethe. What can be done with such people?[415]

In Weimar Klinger wrote the play *Sturm und Drang* which originally bore the title *Confusion*, until Kaufmann persuaded him to change it.[416]

At the end of November 1776 Lenz was banished from the Duchy. In Goethe's diary entry for 26 November we read: 'Lenz's asinine behaviour'. What happened has still not been established, but Herder, Wieland, and Carl August do not seem to have judged the 'asinine behaviour' as harshly as Goethe did.[417] Böttiger writes:

> Goethe's success attracted Lenz here first. He was treated as a real court jester, but when he created a scandal between the old Duchess, who was more than just favourably disposed towards Goethe, and Frau von Stein, the favoured lover, he was suddenly sent away.[418]

The reason for his departure from Weimar had to do with Anna Amalia. Lenz must have told Anna Amalia he loved her. In a letter to Herder at the end of November 1776 Lenz had written: 'How much longer are you going to hang on to form and reputation [Namen]? If only I had understood Goethe's hints. Tell him that.'[419] This is comprehensible if Goethe, Minister and secret lover of Anna Amalia, had made it clear to Lenz that a liaison with the Duchess Anna Amalia was impossible. Lenz must have ignored this, and had to go; otherwise he would have represented a danger to the secret lovers Anna Amalia and Goethe. If Lenz, for whom convention of any kind was anathema, had made a great fuss about his love for the Princess Anna Amalia, it would have become clear, not only to the literary world, that the widow Anna Amalia was a beautiful, desirable woman for a young poet, and accordingly for Goethe as well. Graf Görtz, who had seen through the smoke-screen with Frau von Stein, might have found an opportunity to use Lenz to destroy Goethe at the beginning of his days in Weimar. For this reason Lenz could not be allowed to stay in

Weimar. He was able to stay first with Goethe's sister, then with Swiss friends, but was not capable of grasping one of the many opportunities offered to him for a settled middle-class life. When he visited Bern, completely penniless, he booked himself into an expensive inn, and in August 1777 wrote to Lavater, with whom he was to stay as a guest for several months:

> Lavater, I am here ... and am waiting for you to send me, as soon as you see this, a Louis d'or and a ducat. If you were to delay even one post day I would be plunged into debt and other affairs which are still worse.[420]

In the summer of 1779 Lenz fell into 'apathy and a trance', incapable of speaking and 'staring straight ahead in a state of deep melancholy'.[421] Goethe and Anna Amalia organized and financed his return journey to his homeland Livonia. Lenz had been suffering, in the meantime, from attacks of insanity. His brother, Karl Heinrich Gottlob Lenz, interrupted his studies in Jena earlier than envisaged and travelled in the summer of 1779 to Goethe's brother-in-law Johann G. Schlosser (1739-1799), who had looked after Lenz for a whole year. With his brother he travelled from there on foot to the Ostsee and then by ship to Riga.[422] According to Lenz's brother:

> To help me in this I received, from the magnanimity of the widowed Duchess [Anna Amalia], through Goethe, financial support in cash. ... Also Goethe received me very kindly in his garden house and conversed with me as we walked together ... mostly in endearing terms recalling Jakob Lenz; and even his weaknesses he touched on with great delicacy.[423]

Later, wrongly informed, Anna Amalia writes to Merck on 4 November 1779: 'That Lenz has been made professor seems odd to me; the university that would do this must have become mad and Lenz must have become clever. Anyway, I am very pleased that poor Lenz has recovered.'[424] Lavater did not at all believe the rumour and wrote:

> Believe me, a fool remains a fool,
> In a coach, on a horse, or on foot.
> And so, brother, have no faith in a fool or his penance.[425]

Lenz made his way as a teacher and translator in Riga, St Petersburg, and Moscow. He died in Moscow in 1792 when, as a result of reaction against the French Revolution (1789), brutal police action was carried out against the intelligentsia and the Freemasons.

Klinger, too, did not stay long in Weimar. Anna Amalia endeavoured to find him a post outside Weimar. In line with Klinger's penchant for military life, the Princess Anna Amalia sought for the penniless middle-class man a position as officer and even wrote to King Friedrich II and other highly-placed military men.[426] Klinger wrote to Ernst Schleiermacher (1755-1844) on 7 July 1776: 'You can't imagine how difficult it is to come as an officer amongst troops and be without title or money. May it be left to luck and chance, and to the noble soul [Anna Amalia] who is showing a loyal interest.'[427] When Anna Amalia did not succeed in securing a regular post for him, with Goethe she hit on the plan of arranging for him to go to America as a mercenary. Anna Amalia's father, the Duke of Braunschweig, carried on a lively trade in soldiers and used the income from this not least to finance the upkeep of his many mistresses.[428] Klinger wrote to Schleiermacher on 19 August 1776:

> A glorious project is underway and may chance make it succeed. I want to take part as an officer in the American campaign. Imagine, lad, what a world! What a great new world! To stand on American soil with courage, vision, assurance. Help, eternal gods! A thousand flames are lit in me, and I think I am burning and collapsing. O what a day for me!

On 12 September Klinger writes to Schleiermacher: 'Yesterday I visited Duchess Amalia who gave me great hope that something would come up for me.'[429] That Klinger did not go to America is best explained by the fact that Anna Amalia and Goethe did not want to palm him off as a mercenary. At the end of September Klinger fell out with Goethe and left Weimar. Böttiger reports Bertuch's comment about this: 'He [Klinger] had caused all kinds of gossip about the old Duchess and the young one and was dismissed as a trouble-maker.[430] On 29 August 1789 Klinger explained to Schleiermacher why he left Weimar in 1776:

> A wretched creature [Christoph Kaufmann], whose heart is as bad as his mind is confused, had broken the bond between us [Goethe and Klinger] through his gossip. He believed the awful nonsense. I was too proud to justify myself, and the high opinion I have of Goethe would not allow it, so I broke away.[431]

On their journey to Switzerland in 1779 Goethe and Carl August passed near the property of 'God's bloodhound' Kaufmann, who had just failed in his attempt to settle down as a free farmer. Without seeing him, Goethe wrote the lines:

> As God's bloodhound he was free
> To play his rascally tricks.
> He now has lost the trace of God,
> But still remains the dog.[432]

From Weimar Klinger went to Leipzig. He told his friend Schleiermacher to sell off everything except his underclothes and some books to meet his debts. He intended to keep his head above water for a time with his plays. But shortly afterwards he writes again in a letter of October 1776:

> Don't sell any of my things ... I have been here for three days and out of consideration for my mother I have taken up a post as dramaturg with Seyler. I get 500 Thaler in cash, free board and lodging, and can give my mother 200 annually, which she will receive in a month.[433]

These fairytale conditions of employment were completely unusual, especially for a poet who was not well-known. Wieland wrote to Merck about the 500 Thaler: ' ...And are you not, like me, amazed by the daily more wondrous *mirabilia Dei* [divine miracles] in our time?'[434]

Abel Seyler (1730-1801) and his theatre company had been brought to Weimar by Anna Amalia in 1771 on salary, and only left Weimar because of the fire in the residence in 1774. They left on good terms. It is likely that Anna Amalia had a part to play in Klinger's employment, possibly providing the high salary from her own funds. Through this 'divine miracle' Anna Amalia and Goethe would finally have found the means of settling Klinger outside of Weimar. Later Klinger had success not only with voluminous writing but with a notable career as a Russian officer and in university administration in Dorpat (Estonia). From 1801 onwards Goethe and Klinger corresponded again. On 26 May 1814 Klinger wrote to the friend of his youth:

> The last time I saw you was in Weimar during the first summer of your time there [1776]. This was the time I was hoping, through the mediation of the unforgettable Duchess Amalia, to begin my military career in America.[435]

When Goethe was brought news of Klinger's death he remarked to Chancellor von Müller on 31 March 1831: 'That was an incomparably loyal, solid, and direct fellow.'

Anna Amalia had Goethe as her teacher in 'geology, mineralogy, botany, zoology, anatomy, chemistry, physics etc'.[436] In general, their life is a constant giving and taking through which they grew to be one. Schiller's observation is interesting: according to him, Goethe and Anna Amalia experience the world around them above all through the senses. When Schiller became acquainted with Anna Amalia, he wrote, on 28 July 1787 to his friend Christian Gottfried Körner (1756-1831); ' ... nothing is of interest to her unless related to the senses, which gives her the taste she has or is supposed to have, for music and painting and such like.' About Goethe Schiller writes to Körner on 1 November 1790: 'I don't entirely like his philosophy either. He takes too much from the world of sense, whereas I draw on the soul. His whole way of seeing things is sensuous and, for me, too related to the feel of things.'

Anna Amalia was a very keen student of the painter Kraus[437] and also later of the painter Oeser, who frequently stayed as her guest in Tiefurt. Through hard work she achieved a certain level of competence in drawing. On 6 July she writes to Merck:

> My love of drawing is as strong as ever. I have a camera obscura in which I draw and it seems to me very useful for acquiring a proper knowledge of proportions in nature. It is a great help to me because I have begun rather late in life to dedicate myself to drawing. Experimental physics is a big interest for me this year too ... Drama is progressing nicely as well. Our friend Wolf (Goethe) is loyally making his contribution. Very soon you will receive from Frau Aja [Goethe's mother] a new dramatic piece from the fruitful pen of the Privy Councillor.[438]

In a letter to Merck on 25 April 1784 she reports that she is particularly interested in portrait painting and commissions him to acquire for her drawings of the human head by Petrus Camper (1722-1789): 'Now, to become more competent in this art, I would like to see some drawings such as those [which illustrate] how Camper shows the parts of the human head.'[439] In a letter of 3 June 1784 Merck writes to her with enthusiasm about his meeting with Camper: 'I am one of the happiest of men, if there is such a thing as happiness in this world.' On 25 June 1784 Goethe writes to 'Frau von Stein': 'I am delighted that Merck is so happy.' Goethe had already written to 'Frau von Stein' on 19 June 1784 that he had had part of a letter from Merck to Anna Amalia copied by Fritz. Through the copy of Merck's letter he made it plausible for Fritz to think that in his letters to Fritz's mother he was writing about Camper and Merck. But Frau von Stein, in contrast to Anna Amalia, had no interest in anatomical studies. In addition, Merck was not her friend because he thought her not worthy of a Goethe. He made no bones about this, for example in a letter of 21 July 1779 to Anna Amalia whom he revered. He is writing about his visit to Weimar: 'I have no memory of the people in Ettersburg [the residence] apart from the most notable, and no trace of the others or the unpleasant ones remains. I didn't give a thought to the von Stein family.' Later, as well, Goethe informed his beloved about Camper. On 11 September 1785 he writes: 'Camper even wrote a good letter about the first part of the *Ideas* [Herder's treatise, 1784 onwards]. I want to share all good things with you.' Frau von Stein, on the other hand, though an influential and prudent social figure, was not interested in the programme of constant refinement through science and art. Goethe's characterization of the Countess Leonore Sanvitale through the words of Tasso can be taken as Goethe's view of Frau von Stein: 'No, she was/And remains cunning at heart; she moves/With quiet measured steps where benefit is found' (ll. 2495ff.). Tasso says to the Princess about the Countess (ll. 963ff.):

> I have listened to you, or otherwise
> I would have moved away from her instead of approaching.
> Nice as she can seem
> I don't know what it is, I was seldom able
> To be quite open with her and, although
> She quite intends to benefit her friends,
> You sense what she intends and are put off.
>
> **Princess:** This is not the way to find society,
> Dear Tasso. This path misleads us to wander
> Through lonely woods, through quiet valleys;
> Our inner selves are more and more disturbed
> And strive to build, within, the golden age
> That we are outwardly denied.

Goethe and Anna Amalia's Golden Age is an inner one, leading through lonely woods and quiet valleys. At the beginning of 1782 Goethe wrote the fancy-dress parade *Aufzug der Vier Weltalter*. Anna Amalia appeared in it on 12 February as the Golden Age, accompanied by joy and innocence. The stage direction for the costume was: 'white and gold, simple in Greek taste. The sun on her head'.[440] Anna Amalia spoke the words:

> Gentle as a morning dream I come forth,
> Men don't know me until I've long gone.
> The beauty of youth, the time of blooming
> The heart's first-born are dedicated to me.

Anna Amalia was an art connoisseur of the highest order. On her way to Italy in 1788 she had herself shown around the Munich gallery of the painter Ferdinand Kobell (1740-1799), works of whom she had in her own collection. Kobell expressed his judgement of her in a letter to Knebel: 'Along with her extensive knowledge of painting, she has a love of art and an inquiring eye for every painting – something which painters themselves often lack.'[441] More important for the admirer of Mozart (1756-1791), Haydn (1732-1809), and Gluck (1714-1787)[442] was music. She played piano, flute, lute, harp, and guitar. She appeared as a singer in the amateur theatre and did some composing. She also wrote about the theory, aesthetics and history of music,[443] and this in a century in which women were considered to have no talent for music.[444] She always worked at the development and refinement of her talents, and, in particular, the journey to Italy would open new horizons to her. Her knowledge of languages far surpassed the norm.

Soon after handing over the reins of government to her son she worked at perfecting her language skills. Besides French, English, and Italian she had a command of Latin. Under the guidance of excellent teachers like Wieland and Anse de Villoison (1750-1805) she made continual progress in Ancient Greek. She wrote to Knebel on 23 June 1782, quoting Villoison: 'I am able to read and understand seven anacreontic odes. But I am also "une princesse pleine de génie"! Knebel, what do you say about that?'[445] She writes enthusiastically to Knebel:

> How can I have been so lax as not to have learnt this language of the soul earlier? I feel as if I were in a completely different world. My soul flutters lightly with the lovely dove that pecks his bread from Anacreon's hand.[446]

Precisely in the literary testimony from Anna Amalia's journey to Italy from 1788 to 1790 are Goethe and Anna Amalia to be seen as a like-minded pair. The fact that Anna Amalia was bitterly wounded by her lover's refusal to stay with her in Italy, bringing with it the final refusal to continue their nocturnal love, is evidenced in letters from her lady-in-waiting von Göchhausen passing on messages from her mistress. Anna Amalia read her correspondence, as is clear, for example, from a letter to Wieland on 20 December 1788, in which the tiny lady-in-waiting reports that she has seen a marvellous statue. Anna Amalia adds to the letter: 'Tusnelden's [von Göchhausen's] nose reached exactly the level of its big toe.' Von Göchhausen writes in a letter to Goethe on 22 November 1788:

> If I could buy your presence here with physical pain (or even mental pain) I would be willing and ready ... What I would give for you to be here. If I could buy you with a joint of one of my skinny fingers, I think I would sacrifice the whole finger.

The fact that the lady-in-waiting chooses the exaggerated image of readiness to mutilate herself for the sake of Goethe's presence shows that she is informing Goethe about the suffering of her mistress, for Anna Amalia is suffering from the separation and is still unwilling to accept renunciation. But the stay in Italy is to help Anna Amalia in this. She writes to Merck on 6 January 1788: 'I believe that Italy is to us what the river Lethe was to the ancients. We become rejuvenated by forgetting all the unpleasantness we have experienced in the world and thereby are reborn as new people.'[447] Goethe wrote similarly about his first ten years in Weimar. He said he only wrote *Tasso* to free himself 'from all that was painful and burdensome in my impressions and memories of Weimar.'[448] Quite beautifully Goethe has Anna

Amalia, as the Princess in *Tasso*, mourn when the poet goes to Rome and has to leave her (ll. 1859ff.):

The hope of seeing him no longer fills
The hardly wakened spirit with joyful longing;
My first glance down into our gardens
Seeks him in vain in the shadows' dew.
What a happy feeling was the wish
To be with him on every cheerful evening!
Our time together increased the longing
To know, to understand each other better
And every day our minds were tuned to purer harmonies.
But what twilight now descends on me!
The glory of the sun, the joyful feeling
At its brightest hour, the brilliant presence
Of a world with a thousand facets
Is empty, deeply veiled in a surrounding mist.
Before, every day for me was like an entire life.

In Italy Anna Amalia and Goethe were both interested in a particular death mask. The Princess tried in vain to see the death mask of Torquato Tasso, which was kept in a monastery. In the first of the *Fünf Briefe Über Italien* she writes: 'I regretted that the rules of the monastery prevented me from entering to see these valuable memorials of the great Torquato Tasso.' Goethe had seen them on 3 February 1787. He wrote to Anna Amalia ['Frau von Stein']: 'How I have thought of you today!' He succeeded in acquiring a copy for his beloved. During her stay in Italy Anna Amalia will affirm that renunciation is the right course to follow. Especially in Naples she finds the rejuvenation she hoped for, so that she could return to Weimar as a new person, as a priestess to watch over Goethe's poetic genius.

On 13 September 1789 Anna Amalia writes to Knebel from Naples:

> If only you could see the moonshine here. It is more beautiful than the sunset in Thuringia even on the warmest evenings. It comes up from behind Vesuvius, rests on its peak and greets the whole surroundings, whose glowing purple yields only to the new light. The dark blue sky, whose dazzling stars are a wreath around the moon and seem to dance gracefully with it; the sparkling Milky Way with its millions of stars, which like the girdle of Venus, seem to surround the whole of the earth with love; all this is doubled, reflected in the silver sea, which calmly and quietly receives the beauty which is all around it.[449]

In her description of her sojourn in Italy in the *Fünf Briefe Über Italien* Anna Amalia includes reflections about vegetation, geology, history, administration, social concerns, but, above all, about music, theatre, and literature. Her comments are of a high order and are laced with irony and wit, but also with a discreet criticism of circumstances in Italy. Right at the beginning of the first of the *Fünf Briefe Über Italien*, written to an unidentified 'dear Sister', Anna Amalia describes her visit to St Peter's Basilica:

> At first I thought I had entered a labyrinth. My eyes wandered hither and yon, now to the colossal pillars, now to the enormous figures of saints and popes, to precious works in bronze, glorious tombstones in the finest marble, and to mosaics. I was astonished by all this, but it left me cold, whereas the sight of the Pantheon inspired me with a warm and exalted feeling. Anyone who didn't know that the function of this building [St Peter's] was to be a church could have seen it as a palace or a theatre.

When on 23 November 1788 she was received in an audience with Pope Pius VI (1717-1799), the Protestant Princess found: 'It was a comical and theatrical performance.' Goethe's judgement was similar. On 8 June 1787 he writes about the Roman Church:

> Yesterday was the feast of Corpus Christi [since 1246 the feast of the bodily presence of Christ]. I am now once and for all not able to stomach these church ceremonies. All these attempts to support a lie seem shallow to me and the masquerades which have something impressive for children and sensuous people seem to me, even from the point of view of an artist and poet, petty and lacking in taste. Nothing is great except what is true, and the smallest thing that is true is great.

Anna Amalia is enthused when she walks through the Pantheon. She says of the round temple built by the Emperor Hadrian (76-138) in honour of all the gods and which only survived because it was taken over for use as a Catholic church since 609:

> Through its vaulted ceiling, where the rays of light shine through as if they were God's own eyes, this temple gives the inspiring notion that it is the general dwelling place of the gods and of the architect of the world, whose works are distinguished by inimitable greatness, unity, and simplicity. A holy frisson went through me the first time I saw it. I was raised up to the invisible Being that hovered about me. Here you find a striking proof of how well the ancients could reach their goal with the simplest means and how their ideas matched the greatness of things. The form of this masterly work of art was disturbed by little altars which now replace the antique marble statues, but superstition has not succeeded in destroying the majesty of the building.

Anna Amalia was, like Goethe, a Greek. In feeling she lived in the world of the ancient gods. 'We know how much the Greeks succeeded in the perfection of the senses', says Anna Amalia in her *Gedanken über die Musik* (c.1799), 'by which they were put in a position to produce inimitable works of art'.[450]

Everything that was magnificent attracted the lovers. Vesuvius, for example. Goethe, who had climbed the volcano several times, reports on 8 June 1787:

> Vesuvius, which had burned very strongly since my return from Sicily, finally produced a strong overflow of lava on 1 June. And so I was able to see also this spectacle of nature, although only from a distance. It is a great sight ... I saw simultaneously the moon, the reflection of the moon on the edge of the clouds, the reflection of the moon on the sea and on the edge of the nearest waves, the lights of the light-house, the fire of Vesuvius, its reflection in the water, and the lights on the ships. This light in so many different forms made a unique spectacle.

In a letter of 29 May 1789 Anna Amalia describes the volcano to Knebel:

> Some days ago it [Vesuvius] wore a wreath of clouds, apart from the opening, from which a dark red flame shot up. The glowing stones which it threw out danced lightly in the air, and then came the lava which mingled with the clouds and divided them. The reflection of the lava transfigured the mountain with a dark red glow which lasted deep into the night. It was the most beautiful spectacle I have ever seen in my life, and I did not fail, every evening, to say my evening prayers facing Vesuvius. I can well imagine that there are nations that adore fire [as divine].[451]

Goethe's letter to Anna Amalia of 6 February 1789 shows how similar their range of interests was:

> May Your Highness kindly send for the works that have been written about Paestum, Naples, Pozzuoli, etc ... Furthermore, get copper engravings of Portici from the museum ... and have them give you a selection from the sulphur collection of Abbot Dolce ... It will be a great treasure for us afterwards.

Anna Amalia answered on 18 March 1789:

> I am very glad that your fingers have finally thawed and that after this long time you have given a sign of life. To show that I am not answering like with like I am sending you 1). The copies of Abbot Dolce, 2) those of Pichler ... In the same box you will find all twenty-four Kaysers in sulphur copy which I am sending for the little Prince ... You will also find a little print in red sulphur. Look at it closely. It is the famous stone which was in the cabinet of the King of France ... Stay nice and healthy and think sometimes of the absent ones. My people greet you a thousand times.[452]

Anna Amalia was also not to forget botanical studies. Goethe writes to her on 14 December 1789: ‘May Your Highness bring us all kinds of seeds from that area, no matter what. What is commonplace there is useful for our scientific speculations, one way or the other.’

Anna Amalia delayed her return until her journey would have lasted, like that of Goethe, twenty-two months: ‘We arrived happily in Weimar at 11 at night’, the lady-in-waiting von Göchhausen noted under the entry of 18 June 1790 in the diary of Anna Amalia’s Italian journey. Thus Anna Amalia returns exactly two years after Goethe’s return to Weimar on 18 June 1788 at 11 o’clock at night. Herder wrote to Knebel that Goethe arrived in Weimar at ten o’clock in the evening with the full moon.[453] Against this backdrop it is possible to relate the didactic poem ‘Die Metamorphose einer Pflanze’ unequivocably to Anna Amalia and not to Christiane Vulpius as heretofore.[454] The didactic poem is directed to an unidentified beloved and aims at explaining to her the metamorphosis of a plant, which, according to Goethe, amounts to an attempt to reduce the manifold individual phenomena of the world-garden to one general, simple principle.[455] Goethe worked on it until he could finish it in Jena on 18 June 1798. Ten years after his and eight years after Anna Amalia’s return from Italy Goethe recalls this day by giving the didactic poem to Anna Amalia. It ends with the lines:

> Take joy in today. Love, which is holy,
> Strives to produce the fruit of similar minds
> A similar concept of things, so that in harmonious vision
> The couple are joined and find the loftier world

In this context the meaning of a curious use of the word ‘merkwürdig’, which Goethe weaves into the introduction to the poem, becomes clear:

> This poem was extremely welcome to the real [eigentlich] beloved who had the right to apply the lovely images to herself; and I too felt very happy when the living parable increased and completed our beautiful, perfect affection.[456]

Since the didactic poem was normally taken to refer to Christiane, Goethe speaks here of the ‘real beloved’. On 20 June 1798 Goethe writes to Christiane that when a letter from Anna Amalia’s lady-in-waiting, Fräulein von Göchhausen, arrived it should be sent on by messenger to him in Jena. He was clearly eager to see how the ‘real beloved’ would respond to the beautiful present.

Many in Weimar did not understand Goethe’s thorough scientific studies. Anna Amalia herself complained to Goethe’s mother in Frankfurt that her son was squandering his precious time on useless things. In a letter to Goethe in 1800 in which the Princess wants to draw the poet's attention to a gem with a portrait carved into it, this dissatisfaction is still in the air. She begins with: 'If it doesn't disturb you, dear Privy Councillor, in your philosophical reflections, I would like you to take a little look back at the lovely muses who are so gracious to you.'[457] With the poem 'Die Metamorphose der Pflanze' Goethe wants to counter the lack of understanding, arising from ignorance, that he has met in his scientific work. In his introduction he continues:

> Nowhere was anyone prepared to admit that science and poetry are compatible. People forgot that science developed out of poetry. They didn't take into account that after a turnabout in [historical] periods both can very easily meet again, on a higher level, to the benefit of both.

Only after a hundred years was the scientist Goethe inherited by Rudolf Steiner (1861-1925). As editor of Goethe's scientific writings (1890-1897) Steiner had become intimately familiar with his thinking. He expressly traced his anthroposophy – as Weltanschauung and theory of knowledge – back to Goethe.[458] The didactic poem 'Die Metamorphose der Pflanze' shows how Goethe tries to convince Anna Amalia of the fundamental importance of his scientific studies. In his introduction to the poem he continues:

> [Female] friends who early on would like to have drawn me away from the lonely mountains and from thinking about the stark rocks were also not at all happy with my abstract gardening. Plants and flowers should be distinguished by shape, colour, smell, and now they were disappearing into a ghostly illusion. I then tried to win over these well-wishing minds by using an elegy which may be permitted a place here, where, in the context of scientific elaboration, it may be become more intelligible than if it were to be slotted into a series of delicate and passionate poems.
>
> You are confused, beloved, by the thousand-fold mixture
> Of these flowers scattered around the garden.
> Many names you hear and the barbaric sound of one
> Dislodges another from the ear.
> All the shapes are similar but none is the same
> And so the chorus points to a secret law,
> A sacred puzzle. Would that I could deliver up for you,
> Immediately,beloved, the magic word! ...

The fact that Goethe, despite his renunciation, was attentive to Anna Amalia in such ways right to the end, is indicated by one of the few extant letters of the Princess to the poet in April 1805:

> I have received your consignment with appreciation and gratitude. You have given your dedication – which I think I can say is flattering – a particular magical twist of your own ... Your genuine friend, Amalia.[459]

Anna Amalia will, in encoded form, remain the centre point of Goethe's love poetry. The poet dedicates work to her even publicly, for example, the masquerade *Paläophron und Neoterpe* [The old mind and the new pleasure], a celebration at the end of her birthday. The point at issue is the contrast between old and new, the right relationship between past and future. After a performance on the occasion of Anna Amalia's birthday on 24 October 1800, the theatre Director Goethe stood up and announced to the Princess in verse the masquerade *Paläophron und Neoterpe* as a belated birthday present:

> You have consumed the purest fare of the Muses.
> Now forgive this brightness, painful to the eyes.
> That we have dressed in playful masks today
> The freedom of the boards allows.
> And to this troupe you are well disposed
> For under every mask there beats a heart.
> Could you but see this inner soul unveiled,
> Ideals would stand before your very eyes.
>
> Reverence approaches with open gaze,
> And gratitude with free expanding chest.
> There follows loyalty with enthusiasm – to serve you
> Always is its greatest joy.
> Modesty with nervous daring
> Is conscious of its silent speech,
> On the golden steps our wishes kneel
> To call down happiness on you a thousand-fold.
>
> And so a temple seems to be created here
> Where once the fool's bells had rung.
> The creaking of the boards, the players' nerves
> Take on now a higher meaning.
> This troupe brings you its blessing for a happy life
> And if you smile on the gracious song of the Muse
> You will shortly hear the expression
> Of old times dressed up as new.[460]

With these lines Goethe pays homage to his secret beloved. Under Goethe's mask beats a heart, and if Anna Amalia could see his inner self unveiled, she would see Ideals stand before her, namely, his perfect love. Reverence, gratitude, and loyalty are what Goethe feels for his Princess, and to serve her eagerly is always his greatest joy. But Goethe is not allowed to confess his love openly, and so he does it with 'silent speech' [stummer Sprache] by encoding his declarations of love. The words 'Is conscious of its silent speech' [Ist sich der stummen Sprache wohl bewusst] allude to a crucial line in the 'Prolog im Himmel' of the *Faust* tragedy. The 'Prolog' was written around this time.[461] In this crucial line God says to Mephistopheles (ll. 328f.): 'A good man, in his dark striving, is conscious of the right way to go.' [Ein guter Mensch in seinem dunklen Drange/Ist sich des rechten Weges wohl bewusst.] Goethe also dedicates his collection *Winckelmann und sein Jahrhundert* (1805) to Anna Amalia: 'As a friend receive the loud expression of homage/Which fate almost cut from my lips.' [Freundlich empfange das Wort laut ausgesprochener Verehrung,/Das die Parze mir fast schnitt von den Lippen hinweg.] Of the three fates, which spin the thread of life, preserve it, and cut it, Goethe is referring to the third, since shortly beforehand he had been very seriously ill.

Anna Amalia had not had it easy in her youth. In fact, it was not unusual for the life of a Princess to turn into a nightmare. Her autobiographical writing in *Meine Gedanken*, four double-sided sheets, gives information about her early years. These sheets are dated 1772 and it is thought they were addressed to Wieland, although they were found in Goethe's bequest.[462] *Meine Gedanken* is a kind of personal account towards the end of Anna Amalia's time in office as Regent. It is a brutally honest report:

> From my childhood onwards – the beautiful early days of my life – what did it all add up to? Nothing but sacrifice for other people. ... Oh, the blood that raged through all my veins was too hot. Every pulse beat a feeling of tenderness, pain, remorse in my soul. God! Any prisoner tries to get free of his chains: and I – I am to bear my bonds with patience when my gentle soul is under siege? ... Not loved by my parents, always put down, always second to my siblings, I was called a reject of nature. The fine feeling given me by nature made me very sensitive to the harsh treatment. It often brought me to the point of despair where I once even wanted to take my life.

When taking over government while her son was still a minor, in

> 'those years when for others everything is blooming, for me there was only fog and darkness. ... How happy I would have been if I had had a friend who had profound knowledge of the human heart and who could open up for me what was a mystery to myself and remained locked up so deep inside me. ... Day and night I studied to educate myself and to equip myself properly for my tasks. I felt then how much I needed a friend in whom I could completely confide. There were many who looked for my favour and friendship. Some tried it through flattery. Some, through a false front of truth and pious righteousness, sought to further their own interests; and others sought it out of vanity, as something they could boast about.

She first found an honest friend in the old Councillor Johann Poppo von Greiner (1708-1772), who at her instigation was raised to the nobility:

> From him I got to know and love the truth ... When the ruler and his friend have a noble disposition the only result can be the greatest and noblest friendship ... But there are few great men and few people who have a noble disposition. For rulers, I must unfortunately admit, it is difficult to find real friends, and – if they are real friends – to keep them. Rulers are from their early years surrounded by vermin. This makes them either distrustful of everybody, or they throw themselves into the arms of unworthy people. If they meet someone whom they deem worthy of their friendship, it is very rare that this person does not become puffed up, and the Prince's friendly affection shown by the Prince does not remain friendship for long.

In *Tasso* Leonore Sanvitale characterizes the Princess with the words (ll. 89ff.):

> You are not blinded by transitory appearances,
> Wit does not prejudice you, and false flattery
> Cannot sidle up to you and reach your ear.
> Your mind stays firm, your taste is right,
> Your judgement straight
> Always you give great support to what is great
> Which you know as well as you know yourself.

Meine Gedanken is addressed to a particular person, as is clear from formulations like, 'If I could describe to you my feelings when I became a mother!' The fact that Goethe did not burn these pages found in his bequest is an important circumstance, for he was always carrying out 'autodafés', as he called the destruction of documents.[463] In 1797, for example, he had burned a great number of letters which had been written to him since 1772. Part or all of the letters from the Duke Carl August,[464] his Darmstadt friend Merck,[465] his sister Cornelia (1770-1777), his mother Catharina Elisabeth, perhaps also those of his famous beauty, Corona Schröter[466] – with whom Goethe consorted frequently in his first ten years in Weimar, not least to distract court society from his secret love for Anna Amalia. If Goethe did not burn *Meine Gedanken* it was because he intended to have his relationship with Anna Amalia thought about.

This leads to the question: when did Anna Amalia and Goethe first become acquainted? There are traces leading back to 1772:

> In the autumn of 1772 – according to what is handed down in Goethe's family – in Bad Ems the eye of the young Dowager Duchess Anna Amalia of Weimar, who was acquainted with beauty and was thirsty for it, fell on the radiant young figure – radiant with classical

> beauty, spirit, and joy for living. The lively, witty, open-minded Princess had the stranger introduced to her ..., Wolfgang Goethe from Frankfurt am Main, who was on his way back to his parental home from the Supreme Court in Wetzlar. The Duchess found his witty and sparkling conversation and the whole charming personality of the young son of a Frankfurt patrician so interesting that she gave him a friendly invitation to her Weimar Residence.[467]

Goethe was in Ems around 13 September 1772. In *Dichtung und Wahrheit*, Book 13, he writes: 'I used the pleasant baths a few times.'[468] On leaving Wetzlar he gave back a book he had borrowed from his friend Karl Wilhelm Jerusalem (1747-1772), the son of Anna Amalia's former tutor in Braunschweig and stepbrother of Johann C. Albrecht (c.1736-1803),[469] tutor to the Weimar Princes in Weimar since 1765. The suicide of Karl Wilhelm Jerusalem in Wetzlar at the end of October prompted Goethe to write his epistolary novel *Die Leiden des Jungen Werther* (1774), a novel which made him world-famous. We can see from the Fourier book for the year 1772, in which the names are entered of those who have participated in official events at the Weimar court, that Anna Amalia presided at the princely table in Weimar for the whole month of September.[470] Unless these court entries were falsified, there could have been no meeting between Anna Amalia and Goethe, at least not in September 1772. The decisive point about 'what is handed down in Goethe's family' is that a meeting between Goethe and Anna Amalia is understood to have taken place before his arrival in Weimar in 1775.

Anna Amalia's primary concern in her last years of Regency was the preparation for an appropriate marriage for the Crown Prince Carl August. Accordingly, she could have wished to make the acquaintance, unofficially, of the Princesses who would be in line to marry her son, and to travel to meet them. In the context of a journey of Anna Amalia before 1775 there could have been a meeting with Goethe. In his autobiography for the early years, *Dichtung und Wahrheit* (1811-1831), Goethe could not mention such a meeting without at the same time endangering the state secret. Perhaps it was not just an irony of fate that the decree by which Wieland was appointed tutor to the Princes was signed by Anna Amalia on 28 August 1772, on Goethe's twenty-third birthday. The famous Seyler troupe, which played in Weimar from 1771 until the destruction of the Residence by fire in 1774, must already have attracted Goethe's attention to Weimar: 'Goethe had heard several favourable things about conditions in Weimar even before Knebel visited him for the first time in Frankfurt.'[471] It is indeed strange how natural it seemed for Knebel, who had received his appointment in Weimar just a couple of weeks previously, to visit Goethe at the end of 1774, introduce him to the Weimar Princes, and to work at Goethe's reconciliation with Wieland whom he had mocked in the satire *Götter, Helden und Wieland* (March 1774). Wieland had been so put out by it that to his friends he called Goethe his mortal enemy.[472] When Carl August first invited him, the poet who was celebrated in Germany as author of *Götz* (1771/73) and *Werther* (1774) knew exactly what the seventeen-year-old, who was still under the tutelage of Wieland and Count Görtz, would like to hear: namely, nothing about his writing but about authors 'whose talent was rooted in active life and returned to it immediately with direct relevance'.[473] For this reason he spoke to the Crown Prince about Justus Möser (1720-1794), a statesman and writer in the spirit of the Enlightenment, whose first volume of *Patriotische Phantasieen* (1774), which Goethe already knew, lay on the table in the room in which Goethe was received.

As for Knebel: when the task of tutoring Anna Amalia's second son was ended, Knebel was salaried without any fixed duties – more accurately, without any officially fixed duties, for in fact he was regularly on delicate missions of a diplomatic and secret service nature, for Goethe, for Anna Amalia, and Carl August. Knebel had a function similar to that of Frau von Stein, and every time the situation became tricky in Weimar he stepped in. Frau von Stein and Knebel were close friends, as is evidenced by the life-long correspondence, like her letter of 22 June 1816 to Knebel in Jena:

> Here [in Weimar] they say that in Jena, because of the end of the world caused by the collision of two planets, people have packed up and are holding prayer meetings, but that there was a miscalculation and now this event is postponed until the 25th. I hope the crash will bring good friends closer together and that my house will suddenly land beside yours.[474]

Further evidence that Goethe became acquainted with Anna Amalia before 1775 is gathered from his satire *Götter, Helden und Wieland* (1774), in which Wieland's singspiel *Alceste* (1773), the first serious opera written in the German language, is satirized. Anna Amalia was the inspiration behind this work of Wieland, and so the Duchess, with her enthusiasm for music, deserves the credit for having created the conditions under which the first important German opera came into being at her little court. She is said to have been so intensely interested that she was secretly present at the rehearsals.[475] In his satire, the young Goethe criticized his poet-colleague Wieland because in his opinion the Athenian poet Euripides would have felt that this version of his material was at best mediocre. Goethe poses the question in his satire: for whom is Wieland really writing? – and has him answer: 'For my Princess' [Anna Amalia]. Then comes the reply: 'You should know that princes count for nothing here'. The conversation is taking place in the underworld, where birth and lineage count for nothing. To Anna Amalia, who in *Meine Gedanken* saw herself 'surrounded by vermin' and whose friendship was sought 'through flattery ... through a false front of truth and pious righteousness', Goethe presented himself as a poet who had no need to flatter the ruler. In 1779 Wieland's *Alceste* was parodied in the Weimar amateur theatre. Anna Amalia appeared as Alceste, while Goethe played Hercules who led Alceste from the underworld back to life. Wieland, who had been led to believe he was attending the performance of a different piece, was horrified by the savage and comical reworking of his *Alceste*. He was insulted and ran out of the room. However, at the supper that followed he was ready to make peace.[476]

Goethe received news of Weimar also from the Frankfurt painter Kraus, who through the intervention of Bertuch[477] had been given work in Weimar for some months and in 1775 was given employment there shortly before Goethe's arrival:

> Looking through the extensive portfolios that the good Kraus had brought back from his travels, the most interesting part was when he showed landscape or personal pictures, the Weimar circle and its environs. I, too, was glad to ponder them because it had to be flattering for the young man to consider so many pictures only as the involved and repeated statement of a wish to see me there (*Dichtung und Wahrheit* Book 20).

On this occasion Goethe will have seen at least a sketch for the oil-painting *Anna Amalia* of 1774 in which, in a relaxed posture, she looks like a young girl in love (ill. 1), which is in stark contrast to other depictions of her where she is always seen as a Princess conscious of her position. On a table on which she is resting her arm a flute is to be seen – at that time 'an attribute with sexual connotations'[478] – ; a music score in which part of a line of text reads ' ... make heart and hand'; as well as two books lying open with a closed book between them with the title 'Agathon. Part One'. It is revealing that, along with allusions to love and the erotic, there is an image of Wieland's Bildungsroman *Agathon* of 1766/67, the first significant one in German literature. Anna Amalia is identifying Weimar as a place of self-refinement. Goethe's love relationship with her will later be the foundation on which he writes his Bildungsroman *Wilhelm Meister*. Accordingly, Goethe describes in his novel his breakaway from Frankfurt into the wide world. He was to

> tear himself away from the stagnating, tedious middle-class world ... from which he had long wished to rescue himself. To leave his father's house, his family, seemed easy. He was young and new in the world and his courage to run after happiness and contentment in the world was heightened by love (*Lehrjahre* I, 10).

It is noticeable that every possible contact of Anna Amalia with Goethe before 1775 was later veiled. She met with Merck in 1773, at a time when he was already a close friend of Goethe. Anna Amalia must have met the military advisor Merck when he was travelling through Erfurt. In May 1773 he was accompanying Countess Karoline von Hessen-Darmstadt (1721-1774) and her three daughters to Russia, for according to the wishes of the King of Prussia, Friedrich II, one of the three (Wilhelmine) was to marry the heir to the Russian throne, and another (Friederike) was to marry his own heir to the throne – the same Crown Prince who divorced Anna Amalia's sister. Carl August could have the one that was left (Luise).

The travelling party stopped over in Erfurt and there Carl August, accompanied by his mother, saw the Princesses and was allowed to guess which of them he would one day marry. In a letter of August 1781 Anna Amalia recalls her first meeting with Merck but places it in the year 1778.[479] One cannot help thinking that after a first meeting of Anna Amalia with Goethe before 1775 a network of contacts issued from Weimar in the direction of the young poet even before Carl August, on his journey at the end of 1774, became acquainted with Goethe through Knebel. Frau von Stein, during her visits to the spa, also paved the way for contact with Goethe through the esteemed doctor Zimmermann, whom she knew since 1773. Zimmermann was also the person who recommended Frau von Stein as a confidante to Princess Luise, the future reigning Duchess of Weimar. In a letter to Frau von Stein before Luise's arrival in Weimar in October 1775 he writes: 'I have told this Princess a lot about you. I begged her, as soon as she arrives in Weimar, to make your acquaintance. I have promised her that she will find in you the friend she needs.'

Even Knebel's supposedly casual visit to Weimar at the end of 1774 which led to the invitation of Goethe to Weimar would seem to be part of the plan. Knebel had already spent two weeks in Weimar at the end of 1773 and had made a good impression on Anna Amalia.[480] Count Görtz was opposed to the appointment of Knebel who was a lover of the arts and in contact with many writers. In a letter to Minister von Fritsch of 13 October 1774 Anna Amalia tells him of the successful outcome of the arrangements to appoint Knebel. Negociations had begun in the spring of 1774, and von Fritsch had been the driving force: 'The civil war has ended; yesterday evening Görtz came to me

[Anna Amalia].'[481] Alongside his tutoring of the Princes it had been Knebel's secret task to make sure that the young Crown Prince Carl August, during his journey abroad, which took him as far as Paris, would be enthusiastic about Goethe and then, prompted by Knebel, of his own accord invite Goethe to Weimar. For his part, Goethe seems to have hoped for an invitation to Weimar. In March 1775 an anonymous piece *Prometheus, Deukalion und seine Rezensenten* was published in which critics of Goethe's *Werther* were treated with biting satire, amongst them Wieland. Goethe, since this work was attributed to him, was immediately set on a course of damage limitation. Countess Görtz writes to her husband in Paris: 'There is much wit in this farce, but it betrays an unworthy character. Wieland will give him [Goethe] a short, sharp answer. He is beside himself.'[482] Count Görtz's immediate reply, though he had not read the piece, was: 'This Goethe is a base fellow!' After reading the satire Görtz writes a few days later:

> This is a piece of filth! Far from laughing at it I feel only disgust. Tell my friend Wieland that it is beneath his dignity to involve himself with such fellows. He knows how I am opposed to measures such as the bastinado, but for this fellow I know no other cure. One thing is certain: Goethe and I will never be found together in the same room.

When doubt was voiced about Goethe's authorship, Görtz was still convinced that the satire was Goethe's work. He writes in April to his wife: 'Wieland is very good natured. He doubts whether Goethe is the infamous author of "Prometheus", but I am sure of it.'[483]

Since Knebel sided with Goethe, Görtz intrigued against him. Carl August reported that one day in Paris Görtz came to him several times before going to bed to warn him with great urgency against contact with Knebel.[484] In the meantime Goethe had identified his *Sturm und Drang* poet-friend Heinrich Leopold Wagner (1747-1779) as the author of the satire. Goethe immediately had a public declaration printed which he sent to Paris[485] for Knebel, who was acting as intermediary with Wieland. In the declaration Goethe named Wagner as the author and added: 'I think I owe this clarification to those who love me and accept my word. I was also glad of the opportunity quietly to observe different people in their behaviour towards me.'[486]

After the scandal caused by Wagner's *Prometheus* satire subsided, Carl August and Goethe saw one another again in May in Karlsruhe, where the Prince was pushing ahead with arrangements for his marriage to the Princess Luise. When the newly enthroned Duke Carl August travelled to Karlruhe in September 1775 he invited Goethe, 'on the spur of the moment',[487] to Weimar. The invitation was repeated by the princely couple on their return journey. On 7 November 1775 the young poet entered Weimar and immediately Goethe was seen to be relaxed in Anna Amalia's company. Wieland reported that Goethe 'often rolled about on the floor and made her laugh with his tangle of arms and legs'.[488] With Goethe's arrival, Wieland was so charmed that 'I fell in love with him and really adored him'.[489] Wieland further confided to his friend Böttiger:

> When the doctor and former lawyer Goethe arrived here as favourite of the Duke, the Dowager Duchess also found him extremely charming and witty. Nowhere did he play his pranks and fireworks more madly than in her presence.[490]

When the Counts Stolberg, 'the life-loving and excentric brothers who acted like [*Sturm und Drang*] geniuses and were brimming over with hatred of tyrants,'[491] stopped over in Weimar for a week at the end of November 1775, they said of Anna Amalia:

> The Dowager Duchess, still a beautiful woman of thirty-six, has a good mind, much dignity, an obvious goodness, so completely different from princely persons who seek dignity in stiffness. She is charming in company, speaks very well, jokes with refinement, and is able to pay compliments in the nicest way.[492]

10 | David Heinrich Grave: A Human Catastrophe

> What I possess I would like to retain.
> Change is entertaining, but scarcely of any use.
> I was never led, with youthful desire,
> To try my luck in the stranger's world,
> Or grasp at something to satisfy the needs
> Of my inexperienced heart.
> The Princess in *Tasso* (1790), ll. 1882ff.

> I will resist every fleeting desire, and even the most serious of desires I will lock away in my bosom; no female creature will hear a confession of love from my lips unless I can devote my whole life to her.
> *Wilhelm Meisters Lehrjahre* [Apprenticeship Years] (1796), IV, 20

The transition from a fiery passion between Anna Amalia and Goethe to a special kind of friendship took place during the period of their two sojourns in Italy, each for a period of twenty-two months. In this time David Heinrich Grave (1752-1789) joined the close circle around Anna Amalia. Grave was 'a very knowledgeable young man with a good musical education. He had a fine build and a resonant tenor voice. He was also a talented actor and an especially expressive mimic.'[493] Before his Weimar employment he had performed on several stages, the last of them in Berlin. At the beginning of 1785 he joined the acting troupe of Joseph Bellomo. Even before Goethe's flight to Italy Grave had been discovered and supported by Anna Amalia as a gifted singer. In the spring of 1786 he left Bellomo and became a chamber singer for Anna Amalia, learned Italian with Jagemann, and prepared himself for a journey to study in Italy. In her memoir, Henrietta von Egloffstein reports her gratitude for the teaching she received from Grave in the year 1787:

> She [Anna Amalia] had hardly discovered by chance that I had 'a well-sounding voice' when she sent me her excellent chamber singer Grave – who never taught anyone else – so that my natural ability could be more thoroughly trained.[494]

Karoline Jagemann, in whose house Grave was a lodger, recalls singing lessons with him and adds: 'He was a very handsome man ... a very good actor and a great favourite of audiences, especially of the ladies.'

There is a negative comment from Friedrich Schiller about Grave. Schiller was plagued by basic financial worries and was hoping for a post in Weimar. He speaks of a relationship between Anna Amalia and Grave:

> The Duchess [Anna Amalia] is making a fool of herself here because of an attachment she has for a wretched dog, a singer ... He is supposed to be going to Italy and people are saying that she will accompany him.[495]

This attachment could have had a political explanation. According to Goethe's view, a Prussian intervention was imminent, led by Count Görtz, so that it was possible that Anna Amalia wanted to give the impression that she had many admirers. It is also feasible that after Goethe's flight she sought the company of a capable, witty artist without thinking of the effect that she, as a woman, might have on Grave, a man thirteen years her junior. Grave was in an unhappy relationship. According to Karoline Jagemann he had rushed into a marriage with an admirer 'who was smitten with the stage hero and after the first intoxication had fallen into dissension with the emotional man.'[496] The proximity of the Princess was to have fatal consequences for the singer.

At the beginning of 1788 Grave went to Italy to perfect his singing under the tutelage of the Italian masters.

> Recommendations and advice from his language teacher [Jagemann] brought him the advantage that he had board and lodging almost free, travelled and enjoyed visits to the theatre and to concerts, while he [Jagemann] made use of his attractive reports and reviews for his newspapers.[497]

His reports in the *Gazetta di Weimar* show him as an extraordinary connoisseur of music.[498] In August 1788 Anna Amalia began her journey to Italy. Grave met her in Milan but only joined her travelling party in Rome. Just how attractive the singer Grave was to women can be gathered from a letter of Caroline Herder to her husband. Herder did not himself have the financial means to travel to Italy. When the wealthy Canon Johann von Dalberg (1752-1812) offered Herder the possibility of accompanying him to Italy, he accepted. A further travelling companion was the young widow Sophie von Seckendorff (1755-1820), Dalberg's mistress. Herder was not able to accept for long a situation which meant that he, one of the leading theologians in Germany, might seem to condone by his presence what he saw as an immoral relationship. On 20 October 1788 Caroline Herder writes to her husband:

> An honest woman doesn't act like [Frau von Seckendorff] ... It is a nuisance that you can't cut loose from Dalberg. Be nice and friendly to the Duchess [Anna Amalia]. They say that until now she has been unspeakably good on the journey. I would like her [Seckendorff] to start up a romance with Grave. This would open Dalberg's eyes and he might send her to the nearest spa. Her behaviour is shameless, shameless. At court and around the town people are saying that she can hardly show her face in Germany again.[499]

In a birthday poem on 24 October 1788, Herder called Anna Amalia a sister of the muses:

> Greetings, lovely sun
> Welcome, day of joy,
> To the temple of the Muses.
> Your sister comes to you;
> Gracious Muses, for her service
> Create for us an Elysium.[500]

On 11 April 1789 Herder wrote to his wife:

> Grave is here. He has arrived for the Holy Week music, which, as everyone knows, is unique in Rome, and will probably travel on with us to Naples. He is not lodging with us, and I am sure that the Duchess [Anna Amalia] will [text erased] ... with him.[501]

In a letter to Anna Amalia on 29 May 1789 Herder spoke about Grave as her 'divine singer'.[502] At the beginning of June Grave left for Naples with Anna Amalia's party. He reports to Jagemann from Naples:

> The Duchess is well. She lives without ceremonial with the Queen of Naples as with a sister and is adored by the nobility. She has told me to take lessons with the great singer Aprile, so that I will stay here until the end of the year ... the beauty of the evenings and mornings is indescribable. When you look out the window you are simply ecstatic. If I could die in this paradise I would have lived.[503]

During this time he is thought to have asked Anna Amalia, if he should die, to look after his daughter.[504] On 30 November 1789 Grave is suddenly dead. According to one biographer, in a mood of despair he threw himself into the sea in Naples, because Anna Amalia did not return his love.[505] The suicide motif is correct, but Grave had, in fact, plunged a dagger into his heart. In her memoirs, Charlotte von Kalb records what the returned travellers said:

> Especially in Naples it was noticed that he was in a gloomy mood. The Duchess had travelled with her entourage to Ischia; the doctor, the secretary stayed back with him and waited patiently for her return. – The singer sat in a corner in his overcoat and with his hat pulled down over his eyes. The others spoke about various things relating to the journey and now called on him to say more concretely how it had been. They had looked at him and become aware that he had gone pale. They approached, saw that he was dead, and opened up his coat. In deep silence he had plunged the dagger into his heart.[506]

About this case there are only

> a few very restrained accounts. It is as if people were terrified of saying anything that would have some kind of consequences that could lead to deeper conclusions being drawn, deeper connections being revealed.[507]

In a letter of Grave's wife Louise to Einsiedel, in which she demanded a considerable sum of money, she spoke of 'circumstances which had an unhappy influence on his mind'; if she did not get the money she demanded, she would reveal her story 'unreservedly to the world ... Nothing will prevent me from doing it.'[508]

In the context of Grave's suicide, Anna Amalia's lady-in-waiting Luise von Göchhausen plays a mysterious role. It is thought that her sarcastic comments sparked off his decision: '...Göchhausen fired her darts even at the Duchess's best friends. Young Bury even thought that the sarcasm of the misshapen lady-in-waiting was responsible for Grave's suicide.[509] According to Karoline Jagemann, Göchhausen is supposed to have spun intrigues through which Grave lost the support of Bellomo in Weimar.[510] Karoline's explanation is not plausible, for an excellent artist like Grave had nothing to fear from such intrigues. Nor is it feasible that such a loyal lady-in-waiting would scheme behind Anna Amalia's back. What is important behind this report, however, is the fact that Luise von Göchhausen did play a role in Grave's suicide. On 17 October 1790, just eleven months after Grave's death, Goethe writes to Knebel: 'The Dowager Duchess has been at loggerheads with Göchhausen for a whole year. It is not possible that their relationship will be restored. The Duchess wants to be rid of her – the sooner the better.'

There were also others who thought von Göchhausen guilty of Grave's suicide. Frau von Stein's sister-in-law Sophie von Schardt writes to her nephew Carl von Stein (1765-1837) in a letter of 5 December 1790: 'They say Göchhausen has completely fallen from grace because the Duchess noticed her eavesdropping at her door and annoyed Grave to death. Fine behaviour for a lady-in-waiting.'[511] This means that Anna Amalia could not be reconciled with her lady-in-waiting because of her guilt in Grave's suicide. The fact that she was still not dismissed but only had her duties curtailed indicates that Anna Amalia herself must have felt partly guilty. A letter of Knebel's to his sister confirms that the motive for Grave's suicide was unrequited love:

> Something extraordinary has happened. Grave, the musician, who was in Naples with the Duchess and on whom she showered favours, took his own life there. He was said to have fallen into a confused state of mind, and in fact he was not strong enough mentally to smooth out and combat any inner turmoil by dint of reason.[512]

Grave had fallen hopelessly in love with the Duchess. Schiller had hinted unmistakeably at this before the journey to Italy began. Anna Amalia, who was already a widow at the age of eighteen, was never known to have had a love relationship. It must have been incomprehensible to Grave that this woman, in the autumn of her life, would not give her love to the much sought-after singer, although she showed him her favour in so many ways and clearly wanted his companionship.

From a letter of Friedrich Bury (1763-1823) to Goethe on 22 December 1789 it is clear that an attempt was made to hide from Anna Amalia the concrete details of Grave's death:

> You can't believe how downcast the dear Duchess is after Grave's death. If she found out about his suicide she would be inconsolable. It is true that she has lost a great deal regarding her musical life, which is her whole existence. Particularly when she thinks of herself in Germany again and of the repetitions she would have of all the beautiful things she had heard in Italy and of the great joy she would have [in hearing them again], the good lady sees it all brought to nothing through the loss.[513]

It is probable that Anna Amalia, who bore responsibility for the external welfare of her travelling party, was not fully informed about all the important circumstances. Carl August mentioned the tragic case in a letter to his mother of 5 January 1790:

> I very much regret Grave's death ... It is a pity that he is now not going to bear the fruit of all that you bestowed on him. Now that, on this occasion, a rather considerable sum for his pension falls back into your purse and you will probably spend it on music again, I suggest that you use it to help to maintain a good theatre for us and for the Weimar public, since you no longer have to burden yourself forever with a man one would eventually want to be rid of.

That sounds rather unfeeling, but it is to be seen as a warning to his mother. She should have noticed Grave's condition earlier and reacted accordingly.

In *Tasso*, which is Goethe's superb loving tribute to Anna Amalia, the Princess states regarding the departure of Tasso for Rome that she will never be able to love anyone but this poet (ll. 1882ff.):

> **Princess:** What I possess I would like to retain.
> Change is entertaining, but of scarcely any use.
> I was never led, in youthful desire,
> To try my luck in the stranger's world
> Or grasping at something to satisfy the needs
> Of my inexperienced heart.

She loves only the poet who is minded to leave her (ll. 1888ff.):

> I had to respect him, and so I loved him;
> I had to love him, because with him my life
> Became a life such as I had never known before.'

Accordingly, the poet is described (ll. 230ff.):

> He does not storm wantonly backwards and forwards from one breast to another;
> He does not fasten, in sweet self-deceit, onto beauty and shape, and does not pay
> For swift intoxication with disgust and ennui.

In *Wilhelm Meisters Lehrjahre* (1796) the hero of the novel, Wilhelm – with the choice of name Goethe is paying homage to 'William' Shakespeare – makes a vow (IV, 20):

> I will resist every fleeting desire, and even the most serious of desires I will lock away in my bosom; no female creature will hear a confession of love from my lips unless I can devote my whole life to her.

The plan Goethe conceived in Sicily for a mutual renunciation only meant a heightening of their love. For Grave the Duchess could only offer a bond of sympathy, but not her heart.

Anna Amalia was so affected by the human catastrophe with Grave that, while still in Naples, she had Einsiedel ask Goethe to come to Italy to collect her.[514] The poet accedes to her request and arrives in Venice on 31 March. He waits for her there for more than four weeks, although he could have joined her within a few days. At the very place to which his flight in 1786 had led him and from where he could have boarded ship to sail to the New World, Goethe, now firmly intent on renunciation, waits for the arrival of Anna Amalia. He cannot go any further, for Grave's catastrophe was not to be followed by another one. He had to bear responsibility for Christiane, who in the meantime had given birth to their son; and he was, furthermore, not able to disappoint Carl August, to whom before his return from Italy he had promised unconditional honesty. By waiting in Venice he showed Anna Amalia that there could only be renunciation between them.

The literary fruits of this time are the *Venetianische Epigramme*, which include, amongst other things, a biting satire against clerics, Italy, Germany, love, and other things, and are seen as an 'act of purification' on Goethe's part.[515] For her birthday on 24 October 1790 he gave her a selection of the epigrammes: 'Say, to whom do I give this little book? The Princess [Anna Amalia], who gave it to me,/Who creates Italy for us now in Germany' ('Epigramm 16'). His renunciation is expressed in 'Epigramm 7': 'I had a love which was dearer to me than everything!/But I have it no longer! Be silent, and bear the loss!' Self-criticism is also contained in the *Epigramme*: 'For jugglers and poets/Are closely related; they look for and like to find one another' (Epigramm 47), and : 'I have become impudent, and no wonder. You gods know, but not you alone, that I am pious and loyal' ('Epigramm 74). At the beginning of May 1790 Anna Amalia reached Venice via Loreto, Bologna, and Padua. She writes:

> I can't say how I felt. I became sad and depressed. The great idea one has of it was not there; when I entered the town of canals my sadness increased; it all seemed melancholy; when we got out at the inn I found Goethe and was cheered up again.[516]

They stayed on for a few weeks in Venice before leaving for Thüringen. On 14 May they witnessed

> the solemn wedding of the Doge with the sea ... the sea was still and the sun shone down on the most brilliant event of the Venetian year. The Doge's boat, the *Bucintoro*, was escorted by ships of the War Marine and by hundreds, even thousands, of gondolas; St Mark's Square was 'packed full', cannons were fired and all the church bells were ringing.[517]

On the journey home they made enough stop-offs for Anna Amalia to be able to arrive in Weimar with Goethe on the same day and at the same time as he had done on his first Italian journey in 1788 – on 16 June 1790 at eleven o'clock at night. Thus the end of the passionate love between Goethe and Anna Amalia, the end of the sojourns in Italy that separated them, was marked by a dramatic death. With this difficult inheritance the lovers were sent from Arcadia; heavily burdened they were to make their way, united, back to Weimar, and from now on to renounce one another.

11 | Deception: Letters to 'Frau von Stein'

> I like this Princess Charlotte, | : the cursed name is pursuing me everywhere : | but I have nothing to do with her. I like looking at her, and that's what princesses are there for.
> Goethe to 'Charlotte von Stein' 1 January 1780

> More than ever Frau von Stein is putting on a public show with her friend [Goethe]. In the end, things are much the same as we left them.
> Countess Görtz to her husband 24 December 1780

> 'In the meantime one must admire the skill with which this woman [Frau von Stein] was able to carry on her artificial game, so that even in later years she was considered to be Goethe's lover.'
> Henriette von Egloffstein, *Erinnerungen* [Memoirs]

Between 1776 and 1789 Goethe wrote more than 1,600 love letters, which, while addressed to Frau von Stein, were intended for Anna Amalia,[518] and so in what follows here there will be mention of Goethe's letters to Anna Amalia ('Frau von Stein'), whereby the addition ('Frau von Stein') indicates that they were not intended for Frau von Stein. Anna Amalia's ('Frau von Stein's) letters to Goethe are, significantly, not extant.[519] From 1796 to 1826 Goethe wrote 132 letters to Frau von Stein herself, mostly short and in a distant tone. In this case the replies are extant. Looked at with a critical eye, his letters reveal contradictions, and the individual phases of a cover-up of identity – unavoidable for the lovers, become clear.

There were several ways that Goethe's letters to Anna Amalia ('Frau von Stein') could be delivered. It was important to send some of the letters through Frau von Stein so that in Weimar the comings and goings of messengers would convince the public that Goethe was carrying on a relationship with the lady-in-waiting. These letters would have been handed on by Frau von Stein unopened. To bring her letters that were not directly addressed to her, Anna Amalia could rely on the services of members of her intimate circle, above all, her lady-in-waiting Luise von Göchhausen and her chamberlain von Einsiedel, who were on good terms with Frau von Stein. This is seen from the few existing letters. On 13 January 1789 Luise von Göchhausen writes from Naples to Frau von Stein: 'May we soon see one another again, my love!'[520] Frau von Stein begins an undated letter to von Einsiedel with, 'Dear, excellent [allerbester] Einsiedel!'[521] When Goethe was travelling with Duke Carl August, mail went through his hands. On 2 December 1776 when Goethe wrote a letter to Anna Amalia ('Frau von Stein'), Carl August signed as well. In a poem, Carl August, who had no idea of the cover-up with false identities, made fun of a letter he thought came from Frau von Stein, but which in fact came from his mother:[522]

> However nice and small a thing,
> Someone it will plague.
> Your little letter, for example,
> Makes hussars complain.
>
> A hussar brought one for Goethe
> And swore with great conviction.
> 'Delivering love letters? 'I prefer
> The heat of battle any day.'

In a letter from Goethe to Anna Amalia ('Frau von Stein') of 13 March 1781 we read: 'The Duke has kept back until now the letter a hussar brought me and sends it to me in ten sealed envelopes, one inside the other.' The deceit was so convincingly done at all levels that no one suspected anything. It is likely that many of the little notes were sent by pigeon post, which would also explain their unusual format as well as the fact that often several were exchanged daily. This would also explain why the letters were stuck into folio volumes by an unknown hand,[523] because, by their being pasted in, it could not be ascertained whether the letters had been rolled or folded in a capsule. A letter from Goethe to Anna Amalia ('Frau von Stein') of 21 August 1779 suggests it has been sent by pigeon post. 'Your pigeons don't know what's happening to them when the window won't open for them.' Princess Anna Amalia owned pigeons and fed them herself every morning in Tiefurt.[524] Carrier pigeons could be released anywhere, and they would keep on returning to the dove-cots, making flights over hundreds of kilometers. In ancient Greece, carrier pigeons were used to report back home about victory at the Olympic Games.[525] Thanks to the use of carrier pigeons, Caesar (BC 100-44) was able to consolidate and develop Roman rule in Gaul, for very quickly he was informed about pockets of unrest and so could keep the rebels in check with the aid of a small number of legions. Many empires in the Orient introduced a state carrier pigeon post system. Crusaders brought back knowledge about carrier pigeons to the West,[526] and monasteries 'turned to the cultivation of pigeons with great care and attention'.[527] After his nocturnal visits, Goethe therefore only needed to bring with him some pigeons in the appropriate cages to be able to send a love letter to Anna Amalia from any given place.

Only a portion of Goethe's letters to Anna Amalia are extant. From the lists of post sent it is clear that Goethe sent more letters.[528] One can assume, therefore, that Goethe's letters to Anna Amalia ('Frau von Stein') were sorted. Sometimes only individual passages of letters have been cut out,[529] and often there are explanatory marginal notes written by Fritz von Stein, who inherited the letters of his mother. Goethe and Anna Amalia used a letter seal with the words 'Alles um Liebe'. This is the motto taken from Goethe's drama *Stella* (Act 5) of 1775, and is therefore to be understood as a kind of excuse, for the play deals with the problem of the love of a man for two women, a problem which is solved in the original version by the three living together. The seal 'Alles um Liebe' stands for the idea that love, as the higher maxim for living, justifies a great deal, possibly even infringements of social convention and morality through deceit. In the first letter to Anna Amalia ('Frau von Stein'), probably from the beginning of January 1776, Goethe hesitated to use the seal. He had been in Weimar not quite two months. 'And as I can never tell you of my love, I can also never tell you of my joy ... For that reason I will never use the seal.' But he will, in fact, use the seal for his letters. On 29 January 1776 he is still writing in a letter to Anna Amalia ('Frau von Stein'): 'Curse it, my head and heart are in turmoil about whether I should stay or go.' But on 23 February 1776 he writes to her: 'I am lying at your feet and I kiss your hands.' The last stanza of 'Rastlose Liebe', May 1776, shows what motivated Goethe to stay:

> How am I to flee?
> Into the woods? All in vain!
> The crown of life,
> Happiness without rest,
> Love, that is you!

The closer one looks at Goethe's letters, the more one is struck by absurd inconsistencies. It is not clear why so many letters were written, since Goethe and Frau von Stein lived so close to one another

– from 1781 onwards their gardens directly adjoined one another, whereas Goethe could have no unlimited access to Anna Amalia without incurring the risk of arousing public suspicion. In a conversation with Eckermann on 7 October 1827 Goethe says that after his arrival in Weimar in 1775 he soon found himself 'in passionate circumstances again'. After a rather lengthy sojourn away from Weimar he hesitated 'to visit the beloved. Our affection had already attracted attention, and so, to avoid adding to this, I was careful not to go there during the day-time.' Goethe tried to find plausible reasons to be near Anna Amalia as often as possible, for example, when he was dictating his work to Luise von Göchhausen. But the possibilities remained limited, and correspondence was to compensate for this. There were events which officially brought them into one another's company, above all, their collaboration in amateur theatre. But on these occasions they could not look at one another too often or too intensely without endangering the secret of their love. Only at the very beginning was Goethe able to write to his beloved (24 February 1776): 'Yet again, during the whole of the masked ball I saw only your eyes – and the moth drawn to the light came to mind.' The poem 'Nähe', first published in 1789 shows how they were continually forced to adopt precautionary measures:

> How often you are, beloved little one,
> Somehow a stranger to me!
> When we are in a crowd, with many people
> This obliterates my joy.
> But yes, when everything around is quiet and dark
> Your kisses make you known to me again.

The times when it is 'quiet and dark', and the lovers are together, are relatively short. Far away from Anna Amalia Goethe writes on 25 August 1782:

> Your being and your love are like a sweet melody that raises us up and like a gentle cloud supports us in our cares and pain. I go around amongst all my friends and acquaintances as if I was searching for you. I don't find you, and I return to my isolation again.

Initially Frau von Stein joined in the frenzied activity around Goethe and Carl August.[530] But then she withdrew more and more. Every year she spent the midsummer and autumn on her Kochberg property to the south of Weimar. She also made long sojourns in spas. She often said she was sick or indisposed. This fits with her position as intimate friend of the young Duchess Luise, who also liked to keep to herself and to whom she could in this way demonstrate her supposed affinity.

In character, the Duchesses Luise and Anna Amalia were at opposite poles to one another and came together only in official circumstances. Luise cultivated the company of Herder, who introduced her to his work and gave her lessons in Latin.[531] According to Herder's wife, Luise 'respected him especially because of his strict morality'.[532] Goethe performed the function of a kind of therapist looking after the marriage of the Duke and Duchess Carl August and Luise.[533] A letter written by Luise to Frau von Stein in July 1777 illustrates not only Luise's inclination to withdraw from all social activity but also her relationship to her mother-in-law Anna Amalia:

> The day before yesterday I was in Ettersburg [Anna Amalia's residence] and was bored to death. I assure you I am always afraid to go there, although the mood of my dear mother-in-law is slightly better than in your time. ... When I am in Belvedere [Luise's residence] I am little concerned with human beings and wish they were little concerned with me. ... Goodbye, my dear Stein. I love you with all my heart, be assured of that! ... Come back soon, and don't bury yourself in Kochberg.[534]

A year later she writes:

> I have to scold you for your long absence. What irresistible attraction does your Kochberg hold for you that it keeps you there despite the cold and gloomy weather? Or have you become so indifferent to your friends that it doesn't matter to you whether you see them or not?[535]

In another letter Duchess Luise asks Frau von Stein: 'Are you alone with your oxen and cows, or do you have other company?'[536] But only the execution of the task given her by Anna Amalia kept the loyal lady-in-waiting away from Weimar. If she had been constantly around Goethe this would have increased for her the danger of becoming entangled in contradictions. As it was, when she was in Weimar Goethe had to visit her often to maintain the deception.

Frau von Stein was above all devoted to Anna Amalia, who knew her capabilities and nurtured them. She arranged a good match for her in Josias von Stein, and she gave support to her brothers and sisters and to her parents. When the Princess, in handing over the reins of government to her immature son Carl August, was, with Goethe's help, making sure that the country did not fall into the hands of corrupt flatterers, Frau von Stein was completely at her disposal. From the beginning she was initiated into the 'state secret Goethe'. With all the means at her disposal she took care that it remained a secret, which is the reason she withdrew from public life as far as was necessary. Duchess Luise interpreted it as a sign of their being kindred spirits; for Anna Amalia it was a sign of her unconditional loyalty. Frau von Stein took an active part in the amateur theatre on only a few occasions, as for example in the spring of 1776. For the most part, like Duchess Luise, she stayed away from performances.

It is striking that Goethe's mother wrote only two letters to Frau von Stein (1785/1787) but forty-nine to Anna Amalia (1778/1787). On 10 February 1829 Eckermann notes Goethe's statement about Anna Amalia:

> A perfect Princess, with a perfect human disposition [Sinn] and an inclination to enjoy life. She has a great love for his [Goethe's] mother and wants her to come and live permanently in Weimar. He is against it.

The rumour that Goethe's mother Catharina Elisabeth wanted to move to Weimar was a persistent myth in Frankfurt,[537] but it was never seriously envisaged that she would. She did not even visit Weimar, although Anna Amalia eagerly invited her and welcomed the plans that were being made. On 4 November 1778, for example, she wrote to Catharina Elisabeth about a possible visit to Weimar:

> Friend Wolf [Goethe] wants it, too; recently we have spoken a lot about it. During the stay we want to give his dear old father a lot of pleasure ... I think, dear mother, that your own heart will speak up enough for you to want to see your darling boy [Goethe] again. You can't believe how much I am looking forward to it.[538]

In 1778 Anna Amalia had undertaken a journey to Frankfurt and to the Rhine and had met Goethe's parents. She visited them again in 1780 on her journey to Mannheim.[539] On 3 August 1778, the day after her return from the journey of several weeks to the Rhine, Goethe writes to Anna Amalia ('Frau von Stein'): 'My love, yesterday evening I realized that there is nothing dearer in the world for me to see than your eyes and that there is nowhere I want to be more than with you.'

Frau von Stein, on the other hand, visited Goethe's mother in Frankfurt on only one occasion – in 1789, when the supposed relationship with Goethe was already over. Anna Amalia's letters to Goethe's mother begin with 'Dear Mother!', which becomes 'Dearest [Liebe, beste] Mother!' When Goethe writes to Anna Amalia ('Frau von Stein') on 26 August 1781 'With a good morning greeting I send my beloved [besten] a letter from my mother so that you can take delight in the life that's in it', this could hardly have interested Frau von Stein since as yet she did not know Goethe's mother.

In a letter of 31 November 1781 Anna Amalia tells Goethe's mother that her son is moving to a house Am Frauenplan:

> I have also promised to get him some furniture because he is so nice and good. You will be so kind, dear mother, as to send me some

> samples of chintz for chairs and a sofa, and send me the prices at the same time.[540]

So Anna Amalia was looking for fittings for Goethe's house and paying for them. In a letter of 9 May 1782 Goethe writes to Anna Amalia ('Frau von Stein'): 'How I am looking forward to my new setup! To everything that your love will help to arrange and maintain. May you have as much joy as the happiness you give me.' On 17 October 1782 Anna Amalia writes to Goethe's mother:

> I could tell you a lot of nice news from here. Amongst other things, that the palace of Privy Councillor von Goethe is both inside and outside superbly appointed and that it will be one of the most beautiful in the town of Weimar.[541]

The house am Frauenplan (1709) was, at the time Goethe moved into it, the only one in Weimar that 'could compare in size and architectural excellence with the Wittumspalais'.[542]

Even early letters to Anna Amalia ('Frau von Stein') contain many utterances which point to the motif of nocturnal love and to its prohibition. On 14 April 1776 Goethe sends Anna Amalia ('Frau von Stein') the poem 'Warum gabst Du uns die tiefen Blicke' with the verses:

> And we seem only to be half alive
> The brightest day is only twilight around us
> It is fortunate that the fate that tortures us
> Has no power to change us.

The brightest day cannot show their love because this takes place in secret, in the twilight, and at night. A note dating from around April 1776 has the words: 'We can't be anything to one another, and yet we are too much.' On 24 May 1776 Goethe writes: 'The world that can be nothing to me also doesn't want you to be anything to me.' In a four-line poem of 29 June 1776 he writes: 'My heart, full of the old sorrows, is working in accord with pure, quiet nature. But I am constantly living for the sake of her for whom I am not supposed to live.' This prohibition of their love is a constant theme and cannot easily be explained by the fact that Frau von Stein is married, for it is something insuperable. On 22 July 1776 Goethe writes:

> My fate is so oppressive
> That I am striving for the impossible.
> Dear angel for whom I don't live,
> I live for you in the mountains.

So that no doubt could arise in Weimar about Goethe's supposed love relationship with Frau von Stein, Goethe arranged for an elaborate writing desk to be made for her.[543] Through the careful directives given for its construction the tradesmen were to be convinced that something ethically superior lay at the foundation of this strange relationship. A difficult task, but it was achieved. At first people gossiped eagerly about Frau von Stein's indefinable relationship to Goethe. Countess Görtz writes to her husband that Frau von Stein 'patiently put up with public gossip'.[544] Later, no one criticized the relationship. People believed in the chasteness [Reinheit] of both parties,[545] and the 'lovers', with no spark of passion between them, were avoiding one another's company. Although work was done on the desk from the spring of 1779 onwards, Goethe simply had it brought into Frau von Stein's house while he was away in Switzerland. From a letter of 4 June 1779 the conclusion is drawn that Goethe intended to give her the present earlier:[546]

> I don't know whether you, too, have a note in your calendar about Charlotte. It is in mine, and I had hoped to send you as a morning greeting a sign of my continuing preoccupation with you. It didn't work out, so I am sending you the finest thing I have in the house. I can't let this ominous name-day go by without telling you, differently from other days, that I love you.

It would be impossible for him to write of an ominous name-day to a woman who is called Charlotte and who returns his love. Whereas the word 'omen' can suggest something either good or bad, the adjective 'ominous' refers to a bad omen.[547] Goethe does not use this word very frequently in his work, but where it does occur it has a negative connotation, as for example in *Götz* (1771/73): 'rather the howling of the death-knell or the ominous birds' (Act II). This shows that it is cutting comment to Anna Amalia about the name-day of Charlotte von Stein, and it is also a criticism of the need for a cover-up. A short time later Goethe makes the following entry in his diary for 12 August 1779:

> ... had a strong talk with (☾) [Anna Amalia] which ended up the same way. With relationships which can't be changed certain things must come to a head and finally burst. That happens from time to time. Otherwise it went well.

At the beginning of September 1780 Goethe writes the poem 'Wandrers Nachtlied':

> Above all the peaks
> Is peace,
> In all the tree tops
> You hear
> Hardly a breath;
> The birds are silent in the forest.

Just wait, soon
You too will rest.

Towards the end of the month quite different moods take over in him, for Goethe is madly jealous. He is in Ostheim near Meiningen; on 20 September 1789 he writes in a letter to Anna Amalia ('Frau von Stein'): 'My nature is closing like a flower when the sun turns away', and 'God knows where we will go when separated. Addio'. That the sun turns away from him so that he feels sick cannot refer to Frau von Stein, who is living in Kochberg and is also visited there by Goethe. The sun that turns away from him is Anna Amalia who, together with Adam Friedrich Oeser undertakes a journey to Mannheim. He will not see her for a month, because she and Oeser are to be away until 20 October. Oeser was an important painter, sculptor, and art theorist and had been Goethe's teacher of drawing during his student years in Leipzig. Goethe had described him as an attractive man.[548] He had had an influence on Johann J. Winckelmann (1717-1768) who had applied to classicism (c. 1750-1830), a period which superseded baroque, the formula so loved by Goethe and Anna Amalia: 'noble simplicity and quiet greatness' [edle Einfalt und stille Größe].

In Mannheim there was a famous hall of antiques in which casts of significant statues were on show: for example, the Belvedere Apollo, *The Dying Gaul*, the Castor and Pollux group, and the late hellenistic Laokoon group. This latter portrays a Trojan priest and his two sons at the climax of their vain struggle against two snakes which are crushing them to death. Laokoon had warned against bringing the wooden horse of the Greeks into the city of Troy and for that reason was, with his sons and at the command of the incensed god Apollo, killed by the snakes. The Laokoon group, created by Hagesandros, Polydoros, and Athanadorus of Rhodes, was one of the most important ancient pieces of sculture. It played a central role in the art theory of Winckelmann and Lessing (1729-1781).[549] Goethe, who saw the copy in 1771, wrote about it:

> To grasp the intention behind Laokoon, stand back facing it at a suitable distance, but with eyes closed. Open your eyes and close them again immediately. Then you will see all the marble moving. You will be afraid that, opening your eyes again, you will find the whole group changed. I would say that, as it is now, it is lightning captured, a wave turned to stone the moment it reaches the shore. You get this effect when you see the group at night by torchlight.[550]

Anna Amalia went to Mannheim with a view to seeing these treasures of sculpture with her own eyes and studying them. Lessing recommended artists to visit the hall of antiques, because it offered more advantages

> than a pilgrimage to Rome to see the originals, which for the most part were too dark or too high, or were too hidden amongst inferior pieces, for the connoisseur, who wants to walk around them, feel them, and look at them from several angles, to be able to use them properly.[551]

As a connoisseur of art Anna Amalia was Goethe's equal. In a letter of 6 November 1781 to her friend and art dealer Merck she writes:

> Some days ago I received the first copy of the great Vestal Virgin which was first found in Herculanum and is now in Dresden. The cast is excellent; connoisseurs are comparing it with the great Flora in Mannheim.[552]

Anna Amalia and Goethe possessed several casts and they added to their collection continually. They supported the sculptor Klauer and in 1779 enabled him to study in Mannheim over a long period.[553] Klauer made busts of many Weimar personalities, including frequent ones of Anna Amalia and Goethe (ill. 6-9).[554] He also did a bust of Anna Amalia's lady-in-waiting von Göchhausen, but not one of Frau von Stein.

When his beloved had travelled off to Mannheim with Oeser, Goethe writes in a letter of 21 September 1780 to Anna Amalia ('Frau von Stein'):

> ... the Duchess [Anna Amalia] is going with Oeser to Mannheim. So I will see you again soon. I am longing to be home, the way a sick man longs for his bed. When clouds settle over the earth, you don't want to go outside.

Goethe says further that he and Carl August are climbing high mountains and he thinks of 'the danger of suddenly crashing down'; then they were

> transfigured in such a way that past and future worries about life and its weariness fell to our feet like dross, and we, still clothed in earthly garments, felt the lightness of future blissful wingedness through our still heavy feathers. And now I take leave of you.

The word 'leave' [Abschied] refers clearly to the recent departure of Anna Amalia. It is signed '*G. il penseroso fedele* (the loyal brooder). This designation relates to a performance of the operetta *Kalliste oder der Triumph der Treue*, a version of the *Sposa Fedele* (The Loyal Bride, 1778) by Johann J. Eschenburg (1743-1820). However, Anna Amalia does not appear to Goethe to be a loyal bride, since she is travelling to Mannheim with Oeser; so as a loyal fiancé he has at least to become a loyal brooder who thinks about throwing himself down the side of a mountain.

After a short letter of 24 September 1780 there is pause, and then from 4 October Goethe is staying at Kochberg on Frau von Stein's property. They are joined on 9 October by the Duke, Frau von Stein's husband Josias, and Knebel. Goethe leaves for Weimar on 10 October after his beloved is supposed to have said something hurtful to him – a formulation he had to use, even if the communication had come to him in writing from Mannheim. Goethe is completely churned up and writes, still on the same day:

> What you said to me early today caused me great pain, and if the Duke had not accompanied me up the mountain I would have wept my fill of tears. One ill is heaped on another! ... I won't be satisfied until you have given me a verbal account of the past. ... Have pity on me. All of that was added to the state of my soul which seemed like a pandemonium of invisible spirits; and no matter how uneasy the spectator felt, the spectacle only represented an infinitely empty vault.

The next day Knebel follows him to Weimar and stays with him. This calms Goethe down to some extent, but his jealousy continues to knaw at him. On 13 October 1780 he admits to being jealous: 'It is strange, but that's the way it is, that I am jealous and stupid like a small boy when you are friendly to other people.'

The jealousy was in no way related to Frau von Stein, for she was with him on her Kochberg property; and so Goethe is referring to Anna Amalia and Oeser. On 29 October 1780, when Anna Amalia is back in Weimar and Goethe has realized that his jealousy of Oeser was exaggerated, the poet justifies his behaviour:

> I don't know why, but I feel you haven't yet forgiven me ... That's what happens when a person suffers quietly and does not want to worry his dear ones or give in to weakness himself. He finally is forced to cry out *Eli, Eli lama sabacthani* (My God, my God, why hast Thou forsaken me? – Matthew 27, 46). The people reply, 'You have helped others, help yourself', and the best of them interpret it wrongly, thinking that he is calling on Elias.

Goethe's lamentations, like those of Christ, will be misinterpreted. His fit of jealousy will be seen in relation to Frau von Stein and not Anna Amalia, and so they will not understand why he is suffering. In a letter to Carl August on 25 January 1781 Goethe passes on, not without a degree of satisfaction, the story of a scandal at Anna Amalia's court:

> A propos of artists, Christiane, the nice little chambermaid at your mother's court, became pregnant in Ettersburg and claims that old

> Oeser is the father. The Duchess is going mad and is threatening her with imprisonment. There are already two versions of the girl's account of things.

While Goethe was still jealous of Oeser, he was reflecting about his nocturnal love for Anna Amalia. After a walk in 'infinitely beautiful' moonlight he included a poem in a letter to the beloved on 13 October 1780. He puts the words of the song in the mouth of the elves, but he is also referring to his nocturnal love, for they are only allowed to be lovers under the protection of night:

> At midnight
> When people are asleep
> Then the moon shines on us
> The stars twinkle for us.
> We go around singing
> And loving to dance.
>
> At midnight
> When people are asleep
> In meadows at the erl trees
> We find our space
> We go around singing
> And loving to dream.

The fact that their real life in common begins at night is clear from a letter to Anna Amalia ('Frau von Stein') on 19 November 1784: 'I'll come again tomorrow evening and we will continue our life'. On 25 October 1780 Goethe writes about a short meeting he had with Merck in Mühlhausen in Thüringia: 'I spent a very good day and a couple of nights with Merck. But the dragon is putting me in a bad mood. I feel like Psyche when she saw her sisters again.' The fairytale *Amor and Psyche* by Apuleius (c. 125-161 AD) is of quite central importance, since it recurs in many of Goethe's works. Knebel had given a reading of the fairytale about the 'socially unequal' match on 10 February 1780 in Tiefurt. The god Amor is the husband of the mortal Princess Psyche. She has never actually seen him, because they are only allowed to meet at night and in complete darkness. Since Psyche's sisters are envious they tell her that her husband is a dragon, and so Psyche defies the prohibition and shines a light on Amor's face. A drop of hot oil falls and wakes Amor, who punishes Psyche by leaving her. Only after severe trials, amongst them a dangerous sojourn in the underworld, are the lovers reunited, with Psyche being raised to the ranks of the gods.

Merck, who knew nothing of the deception, echoed the view of many when he disapproved of Goethe's 'relationship' to Frau von Stein. The main requirement of *Sturm und Drang* was that the poet express all he encountered in life realistically and naturally. The alleged love relationship of the brilliant young 'genius of geniuses' with the married lady-in-waiting von Stein seemed to bear no literary fruit, and in fact Goethe's literary output was slowing down. Merck wanted to make it clear to Goethe that, in the words of the fairytale, Frau von Stein really was a dragon and that he was acting unworthily of his extraordinary capabilities. In fact it is the Princess Anna Amalia who is hidden behind the dragon's form of Frau von Stein. If light were shed on his hidden love for the Princess and if their relationship were to become known, they would be separated like the lovers in the fairytale.

In the letter of 1 October 1781 Goethe writes of a gem, a jewel with an image cut into it which he had acquired in Leipzig: 'It depicts Psyche with a butterfly on her breast in yellow agate. It is as if I always called you my beloved soul [Psyche].' Goethe had the stone set in a ring for his beloved (letter of 2 October 1781) and she sealed her letters with it (letter of 27 November 1781). Since the fairytale of *Amor and Psyche* was of great importance for the lovers, Anna Amalia translated it for her *Tiefurter Journal* (dating from November 1781). On 29 January 1782 Goethe writes to Anna Amalia ('Frau von Stein'):

> After surviving the day's work I hurried to you ... I didn't find you, grumbled for a moment and then went out walking in the beautiful moonlight and found your lovely word, for which I thank you. Psyche was not silent, my love!

Anna Amalia decorated her residence in Tiefurt with, amongst other things, coloured prints telling the story of Amor and Psyche, made in 1693 by the famous copper engraver Nicolas Dorigny (1658-1746) in imitation of Raphael's frescos in the Villa Farnesina.[555] Goethe owned these prints as well. Anna Amalia seems to have given them to him in August 1778.[556] On 18 November 1786 Goethe writes to Anna Amalia ('Frau von Stein') that he has seen Dorigny's models: 'Today we saw in the [Villa] Farnesina the story of Psyche which you know from my rooms.' On 16 July 1787 he reports the same thing:

> Yesterday I was with Angelica in the [Villa] Farnesina where the fable of Psyche is painted. How often and in how many situations have I you, looked with you at the bright copies of these pictures in my rooms. I was reminded of it because through the copies I almost know them by heart.

Goethe also tracked down Raphael's (1483-1520) early sketches and studies for the Farnesina frescos. On 6 May he writes to Carl August from Florence:

> On the day before yesterday [in Rome], for a small sum I bought for you something that is sure to give you pleasure. The story of Psyche

> in the thirty-two pages of drawings by Raphael. From these he afterwards took the subjects for the Farnesina [frescos], and for that reason they are doubly interesting.

In *Tasso* the poet and his Princess are linked to the fairytale (ll. 228ff.): 'It is the youth [Amor] who married Psyche and who has his place and a vote in the council of the gods.' The first edition of *Tasso* (1790) was adorned with a picture of the bound Psyche painted in Rome by Julius Heinrich Lips (1758-1817).

Since the pair of lovers are only allowed to see one another secretly under the protection of night, Goethe often complains that he cannot be near his beloved enough. Again, this cannot refer to Frau von Stein, since Goethe had relatively free access to her company. In a poem sent to the beloved on 16 December 1780, he writes:

> Beloved trees, to you I say
> ...
> You know how much I love
> The one who returns my love,
> Who responds to the finest of my urges
> With even greater fineness.
> ...
> Provide shade, produce fruit
> New joy every day
> As long as I may write and write for her
> Near in every way

In April 1776 Goethe began some reconstruction on his garden house and planted lime trees in front of it. On 1 November 1776 it was Anna Amalia who took a walk to Goethe's garden and held the young lime trees upright for him as he was about to plant them. In Goethe's diary there is the entry: 'Dowager Duchess with Göchhausen across the meadow. Planted lime trees.'[557] Goethe seems to be referring to these trees in his poem.[558] But it was an exception for Anna Amalia to be at his house in such a relaxed way. It was not possible for the lovers to visit one another at will, because the Princess Anna Amalia had to take part in a regimented court life. In her own widow's court with its ladies-in-waiting, cook, pastry cook, chambermaids, librarian, and private secretary there were in all up to thirty personnel.[559] The court of the ruling Duke and Duchess also made corresponding demands on her. Every Sunday Anna Amalia had herself driven in a glass carriage to the court of her son Carl August.[560] She made short journeys also in her sedan-chair (ill. 11). Every step she took outside of her private area was accompanied by servants:

> Every door she went through during court functions could only be opened and closed by a page. If the Duchesses went anywhere one [of

> the servants] had to ride hanging from the coach door and another had to carry her train.[561]

That Frau von Stein could not have been Goethe's lover is seen also from the fact that Goethe did not wait for a few days until 25 December – her birthday – before presenting her with the poem written on 16 December 1780. Instead of that he writes on her birthday that Christmas Day for him is also a birthday occasion. From 1775 until 1785 only once, in a postscript to a letter, is there mention, namely on 25 December 1781, of Frau von Stein's birthday: 'Happy birthday!' This from the poet who seemed to be sending Frau von Stein an avalanche of letters. When there is a further mention on 26 December 1785, this does not necessarily refer to her. Goethe could just as easily be referring to a Christmas present for Anna Amalia: 'I knew that on Christmas Eve I had a present for you, but I couldn't think what it was. I am sending it on now.' The year 1782 shows quite forcibly that for Goethe Frau von Stein's birthday was of no importance. In a letter to 'Frau von Stein' on 25 December 1782 he does not mention her birthday. But on 24 October 1782, Anna Amalia's birthday, he gave his beloved a special present. In a letter to Knebel on 8 November 1782 Anna Amalia writes: 'Goethe gave me great pleasure by making me a present of all his unpublished writings. Would not anyone find that flattering, dear Knebel? But it also makes me very proud.'[562] Goethe saw his work as inseparable from Anna Amalia. He wants to lay at her feet his future creations which are to glorify her in many different ways. From his first decade in Weimar there is no sign that Goethe celebrates Frau von Stein's birthday. Between 1776 and 1785 eight of Anna Amalia's birthdays can be shown to have either been celebrated by Goethe or mentioned by him. Goethe biographers have noticed this, but they were unable to explain it.[563] In later years, even after her death, Anna Amalia's birthdays are regularly mentioned. On the other hand Frau von Stein, who survived her mistress Anna Amalia by twenty years, is mentioned or visited by Goethe on only three of her birthdays, the last of them being 1815.[564]

On 12 March 1781 Goethe expresses his wish to marry his beloved:

> My soul has become closely entwined with yours, I don't want to talk about it. You know that I am inseparable from you and that there is nothing high or low that can make me part from you. I wish there were a vow or a sacrament that could make me yours visibly and by law. How much that would mean to me. And my noviceship was long enough for me to reflect on it.

For Frau von Stein there would have been the possibility of a divorce, which in those days and at this social level was not uncommon. But

Goethe's statement 'I wish there were' implies that there is in fact no vow or sacrament that could outwardly manifest that his beloved belonged to him. Goethe was not able to marry Anna Amalia, although she was a widow, because the barriers of class were insuperable. In his autobiographical novel *Wilhelm Meisters Lehrjahre* (VIII, 9) Goethe encodes this situation. In relation to the harpist Augustin we read: He should realize that he is not living in the free world of his thoughts and ideas but within a constitution whose laws and conditions have taken on the unassailable character of a natural law.' On 8 July 1781 Goethe writes: 'We are indeed married, i.e. joined by a bond where love and joy are the paper but the entry is the cross, worry, and wretchedness. Goodbye. My greetings to Stein. Help me to believe and hope.' The abrupt mention of Josias von Stein when Goethe has just said he is in fact married to the man's wife has received no convincing explanation from the biographers.[565] It is explained satisfactorily, however, if the letter was addressed to Anna Amalia. She has to help the inconsolable poet, who is plagued with doubts, to think of and to hope for a future they can share. 'Cross, worry, and wretchedness' show that Goethe sees no way out of this social mismatch, which can only be lived inwardly and has to be protected outwardly by deception because there is no possibility of external legitimation.

According to plan, Goethe frames his love letters to Anna Amalia with sentences which relate to Frau von Stein's family circumstances. Frau von Stein can therefore show these letters to her circle of friends. Besides, if the letters were to fall into the wrong hands, for example, when sent by carrier pigeon, there would be no danger; and so the correspondence is carried on in such a way that anyone who looked at the letters, legitimately or otherwise, would not immediately see that Anna Amalia was Goethe's lover. The references to Frau von Stein's family and the places she stayed are only deception, planned additions meant to hide the identity of the beloved. When Frau von Stein is asked in these additions to do something for Goethe, Anna Amalia understands it as a request for her to have Frau von Stein carry out the task promptly.

The lovers considered these and other precautionary measures necessary, because Goethe's 'indefinable' relationship with Frau von Stein was arousing ever more interest. Lavater's brother-in-law, the theologian and translator Georg C. Tobler (1757-1812), visited Weimar in 1781, remained several months and took an intense interest in Frau von Stein. Lavater had recognized Goethe's greatness early on. For him, Goethe was a 'unique genius'.[566] But he adopted an increasingly intolerant attitude to people of other faiths and eventually undertook extended journeys as a wandering prophet.[567] Lavater gave his compilation *Pontius Pilatus* (from 1782) the motto: 'He who is not for us is against us.'[568] In his *Jesus Messias* (from 1783) Lavater used Goethe's image for that of the devil/tempter, which was to estrange Goethe from him completely. In a letter to Anna Amalia ('Frau von Stein') of 14 June 1786 Goethe asks: 'What does the author of *Pontius Pilatus* matter to me? – apart from his other qualities.' When Lavater sent Goethe his *Nathanael* (1786), a story of conversion, with the dedication 'noble, guileless, dear, dear man!', Goethe angrily scribbled a note: 'You've come to the wrong man with your pious claptrap. I am no Nathanael. Get packing, you sophist or else we'll come to blows.'[569]

Goethe had made the acquaintance of Lavater's brother-in-law Tobler on his journey to Switzerland with Carl August. At that time Goethe wrote about Tobler to Lavater on 2 November 1779): 'My mind is close to him but my heart is not ... We were not comfortable with one another.' Lavater was now interested in Goethe as well as in the woman he loved. Tobler was to find out why Goethe cultivated a love relationship with a married woman of all things. Goethe wrote to Lavater on 20 September 1780:

> The talisman of that beautiful love with which she [die St(ein)] spices my life does me a lot of good. She has gradually inherited my mother, my sister and my lovers, and a bond has been formed like the bonds of nature.

In the same letter Goethe answers a question of Lavater's regarding the latter's friend, the widow Maria Antonia von Branconi (1746-1793), with whom Lavater would like to have matched Goethe: 'God protect us from a serious bond with which she would extract the soul from my body.' Frau von Stein's friend Zimmermann called Frau von Branconi 'the greatest miracle of beauty that exists in nature'.[570] When Goethe visited Lausanne he met her and wrote with cutting irony to Anna Amalia ('Frau von Stein') on 23 October 1779 – the day before Anna Amalia's birthday – : 'She seems to me so beautiful and pleasant that I silently asked myself several times in her presence whether it was possible for her to be so beautiful.' From 1767 Frau von Branconi had been the mistress of Anna Amalia's brother, the Crown Prince Carl Wilhelm Ferdinand (1735-1806), and had born him a son in 1776. When Goethe accepted Frau von Branconi's invitation to visit her at her little residence in Langenstein and arrived with little Fritz von Stein, he wrote in a letter to Anna Amalia ('Frau von Stein') of 20 September 1783: ' ... she [Frau von Branconi] didn't know where she was with me, and I would like to have said to her: I love, and I am loved, and I don't even have room for friendship anymore.' Frau von Branconi was interested in Goethe but could not understand him. He spurned her, a famous beauty, and instead seemed to remain faithful for years on end to a certain Frau von Stein about whom nothing particularly significant could be said.

An enormous curiosity was in this way aroused among many people, and accordingly Tobler's attention was directed to Frau von Stein and her relationship to Goethe. In a letter in May 1781 Tobler writes to Lavater:

> The most pleasant and the most socially gracious of them is Frau von Stein. But I see no basis for admiring her specially; nor do I see that she has any high degree of tenderness for Goethe ... Goethe took me aside yesterday evening and said that I shouldn't chat too much about the way things were in Weimar.[571]

Tobler was lodging with Knebel who, here too, performed his diplomatic duties admirably. His guest said about him in a letter to Lavater on 7 May 1781: 'I can be open with him.'

The precautionary measures in Goethe's letters are increased on 1 May 1781 when the name Lotte is introduced: 'Adieu dear Lotte ... ' Goethe did use the name Lotte from now on, but in his letters only one month later, on 1 June 1781, another name crops up in a poem. He refers to the beloved as Lydia and later Lida. His letter concludes with the words: 'In this world, my dearest, no one has a better harvest than the dramatic writer, and the wise men say: don't judge any man until you have stood in his shoes.' The poem in which the name Lydia occurs for the first time and is later to receive the title 'Versuchung' is as follows:

> When once our mother Eve handed the harmful fruit to her husband
> The whole of our race became sick from the foolish bite.
> You, Lydia, good, lovely child doing penance
> Only taste of the holy body which nourishes and heals our souls.
> And so I send you in haste the fruit full of earthly sweetness
> So that heaven will not withdraw you from your beloved.

By using the name Lydia it was possible for Goethe to avoid having to use the name Lotte in his writing. When he uses the abbreviation L., which he frequently does, it is not clear which name he actually means. Poetry is for Johann Georg Hamann (1730-1788), a philosopher whom Goethe admired, the mother tongue of the human race. It is the purest echo of divine language and can only stand in the service of truth. In the letter of 1 September 1781 Goethe mentions his poem 'Der Becher' in which he addresses his beloved as Lida and compares her with Psyche: 'No, such a vessel no god apart from Amor has formed or possessed!' A poem of 9 October is the only one in the first version of which the name Lotte appeared; it was then crossed out and the name Lida inserted. The crossed-out name of Lotte is of great symbolical significance. The first lines read: 'The unique one, ~~Lotte~~ Lida, whom you can love/You demand entirely for yourself, and rightly/For he is solely yours.' In a four-line poem which Goethe sends with a letter on 12 April 1782 to Anna Amalia ('Frau von Stein') it is unmistakeable that the addressee is a Princess: 'Here, dearest, an epigramme. It is your poem:

> They say that nature has given kings longer arms
> Than other mortals for safeguarding of the realm.
> But to my lowly self she also gave that royal privilege,
> For from afar I reach out to you, my Psyche, and hold you tight.

Later Goethe changed the name Psyche to Lida which he uses synonymously. In this way he makes it clear that the woman he addresses is also a Princess.

In the letter of 1 September 1781 Goethe announces to the beloved his present of a precious stone of yellow agate on which Psyche is represented: 'In Leipzig I saw *Das Öffentliche Geheimnis* [The Open Secret] and my conscience warned me.' The theme of the play is 'the secret poetic language of two lovers in lines where the initial words yield up a meaning of their own'.[572] The 'warning' refers to Goethe's worry that his secret could become known. He says in the next sentence of his letter:

> My dearest, I have always conversed with you and through your boy have shown you love and kindness. I have kept him warm and made him comfortable in his bed; I have had my delight in him and thought about his education.

If the warning about the discovery of the secret was to be taken seriously further precautionary measures were necessary. What better way than to take Fritz, Frau von Stein's son, into his care, especially since it was greatly appreciated. Fritz made Goethe's pretended love for his mother incomparably more feasible. Goethe was to take him to his heart so warmly that people believed he would make him his heir. After the move from the garden house to the house am Frauenplan in June 1782 Goethe took over the care of Fritz entirely, so much so that Fritz was the envy of Weimar. Goethe educated him and often took him with him when travelling. Quite literally, this spread the plausibility of his strange relationship [with Charlotte von Stein] all over the duchy. At the same time, Goethe enjoyed it because he loved children. From his time in Wetzlar in the summer of 1772 it is reported:

> The eyes of all Wetzlar were on a man they could not comprehend, who on one market day bought up all the cherries in the whole market, rounded up all the children in the town and then led the

> whole procession to [Charlotte] Buff's house, where he arranged them all in a circle around the baskets, and Lotte served them bread and butter as well.[573]

In Weimar as well he liked to surround himself with children and arranged feasts for them. For a young boy who needed a lesson in patience he resorted to an unusual remedy: Goethe covered him up to the neck in a pile of sand.[574] But the children in Weimar were especially enthusiastic when he had them perform in the amateur theatre, for example, for those who were having dancing lessons, in the ballet *Der Geist der Jugend* (1782).[575]

On 23 August 1782 the precautionary measures in Goethe's letters were further intensified. In the sixth year Goethe suddenly begins to thematize the journeys of Frau von Stein to her Kochberg property: she is to return, he is so alone, he misses her. Frau von Stein came for a few days to Weimar; Goethe made brief trips to Kochberg several times in September or to wherever she happened to be staying. At this time, from May 1782 until the spring of 1783, the Frenchman Anse de Villoison was staying in Weimar.[576] He was an expert in ancient Greek and the author of a Homer-Dictionary.[577] Carl August and Knebel had become acquainted with him on their journey to Paris (1774/75). In Paris '[Villoison] besieged the Duke and mobilized himself to write a poem celebrating his marriage, because he believed it might earn him an Order or fine-sounding title'.[578] And now he settled down at the court in Weimar and it seemed as if he never wanted to leave, although he received several hints about it, especially in the way his extraordinary appearance was made fun of.[579] He stayed unnecessarily long in Weimar, making undue demands on hospitality, so that Goethe became suspicious of him. He was often with Anna Amalia in Tiefurt, where he gave her lessons in ancient Greek. It was not far-fetched to think that someone who had an inkling of their secret had set on them this puzzling scholar who 'bought up all the philological books he could lay his hands on and sent boxes of them off to Paris'.[580] In October 1782 Countess Görtz also visited Weimar and wrote freely to her husband about the forbidden love.[581] Goethe had to be careful. The senior Prussian diplomat could have been intriguing to revenge himself on Anna Amalia and Goethe as 'the cause of our torments', as Görtz called Goethe in a letter to his wife in 1776.[582] Proof of a forbidden love between the poet and the Princess would have been useful for blackmailers, but also for political purposes. The lovers had to be prepared for break-ins, for bribing of servants and other kinds of inroads into their privacy. In *Tasso* Goethe has the Duke say in relation to the poet (ll. 315ff.):

Of many
He is suspicious, who I am sure,
Are not his enemies. If it happens
That a letter goes astray, that a servant
Leaves his service for another,
That a paper of his goes missing,
Immediately he sees a plan, betrayal
And malice that undermines his future.

Goethe and Anna Amalia become even more cautious. The deception is increasingly refined, for they are constantly worried about making a fatal error. In the letter of 4 May 1783 – the strange Villoison had long since left – Goethe wrote:

> The way you told me yesterday evening that you had a story to tell me worried me for a moment. I was afraid it had something to do with our love, and, I don't know why, but for some time I have been worried. How strange it is that the weight of a person's whole happiness hangs from a single thread.

These worries make no sense if seen in relation to Frau von Stein. The discovery of Anna Amalia's and Goethe's secret, on the other hand, would have led to their separation. The big gaps in Goethe's diary – for the period from July 1782 to August 1786 no entries are extant – can be explained by Goethe's and Anna Amalia's ever increasing caution. The use in his diary of symbols from the planetary system for referring to his closest friends had precisely the function of allowing him to continue the diary without spoiling the cover-up. Along with the use of the sun symbol (☉) for his visits to Frau von Stein he can use the same symbol when the moon symbol (☾) would be compromising, as on 13 February 1778: 'Night to (☉) walking with her again in the moonlight'. But to avoid the danger of a fatal contradiction Goethe probably preferred to discontinue the diary.

On 23 June 1784 there is another significant four-line poem referring to their nocturnal love and introduced with the words: 'If only I could conjure up from somewhere a memento for you. I was planning to have it carved into a rock:

What I deny but confess, reveal but hide
Is my only good, is sufficient treasure for me.
To the rock I entrust it so that the lonely man can guess
What gives me joy in loneliness, joy in the world.

Goethe's 'love' for Frau von Stein need not be committed to the rock, because there is nothing to guess about. The poem only has meaning if it refers to someone else. On 20 September 1784 he laughs about the deception in a letter which begins: 'We fulfill our duty so conscientiously, my dear Lotte, that in the end doubt about our love could arise'.[583] From this letter it is also apparent that a visit of Fritz Jacobi to Weimar is gradually becoming a problem. Goethe continues in ironic vein to Anna Amalia ('Frau von Stein'):

> The presence of Jacobi would be doubly valuable to me if you were with us. It is impossible to speak with anyone at all about you. I know that I would always say too little and I am afraid of saying too much. I wish that everyone knew you and could feel the joy I feel without daring to express it. It is really an abuse of friendship to be with a man like Jacobi, with such a true and sensitive friend, without letting him see into my heart and without his becoming acquainted with the treasure from which I am nourished.[584]

Goethe had not seen Jacobi for nearly ten years. His visit was to be a sign of reconciliation after a 'book crucifixion', for in 1779 in Ettersburg Goethe had mocked and then nailed to a tree a copy of Jacobi's novel *Woldemar*, which in bloated fashion imitated his *Werther* (1774). Jacobi wrote his novel when he thought Goethe guilty of disloyalty as a friend.[585] Goethe, on the other hand, seems to have been unable to tolerate for long Jacobi's exaggerated sentimentality. When Jacobi heard of the 'book crucifixion' he broke off contact with Goethe. Only in 1782 did it come to a written reconciliation, prepared by Knebel in consultation with Anna Amalia and indeed Goethe himself.[586] Anna Amalia had become acquainted with Jacobi in Düsseldorf in 1778 on her journey to the Rhine. Her impression of him could not have been very good, for during Goethe's trip to Switzerland (1779) she had his satire of Jacobi's novel printed. Anna Amalia liked the satirizing of vanity and self-complacency in the German literary world, for a year earlier she created the music for Goethe's second version of the *Jahrmarktsfest zu Plunderweilern* (1778).[587] After the reconciliation Jacobi was especially interested in Goethe's friendship with the mysterious 'lover' Frau von Stein. It is in this context that the sentence, 'We fulfill our duty so conscientiously, my dear Lotte, that in the end doubt about our love could arise', is to be read. Goethe turns to Anna Amalia and asks for a more strenuous effort regarding the deception, otherwise Jacobi could see through his pretended love relationship with Frau von Stein.

A letter of Goethe's on 24 October 1784 is clearly directed to Anna Amalia and not to Frau von Stein. This letter also shows that it can be delivered directly to Anna Amalia herself. Goethe writes on Anna Amalia's birthday (ill. 23):

> It will depend only on my Lotte how and where I am to spend my time today. If she stays at home I will come to her and bring my work

> and some nourishment for midday and evening. If she wants to dedicate herself to the outside world I will stay at home, work hard and enjoy the happiness of her company when the court leaves her free. Adieu, my dearest. 24 October 1784.

On this day Frau von Stein was on her Kochberg property 35 kilometres to the south of Weimar and could not possibly have attended any function at court. The editors of the Weimar edition of Goethe's work (1887-1919), convinced that Frau von Stein was Goethe's beloved, dated the letter as 1785, with the comment:

> On 24 October 1784 Frau von Stein was in Kochberg. The supposition that the letter was written in 1783 is to be rejected because experience tells us that erroneous writing of the date of a future year seldom comes about.[588]

A mistake in writing the date of a previous year is also seldom. Before and after this letter there is mention of Frau von Stein's staying in Kochberg. On Anna Amalia's birthday on October 24 1784 Goethe uses the agreed name Lotte, and for this reason the letter was not suppressed; but he writes it in conscious contradiction with the facts of Frau von Stein's whereabouts. This letter shows Goethe's nervous state of mind towards the end of his first decade in Weimar. He tells his beloved on her birthday that the deception is dangerous to their relationship. Even if Frau von Stein had been in Weimar the letter of the 24 October would have appeared strange, for from 1776 to 1783 Goethe had either mentioned six of Anna Amalia's birthdays or joined in celebrations of them. Therefore in 1784 he could not have used his time at will, since Anna Amalia had invited all of the cultured circle to Tiefurt to celebrate her birthday. On 28 October 1784 Goethe wrote to the Duke: 'Your mother was happy and cheerful on 24 October. Every poetic plume had been active and all kinds of harmless little offerings were made.'[589] The editors of the Weimar edition have brought Goethe's letters, particularly most of the undated ones, into harmony with Frau von Stein's life, which had the effect of deepening the secret even further.

From 1784 onwards nearly every letter mentioned the name Lotte or L. A continual theme is that he is hoping she will return from Kochberg soon. In a letter to Knebel on 20 April 1785 Frau von Stein writes almost openly about the hopeless situation:

> It is strange that even as I receive your letter I have been thinking sadly to myself about the same subject. But, unfortunately, where our friend [Goethe] has given up hope, nothing can be changed because there *is* no hope, and a morally wrong measure [Takt] and tone are

> dominant in our system. But as a wise man he will in time come to terms with it.[590]

For Frau von Stein, who is hardly speaking of herself, nothing can be changed regarding Goethe's forbidden love. Nothing can be changed because of the 'morally wrong measure and tone' in the system.

Not until shortly before and during his flight to Italy do Goethe's letters again make reference to the secret. On 25 June 1786 he writes: 'I am revising my Werther and find that the writer was wrong in not shooting himself when he had finished writing it.' Something very serious must have happened, otherwise such a sentence written to the beloved cannot be explained. Anna Amalia was thought to be seriously ill at this time, and in May and June there seems to have been reason to fear for her life.[591] It is possible that Fritz, the 'traitor', had already indicated anonymously that he knew about Goethe's secret. On 9 July Goethe writes about the Weimar African affair – a solution for the problem of his forbidden love that must often have gone through his head. Councillor [for Mining] von Einsiedel (1754-1837), a brother of Anna Amalia's Chamberlain, after one failed Africa expedition in May 1785 started out on another in search of gold mines. At the same time news arrived in Weimar that the married Emilie von Werthern-Beichlingen (1757-1844) had died. The truth was that she had had a doll put in her coffin so that she could flee to Africa with Einsiedel. In Tunis they were forced by the plague to return home.[592] As early as 11 June 1785 Goethe wrote to Anna Amalia ('Frau von Stein') about indications that the Baroness was still alive:

> I wouldn't begrudge the little W[erthern] a dwelling place with her beloved in Africa rather than in the grave. I don't believe it. In this day and age such a decision is rather rare. We would also soon be reading about it in the newspapers.

When the 'African' Emilie returned to Weimar in 1795 Anna Amalia received her kindly and sympathetically. Frau von Stein wrote:

> Also the Duchess's [Anna Amalia] behaviour was special. She went to the Herders and summoned Einsiedel and there was more joy in the Father's house in heaven over the one sinner who did penance than over the thousand just.[593]

Goethe takes up the story on 9 July 1786 and says to his beloved:

> And now our refugees! How dreadful! To die, to go to Africa, to begin the strangest romance and to end in the most ordinary way by divorcing and marrying again. I found it terribly funny. In this work-a-day world nothing out of the ordinary can happen. I have the desire to tell you this and other stories, though I am never really in the mood for writing.

Goethe's and Anna Amalia's interest in the failed flight to Africa comes from the fact that they, too, were thinking of escaping together. Directly before Goethe's flight to Italy there are several mentions of this. On 16 August 1786 he says: 'You should always be with me, we should have a good life.' On 23 August 1786 the planned flight of the pair to America is touched on: 'And then [in a week] I will be living with you in the free world, and, in happy isolation and with no name and rank, come closer to the earth from which we are taken.' In a letter of 2 August 1815 Goethe confided to Boisserée that he had planned around this time to emigrate to America: 'What would have happened if I had gone to America with a few friends thirty years ago and had heard nothing of Kant etc?'[594] Carl August frustrated these plans. Goethe's flight with Anna Amalia would have had consequences for him and the tiny duchy. Furthermore, Carl August would have lost the two people whose advice and support he needed. For reasons of state he would also possibly have needed to condemn them publicly.

When during his stay in Karlsbad in August 1786 Goethe told Carl August of his love relationship with Anna Amalia and discussed his fears regarding Prussia and Count Görtz, Carl August insisted that his mother must stay in Weimar. On Goethe's birthday on 28 August Carl August left Karlsbad. A few days later, on 3 September 1786, Carl August's birthday, Goethe fled to Italy. In a letter to Carl August from Italy on 14 October 1786 Goethe refers back to this conversation:

> I can't tell you how strange I find it thinking about our time together in Karlsbad – that in your presence I had to give you an account of a large part of my past life and all that was connected with it.

For this reason, after his two-year sojourn in Italy he promised Carl August on 17 March 1788 regarding their future collaboration: ' ... I am coming ... My first and most important expression of gratitude has to be unconditional honesty [with you].' It follows that until this time he had been only conditionally honest.

It seems it was December before Anna Amalia found out where Goethe was. Carl August wrote to his mother on 14 December: 'At last you know where Goethe is staying. May the good gods accompany him. I wrote to him yesterday and asked him to stay away as long as he himself wanted to.' Goethe wrote to Anna Amalia ('Frau von Stein') from Rome on 23 December 1786:

> The fact that you were sick, sick through my fault, makes me sadder than I can say. Forgive me. I myself am struggling with death and life and no tongue can express what I was feeling. This fall has brought me to myself. My love! My love! ... Yours in life and death.

On 17 January 1787 Goethe writes to Anna Amalia ('Frau von Stein'): 'Since the death of my sister (1777) nothing has saddened me so much as the pain I caused you by my departure and silence.' In *Tasso* he refers to the poet's planned departure for Rome as 'the dark door of a long period of mourning' (ll. 2229). The circumstance that Tasso's secret love of the Princess has been discovered and that he therefore must leave makes him say (ll. 3370ff.):

> I feel my innermost self
> Shattered and I am alive to feel it.
> Despair attacks me in a full onslaught
> And hell's torture annihilates me.

It was Carl August who, like the Prince in *Tasso*, forbade any contact until further notice. Once they knew that there was no imminent danger Anna Amalia still had hopes for a future with her lover. Even in 1787 she wanted to follow him to Italy. When this plan failed she wanted him to stay on in Italy when she came there in 1788. But Goethe would not accept this either.

The deception regarding identity had been kept up for more than ten years. It was now no longer necessary. As can be seen from Goethe's diaries, because of their renunciation they can be together until the time of Anna Amalia's death, but their passionate love is turned into a special kind of friendship. With four letters in 1789, for the benefit of the public, Goethe ends his 'relationship' with Frau von Stein. The climax of these letters is a coffee scene in the second last of them on 1 June 1789. Goethe has to make the break seem plausible. After his return from Italy Goethe lived with Christiane Vulpius, which Frau von Stein is supposed to have found out only some months later, and that through her son Fritz, the 'traitor'. Fritz is supposed to have found that Christiane was in Goethe's house and immediately brought news of it to his mother, since, as his brother Carl said, he prided himself on being a guardian of morality.[595] While Frau von Stein, in the company of people at court, expressed her horror at the union between Christiane and Goethe, Goethe reproached her in four letters which this time were really addressed to her so that she could show them to her circle of friends:

> I hesitated ... to write because in such cases it is difficult to be honest and not to be hurtful ... I saw Herder and the Duchess [Anna Amalia] travel off. The seat in the coach which they had earnestly offered to me was empty. I stayed behind for the sake of my friends, just as I had come back for their sake, only to hear them persist in saying, at that very moment, that I should have stayed there ... It was something of a miracle that I should have lost the deepest, most intimate relationship with you. ... But I want to say that I cannot

> accept the way you have treated me until now. If I made conversation, you shut me up. When I was communicative you accused me of indifference. You examined every expression of mine, you criticized they way I move, my whole attitude. I would like to go on but I fear that in your frame of mind it would insult you rather than lead to reconciliation.

What follows now is the coffee scene:

> Unfortunately, for a long time now you have spurned my advice about coffee and followed a diet which is harmful to your health. As if it is not difficult enough to cope morally with certain moral impressions, you strengthen the power of hypochondria to plague you with its gloomy ideas by resorting to a physical means, the harmfulness of which you have known about for some time. For love of me you avoided it and felt the ensuing benefit. ... I do not entirely give up hope that you will once again know me properly. Good bye.

The comedy of this conclusion would be hard to beat. 'Coffee' featured in their relationship from the beginning. In May 1776 Goethe invited Frau von Stein to his garden house for coffee.[596] One commentator talks of a 'laughable, absurd detail',[597] another judges the 'extraordinarily strange letter' to be 'a deliberate insult'.[598] Considering that this is the reason for their separation, the relationship between Goethe and Frau von Stein can only be seen as 'symbolic',[599] a category deliberately designed to fit this supposed pair. Goethe, who sent coffee from Italy back to Weimar, staged this comical separation only for the benefit of the public. On 5 October 1786 he had written from Italy to Anna Amalia ('Frau von Stein'): 'Since I promised you coffee from Alexandria I'm sure you didn't think I would be getting it for you in Venice. I have enquired in different places and used the help of connoisseurs.' On 13 October he writes again:

> The first stage of my journey is over. May heaven bless the remaining ones and above all the last one, which will bring me back to you. I have put enclosures and drawings in the box which is to bring the coffee to you. It is the most exquisite Alexandrian coffee that is available here.

We know that Frau von Stein herself was in fits of laughter over the coffee scene. In her tragedy *Dido* (1794/95) she has the unfaithful Ogon [Goethe] make the following reproach to the faithful Elissa [Frau von Stein], which causes Elissa to laugh (p. 508):

> These false notions come from a drink which is injurious to you and which I always warned you against. Just enjoy the right spiritual product of the earth and you will soon learn to accept the fine image you have of me. Elissa: (*laughing*)

To make the separation between the 'lovers' believable Frau von Stein occasionally spoke badly about Christiane Vulpius. In this way, for the benefit of the gossip-loving Weimar society, she made visible her supposed sadness over the end of her relationship with Goethe; but in writing to those initiated into the secret she sounds in a relaxed and contented frame of mind, as when she writes to Knebel on 3 July 1790: 'The Duke has summoned Privy Councillor von Goethe to Silesia. No doubt he would prefer to be here with his little Christiane.'[600]

The need to keep up the deception with more and more lies was finally over in 1789. It was necessary, however, for Frau von Stein strenuously to keep up the act, since right up to her death attention was drawn to her as the former lover of Goethe and she was forced to act out the role. A report from Eduard J. d'Alton (1772-1840) to Knebel on 13 March 1810 about his visit to Goethe's former 'lover' gives an impression of how Frau von Stein treated such visits:

> My stay in this area is the most instructive of my life. Never have I been abused with such confidentiality as here. For example, the old Stein confided to me all her secrets because she thought her mistakes brought her honour. She complained about Goethe's unfaithfulness. He had promised to make her son in Breslau his heir, not to marry, and God knows what else.[601]

Part of Frau von Stein's artificial game was to show Goethe's letters to visitors who were interested in the indefinable love relationship. Charlotte von Kalb, for example, was very interested in making the acquaintance of the famous Frau von Stein. Herself unhappily married and since 1784 Schiller's lover, she moved to Weimar a few weeks after Goethe's flight to Italy in 1786. Frau von Kalb writes about her first meeting with Frau von Stein: 'Soon after I first saw her she showed me different things of Goethe's that were published later or that were not published at all ... Eagerly I read manuscripts, and also letters were entrusted to me.'[602] At first this exaggerated confidentiality suppressed any doubts. Especially convincing for Frau von Kalb were Goethe's words to Wieland in the spring of 1776, at a time when Goethe and Anna Amalia were trying to explain to him the supposed relationship to Frau von Stein in terms of the transmigration of souls:

> I can't explain the importance – the power this woman [Frau von Stein] has over me except through the transmigration of souls. – We were once man and wife! Now we know about one another – veiled, in a world of spirits. – I have no name for us – the past – the future – the cosmos.[603]

Goethe stretches to the point of satire the idea of reincarnation, a pet concept for Wieland, in order to convince him. This shows how focused and imaginative Goethe and Anna Amalia were in deceiving key figures in Weimar society. Wieland had warned his young poet colleague Goethe about entering a relationship with the married Frau von Stein. Caught up with the thought of the reincarnation, Wieland managed to show understanding for the strange pair with its indefinable bond. Frau von Kalb, on the other hand, was no longer convinced that there was a relationship between Goethe and Frau von Stein. Her view was that in *Tasso* the Duchess Luise and Frau von Stein were depicted in their relationship to Goethe. Her assumption was that Goethe had an illicit love for the Duchess Luise and that the lady-in-waiting, Frau von Stein, was presented as the lover – a front to protect the young Duchess.[604]

Frau von Stein acted similarly with Henriette von Egloffstein, who in her *Erinnerungen* writes about a visit in 1787:

> I thought it was impossible that the celebrated poet would not have looked for a younger and more beautiful lover [than Frau von Stein], but gradually this doubt disappeared when I visited her in her house and saw her there surrounded with nothing but mementos of her friend who was at that time living in Rome. She led me to a picture of him, read me his poetry, and tried to prejudice me in favour of him by the description of his lovable nature.

Later Henriette saw through Frau von Stein's deception: 'Now you would have to admire the skill with which this woman played her artificial game, so that even in later years she was thought to be Goethe's lover.'[605] Frau von Stein's artificial game convinced many uncritical visitors. In a letter of 2 November 1789 the writer Caroline von Lengefeld (1763-1847) writes to her future brother-in-law, Friedrich Schiller:

> During the last days of our time together I got on better with Stein. She had sunk into a quiet sadness about her relationship with Goethe and she seemed to me more true, more harmonious than in the unnatural mood of indifference or contempt. A tender relationship that has lasted twelve years cannot be dissolved into such hostile feelings.[606]

Even after the pretended love relationship was long since a thing of the past, friends wanted to see letters of Goethe's dating from this period, as, for example, Schiller's wife Charlotte (1766-1826), one of the closest friends of Frau von Stein. After persistent requests, Frau von Stein showed her some letters. Charlotte von Schiller wrote about them to Carl August's daughter Princess Caroline Luise (1786-1816) on 5 February 1812:

> I saw into the soul [durchblickte] of this wonderful human being [Frau von Stein] and lamented the fate of our friend ... How interesting the master was early on, how soft, how he loved, and how could it change! This nature is a mystery to me. How poor Charlotte had to suffer.[607]

From September 1796 Goethe resumed correspondence with Frau von Stein. The letters reflect the tone that was now dominant between them. There are forty-two letters, full of insignificant, brief exchanges. This continues until a letter of 18 April 1807 – Frau von Stein inserted the date herself. A change can be observed here. Anna Amalia had died on 10 April. From 18 April until December there are fourteen letters, some of them several pages long. Goethe gives the impression he needs support. In the first of the letters he writes: 'The drop in the barometer has taken revenge on my lack of faith by signalling a great misfortune. From two days ago until yesterday I had an attack as bad as any so far.' Johanna Schopenhauer (1766-1838) writes to her son on 28 April: 'Disaster has hovered over us ... Goethe has been close to death.'[608] Goethe had nearly followed his deceased beloved. On 24 May 1807 Goethe writes to Frau von Stein about her son Fritz's visit to him in Jena. Around this time Goethe began dictating his autobiographical novel *Wilhelm Meisters Wanderjahre oder die Entsagenden*. (The 'betrayal' by Fritz had been the catalyst for the renunciation.) In the letter he says about Fritz: 'I found his good, natural, steady, intelligent, and cheerful attitude refreshing. He showed me again that the world is only as you take it.' On 25 May 1807 Goethe left unusually early for Karlsbad. Carl August followed his friend on 6 June, announcing:

> It is not likely that between now and the first six weeks anything is likely to happen that would absolutely demand my presence here ... so I have decided to leave and hope to arrive in Karlsbad on Saturday evening.

According to Goethe's diary, many conversations with Carl August took place.

Frau von Stein's letters to Goethe after 1796 show that she was unable to find a personal tone in writing to her Olympian friend. She addressed him usually with 'lieber Geheimderath' [his official title], or 'allerbester liebenswürdiger Geheimderath' [adding 'dearest, kindest' to the title] or 'lieber bester verehrter Meister' [dear best esteemed Master], but only seldom with 'dear Goethe', which is the very least one might expect from a former lover.

After Frau von Stein had attended a performance of *Tasso* on 20 March 1811 she wrote a note to Goethe that evening to tell him that she found the piece 'ever more heavenly' and signed herself not 'Your Lotte' but 'Your loyal admirer von Stein'. This is not the woman Goethe immortalized in Tasso's Princess. Her role is that of the lady-in-waiting, Leonore Sanvitale. It is different with Anna Amalia. The few extant letters to Goethe give evidence of a complete equality. A letter of 1793 closes with the very personal 'Addio Amalie';[609] another from the year 1806 closes with 'I wish you a very good day. Amalia'.[610] In a letter of 1798 she writes: 'I will come with great pleasure to the opening of the theatre on Sunday. Enjoy the fine weather. Amalie.'[611] In 1801 the Princess turns to Goethe as Theatre Director in support of one of her protégés:

> Forgive me, dear Goethe, if I repeat my request regarding Kappelmeister Kranz. I have spoken with him ... I rely completely on your friendship, which gives me hope, dear Goethe, that you will give deep consideration to my request and wishes and will thereby make me infinitely indebted to you. Your true friend Amalie.[612]

On 25 December 1815 Goethe sends Frau von Stein a poem which ends with the lines: 'I who, as before, am as far away as the sun,/In silence love, suffer, and learn'. On 28 August 1826 Goethe adds to the poem 'Den Freunden' some personal lines for Frau von Stein:

> The enclosed poem, my dearest, should really close with: 'To see the affection and love of two people living as next-door neighbours endure through so many [changing] times is the most sublime thing that can be granted to a human being.' And so on forever and ever!

Neighbourly affection and love defines the relationship between Goethe and Frau von Stein – but they were also as far from one another as they were from the sun. In her last letter to Goethe on 28 August 1826, when her death was not far off, she signs herself 'Charlotte von Stein, née von Schardt'. As if struggling to free herself from the burden of her secret, she expressly directed that her funeral procession should not pass by Goethe's house but should take another route. Her directive was not followed.[613] After her death Goethe hardly mentions her. In a letter of 13 March 1827 to the trustee of her bequest Goethe asked to be given back a folder containing his own drawings. In it he refers to the deceased 'Frau Oberstallmeister von Stein', and later in the letter he refers to her as his 'noble friend'.[614] Carl August summed it up in 1828: 'Frau von Stein was a very good woman, but not a shining light.'[615]

12 | Frau von Stein's Literary Works

> I obeyed you, otherwise I would have moved away
> From her instead of, as you wished, approaching.
> Lovable as she may appear,
> I don't know what it is, I could only seldom
> Speak openly with her; and even when she plans
> To be of service to her friends
> You sense the plan and feel estranged.
>   Tasso to the Princess in *Tasso* (1790), ll. 963ff.

> Silence has done more good than telling the whole truth ...
>   Charlotte von Stein, *Die Zwey Emilien* [The Two Emilies] *(1803)*

Frau von Stein's literary work opens a special perspective on the forbidden love. The four works of hers that are still extant – a story and a comedy are considered lost – serve for the most part to portray the tragic love between Goethe and Anna Amalia. Frau von Stein found herself in the middle of it and her help was to be invaluable.

In the play *Rino* (1776), comprising sixty-six lines, there are four women and Rino (Goethe). Adelhaite (Anna Amalia) says to the other women, among them Gerthrude (Frau von Stein):

> My friend [Goethe] comes to me today
> And he's not for you, nor you, nor you.
> I want him for myself alone,
> And you can only watch.

Anna Amalia's attraction to Goethe, referred to here, did not remain unnoticed at the Weimar court. But Frau von Stein was immediately identified as Goethe's beloved. Duchess Luise's lady-in-waiting von Wöllwarth claims that Goethe moved away from Anna Amalia. In a letter of 9 July 1781 she writes to Countess Görtz:

> Grandmother's (Anna Amalia) heart is bleeding because her idol, the poet, plans to leave her with a view to coming closer than ever to the divine Lotte. It is unbelievable that this love is lasting so long, because she is ageing visibly.[616]

In the winter of 1794/95 Frau von Stein wrote the *Dido* tragedy which was forty-five pages in length. Queen Dido is the mythical founder of the city of Carthage immortalized in Virgil's (BC 70-19) *Aeneid* (from BC 19) as the 'Dido, radiating beauty'. In Frau von Stein's version Dido commits suicide because she rejects a marriage of convenience with the African King Jarbes who, unless she marries him, threatens to take Carthage by force of arms.[617] Despite Schiller's encouragement to have the play published, *Dido did* not appear until 1867.[618] It was only passed around within her circle of friends. The play became known to a certain extent because of the figures Elissa and the poet Ogon, who represented Frau von Stein and Goethe. The belittling portrayal of Ogon was interpreted as a sign of Frau von Stein's bitterness over the supposed separation from Goethe (1789). Frau von Stein confirmed the official version of her love story with Goethe. Ogon says: ' ... you know that I once loved you. It is hard to speak the truth without being hurtful, but human nature is like a snake: an old skin has to be shed after many years! In my case that has happened.'[619] Frau von Stein wrote this confirmation for the benefit of the Weimar gossip. In *Dido* the relationship between Elissa (Frau von Stein) and Queen Dido is crucial. Dido stands for the Princess Anna Amalia, who read the *Aeneid* in the original. While living in Italy the Princess mentions Virgil's *Aeneid* in the third of her *Fünf Briefe Über Italien*. In a letter to Knebel of 29 May 1789 she writes: ' ... dear Knebel, read the sixth canto of Virgil's *Aeneid*. You will find everything in it that I have almost constantly before my eyes.'[620] Frau von Stein characterizes herself, through Elissa, as a loyal companion of Queen Dido (Anna Amalia): 'I will follow you, even into the underworld;' 'Dear friend, as I only live for you'.

> **Queen:** Are you ready to depart?
> **Elissa:** Ready for everything, wherever you lead me.[621]

In this way the lady-in-waiting von Stein justifies herself for lending her name to the cover-up of the love relationship of her Princess: her motive was unconditional loyalty to her Princess.

The forty-page-long comedy *Neues Freiheitssystem oder Die Verschwörung Gegen die Liebe* (1798) deals in code with the state secret. Not published until 1867, the play had little public resonance. Since people had no knowledge of the forbidden love, the work could only be seen as autobiography. The play has four scenes switching between a German spa and a Schloss Buchdorf. Two actresses, Luitgarde and Florine, are mistaken for two noble ladies, Theodora and Menonda. Daval, the brother of Menonda, tries fanatically to rid the world of love. He is the owner of the Junker property Buchdorf (Book Village), a satirical reference to the small Weimar duchy, in which only printed products achieved economic success. Attempts to develop new sources of income through special methods of field cultivation and cattle raising, through mining ventures or the introduction of industry failed sooner or later. But it was different with books and newspapers, for along with Goethe, Schiller, Wieland, Musäus, and Herder there were other writers in Weimar. August von Kotzebue (1761-1819), a son of Anna Amalia's secretary, wrote around 200 plays. Christian August Vulpius wrote, along with numerous versions of plays for the stage, about sixty entertaining novels, among them the successful robber novel *Rinaldo Rinaldini* (1791). Weimar had other writers to show, including Schiller's sister-in-law Karoline von Wolzogen (1763-1847), who wrote a successful novel *Agnes von Lilien* (1798).

Daval, the owner of Buchdorf, stands for Duke Carl August. His marriage to Luise was unhappy. His numerous extramarital relationships became a state problem, not least because of the many illegitimate children.[622] Charlotte von Stein's comedy is written at a time when Carl August had a love relationship with two singers. The first was with Luise Rudorff (1777-1852) who was engaged as a chamber singer in Weimar on the basis of a recommendation written by Anna Amalia's unfortunate sister, Elisabeth Christine Ulrike.[623] Knebel married Luise in 1798 after she had borne Carl August an illegitimate son. In his story *Die Fee Urganda* Lenz had portrayed Knebel as a misogynist who hated the 'very vivacious beautiful sex with its make-up and frippery'.[624] In a gentle way Luise Rudorff had attracted Knebel's attention. After the opera *The Marriage of Figaro* staged by Goethe on 24 October 1793 for Anna Amalia's birthday, Anna Amalia issued invitations to a small evening meal. At Goethe's suggestion Luise repeated arias, took the blushing Knebel by the hand and sang a magical 'In every place I'll be at your side'.[625] Knebel's marriage to Luise was also a reproach to Carl August because he became the father of Carl August's illegitimate son Carl Wilhelm (1796-1861). In Knebel's eyes, Carl August, through his sexual excesses, abused his position as ruler of the land, without concern for the horrendous consequences for the young women and their illegitimate children. This resulted in a cooling of the relationship between Carl August and Knebel.[626] When Carl Wilhelm von Knebel, through an indiscretion, found out decades later who his real father was he is said to have been shattered.[627]

After Luise Rudorff, Karoline Jagemann, the daughter of Anna Amalia's librarian, became Carl August's favourite. When a position in the opera became vacant which Anna Amalia wanted given to Luise Rudorff, Carl August insisted that the post be given to his new flame Karoline. She had made her first successful appearance in Weimar in 1797 and was to become an important actress and opera singer. In 1798, when Frau von Stein was writing her play, it was clear that only through a quasi marital relationship with Karoline could Carl August be dissuaded from indulging in a succession of love affairs and sexual excesses. For the good of the state Carl August's wife Luise approved the relationship and is supposed to have made a written agreement.[628] The Duke had several children by Karoline, who since 1809 had the title von Heygendorf.[629] But she was continually made to feel the illegitimacy of her position. Frau von Stein writes in a letter to her son Fritz on 29 May 1812 that the words 'Sachsen Weimarsches Bordell' [Saxon Weimar brothel] were written on the walls of Karoline's house.[630] One of the two marriages at the end of Frau von Stein's comedy allude to this love relationship: the one between Luitgarde and Daval. The second marriage relates to Goethe and Anna Amalia. Daval (Carl August) intrigued against the imperial captain of the cavalry Avelos (Goethe), for Avelos was madly in love with Menonda (Anna Amalia). He received a letter from her, forged by Daval, which spoke of their love being an error. 'This letter drove me out of my fatherland and made me unhappy for many years.' Asked where Menonda was, Daval replied: 'I have heard nothing from her for a long time. She, too, left her fatherland.'[631] This creates the link to Goethe and Anna Amalia, since they too went to Italy, each of them for twenty-two months. Daval falsified the letter for 'reasons of a higher order'.[632] In Frau von Stein's view, the separation of the lovers was due not to her son Fritz but to reasons of state.

A further encoding in the comedy is the seemingly gratuitous naming of five books and a manuscript in Daval's library.[633] Of these, some really exist and others have fictional titles. Regarding the manuscript, named as the fourth work, we read: 'Menonda (*takes a manuscript out of a book. Silent amazement*): *Poems of A. G. T.* – Strange, how did you get here, dearest of all handwriting. You were my property, I take you back. (*She tucks the poems away*). The letters A. G. T. stand for Amalia – Goethe – Tasso. Frau von Stein is referring to *Tasso* as representation of a forbidden love. At the end of the comedy Avelos and Menonda are reunited and can now enjoy happiness together, but Frau von Stein has one of the characters say: 'Live happily, Hector and Andromache.'[634] In Greek mythology Achilles drove a lance through Hector's throat (*Iliad*, XXII, ll. 319ff.) and then dragged him several times around the grave of his friend Patroclus whom Hector had previously killed (XXIV, ll. 755f.). His wife Andromache had been carried off with her child into slavery (XXIV, ll. 731ff.). This 'live happily' wish has no meaning in the play. On the contrary it points to profound unhappiness for the pair. Something similar would have happened if the middle-class Goethe had married a Princess. Goethe was, of course, raised to the rank of nobility but on the lowest rung, which would in no way have justified a union with a Princess. A public union would have been seen as an affront to the monarchy, a main pillar of which was the bequeathing of power only to the few families that belonged to the higher nobility. According to Frau von Stein, a cruel fate would have awaited Goethe for his presumption, a warning that the social divisions in a monarchy, the separation between the 'two worlds', was to be seen as deadly serious. Anna Amalia would have suffered a sad fate similar to that of Andromache – probably, like her sister Elisabeth Christine Ulrike, banishment.

Attempts to challenge the rigid barriers of the higher nobility often had a tragic end. In 1435, Agnes Bernauer, who had secretly married Prince Albrecht III (1401-1460), was sacrificed to the dynastic interests of Bavaria. Her father-in-law had her drowned in the Danube to make way for his son to marry a person of appropriate social rank.[635] Since then the tragic fate of the barber's daughter has fascinated artists and historians, who have interpreted her as a witch, a whore, or a saint.

The sister of Anna Amalia's sister-in-law Karoline Mathilde, Queen of Denmark, was banned for ignoring the monarchical barriers. Her mentally ill husband had, in 1769, sent for the German doctor Johann Friedrich Struensee, who brought him some relief in his suffering. The doctor fell in love with Mathilde. From 1771, as Count von Struensee, he was the Minister in charge of administrative affairs and introduced reforms such as the abolition of torture and of censorship of the press. In 1772 he fell from power and, since he had had a child with the Queen, was executed.[636]

When Duke Ulrich von Sachsen-Meiningen married the lady's-maid Philippine Cäsarea Schurmann, a Hessian Captain's daughter, who bore him two sons (1716/17), Emperor Charles VI refused to recognize them as legitimate successors to the Duke. After tough negotiations between the chancelleries, the Emperor yielded and granted:

> in 1727 the requested elevation in rank, but with the added warning to avoid such mis-marriages in future; but in 1744 Emperor Charles VII declared the marriage a real misalliance and the children issuing from it as incapable of succeeding to the noble imperial fiefs, land, and people. And this is how it remained.[637]

We have another example in the Prince of the Empire Carl Anselm von Thurn und Taxis who, as principal deputy, represented the Emperor at the Imperial Diet in Regensburg.[638] His first wife, the Württemberg Princess Augusta Elisabeth, had made three attempts on his life. In the last attempt she also wanted to poison her brother, the Swabian Duke Karl Eugen, the Prince who forced Schiller to emigrate from the Duchy. Carl Anselm's wife was banished and virtually imprisoned, and after her death he married Elisabeth Hillebrand, a woman of the middle classes. She was elevated to the nobility, but the delegates of the Imperial Diet in Regensburg protested vehemently against this union. The reason they gave was that Elisabeth Hillebrand had been a prostitute.[639] The delegates themselves, with few exceptions (among them Count Görtz), together with their wives, were all involved in sexual excesses. When Napoleon dissolved the Imperial Diet in 1806 he called it 'a house of apes, ridiculous and full of bestial malice'.[640] In any case, Elisabeth Hillebrand was not accepted as their peer. The marriage failed and she was banished.

Frau von Stein consciously sets up parallels between the pairs Anna Amalia and Goethe, and Karoline Jagemann and Carl August. Though Karoline was Carl August's 'second wife' for about thirty years and lived with him, they were not able to appear officially as a couple.[641] The situation with Goethe and Anna Amalia was even more dramatic, for even their friends and nearest relatives were not to have an inkling of their relationship.

The comedy in five acts, *Die Probe* (1809), attributed to Frau von Stein, was long thought to have disappeared. Thanks to progressive digitalization of library holdings a copy has in the meantime been found in the Netherlands. As far as can be seen, the play is a translation from the English by Carl von Stein and deals with mistaken identity and disguise.

The question remains why Frau von Stein wrote literary works depicting her relationship to the secret lovers. The Steins were always short of money and deeply in debt. The education of their children was a financial problem because their country estate in Kochberg was badly managed. After her husband died in 1793 Frau von Stein lived on a small salary, which Duchess Luise supplemented.[642]

Fritz von Stein, who for a long time was thought to be Goethe's heir,[643] had apparently rejected the offer of a paid position in Weimar and went first to an unsalaried post in Breslau, where his career prospects became increasingly poorer. This was partly due to his limited ability. Goethe's friend, Wilhelm von Humboldt (1767-1835), who had sent for Fritz to help him with the reform of the Prussian education system, was soon disappointed with him:

> Stein is a very good man but he is only moderately useful when it comes to work ... hardly anything he does is sound. It always has to be changed, and one doesn't know where to start because it really ought to be all crossed out.[644]

His brother Carl von Stein frivolously threw away the favour of his patrons in Braunschweig and, as a student, lived beyond his means. 500 Thaler a year were not enough for the twenty-year-old. At this time many country school-masters had to manage on a yearly income of twenty-five to fifty Thaler.[645] The famous writer Gotthold Ephraim Lessing was employed by Anna Amalia's father as librarian in Wolfenbüttel for a salary of 300 Thaler per annum.[646] But Carl von Stein took it for granted that, as a student, he could live expansively. He was also the father of an illegitimate son.[647] Goethe was the one asked to write the student 'a long letter to chastise and warn him'.[648] And when the careers of the brothers of Frau von Stein faltered and they were passed over for promotion, Charlotte turned to Goethe, asking him to intercede with the Duke. Carl von Stein was not capable of managing the Kochberg property successfully, although he was involved with it full-time as lord of the manor, feudal lord, and magistrate. He took on the obligation of buying out, over a period of time, his brother Fritz's share in the property for 40,500 Thaler. This brought his debts to 101,000 Thaler[649] – more than the value of the entire property. During her work on *Neues Freiheitssystem* (1798) Frau von Stein wrote to her son:

> [Frau] Wolzogen is giving me strong encouragement to do it and describes to me her blissful feeling and new enthusiasm when she sees the many Louis d'or for her writings counted up and lying on her table ... So I would have a means of income if the French chase us away or the brothers Stein go bankrupt.[650]

Whereas Frau von Stein had strictly refused to have this work, or earlier, her *Dido*, printed, in a crisis situation she wanted to use them to have access to not inconsiderable funds. When French soldiers plundered Weimar in October 1806 Frau von Stein in fact lost 'just about everything of value'.[651] However, when her son Fritz was facing bankruptcy in 1808 she was able to come to his rescue.[652] According to her will in 1808 she had jewellery, books and 'beds, linen, silver, furniture and porcelain ... clothes, underclothes, lace etc'.[653] The losses sustained by the French plundering two years previously had been quickly recouped, which could be explained by special aid coming from the Ducal family.

Through her writings, Frau von Stein must have emphatically drawn the Ducal family's attention to her deserts. The well-being of her family was at stake. The fate of loyal ladies-in-waiting when they were no longer needed is seen from the treatment of Luise von Göchhausen, who was in Anna Amalia's service for over thirty years. After the death of Anna Amalia (1807) she was dependent on a small pension. When she was required to move from her attic room in the Wittumspalais to an apartment in the 'Schweins Marckt' she was deeply upset and worried about her ability to pay for it. On 13 July 1807 she writes in one of her last letters:

> In general I am afraid that my new domestic situation bears similarity with the battle of Jena, which, according to people in the know, was lost three days before it was fought. I am afraid I am looking at bankruptcy before I begin to try to manage.

Shortly before her planned move to the 'Schweins Marckt' she died.

In addition to the motif of loyalty and the protection of justified interests there is another: Frau von Stein is not certain that the deception of so many people through the use of her name was right. She looks for ways of justifying her own actions. In her novel *Die Zwei Emilien* (1803), the reworking of an English text (1798), we read sentences like: 'Silence has done more good than pure truth',[654] or the words with which the novel ends: 'So we can only find happiness when we can give ourselves an account of our deep innocence.'[655] The novel is 142 pages long. Frau von Stein has simplified the action of the novel by comparison with the English original. Only in two scenes does she use words directly from the original; otherwise the whole dialogue of the novel, which is set in Naples, stems from her pen.[656] What is striking here is the motif of mistaken identity and disguise as the central theme of the action. A distinction has to be made between truth on paper – because the hero has married the wrong Emilia by mistake – and inner truth, the love for the right Emilia: the second one, the 'beautiful soul' [schöne Seele]. A fantastic piece of jewellery is introduced in the first half of the story. At a masked ball the wrong Emilia wears the jewellery which really belongs to the right Emilia, who, however, has been forced by blackmail to relinquish it.[657]

> No Princess here has such brilliant jewellery, not even the Queen. Other young ladies would show off with it differently. When I was bringing it back from the jeweller half the town was in his house to see it.[658]

The talk of jewellery and precious stones for jewellery is reminiscent of the fabulous diamond necklace in the Paris necklace affair. In this way Frau von Stein is offering an important pointer to the Weimar state secret.

In his comedy *Der Grosskophta* (1791) Goethe treated the material of the necklace affair (1785), introduced into it the story of his own forbidden love, and represented himself as a better swindler than the infamous Count Cagliostro (1743-1795). Count Cagliostro, in reality Giuseppe Balsamo, was an imposter from Palermo, who progressed from adventurer to miraculous healer and head of the Freemasons. He played a dubious role in the necklace affair and was also arrested. During his sojourn in Sicily Goethe visited his family in Palermo (13/14 April 1787). In doing this he was himself a deceiver, for he tells one lie after another. To gain entry to the family, which is living very privately, he pretends to be an Englishman, maintains that he is bringing news and a greeting from Cagliostro from London. He says he is prepared to have a letter delivered to Cagliostro. When asked whether Cagliostro really rejects his family in Palermo, he replies that with 'friends and acquaintances he makes no secret of the fact'. Referring to Cagliostro as 'one of the strangest monsters', Goethe leaves room for further monsters, above all, himself, because his genius had to put itself in the service of a finely wrought deception. With the title Grosskophta Goethe is referring to himself. This can be seen from the fact that, when Goethe was writing the play Count Cagliostro had long since become a tragic figure. In the necklace court-case he was pronounced innocent, and from London he found his way by a circuitous route to Rome, but when the French Revolution broke out the Ecclesiastical State made an example of him as a secret conspirator, and the 'arch heretic' was condemned to death by the Inquisition. Anna Amalia's librarian Jagemann translated the Roman records of the trial into German (1791). Pope Pius VI commuted Cagliostro's death penalty to life imprisonment, and there he died in 1795 in unclear circumstances.

Goethe's comedy *Der Grosskophta* is set immediately before the beginning of the French Revolution. Goethe makes a connection between the epoch-making political changes and the crisis of the Christian teaching of redemption,[659] for only the presumptuousness of Cardinal Rohan as the highest Church dignitary under the Pope made it possible for the necklace affair to happen at all. For Goethe this was the breeding ground of the French Revolution. When critics found fault with the play for being too loosely structured and lacking in tension, Goethe mockingly wrote in his *Kampagne in Frankreich* (1822) in the entry for November 1792 and thinking of the long years of deception: 'I enjoy a certain malicious satisfaction when people whom I have seen often enough exposed to deception rashly maintain that a person cannot be *so* grossly deceived.

In Goethe's *Grosskophta*, as also in Weimar, the deceit does not result in public scandal. In the play, the vain struggle to be virtuous plays an important part as it did with Goethe in the early days of his forbidden love for Anna Amalia. Thus the niece does try, in the Venushain, to play the Princess, but she has already been seduced by the husband of the Countess who cheated the Cardinal. The noble knight also finally betrays his friends and his brothers in the Lodge and in this way opens up excellent career opportunities for himself. The play ends with a scene similar to that at the end of *Tasso* where the poet embraces the Princess. The arrested Canon, who stands for Cardinal Rohan – but also for Goethe, insofar as he desires a woman he is not allowed to have – will say at the end of the play:

> Still less will they tear out of my heart the passion I feel for my Princess ... Tell her that all the humiliations are nothing compared to the pain I feel at having to go even further away from her ... but her image and [my] hope will never leave my heart as long as I live.

Since both plays end with a Princess scene they have a complementary function. There is no question of parody.[660] Goethe's challenge to look at the play more carefully holds good for today. In the poem 'Künstlers Fug und Recht' (1792) he wrote with reference to the critics of his comedy:

> It was his wish and his intention
> To make us think [Dass man dabei was denken sollt].

13| Love Poetry: Belonging to One Alone

This evening she gives me more pleasure; before the firewood
Burns down low and ashes begin to form
My dear girl comes to me. Then the twigs and logs catch fire
And the heated night becomes for us a brilliant feast.
She is busy in the early morning, rises up from love's bed
And from the ashes stokes the flames anew.
Römische Elegien (1790), IX

One turns into many,
Is thousandfold, and ever, ever dearer.
'Elegie' (1823)

At midnight the shining stars lead me
In a lovely dream to the threshhold where she sleeps
O may it be possible for me to rest there too!
However it is with life, it is good.
'Der Bräutigam' (1828)

From 1775 onwards Goethe's love poetry speaks of his forbidden love for Anna Amalia. The high points are, along with individual poems, *Tasso* (1780-1790), the *Römische Elegien* (1788-1790), *Pandora* (1807), the *Sonettenkranz* (1807/08), the *West-Östlicher Divan* (1814-1819), the *Trilogie der Leidenschaft* (1823/24), and the *Dornburger Trilogie* (1828). In the *Römische Elegie* XIII Amor, the god of Love says to him (l.3f.): 'You have dedicated your life and writing – I gratefully acknowledge – to my honour.' Amor later adds: 'Where do you find material for your song? I have to give it to you, and only love teaches you the higher style.' When Goethe begins to write a love poem, it is for one woman alone and he repeatedly makes this clear.

The *Römische Elegien* were written between the autumn of 1788 and the spring of 1790, more or less during the time that Anna Amalia was away in Italy. Anna Amalia is the first of two women celebrated in the poems. Since her real meaning for Goethe's life was not known, until now it has generally been thought that the poet was celebrating either Christiane or Roman women. One commentator referred to a 'strange, confusing game that the poet plays with the reader'.[661] On closer inspection it is possible to see that the women in the elegies are clearly identifiable. The elegies look back at the decade of Goethe's early love for Anna Amalia. 'Elegy XVIII', however, refers to Christiane Vulpius, whom Goethe calls Faustine. Traditionally an elegy is a 'poem of lament, sadness, and melancholy over the loss, the passing, or decline of something'.[662] After their Italian journeys Goethe and Anna Amalia face one another as lovers who have had to renounce their physical love because of the social system.

Goethe's model for the *Elegien* is Propertius (c.50-16 BC). On Anna Amalia's birthday on 24 October 1788 Knebel gave Goethe a copy of the love poems of the Roman lyric poets Catullus, Tibullus, and Propertius. These were generally published in one volume, which is why they were known as the three-leafed clover. Catullus had taken as his model the Greek poetry of the Hellenistic period. Building on this, Tibullus and Propertius created the classical form of the Roman elegy. On 25 October Goethe writes thanking Knebel: 'Thanks for the trio of poets. I didn't have them until now.' In a letter, also on 25 October, Luise von Göchhausen writes to Knebel from Rome: 'She [Anna Amalia] sends you her warm greetings and is soon going to write to you herself.' On Anna Amalia's birthdays nothing happened by chance in the circle of those who were initiated into the state secret. So Knebel could have been responding to Anna Amalia's wish to give the volume of poems to Goethe to inspire him to write elegies celebrating their physical love: 'How happy we once were/ they now need to know through you', Goethe writes in introducing the *Elegien*. Anna Amalia herself occasionally translated ancient poets into German, as, for example, Bion (2nd century BC) and Theocritus (3rd century BC). She especially liked to work at translating the *Elegies* of Propertius,[663] because this was the form in which she herself had been celebrated by Goethe.

Because Carl August feared that the *Elegien* could reveal the forbidden love, he did not want them published. At the very least they should be revised.[664] Some contemporaries were outraged over what they saw as the 'whore-house nakedness' in the *Elegien*.[665] Carl August cannot really have been upset by this. In this context Frau von Stein makes the sarcastic comment: 'I don't understand how our gracious

Lord could, even for a moment, have been subject to this attack of moral pedantry.'[666] For Goethe, Rome is only the backdrop he uses to disguise the fact that he is writing about Weimar. One of Goethe's means of keeping the secret is to awake the impression that the *Elegien* concern events he experienced in Rome, which is why he initially calls them *Erotica Romana*.

From 'Elegie I' to 'Elegie XVII' Goethe celebrates Anna Amalia. He says of her in 'Elegie III': 'Beloved, don't regret that you gave yourself to me so quickly!/Believe me, I don't think of you as forward or cheap.' Shortly after Anna Amalia, scarcely thirty-six years old, was freed of the duties she performed as Regent for nearly twenty years in the Duchy, Goethe, the chief *Stürmer und Dränger*, arrived in Weimar like a volcano of passion continuously erupting. Anna Amalia, like the Princess in *Tasso*, must have immediately succumbed to the charms of the young poet (ll. 1891ff.):

> First I said to myself, keep away from him!
> I withdrew, withdrew, only to come closer,
> So charmingly attracted.

When the poet Johann W.L. Gleim (1719-1803), who modelled himself on the Greek poet Anacreon (6th century BC) and wrote about love, wine, and nature, visited Weimar in the summer of 1777, he was invited by Anna Amalia to an evening gathering. Gleim was reading from his *Göttinger Musenalmanach* when a young man offered to give him a rest. This young man suddenly read after a while

> poems which were not at all in the Almanac. He moved through all possible keys and melodies. Hexameters, iambs, doggerel, and whatever came to mind, everything mixed up and in no order, as if he was just shaking it out [of his sleeve]. What didn't he produce with his fine humour and fantasy on this evening!

The enthusiastic Gleim called out to Wieland: 'That is either Goethe or the devil!', to which Wieland replied: 'Both'.[667]

The poet's imagination was inexhaustible when it came to impressing Anna Amalia. On 22 August 1778, for example, he issued invitations to an evening beside the Ilm after a discussion at Anna Amalia's Court of Muses about the effect of light in the paintings of Rembrandt.[668] Wieland reports to Merck on 27 August 1778:

> Last Saturday we drove out to Goethe who had invited the Duchess [Anna Amalia] to an evening in his garden to regale her with all the poems he had produced on the banks of the Ilm during her absence. We dined in a very charming hermitage ... we drank a bottle of 1760s Johannisberger, and then as we stood up and the doors opened, behold we were greeted with a sight created by the secret arts of the

> arch-magician [Goethe] which resembled more an artistically created vision than a natural scene. The whole bank of the Ilm [was] lit up exactly à la Rembrandt, a wonderful magic mixture of light and dark, the general effect of which beggars description. The Duchess [Anna Amalia] was as delighted as we all were ... Out of sheer love I could have eaten Goethe.[669]

Anna Amalia wrote to Goethe's mother on 29 August 1778:

> In the past week Dr Wolf [Goethe] gave a supper for me in the Stern where the new building improvements have been done. They are nice, glorious. After the evening meal there was a small illumination quite in Rembrandt's taste, where the whole effect was light and shade.[670]

In 'Elegie IV' ll. 29ff. we read about the beloved:

> And I didn't mistake her, caught her as she hurried by,
> Gently, docilely she returned my kiss and embrace.
> O how happy I was! – But hush, that time is past.'

In 'Elegie V' ll. 11ff. we read:

> If by day my beloved steals from me some hours,
> By night she gives me hours in recompense
> It's not just that we kiss, we have sensible discussions;
> When sleep overtakes her I lie there thinking a lot.
> I have often composed in her arms
> And with my fingers tapped the hexameter's metre
> On her back.

He could have good discussions about his poetry with Anna Amalia who, as a fine connoisseur of the classics, could stimulate his creativity. In 'Elegie VI' Goethe is clearer, for his beloved is a widow. Frau von Stein made an ironical comment about this in a letter to Charlotte Schiller of 27 July 1795: 'In this one [elegy], the sixth, there was something resembling inner feeling.'[671] In this elegy there are the words (ll. 3ff.):

> If the people accuse me, I must accept it! And am I
> Indeed not guilty?
> But still, I am only guilty with you!
> These clothes are witnesses to the envious neighbour,
> That the widow is no longer lonely, weeping for her husband.

In the elegy the widow refers to two famous names from Roman noble families who had been seeking her favour. Since these families really existed, people saw in the elegy slanderous statements by Goethe;[672] but Goethe used these only as a Roman equivalent to the high German aristocracy. In 'Elegie VIII' there is a further link:

> When you tell me, beloved, that as a child, you were not liked
> And that your very mother spurned you
> Until you grew up and quietly developed, I believe it:
> I like to think of you as a special child.
> Shape and colour are missing from the vine
> When the grapes have matured and been a delight to men and the gods.

This description refers to Anna Amalia's statements in her autobiographical writing *Meine Gedanken* found in Goethe's bequest: 'Not loved by my parents, always pushed back, second to my brothers and sisters in every respect, I was called a reject of nature.' Anna Amalia was, therefore, the lovely girl who comes in the evening to the poet ('Elegie IX' ll. 5ff.). After a newly enkindled flame of love the lovers have to part again so as not to be discovered. 'Elegie X' ll. 1ff. shows the quality of his 'girl':

> Alexander and Caesar and Heinrich and Friedrich, the Great Ones,
> Would gladly give me half of the renown they attained
> If I could grant them but one night each in this bed.

Friedrich is not the Prussian King Friedrich II, Anna Amalia's uncle,[673] who was not interested in women, but Emperor Friedrich II of Sicily (1194-1250), one of the most outstanding figures in European history. For him and the other outstanding rulers the 'girl' would be so desirable that they would gladly give half of the 'renown they attained' to spend a night with her. A woman because of whom he would be the envy of the great men of history would not only have to be beautiful and loyal but great herself. This cannot be Christiane Vulpius or an unknown Roman woman. On 25 January 1787 he wrote to Anna Amalia ('Frau von Stein') from Rome: 'I had to laugh about the warning of Franckenberg [a friend who was Minister in Gotha] not to fall in love here: you have only one rival here, and I will bring her back with me for you: the colossal head of Juno.' Juno, the highest Roman goddess, is the only woman in Rome on the same level as Anna Amalia, for only an elevated being can be competition for her. One lover of the rulers mentioned is still known to us today: Cleopatra (69-30 BC), Queen of Egypt (47-30 BC), who had a relationship with Caesar and later with his successor Mark Antony (c. 82-30). Goethe compares Anna Amalia with women such as these. His very motto 'All for Love' with which they sealed their love letters is reminiscent of John Dryden's (1631-1700) *All for Love* (1678), one of the few representations of Cleopatra as a deeply devoted lover.

In 'Elegie XV' there is an important sign that further helps to identify the lover. In a Roman inn he meets her in the company of her uncle (ll. 14ff.):

> She spoke louder than Roman women here, decanted,
> Turned her gaze on me, poured, and missed the glass.
> Wine poured over the table, and she, with a delicate finger,
> Drew on the wooden surface circles in the dampness.
> She swallowed my name up with hers; with desire
> I followed the movement of her finger, and she noticed.
> Finally she quickly drew the figure of the Roman five
> And a little stroke before it. Quickly, as soon as I'd seen it
> She drew circle upon circle to delete the letters and figures
> But the precious *four* remained impressed on my mind's eye.

With the image of the spilt wine in which the beloved draws letters and numbers, Goethe ingeniously encodes something important – another reason for Carl August to advise against publication of the *Elegien*. The Roman five with the small stroke before it is important. It is the only concretely described sign, ostensibly referring to four o'clock, the time of night that the poet is to visit his beloved. But Goethe speaks of 'letters and numbers'. The Roman five with the little stroke in front of it, arranged differently, produces the letter 'A'. The 'little stroke' only fits the letter 'A', for only here is the cross-stroke small, while in the number IV all three strokes are of equal length. That Goethe is referring above all to the letter 'A' is shown by the time at which the secret meeting with the beloved is supposed to take place, for shortly before sunrise is hardly the time for a rendez-vous. The letter 'A' for Goethe stands for Anna Amalia. He is continually describing or drawing this letter, sometimes openly, sometimes in coded form. In the entry in his *Tag- und Jahresheften* for 1804 he describes how, at the end of June, amongst the many midsummer fires around the Jena mountains, he noticed one very particular one:

> On the summit of the Hausberg, which, seen from the side, rises up like a cone, an impressive flame climbed up steadily, but it had, as it were, a rather active and restless character. Only a short time passed before it could be seen flowing down the sides of the cone in two streams. These, joined across the middle by a fiery line, showed a colossal shining 'A'. At its peak a strong flame like a crown appeared and indicated the name of our revered Dowager Duchess.

Furthermore a drawing of Goethe's, portraying a person who is sitting in front of a grotto in the shade of a tree (ill. 31), refers to Anna Amalia. The preliminary sketch (ill. 30) which, like the drawing, is dated between 1807 and 1810, clearly forms, with a tree, a cross beam, and a pillar-like stone, the letter 'A'. The drawing is done in such a way that an 'A' only becomes distinguishable by reference to the preliminary sketch. In a similar way Goethe also encodes his literary works in which Anna Amalia is the main female character.

'Elegie XVI' is again a superb example of ambiguity. In the foreground is a lover who is prevented from keeping a rendez-vous in a wine garden when he mistakes a scare-crow for the lover's uncle. An uncle of Anna Amalia was the King of Prussia, Friedrich II, who died on 17 August 1786, the time in which Carl August was initiated into the state secret and plans were laid for Goethe's flight to Italy. Previously the 'traitor' had revealed that he knew the secret, which led to fear that in connection with the change of ruler there might be a Prussian intervention. This fear, which turned out to be unfounded, was aroused in Goethe by Anna Amalia, who was mindful of her unfortunate sister Elisabeth Christine Ulrike and the unscrupulous behaviour of her uncle Friedrich II and his heir. In this elegy the beloved asks:

> 'My love, why did you not come to the garden today?
> Alone, as I promised, I waited up above for you.'
> 'My dearest, I was already there; then luckily I saw your uncle
> Beside the vines and looking eagerly hither and thither.
> I crept hurriedly out!' – 'O what an error took hold of you!
> It was only a scare-crow that chased you away! This shape
> We created from bits of old clothes and reeds.
> I myself worked busily at it, worked at harming myself.'
> Now the old man's dream is fulfilled. Today he chased off
> The profligate who stole from him his garden and niece.

In a letter to Merck of 14 November 1781 Goethe characterizes Friedrich II as follows:

> ... just as in his shabby blue coat and with his hunched figure he performed great deeds, so he controlled world affairs with his capricious, biased, incorrigible view of things.

Shortly afterwards Goethe refers to his secret love: 'I am making my way in this world without deviating so much as by a hair's breadth from what sustains me inwardly and makes me happy.'

In 'Elegie XVII' Goethe deals with the 'betrayal' responsible for the mistake. He compares the 'traitor' Fritz von Stein, the son of his neighbour, with a dog that reminds him of the time with his girl, the widow 'A':

> There are many sounds which annoy me, but worst of all
> I hate the barking of dogs; their yelping destroys my ears.
> One dog alone I hear often in comfort and joy, his barking and
> yelping –

The dog my neighbour has trained.
For once it barked at my girl when she stole secretly to me
And almost betrayed our secret.
Now if I hear its barking I always think: she's here!
Or I think of the time when she came as expected.

The result of the 'betrayal' was the flight to Italy, bringing an end to the nocturnal love which was only made possible when protected by deception. After his return from Italy Christiane Vulpius came into the life of the poet who was now renouncing his love for Anna Amalia. So 'Elegie XVIII' is devoted to Christiane. To mark the change of identity from that of the previously sung widow 'A', Goethe introduces Christiane in this elegy with the name 'Faustina'. He explains her significance as follows:

One thing I find irksome above all; another
Revolts me, disgusts every fibre of my being –
Just the very thought. I will admit it, my friends.
To sleep alone at night I find irksome,
But on love's path what truly disgusts me
Is fear of snakes, and poison under the roses of pleasure,
And when, in the most beautiful moment of joyful surrender,
Lisping worry approaches with its whisperings.
That's why I find happiness with Faustina; she gladly shares my bed
And is totally loyal to her loyal friend.

Above all, Faustina helps the poet to avoid contact with sexual diseases, referred to in the poem as 'snakes' and 'lisping worry'. The poet further celebrates the sensual happiness given him by Christiane (ll. 13ff.):

What bliss it is! We exchange carefree ['sichere'] kisses,
Without worry ['getrost'] we draw in one another's breath and life
And so we enjoy the long nights, we listen
Bosom to bosom, to the storms and the downpouring rain.

Christiane, whom Goethe's mother for a long time referred to as his 'Bettschatz' [literally bed treasure], though from now on not treated by the poet as an equal partner, will still be an honest and loyal companion for life.

In 'Elegie XX' Goethe refers to the state secret and how he intends to handle it:

If strength and an open courageous character graces the man
Deep secrecy perhaps becomes him still more.
Reticence, you conqueror of cities! Princess of the peoples!
Precious goddess, who leads me securely through life,
What fate is mine! In fun the muse, like Amor,
The villain, opens my closed lips.

It was always difficult to hide the shame of kings.
Neither the crown nor the Phrygian alliance could hide
Midas' elongated ear; his nearest servant discovered it
And the secret made him anxious and depressed.
It would have relieved him to bury it in the ground
But the earth does not keep such secrets.
Reeds spring up and rustle and lisp in the wind:
'Midas! Midas, the Prince,has an elongated ear!'
It is still harder for me to keep a lovely secret;
The fullness of my heart pours easily from my lips.

King Midas of Phrygia, the western part of central Anatolia (Turkey), dared to value the music of Pan above that of the superior god Apollo. To punish him Apollo made asses' ears grow on him. Out of shame Midas covered them with his headdress. He threatened to kill his hairdresser – from whom he could not hide his ears – should he betray his secret. Since the hairdresser could not bear the weight of the secret he dug a hole and shouted the secret into it. On this spot rushes grew which, rustling in the wind, repeated the secret: 'Midas, Midas, the Prince, has an elongated ear!' Goethe's poems, too, entrusted with his secret, rustle and whisper like the rushes, so that finally his secret will become known:

I can confide in no lady – she would scold me;
No friend: perhaps he would put me in danger.
To you, hexameter, to you, pentamenter, let it be told
How she delights me by day and at nights makes my happiness.
Sought after by many men she avoids the traps laid for her –
Openly by the daring and secretly by the cunning.
Cleverly, gracefully she slips by them and knows the paths to her lover
She knows is listening and waiting eagerly to receive her.
Moon, she is coming, hold back so that the neighbour won't see her;
Rustle, breeze, in the branches, so that no one hears her tread;
And you, beloved songs, grow and bloom and cradle yourselves
On the lightest breath of the balmy loving air,
And finally reveal to the people, like those garrulous rushes,
The beautiful secret of the happy pair.

In his poetry Goethe communicates the 'shame of the kings', the secret. He had already said in 'Elegie XII' (ll. 23f.):

And what was the secret, if not that the great Demeter
Was happy to take her pleasure with a hero.

A goddess fell in love with a superb mortal. The limits are comparable with those of the monarchy which forbade a Princess to marry a man from a lower social class, even if he was a unique poet like Goethe. In the face of all impediments Anna Amalia as the goddess of fertility chose Goethe as her hero, but, since in doing this she was ignoring the law, she had to do it secretly. Both had undertaken to keep the state secret, but Goethe's 'beloved songs' were 'finally' to make discovery possible for his readers.

With Anna Amalia's and Goethe's separation the love poetry based on their renunciation and pain begins, which until now could not be known as such. Goethe develops it in many poems and in the novel of renunciation *Wilhelm Meister*. After their return from Italy both collaborated again on the idea of a theatre that should ennoble people. From 1775 until 1784, together they had directed the amateur theatre. Then Bellomo's troupe of actors was engaged, and when the troupe moved on in 1791 Goethe was given responsibility for the artistic direction of the standing court theatre with professional actors. During her Italian journey (1788-1790) Anna Amalia had made a special study of comic opera with a view to introducing it in Weimar like everything else that could contribute to the improvement of its theatre: '... in the different theatres Anna Amalia examined the acoustics, hygiene, and the lighting'. As a music expert she was familiar with the work of Domenico Cimarosa (1749-1801). In Naples Anna Amalia became acquainted with Giovanni Paisiello (1740-1816), another important exponent of *Opera Buffa*.[674] For Anna Amalia's fifty-second birthday Goethe mounted a production of Cimarosa's comic opera *Die Theatralischen Abentheuer* in his own version of the text. On 24 October 1792, on his return from the campaign of the Coalition army in France where several times his life was in danger, he dedicated to Anna Amalia the first adequate interpretation of the Igel pillar (c. AD 250) in Trier. On 24 October 1793 Goethe was able to present to the Mozart admirer a performance of the *The Marriage of Figaro*. Shortly before this, Anna Amalia's younger son had been killed during the Coalition army's campaign in the Pfalz. Carl August asked Goethe to break the news to Anna Amalia and he devoted a lot of time to consoling her. Goethe writes to Knebel on 27 September 1793: 'The Dowager Duchess indicated yesterday that she would like to go to Jena.' On 11 October 1793 he wrote to Jacobi: 'As an old friend in need I have been able to provide the Duchess with different kinds of diversion.' A year later, on 24 October Goethe mounted for Anna Amalia a performance of Cimarosa's comic opera *Die Vereitelten Ränke*, using his own version of the text.[675]

For Goethe, Anna Amalia's birthdays are always of supreme importance. Shortly after her death a sentence is found written by Goethe on 16 May 1807 which sounds like a rejection of the tragic fate he has suffered: 'There is nothing opposed to God except God himself.'[676] In *Dichtung und Wahrheit* Goethe makes a direct link between this 'strange and monstrous statement' and his *Egmont* play (1788), in which the hero wins the 'tacit affection of a Princess, [and] the express affection of an unsophisticated girl [Naturmädchen]' (Book 20). According to Goethe the statement is explained in reference to the hero's relationships to daimonic persons. Egmont [Goethe]

> knows no danger and is blinded to the greatest danger that approaches. Surrounded by enemies we can cut through them; the nets of state shrewdness are harder to break through.

Reasons of state, the necessity to yield to the inexorable laws of the monarchy, brought about Goethe's downfall. There follows a passage about the daimonic:

> For the sake of some of my dear readers ... I will talk about something of which I became convinced only much later ... The daimonic appears in its most frightening form when it is dominant in some person. During my life I have been able to observe several such, either at close quarters or from a distance.

In a conversation with Eckermann Goethe mentions amongst these 'several' Carl August and Friedrich II,[677] those representatives of the monarchy who forced his love for Anna Amalia to be nocturnal and made his renunciation of her a necessity:

> ... a monstrous force radiates from them ... all the combined forces of morality cannot influence them ... nothing can beat them except the universe itself against which they have chosen to do battle; and from such observations that strange but monstrous statement must have originated: nemo contra deum nisi deus ipse [no one against God except God himself] (IV, 20).

The court sculptor Carl Gottlob Weißer (1779-1815) made a death mask[678] of Anna Amalia, who died on 10 April (ill. 34). For the first and only time in his life Goethe overcame his abhorrence of face masks and had the same sculptor make one of him in October 1807. The eyes are closed, and so the effect is that of a death mask (ill. 35).[679] This mask was produced in two sittings, one on 19 October, the first anniversary of his wedding. An entry in his diary reads: 'At four o'clock to Weißer'. The final sitting took place on 24 October, the first birthday of Anna Amalia after her death. The entry in the diary reads: 'Afterwards with Weißer'.[680] On both of these days Goethe presented himself as a dead man. In the view of his long-time colleague Kräuter: ' ... the seriousness of the features has something you'd have to call dark'.[681] 'The forms here are completely exact', wrote Goethe years later in a letter to Boisserée of 27 February 1820. Using the masks he had made of Goethe and Anna Amalia, Weißer made busts of both of them (ill. 38 and 39). To this pendant Goethe was determined to add another by Christian Friedrich Tieck (1776-1851). Tieck was an innovative sculptor, full of inspired strength, and was considered amongst the best of his time. In 1807/08 he was in Rome occupied with making a bust of Goethe, commissioned by the Bavarian Crown Prince Louis (1786-1868) (ill. 36), who, since the beginning of 1807, commissioned busts of famous Germans to bring them together in a temple of fame, the later Walhalla (1830-1842) in Regensburg. Tieck was also therefore to make a bust of Anna Amalia. Probably through Weißer Tieck had a copy of Anna Amalia's death mask sent to him in Rome.[682] The bust he made is even more faithful to the death mask than that of Weißer (ill. 37).[683] The mask of Goethe made by Weißer became the basis for most of the Goethe-busts modelled in later years.[684]

After Anna Amalia's death Goethe wrote the official obituary *Zum Feyerlichen Andenken der Durchlauchtigsten Fürstin und Frau Anna Amalia*,[685] a masterpiece which was read from all the pulpits of the Duchy and was published. Subsequently he fell seriously ill and went to Jena and from there to Karlsbad. There he began to dictate *Wilhelm Meisters Wanderjahre*, a work which offers deep insights into his biography of the first decade in Weimar. Goethe finds the strength to transform the love poetry of renunciation into the love poetry of transfiguration. At the end of the prologue written for the opening of the Weimar Theatre on 19 September 1807, Goethe makes it known that he feels himself a widower:

> But always be mindful of the departed, whose glorious time on earth
> (*In the background is seen in ciphers the memorial to the deceased Dowager Duchess, surrounded with glory and the circle of those she has left behind.*)
>
> Veiled in clouds, was purified and transfigured in glory,
> In brilliant immortality, no longer prey to chance;
> Around her gather her beloved race
> And all whose fate was hers to rule;
> Here as always she was like a mother.
> In sorrow and in joy be always mindful of her,
> Taking on joy, deprivation, hope, pain, and separation
> In human fashion, but manly too.

The last two lines are, of themselves, not comprehensible. In them, Goethe is summing up his tragic love for Anna Amalia. As her man, he experienced joy, but had to do without her as his beloved, until he was separated from her by death. Goethe refers to himself as a widower in the poems of the *West-Östlicher Divan* (1815) as well as in *Pandora*.

Goethe began to write down the text of *Pandora* for a festival performance. In it he compares Anna Amalia with the beautiful Pandora, who, according to Greek mythology, was created by the gods as the most beautiful woman. But the highest of the gods, Zeus, gave her a box in which all the evils of the earth were contained so that human beings could not become equal to the gods. In Goethe's version the box contains the promise of love, dignity, beauty, and later of science and art. Goethe is Pandora's abandoned husband Epimetheus:

> I was intoxicated in receiving the lovely bride.
> I then approached the mysterious dowry
> ...You don't deceive me, Pandora, you the only one for me!
> I want no other happiness, real
> Or conjured in the air. Stay, be mine!

But Pandora disappears: 'She was gone! I have never seen her again.' The pain of separation expressed in *Pandora* is of devastating depth. The poet mourns an enormous loss:

> He who is condemned to part from his beautiful one
> Let him flee with averted gaze!
> Just as he, when looking at her, is enflamed deep within,
> So she draws him, drags him eternally back.
>
> Don't ask yourself in the sweet one's presence:
> Is she parting, am I parting? A black sorrow
> Grasps you, constricts you; you lie at her feet
> And despair tears at your heart.
>
> If you can weep and you see her through tears,
> Tears which make her seem far off,
> Stay! It is still possible! Night's most immovable star
> Bends down to the love, to the longing.
> ...
>
> For lovers the best consolation is to have none;
> To search for what is lost is more gain
> Than to snatch up what is new. But woe, vain labour
> The attempt to bring back what's gone far away,
> What cannot be restored is an empty, distressing torture!
>
> With anxious endeavour the mind searches deep
> In the night, seeking this figure in vain. How clearly
> She stood by day exposed to my gaze.

> Her image now appears to waver;
> Just like this was her approach!
> Does she approach me now, does she take hold of me?
> She drifts by like a wisp of fog.
> ...
> Another attempt, my spouse,
> To draw you to me! Have I caught her?
> Is it mine again, this happiness? – Just image,
> Appearance. It flees, escapes, flows away and dissolves.

A second part to *Pandora* that Goethe was thought to be planning was never written. With *Pandora* he only wanted to express his immediate sorrow at the loss of Anna Amalia. How he can see her again will be the subject of his future writings, reaching a climax, for example, in *West-Östlicher Divan* (1815). After the *Pandora* fragment Goethe turns to his novel of renunciation, *Die Wahlverwandtschaften* (1808/09), which was originally planned as a novella for the novel *Wilhelm Meisters Wanderjahre* (1821/1829) and shows similarities with another novella in the *Wanderjahre*: 'Der Mann von Fünfzig Jahren', an ingenious encoding of his forbidden love.

Along with *Pandora* Goethe wrote the *Sonettenkranz* around 1807/08. Though these sonnets are assumed to have been written for Wilhelmine Herzlieb (1789-1865), the assumption cannot stand up to critical scrutiny. Wilhelmine came as an eight-year-old orphan from Züllichau to the Frommanns in Jena, who became her loving foster-parents. Goethe, who was a regular visitor in the house, immediately became aware of the melancholy child and her sad fate. The significance of the harmless relationship was exaggerated because it seemed hard to believe that the sonnets were not founded on a love relationship – which there never was between Goethe and Wilhelmine. Not knowing that Anna Amalia was the beloved always celebrated by Goethe, biographers searched for a person whom he had celebrated at least platonically: 'It is understandable that Goethe so often took to such twilight, innocent ['unberührbar] figures. They give him a guarantee against the relationship becoming too passionate.'[686] An attempt was even made to reduce Wilhelmine's many-facetted and eventful life to a passing encounter with Goethe.[687] In reality, Wilhelmine referred to Goethe as 'the nice old gentleman' and showed him great reverence and respect. Goethe, on the other hand, called her lovingly 'Minnchen'. On 10 February 1808 the eighteen-year-old Wilhelmine wrote to a friend:

> Goethe had come over from Weimar to be able to work undisturbed on his beautiful ideas for humanity and to help on their way those who are trying so hard to be better by giving them nourishment for

> mind and heart ... many an evening when I came to my room ... and pondered what golden words I had again heard from his mouth and thought what people can make of themselves, I burst into tears and could only calm myself [with the thought] that not all people are born on the same level ... and there's an end of it.[688]

When Wilhelmine dissolved her engagement Goethe wrote to the painter Louise Seidler (1786-1866) on 24 February 1813: 'Give Minnchen my greetings. I have always believed that this dear spirit belonged in a world where there is more loyalty.' Wilhelmine seems early to have fallen in love with a Count who, for reasons of social rank, was unattainable for her.[689] Later, she and her family energetically denied conjectures that she had a liaison with Goethe. According to her brother it was 'a much overrated episode in Goethe's life'.[690]

The poet loves the woman celebrated in the *Sonettenkranz* unconditionally. At the end of the second sonnet 'Freundliches Begegnen' we read: 'So that was it!/I could not remain covered in my cloak,/I threw it away. She lay in my arms.' The true feeling of love expressed in the sonnets relates to Goethe's first ten years in Weimar and to his love relationship with Anna Amalia. When Goethe, starting with Wilhelmine Herzlieb's name, reflects on the heart and on love he is distracting from the identity of his true beloved, which it was his duty to do. In his grief over the loss of Anna Amalia, in the sonnets the poet transforms his pain into love poetry. He says in sonnet XV:

> The poet is accustomed, not to avoid creating boredom, to dig over the foundations of his inner self;
> And yet he knows how to ease the burning wounds,
> With magic words to heal the deepest of them.

The first sonnet, 'Mächtiges Überraschen', with the motif of a stream formed into a lake by a dam, points to the effect Anna Amalia had on his writing (ll. 9ff.):

> The wave is turned to spray, rolls back amazed, and yields,
> Swells up, and ever drinks itself.
> Its striving to the ocean [zum Vater] is held up
>
> It reels and comes to rest, dammed back to be a lake;
> Stars, when mirrored, observe the lapping of the waves
> Against the rocks, a new life.

A drawing of Goethe's in 1806 showing a gigantic 'A' before a mountain lake (ill. 29) is a visual equivalent of the sonnet. The gigantic 'A' clearly stands for Anna Amalia. At the beginning of the poem the stream of Goethe's *Sturm und Drang* poetry is still rushing to a union with the ocean in which it loses itself: 'Whatever may be mirrored in the stream at any stage,/It moves irresistibly on to the valley.' Through Anna Amalia's love and influence the stream of poetry is held back as if by a dam and the stars can mirror themselves in it. With his love poetry Goethe now reaches the stars so that the poetry becomes immortal.

In the sonnet 'Abschied' the theme is Goethe's flight to Italy, since after the separation the sea limits the horizon of the poet:

> I was insatiable after a thousand kisses
> And finally had to part after only one,
> After the deeply felt sufferings of a bitter parting.

Goethe had to leave his Princess after only one kiss. In the sonnet 'Epoche' – the period of his love to a living woman is at an end with the death of Anna Amalia in 1807 – there is an important comparison between Petrarch's Laura and Goethe's Anna Amalia:

> One Good Friday, of all days,
> Was inscribed with fire in Petrarch's breast.
> For me, I can well say,
> It was Advent eighteen hundred and seven.
>
> I did not start, I only continued on to love
> Her whom I carried early in my heart
> Then sagely put her from my mind.
> Now to her heart I am driven again.
>
> Petrarch's love, infinitely lofty,
> Was sadly unrewarded, sorrowful.
> An aching heart, an eternal Good Friday.
>
> But may her arrival now and ever,
> Sweet and celebrated with palms –
> The arrival of my mistress –, be an eternal day in May

Francesco Petrarca (1304-1374) linked Good Friday, the day of Christ's crucifixion, with his beloved, because he saw Laura for the first time on that day, 13 April 1327. Goethe associates Advent, the time of the coming of Christ, with his beloved. Anna Amalia is elevated to the level of Petrarch's Laura; the loyal poet wants to raise his beloved to the stars. In *Tasso*, the memorial to his love for Anna Amalia, he has the poet say (ll. 1937f.): 'Is *Laura*, then, the only name /That should sound on every tender lip?' Goethe also wants to see his Princess included here, and to this end he dedicates all his love poetry to her. As early as the second sonnet, 'Freundliches Begegnen', Goethe compares his beloved to the two famous women of literature, Beatrice and Laura, both of whom were celebrated by their poets in sonnet form:

> There came a girl, heavenly to see,
> As fine as those lovely women
> Of the poets' world.

When one day the true identity of his beloved would become known future generations would name Anna Amalia alongside Beatrice and Laura. For Petrarch the love experience with Laura was 'sadly unrewarded, sorrowful'; for Goethe, despite the nocturnal love and the renunciation, it was a fulfilled love. Now he is living in anticipation of her arrival, of a reunion with her, first in his writing and then in the afterlife.

In *West-Östlicher Divan* (1819), a collection of poems written mainly in 1814 and 1815, Goethe starts to work on a magnificent volume of love poetry. This unique collection will be the climax of his transfiguration of Anna Amalia. The *Divan* is divided into twelve books and is accompanied by the poet's commentary. If this work can be compared to a symphony,[691] Suleika (meaning 'seductress' in Arabic), the poet's beloved, is the ever-recurring leitmotiv. The longest book in the collection is devoted to her – 'Buch Suleika'.

Today it is generally agreed that Goethe's Suleika was Marianne von Willemer (1784-1860). Since no one related Goethe's love experience, as expressed in the *Divan*, to his deceased lover Anna Amalia, Marianne was able to foster the ambition that, after Goethe's death, she might be thought of as his former beloved. In September 1814 Goethe became acquainted with the former actress and singer Marianne Pirngruber. In the same month, out of affection and the need for propriety,[692] she married her foster parent, Johann Jakob Willemer (1760-1838), raised to the nobility in 1816. Willememer was already twice a widower, and Marianne had already been living with him for over ten years despite being exposed to social hostility. In a conversation with Sulpice Boisserée, Goethe judged the 'rescue [through marriage] of the endearing little woman [Marianne] as a great moral good'.[693] In 1815 Goethe travelled to Frankfurt again, aiming at nearly completing the *Divan* between May and October. During that time he often stayed with the von Willemer couple who did what they could to support his work. They even decorated the Gerbermühle (their summer house outside the walls of Frankfurt) in oriental style.

Through Herman Grimm (1828-1901), who in 1869 published his chatty and popular essay 'Goethe und Suleika',[694] Frau von Willemer became famous overnight as Goethe's Suleika.[695] In fact, Marianne knew that Goethe was celebrating another woman in his poems and even asked him for hints about this person's identity. After reading the novella 'Der Mann von Fünfzig Jahren' in *Wilhelm Meisters Wanderjahre* she asked Goethe in a letter of 7 August 1829:

> ... perhaps Wilhelm [Goethe] will tell me something in confidence about that interesting widow. How many questions I have to which [the answers] can neither be demanded nor given in correspondence. You would be perhaps amused if you knew how carefully I scrutinize all the relationships and hints that could help me to know the poet from his work and to come to an understanding of him. It is undeniable that he dips his pen into his heart's blood, but despite all the sympathy one has for the deeply beloved friend and for his wounded heart, the uncertainty is almost unbearable when one tries to guess when, how, and by whom these wounds were inflicted.[696]

On 19 April 1830 Goethe gave Marianne the following answer:

> Information about the riddles which occur in my small poems and in the bigger works could be communicated face to face but not in writing. But the result would certainly be that somewhere something *striking* [ein Vorzügliches] would emerge, most extraordinary with respect both to depth and duration.

During the days Goethe and Marianne were together in the summer of 1814 and 1815 they were in company. The few moments they might have had to themselves Goethe preferred to use to explain to Boisserée, at night, his theory of colour. Boisserée makes an entry in his diary on 18 September 1815:

> Herr Willemer fell asleep, was teased about it. We stayed together all the longer until 1 o'clock. Moonlit night. The old man [Goethe] wants to keep me in his room – we chat. He gets the idea of showing me his experiment with coloured shadows. We go onto the balcony with a candle. The little woman [Marianne] is eavesdropping at the window.[697]

Only the exchange of some harmless coded letters with 'the little woman' in 1815 – little cards with only numbers on them referring to page and line of a translation (1812/13)[698] of *Der Divan von Hafis* which they have agreed to use [Hafis being the most important Persian poet (1326-1390)] – has to serve as a basis for maintaining that there was a great love between Goethe and the married Frau von Willemer. After 1815 Goethe always, though kindly, avoided acceding to Marianne's wish to see him again. He never addressed his letters to her personally, but rather to her step-daughter at first and then finally to her husband.[699] Marianne then realized that she had entered 'that magic circle of women not to stay in it, but as soon as she had been sworn in, to leave it for the lonely path again'.[700]

After Goethe's death, Bettina von Arnim (1785-1859) published *Goethes Briefwechsel mit einem Kind*, described by Goethe's friend and collaborator Riemer as 'in a word, a novel'.[701] Here she tries to present herself as the beloved and muse of the poet, as the woman for whom Goethe wrote his sonnets and songs, and as his Suleika. Amongst the voices who rejected these claims was that of her friend Marianne von Willemer who referred to them as a compendium of lies and deceit.[702] For Riemer, Bettina's 'presumption was incomprehensible, a way of taking the arm of a man and accompanying him on his path to immortality'.[703] Many women sought to be near the famous poet. Henriette von Egloffstein, for example, told one of her daughters to mirror herself 'as often as possible in the last rays of this sinking sun':

> Don't neglect to come as close as possible to Goethe ... You may realize too late the meaning of 'je ne suis pas la rose, mais j'ai fleuri auprès d'elle!' (I am not the rose but I bloomed in its presence). All Goethe's words will shine like jewels after his death and give value to those to whom they are directed.[704]

Marianne von Willemer acted even more cleverly that Bettina von Arnim when she saw her great chance of entering literary history as Goethe's Suleika. When Goethe was feeling close to death he sent back to his friends the letters they had written to him. He did this with Marianne von Willemer on 3 March 1832. In these letters there are supposed to have been four poems which Marianne claims to have composed herself and which Goethe wove into the *Divan* as his own. These are poems which are considered amongst the best in the collection and in which Suleika speaks to the poet Hatem.[705] The originals of Marianne's letters to Goethe are not extant, for she destroyed them at the beginning of the 1850s. Previously she had had a copy made by an unidentified person. Despite 'the most careful inquiries' by relations and friends it was not possible to find out who this person was.[706] But through making a copy [Abschrift] of her letters she could change the content at will, and equally at will she could include poems of Goethe's copied from the *Divan* (printed 1819), changing them slightly after having had a period of thirty years to reflect on it. On 21 January 1857 she sent Grimm a copy of 'her' *Divan* poem – the first line of which was 'Was bedeutet die Bewegung?' – with the comment: 'there is only one [strophe] that G. [Goethe in the *Divan*] changed, and I don't really know why. I really think mine is nicer'.[707] What is crucial here is that the person given the task of copying is not named and cannot otherwise be traced. She gave no reason for destroying the original letters to Goethe, although 'he' had held them in his hands and she treated his letters like holy objects. When Marianne left the house she always took his letters with her sewed into her clothing. The destruction of her original letters, therefore, had no other purpose than that she could write them [again] showing herself as the author of the Suleika poems.

Frau von Willemer's clever swindle could have been seen through, because she made mistakes. When she sent Grimm the 'copy' of her letter to Goethe containing the poem 'Was bedeutet die Bewegung?' this letter was dated 6 October 1815. Goethe's original draft of the poem was dated 23 September 1815. To judge by this, the incomparable poet Goethe must have deliberately predated the poem to appear as author of a poem written by Marianne von Willemer, a woman who, before and after the four poems she says she sent to Goethe, had never written anything of significance. 'A charming little song' Goethe says in 1832 of a poem written by Marianne and sent to him by Willemer.[708] Although Marianne had made the not exactly harmless statement that Goethe had included her poems in the *Divan* as if they were his own, people passed over this and other contradictions. Grimm maintained that Frau von Willemer, 'who had such a great interest in the *Divan*, [had little knowledge of] the work as a printed book'. Grimm goes on to say in his essay 'Goethe und Suleika': 'That her memory sometimes deserted her, is clear ... We must not forget that Marianne was over seventy when she told me these things.'[709] For years previously Marianne had woven a web of most beautiful words around her friend Grimm. Besides Goethe, Clemens Brentano (1778-1842), and Boisserée she had another friend. She says to Grimm in a letter of 3 June 1855, 'and another, and another, and you? Isn't it so?'

Only recently it has become known that Marianne von Willemer was involved in forgeries. She was née Pirngruber but maintained that her name was Jung. In this way she covered up the fact that her birth was illegitimate – a severe handicap at that time. She was the daughter of a Dutch teacher of dance, van Gangelt, living in Linz, and a Viennese actress M.A.E. Pirngruber. She never handed in the marriage documents which she was supposed to lay before the Frankfurt authorities. A final deadline given her by the town council for presenting the documents was not observed by Marianne – who was by now extremely wealthy – so that in Frankfurt she was always a foreigner.[710]

Marianne von Willemer was a woman adored by many men. According to one view, out of love for her her stepbrother is supposed to have found his death in a duel.[711] For Goethe she wanted to be more than a passing inspiration and a pleasant hostess. When he did not come to Frankfurt again after 1815, for years she was sick, feeling humiliated and hurt by his lack of interest.[712] With false modesty she asked her young friend Grimm not to publish her love story with Goethe until after her death. According to Grimm: 'This seems to me to be one of the best traits in Marianne's character: the complete unwillingness to have her name linked publicly with that of Goethe.'[713] Her 'correspondence' - Goethe's letters to her as well as the 'copy', by an unknown hand, of her letters to Goethe which she destroyed around 1850 – was, according to her last will, not to be published until twenty years after her death.[714] With the late publication of the letters showing her as Suleika she made sure that no close collaborator or friend of Goethe could challenge the presumption as Riemer had done in the case of Bettina von Arnim.[715] Today we read about Marianne von Willemer:

> The history of literature and of the human mind has hardly ever seen the case of a dialogue which takes place on the highest poetic level. It is a face to face dialogue, using the same sounds, the same words, and the same rhythm. It is a very personal secret, closely kept by both, the most strange masquerade on Goethe's part ... The game went on long after his death, and if Marianne, as an old woman, had not herself told her young friend Grimm about it it would have remained completely hidden.[716]

Frau von Willemer's swindle could only remain undiscovered as long as the mysterious woman who had once and for all conquered Goethe's heart remained unknown. To the critical eye the *Divan* was therefore 'a perfect example of cool "commissioned [kommandierter] poetry" in which Marianne is, as if on cue, to occupy the place long reserved for a beloved'.[717] With the discovery of Anna Amalia as the mysterious woman to whom Goethe's heart entirely belonged it has become possible to read the *Divan* from a biographical perspective.

In the *Divan* Goethe celebrates the love of his life. Here he gives witness to his absolute loyalty to Anna Amalia, for whom his love poetry was written since 1775. It is true that the poet constantly uses different names, but under these only the one woman is to be found. In the thirty-second poem of the 'Buch Suleika' Goethe finds an image for this:

> Let water, springing, surging,
> And may the cypresses confess:
> From Suleika to Suleika
> Is my coming and my going.

Goethe goes from Anna Amalia to Anna Amalia. The cypresses are to confess it to the beloved, for as early as the Romans the cypress was known as the tree of death. With the *Divan* Goethe has as his goal, at least for a short time,to see his lost beloved again in the land of poetry. On these wings Goethe writes his *Divan* songs. In retrospect he says to Eckermann (11 March 1828): 'When the poems of the *Divan* had me in their power ...' In the twenty-first poem of the 'Buch Suleika' Goethe refers to himself using the image of a volcano: 'Under snow and a thick veil of mist/An Etna rages up in you.' In June 1814 Goethe begins work on the *Divan*, and a short time later he goes on a journey to Frankfurt and the Rhine. The 65-year-old spends time at the scenes of his youth, where he had also experienced his early love for Lili Schönemann[718] before going to Weimar and finding Anna Amalia as the love of his life. Through proximity to the place of his early dreams and love and through friendly people who showered honours and attention on him, he found himself in an atmosphere which proved favourable for work on the *Divan*.

In the thirtieth poem of the 'Buch Suleika' Goethe justifies its length by saying that he was in a love-crazed condition. His song is meant for one sole person, the 'star of stars', as he calls Suleika in the fortieth poem 'Wiedersehen', but she is no longer on earth. Goethe characterizes the *West-Östlicher Divan* with subtle irony as 'the veil of earthly love ... which seems to cover up loftier relationships',[719] for these do not take place on earth. The poet Hatem resides after the death of the beloved in the 'quiet widower's house' (as in the poem 'Abglanz'), for he sees Suleika only as a spirit when he stands before the mirror. Goethe's wife Christiane was still alive when Goethe wrote 'Abglanz'. Three days after Anna Amalia's birthday, on 27 October 1815, he sent it to Frau von Willemer.[720] Goethe makes it clear in the twenty-first poem of the 'Buch Suleika' that Hatem stands for Goethe: only if, in verse three, one replaces 'Hatem' with 'Goethe' does it rhyme:

You turn to crimson	Du beschämst wie Morgen*röte*
The forbidding mountain side,	Jener Gipfel ernste Wand,
And once again Hatem feels	Und noch einmal fühlet Hatem [*Goethe*]
Spring's breath and summer's heat.	Frühlingshauch und Sommerbrand.

The introduction to 'Buch Suleika', chosen by Goethe from the collection of the oriental Sultan and poet Selim I (c. 1467-1520), contains a familiar motif:

I thought during the night
I saw the moon in my sleep;
But when I awoke
Surprisingly the sun rose.

Goethe uses the symbol of the sun (⊙) in his diary to create the deception with Frau von Stein. He uses the moon symbol (☾) to refer directly to Anna Amalia. During his sojourn in the Swiss Alps Goethe marked Anna Amalia's fortieth birthday, 24 October 1779, with a sublime description of a sunset which occurred simultaneously with the rising of the moon. The continually stressed uniqueness of the beloved Suleika excludes the possibility that he was celebrating any woman other than his deceased Anna Amalia.[721] In the nineteenth poem we read: 'All happiness on earth/I find together in Suleika alone.' In the third poem in the 'Buch des Paradieses', 'Auserwählte Frauen' Goethe raises the importance of his beloved to the nth degree, for only four women are already to be found in paradise: Mary, the mother of Jesus; Chadidja, the wife of the Prophet Mohammed; his daughter Fatima; and Suleika. Because the poet has celebrated these ladies in his song he is allowed to enjoy their company in paradise.

On 24 October 1815 Goethe writes the poem 'Vollmondnacht' as the forty-first in the 'Buch Suleika', which begins with the line: 'Mistress, tell me, what does the whispering mean?' Thus, on Anna Amalia's birthday he calls Suleika his 'Mistress' [Herrin]. This poem is not just like any other of the hundred poems in the collection. It is 'the key poem of the whole cycle',[722] because in it the beloved Suleika, like Helena in *Faust* (1772-1831), is invoked. In 'Vollmondnacht' Hatem [Goethe] turns to Suleika. Since she is dead the refrain in the first two stanzas is kept in the past: 'I want to kiss, kiss! I said.' That is the climax of an appeal which is prepared by many poems. Now Suleika is to materialize. The third and final stanza is now in the present tense. Suleika has appeared: 'I want to kiss, kiss, I say.' Just before, in another poem 'Nachklang', the poet had cried out in pain and despair: 'My cheeks are pale and gaunt/And my heart's tears are grey./Don't leave me to the night and to my pain,/My most beloved, my face in the moonlight.' Now he can receive the reward for his song of love, and the singer can expect, in the land of poetry, a glowing night of love. The fact that 'Vollmondnacht' was written on 24 October 1815, on Anna Amalia's birthday, shows that Suleika stands for Anna Amalia. But the full moon in question occurred on 18 October. In a letter to the Willemers Goethe refers to the full moon on 18 October: 'Seeing it, lovers must always feel strengthened in their unbreakable bond.' With 'lovers' Goethe means, on the one hand, the Willemer couple he is writing to, and, on the other hand, himself and his deceased Anna Amalia.

Anna Amalia's birthday is an extremely important part of Goethe's encoding strategy, which is why the poem that follows 'Vollmondnacht' is called 'Geheimschrift'. Using this title Goethe points to 24 October as an encoding for the true identity of his mistress: 'The cipher for my sweet Mistress/ Is to hand', says Hatem in 'Geheimschrift'. On 24 October 1826, the fiftieth since the first one they celebrated together in 1776, Goethe sends Marianne von Willemer a brightly embroidered cushion with a four-lined poem. The famous poem 'Gingo Biloba' from the 'Buch Suleika' reflects Goethe's sad fate at not being able openly to declare his love for Anna Amalia: 'Are there two who choose one another/To be known as one?' Only Goethe is known, and the second half, Anna Amalia, is not seen. But to read his poetry without Anna Amalia adds up to understanding only half of it: 'Do you not feel in my songs/That I am one yet two?' In his letter to Anna Amalia ('Frau von Stein') of 11 March 1781 Goethe gave expression to his feeling of oneness with her:

> And all my observations about the world and myself are directed, not, as with Mark Antony, to myself, but to my other self. Through this dialogue, since I always think what your opinion would be, everything becomes clearer and more important.

Expressing virtually the same thing, Goethe writes to Anna Amalia ('Frau von Stein') from Eisenach on 28 June 1784:

> Now it has become clear to me that you are and remain one half of myself. I am not an individual, self-sufficient being. In all my weakness I have leaned on you, my vulnerable sides have had your protection; you have filled in the gaps. Now that I am far from you I feel quite strange. On one side I am armed and steeled, on the other like a raw egg because there I have neglected to put on armour where you are my shield and protection. I am happy that I belong entirely to you.

In the thirty-fourth poem the poet Hatem expresses the importance of Suleika. He wants his song to reach her as his muse without the distance – the other world in which there is no tone or sound – hindering him:

> You woke this book in me, it was your gift;
> For what I joyfully spoke from the fullness of my heart
> Was echoed back to me from your lovely world,
> Like one glance to another, as rhyme follows rhyme.
>
> Now let it sound for you; even from the distance

The word will reach you, without tone or sound.
Is it not still the cloak of the sown stars?
Is it not the transfigured cosmos of our love?

Time and again Goethe points to the one unique love in his life. So the 71-year-old poet tells his readers in October 1820 in the poem 'Zwischen beiden Welten' that he belongs to only one woman:

To belong to one alone
To venerate one alone
What unity of heart and mind!
Lida! Joy so intimate and close,
William! Star that shines so high,
You I thank for what I am.
The days and years have disappeared
And yet the full value of all my work
Rests on those hours.

Next to William Shakespeare (1564-1616), who as a writer showed him the way to the stars, there is only Lida – one of the many names in Goethe's work standing for Anna Amalia. Since her role in Goethe's life was unknown, his statement was not understood. It was suspected that the last three lines were added in 1820 as a seal [Siegel], that 'Lida' referred to Frau von Stein, and that they were written in the first decade of his Weimar years.[723] To judge by this, Goethe is supposed to have confirmed in 1820 that he belonged only to Frau von Stein, who, for example on 21 February 1816, complained in a letter to Knebel that Goethe treated her like a ten-year-old child:

> Yesterday we were with the Duchess [Luise] and Goethe was reading us Persian poems. I hadn't seen him for a long time. I wish there was some of your warmth in his character. It is so nice exchanging ideas and feelings with you! For the least thing you say, if it is not the way he sees it you receive a rebuff. I asked him whether these poems were by one oriental poet or by different ones ... He answered: 'Dear child, no one is going to find that out from me.' As if I were a ten-year-old child![724]

In October 1820 Goethe wrote the poem 'Gegentoast der Schwestern. Zum 24. Oktober 1820, dem Stiftungs- und Amalienfeste'. The poem is about the Freemason members who were meeting in Weimar to celebrate the foundation of the Anna Amalia Lodge and were surprised there by their women-folk who were not entitled to membership. Under the pretext of attending a feast in honour of Anna Amalia they found their way through to their astonished men. For Goethe, who was only allowed to celebrate the birthdays of Anna Amalia through encoding, this was a welcome opportunity to commemorate her birthday for the forty-fourth time since 1776 – this time publicly, without using any code. But he was only told about the event itself, since, according to his diary, he was not at the Lodge but in Jena. In the poem Goethe raises the question: What is a man without his woman? The following verses (9ff.) are put into the mouths of the Freemason sisters:

> But speaking to Amalia, the majestic,
> Who also seems to you transfigured,
> Singing her praises
> We are united with you.
>
> And while we don't intend
> To interrupt your songs,
> All the Brothers are asking
> What if there were no sisters?

In the poem 'Zwischen Zwei Welten' [between two worlds], which Goethe wrote around the same time, he answers for himself the question: 'What is a man without his woman?' Because he owes 'the full value of all my work to her' he belongs to 'one unique person'. On 20 July 1781 Goethe wrote to Anna Amalia ('Frau von Stein'): 'I can't wait to kneel before you and say a thousand, thousand times that I am eternally yours.'

In the Marienbad 'Elegie' (1823), later to be the middle part of the *Trilogie der Leidenschaft*, Goethe again finds sublime verses to celebrate his Anna Amalia. The supposition that the 'Elegie' was for Ulrike von Levetzow cannot stand up to critical scrutiny of the sources. In 1823 Goethe was in Marienbad near Karlsbad for a cure. According to his diary he and Carl August arrived in Marienbad at almost exactly the same time. For 11 July we read: 'Frau von Levetzow and daughters'. Goethe had already become acquainted with the family von Levetzow two summers previously and had enjoyed their stimulating company. It did not escape Carl August's notice that Goethe liked seeing Ulrike von Levetzow, whom he addressed as his 'dear little daughter', and came up with an idea. 'The presence of the Grand Duke brought life and fun into the whole colony', Goethe wrote to Meyer on 13 August. Carl August hit on the idea, without consulting Goethe, of making an offer of marriage on his behalf.[725] He offered Ulrike considerable privileges, and, in the case of Goethe's death, a generous widow's pension. The Levetzow family took the offer as a joke, 'thinking that Goethe was certainly not thinking that way, which he [Carl August] contradicted, often repeating [the offer]'.[726] For 7 August there is an entry in Goethe's diary: 'On the terrace. Much walking back and forth. Early with the Grand Duke [Carl August]. Engagement discussed on the spur of the moment.' On 7 and 8 August

1823, Goethe, thrown by Carl August's plans for his marriage, falls sick. In the diary: 'bad night'. As Minister, Goethe was not in a position to contradict his Prince publicly, but by saying nothing about the marriage he made it clear to the von Levetzow family that he had no intention of marrying again and that the offer was merely a bad joke on the part of the Duke. Something similar must have happened in Silesia in 1790 when, as report would have it, Goethe is supposed to have made an offer of marriage to the 21-year-old Henriette von Lüttwitz – Goethe had not a word to say about it.[727]

The 73-year-old poet calmly accepted being suddenly exposed, for a period of months, to public mockery. As early as 12 August Caroline von Humboldt reported to her husband: 'There is a lot of talk here about two Fräuleins von Levetzow ... It is even said that last week he [Goethe] married the eldest of them.'[728] This confirms that Carl August made the offer of marriage around 7 August and immediately made it public.[729] Caroline von Wolzogen writes in a letter of 24 September 1823: 'Everyone is preoccupied with Goethe's love story, and his family feared he would even marry.'[730] Because Goethe was annoyed about some of the reactions, above all those of his son and daughter-in-law, he did not object to the long speculation about his marrying Ulrike. Accordingly, his friend, the diplomat Carl Friedrich von Reinhard (1761-1837), said in a letter of 2 November 1823:

> He became acquainted at the spa with a pretty young person [Ulrike], and they were saying that he invited her to come to Weimar and that he wanted to marry her. There is nothing in it, but since the excitement annoyed him he took pleasure in prolonging it.

Since Ulrike von Levetzow was so present in the foreground, in the 'Elegie', which he wrote during the journey back to Weimar, Goethe was able to glorify Anna Amalia more openly than usual. While speculation about a second marriage was doing the rounds in Germany, Goethe devoted himself completely to the bewitching piano-playing of the beautiful Countess Marie Szymanowska (1789-1831), who in this reminded him of Anna Amalia. Of all the instruments that Anna Amalia played she achieved most with the piano, so that the Princess even performed 'fairly publicly'.[731] Maria Szymanowska was court pianist of the Tsarina; Cherubini (1760-1840) and Rossini (1792-1868) praised her as the leading female pianist of the era.[732] On 14 August 1823 Goethe writes in his diary: 'To Madame Szymanowska, who played the piano gloriously. Went walking with her towards the mill.' On 16 August we read: 'Poem for Madame Szymanowska. Midday at home. Visited Madame Szymanowska at 4 pm. She played exquisitely.' The poem was to become the third part of the *Trilogie der Leidenschaft*. Around this time Goethe was working on the *Wilhelm*

Meister novella, 'Der Mann von Fünfzig Jahren', an ingenious encoding of his forbidden love for Anna Amalia. Surrounded by music Goethe wallowed in the memory of Anna Amalia. On 24 August 1823 Goethe writes to Zelter:

> The enormous power music has over me these days! The voice of Mildner, the rich sounds of Szymanowska, even the public exhibitions of the local fusiliers open me up in the way one relaxes a clenched fist into a friendly hand.

The people to whom Goethe first gave the 'Elegie' to read – for example, Eckermann on 27 October or Wilhelm von Humboldt on 19 November 1823 – saw it, as might be expected, in relation to Ulrika von Levetzow.[733] It is a middle piece of the *Trilogie der Leidenschaft*. The first piece is 'An Werther' (1824), and the third poem is 'Aussöhnung' (1823). Explaining the genesis of the trilogy, Goethe says to Eckermann:

> My so-called *Trilogie der Leidenschaft* only gradually, and somewhat by chance, became a trilogy. At first, as you know, I only had the 'Elegie' as a piece in its own right. Then Szymanowska visited me ... The stanzas which I dedicated to this friend were written completely with the metre and in the tone of the 'Elegie'. Then Weygand wanted to arrange for a new edition of my *Werther* and asked me for a preface to it. This was a very welcome stimulus for me to write my poem 'An Werther'. But since there was still a remnant of that passion in my heart the poem took shape, of its own accord, as an introduction to the 'Elegie'. So it came about that all three of the linked poems were imbued with the same feeling of love and pain, and the *Trilogie der Leidenschaft* was formed without my knowing how.[734]

In the same conversation Goethe says what a trilogy is for him:

> It is a question of finding material that allows of being treated in three parts, so that in the first there is a kind of exposition, in the second a kind of catastrophe, and in the third a conciliatory resolution.

In 'An Werther' the exposition recalls the 'much wept-over shade', for Werther is the young man who, in the epistolary novel *Die Leiden des Jungen Werther* (1774), chooses suicide because of his unrequited love. With this theme Goethe announces the dramatic action of the 'Elegie': 'I have been chosen to remain, you to depart,/You went ahead of me – and you lost very little.' The final lines of 'An Werther' take up the concluding verses of *Tasso* (ll. 3432f.): 'Entangled in such torture, half guilty./May a god let him say what he suffers.' Then the 'Elegie' begins, almost verbatim, echoing the lines from *Tasso*: 'And whereas man falls silent in his pain,/A god gave me the power to say what I suffer.' Werther's sufferings, therefore, provide the exposition for Goethe's sufferings. Through the reference to *Tasso* Goethe is indicating that the catastrophe which is central to the *Trilogie* is none other than his dramatic love story with Anna Amalia. With the final lines of *Tasso* Goethe had given himself, in 1790, a programme of work for the future: to celebrate Anna Amalia with his incomparable writings about love. Now, when nearly thirty years had passed since the composition of the *Tasso* verses, the poet could look back on the unique works which he had dedicated to Anna Amalia.

In the 'Elegie' his deceased Princess Anna Amalia appears to him as a figure of light (l. 5f.): 'No further doubt! She comes to the gate of heaven,/She lifts you up to her embrace.' Other women are for Goethe only 'a mirage' that can hold his attention momentarily, for his life is devoted to one person alone, and he begins his glorification of her (ll. 43ff.):

> But only for moments may you attempt
> To hold fast a mirage in her place;
> Back to your heart! That's where you will find it better,
> That's where she lives in changing forms:
> The one is transformed into many,
> A thousand, and each one dearer and dearer.
> ...
> So clearly is the image of the beloved
> Burned with flames into the loyal heart.
>
> Into the heart, which strong like the
> High crenellated walls, keeps itself for her
> And preserves her in itself,
> Is glad, for her, that it survives,
> Knows nothing of itself except when she appears,
> Feels freer in such beloved walls
> And only beats in thanks for what she gives.
> ...
> If ever love gives inspiration to the lover
> Most lovingly, this was done for me,
>
> Of course, by her.

In the lines that follow, Goethe intensifies the homage to his Princess further and further. In the final lines of the 'Elegie' the catastrophe of his life is summed up again: the loss of his Pandora, his Anna Amalia (ll. 133ff.):

> I have lost the world [das All], I have lost myself,
> I who was once the favourite of the gods;

> They tried me, gave me Pandora for a while,
> So rich in good things, richer still in dangers;
> They gave me a mouth endowed with many gifts,
> They put me aside, and now they work my downfall.

At the end of the Marienbad 'Elegie' Goethe established a link with *Pandora*, which he wrote in the autumn of 1807 as an expression of his sorrowful parting from his recently deceased beloved. In the third part of the *Trilogie* there is a 'conciliatory resolution' which leads into the realms of music. The poem 'Aussöhnung' is dedicated to the pianist Marie Szymanowska. Music brings him the resolution of the catastrophe, music, in which he had sought solace after Anna Amalia's death. In a letter to Zelter from Karlsbad on 27 July 1807 he expresses to the Berlin composer a wish which shows the particular way he tried at the time to approach his deceased beloved: 'So I would like to leave this world to itself and withdraw back into the sacred sphere, and there I would like every week to have sacred songs, in several parts, performed in my house.' As soon as he returned to Weimar, he did, in fact, start a house choir which gathered on Thursday evenings to rehearse and to perform such songs.[735] The programme was highly ambitious, and again and again house concerts were given on Sunday mornings to a small circle of people. Canons by Mozart and Ferrari or songs by Haydn and Jommelli were performed, all under the direction of Zelter's pupil Carl Eberwein (1786-1868).[736] Occasionally Goethe played the bass in an ensemble. He invited Marie Szymanowska to Weimar, and she came on Anna Amalia's birthday on 24 October 1823. An entry in the diary for that date reads: 'Foundation day of the Lodge [Anna Amalia] ... report of Madame Szymanowska coming from Dresden and Leipzig ... Madame Szymanowska and sister at dinner. Playing was both pleasing and excellent.' Chancellor von Müller noted: 'Bewitching pianist ... brown dress, white lace top, white cap with rose.'[737] The next day von Müller wrote to a [lady] friend:

> Madame Szymanowska, the beautiful Pole, the incomparable pianist, to whom Goethe felt so attracted at the spa and for whom he wrote the glorious poem, is here with her sister since early yesterday ... Her childlike veneration of Goethe is expressed most simply, without any affectation, and so Goethe's image of her is quite fitting: 'that she is like the most cheerful ethereal breeze that flows around one without one being able to grasp it'.[738]

Anna Amalia had once said: 'Music is like a cordial for heavy blood, for it says in the Bible that King Saul drove away his black melancholy with it.'[739] Like Anna Amalia, the Princess in *Tasso* also sought solace in music (ll. 1806ff.):

One thing
Delighted me in my isolation:
The joy of song; I entertained myself
And with gentle sounds put to rest sorrow and yearning
And every wish.
And so suffering often turned to joy and even
Sad feelings to harmony.

Two weeks later Madame Szymanowska departed and Goethe became seriously ill. The beginning and end of the poem 'Aussöhnung' are as follows:

Passion brings suffering! – Who soothes you, anxious heart,
Who have lost too much?

And so the heart, relieved, is now aware
That it is still alive, and beats and wants to beat,
In gratitude for the most generous of gifts,
To give, in answer, willingly, itself.
Then there was the feeling – O may it last forever –
The double joy of music [Töne] and of love.

With the loss of Anna Amalia, Goethe's heart has lost too much and now he only lives to glorify his Princess in his works. The 'divine gift' of music, as Anna Amalia once wrote in her *Gedanken über die Musik* (c.1799),[740] consoles the poet in his bitter separation. Goethe once said to a young visitor: 'Paradise belongs to tender souls. The damned are only those who are unable to love anything.'[741]

Three poems written in 1828, which emerge as a trilogy for Anna Amalia, are amongst the finest of Goethe's love poems. When Carl August died on 14 June 1828 Goethe withdrew to the Dornburg residences near Jena for a prolonged stay. There, high above the river Saale, he wrote the love poems which can be referred to as the *Dornburger Trilogie*. [...[742]] The first, untitled poem links up with the *West-Östlicher Divan* and shows the happy/unhappy lovers:

Suleika, you are resting
On the delicate pillow,
That I prepared and decorated for you.

The end of the poem leads from the introduction to the catastrophe with the lines: 'It hovers there, the golden lyre,/Come, old friend [female], come to my heart.' The middle piece bears the title 'Der Bräutigam'. During his first ten years in Weimar, Goethe felt he was Anna Amalia's bridegroom. The prohibition against marrying Anna Amalia was valid only on earth, not in the other world [Jenseits]. In the other world Goethe and Anna Amalia can finally be a couple. In the first and second stanzas the poet looks back on their nocturnal love which, during the day, became a deception. The third stanza deals with his parting from the beloved through her death. In the last stanza, through the transfiguring love poetry dedicated to Anna Amalia, the aged poet overcomes the pain caused by his tragic fate. He hopes now, as a reward for his fidelity, to cross the threshhold of death as bridegroom, finally to be united to his Anna Amalia:

> **'The Bridegroom'**
>
> At midnight I slept. My loving heart was awake
> In my bosom as if it were day.
> The day appeared, and I felt it was night.
> What does it matter to me, whatever it brings?
>
> She was missing! My industry and striving –
> For her alone I could bear it
> In the burning heat of the day. But what refreshing life
> In the cool evening! – it was rewarding and good.
>
> The sun sank, and bound hand in hand
> We greeted the last blessed sight,
> Eye spoke, meeting eye:
> From the east, we hope, it returns.
>
> At midnight, the brilliance of the stars
> In a sweet dream leads to the place where she rests
> May a place for me also be prepared there!
> Life, however it may be, is good.

In the third poem entitled 'Dem Aufgehenden Vollmonde' the conciliatory resolution takes place. Goethe, who in his first ten years in Weimar used the moon symbol (☾) to refer to Anna Amalia, feels very near to her when the moon is full. In the *Divan* poem 'Vollmondnacht', written on 24 October 1815 at the climax of the magic incantation cycle, the appearance of the deceased beloved and a night of passionate love came about in the world of poetry. The poem 'Dem Aufgehenden Vollmonde' is another poetic meeting with Anna Amalia. In just a few sublime moments the poet can feel the presence of his beloved. Around this time Jenny von Pappenheim (1811-1890), the illegitimate daughter of Napoleon's brother Jérôme, describes the aged Goethe in Tiefurt:

> Goethe got out, put an arm around each of us and led us back to the Ilm, regaling us with Tiefurt's brilliant days and with stories about the Duchess Anna Amalia. At a square [Platz], oblong in shape and lined with old trees, he stopped. It was the place where the noble

> Princess used to have tea served. A bit further on he showed us the places which inspired 'Die Fischerin' he had written and where it had been performed. I never saw him so soft and mild. The whole day was so harmonious.[743]

Goethe's 'conciliatory resolution' in the third part of the trilogy is the certainty that his Anna Amalia is linked with him and will soon be united with him in the other world:

'Dem Aufgehenden Vollmonde'

Do you want to leave me straight away?
For a moment you were so close!
Dark clouds surround you
And now you are no longer there.

But you feel how sad I am,
Your rim is visible as a star!
You show me that you love me
No matter how distant my beloved is.

So rise up then! Bright and brighter
On your pure course, in fullest glory!
If my heart beats fast and full of pain,
The night is full of bliss.

As early as 22 March 1781 Goethe had written to Anna Amalia ('Frau von Stein'):

> Your love is for me like the morning and the evening star. It goes down with the sun and rises again before the sun. It is like a star at the pole which, never setting, weaves an eternally living wreath above our heads. I pray that the gods will never darken it during the course of my life.

In Goethe's official obituary *Zum Feyerlichen Andenken der Durchlauchtigsten Fürstin und Frau Anna Amalia* (1807) he concludes:

> It belongs to the excellence of noble natures that their departure to higher regions works as a blessing as did their time on earth, that they shine on us from there like stars, guiding us wherever we must go on our journey, which is all too often interrupted by storms.

14 | *Wilhelm Meister*: 'There is life in it!'

> There are books which tell you everything but which make nothing intelligible.
>
> *Maximen und Reflexionen*. From the bequest

> Eternally he will be for you the one who divides into many
> And yet one who is eternally unique.
> Find in the one the many, feel that the many are one;
> There you have the beginning as well as the end of art.
>
> *Weissagungen des Bakis* [Prophecies of Bakis] (c.1800), 32

In a conversation with Eckermann on 25 December 1825 Goethe points out very significantly that his autobiographical novel *Wilhelm Meister* can be read on two levels:

> The seemingly insignificant details of *Wilhelm Meister* are always based on something higher, and it is only a question of having eyes, knowledge of the world, and an overview to become aware of the greater things in the small details.

The first phase of his work on the Bildungsroman and Erziehungsroman *Wilhelm Meisters Theatralische Sendung* lasted from 1777 until 1785. Since Goethe was not satisfied with this still unfinished version, between 1793 and 1796 he reworked it into *Wilhelm Meisters Lehrjahre*. He wrote to Herder in May 1794:

> ... I am tempted to send you the first book of my novel. Now that it is revised it needs a few more strokes of the pen, not to become good but to unload it from my heart and from around my neck as a pseudo confession.

The *Lehrjahre* as a novel is a pseudo confession,[744] not a genuine confession because Goethe has to encode the biographical content. Goethe never swerved from his principle of transforming everything that gave him

> joy or pain, or that otherwise preoccupied him, into an image, a poem, and thereby to have closure with it ... All [my works] that have become known, therefore, are fragments of a great confession' (*Dichtung und Wahrheit*, Book 7).

After a ten-year-long planning phase,[745] shortly after Anna Amalia's death on 10 April 1807 Goethe begins work on the second part of the novel under the title *Wilhelm Meisters Wanderjahre oder Die Entsagenden*. In 1821 a first version of the work appeared. In the meantime Goethe published individual parts of it in advance. In 1829 a fuller version appeared. On 19 October 1821 Goethe wrote about the *Wanderjahre* in a letter to Zelter: 'I can proudly say that not one line of it was not either felt or thought. The genuine reader will be able to relive and re-think it all.'

Goethe wanted the confession contained in *Wilhelm Meister* one day to be decoded as his biography. In a letter of 29 March 1801 he writes to his poet colleague Johann Friedrich Rochlitz (1769-1842): 'I can thank God that I was in a position to put so much substance into it [the *Lehrjahre*] that feeling and thinking people would attempt to draw it out [of the novel] again.' But until now the autobiographical aspect of the novel could not be unlocked. Though it was written in an article that '150 years had to pass until readers knew how to value the bequest which Goethe left to them openly hidden [öffentlich verborgen],[746] it was still considered as one of the 'most mysterious works of world literature'.[747] The first part, the *Lehrjahre*, was considered a ground-breaking work because with it, on the basis of pedagogical thinking coming down from antiquity, Goethe outlines a general plan for rearing and educating children, but the encoded biography of the poet provides the supporting framework of the novel. Anna Amalia, in a letter to Goethe's mother on 22 February 1784, writes about the earliest part:

> How did you like 'Wilhelm Meister'? It will become a masterpiece of our Herr Wolf [Goethe]. There is life in it! He is a Prometheus who creates for himself his own small world. Adieu, dear mother! I kiss you a thousand times.[748]

Without knowledge of the biographical aspects, *Wilhelm Meister* remains in the long run inaccessible. This is especially true of the *Wanderjahre*, which, because of the premature publication of individual parts of it, has been looked on as patchwork. Even Franz

Grillparzer (1791-1872), a poet whom Goethe, after a visit in 1826, would like to have kept in Weimar, said about the *Wanderjahre* that Goethe was misled

> into forcing into one volume parts and fragments which were not originally thought to belong together, and [he] left to the admiration of the ages and the power of his name the worry of establishing a unity of the whole.[749]

It was part of Goethe's encoding strategy to give the impression that in the *Wanderjahre* he had merely used again various smaller works: 'Hardly any work of Goethe's met with so much misunderstanding, puzzlement, even aggressive rejection as this late novel.'[750] In the *Morgenblatt für Gebildete Stände*, Goethe expressed his gratitude for attempts to interpret the *Wanderjahre* (21 March 1822):

> For the moment, the only answer I have for these esteemed friends is that it is deeply moving for me to see the problem of my life, which I am myself sometimes at a loss to understand, so clearly and cleanly unravelled for public view.[751]

This statement of Goethe's is an example of his famous irony, about which his collaborator Riemer said that 'it is not understood by everyone; some don't even suspect it'.[752] The 'problem' of his life that Goethe refers to is that he has to perform the splits between the secret imposed on him about Anna Amalia and the need to communicate his biography as a means of interpreting his work. The *Lehrjahre* and the *Wanderjahre*, in reality, deal with the first decade in Weimar, sprinkled, as in the biography of his earlier years in *Dichtung und Wahrheit*, with reflections about the period before 1775 and after 1786. In 1821 Goethe prefaced the first version of the *Wanderjahre* with the poem 'Wandersegen':

> The journeyman's years have now begun
> And every step of the wanderer is critical.
> It is not his custom to sing or pray;
> But as soon as the path becomes treacherous
> He turns his serious gaze, where mists obscure it,
> Inward to his heart and to the heart of his beloved.

Immediately after Anna Amalia's death on 10 April 1807 Goethe composed her official obituary, suddenly sought contact with Frau von Stein on 18 April, became seriously ill, went to Jena, and finally left from there to go to Karlsbad for a cure. Besides that, he began to dictate the *Wanderjahre*. He writes to Zelter on 27 July 1807: '... dictated small stories and fairytales which I have been carrying around in my head for a long time'. In the entry for the year 1807 in his *Tag-*

und Jahresheften – Als Ergänzung Meiner Sonstigen Bekenntnisse, written between 1817 and 1830, he reports:

> Very soon after the performance of *Tasso*, such a pure representation of tender, witty, and loving scenes to do with court and the world, Duchess Anna Amalia, to the sorrow of everyone and to my own special grief, left the fatherland that for her was utterly shattered, even destroyed. A hasty essay [*Zum Feyerlichen Andenken der Durchlauchtigsten Fürstin und Frau Anna Amalia*], more like an official form [Geschäftsform] than something written with higher, more inward meaning, was only to be a confession of how much more I was obliged to dedicate to her memory.

Later in the same entry Goethe mentions what he has written 'with higher, more inward meaning':

> This season was rich in smaller stories, conceived, begun, continued, and completed. All of them, intertwined by a romantic thread under the title of *Wilhelm Meisters Wanderjahre*, were to form a strangely attractive whole. Among these are: the conclusion to the 'Neue Melusine', 'Der Man von Fünfzig Jahren', 'Die Pilgernde Törin'.

In Goethe's *Unterhaltungen Deutscher Ausgewanderten* (1795) we see what he means by 'intertwined stories': 'I love parallel stories. One points to the other and explains its meaning better than many dry words.'[753] The novella 'Die Pilgernde Törin' is a translation and enhancement of a French story by an unknown author which Goethe read for the first time in 1789. It is the story of a mysterious woman who finds herself alone on a kind of pilgrimage. There are many parallels to Anna Amalia's life.

The novella *Der Mann von Fünfzig Jahren*, a densely written piece, deals with Goethe's forbidden love for Anna Amalia and is of central importance. In his diary entry of 5 October 1803 the 54-year-old poet mentions the novella for the first time: 'Early thought through Mann von Fünfzig Jahren.' Goethe worked on it over a period of two decades, and from June 1807 he dictated the novella. An entry in the diary for 4 August 1807 reads: 'Mann von Fünfzig Jahren up to a certain period.' In 1827, expanded by the addition of further 'periods', the novella is completed. Around the fiftieth recurrence of Anna Amalia's birthday since Goethe arrived in Weimar in 1775 he was working on it intensively, as is shown by many diary entries. On her birthday, 24 October 1826, he writes: 'The outline for the Mann von Fünfzig Jahren.' In his conversation with Eckermann on 25 December 1825 – the birthday of Frau von Stein – Goethe says, when asked if in his creative writing he portrayed his actual experiences:

> There are, in fact, few people who have an imagination which grasps the truth about the real; instead, they like to be in strange countries and circumstances of which they have no understanding and which their imagination can concoct for them. And then there are others who cling to the real and, because they are altogether lacking in poetry, make demands on it which are too narrow.

The novella tells the story of a Major and his son Flavio, both talented poets, who alternately fall in love with the girl Hilarie and a beautiful young widow. The Major is Hilarie's uncle and wants a marriage between her and his son Flavio. However, Flavio loves the beautiful widow. When the Major finds that Hilarie is in love not with Flavio with the Major himself, he thinks he can marry his niece and is therefore happy that his son will want to marry the widow. Hilarie and the widow both prefer the Major to the young Flavio. When the beautiful widow refuses a marriage with Flavio, Hilarie comes closer to him, but since this has the appearance of sin attached to it, at the end of the novella she turns back again to the Major. In his writing, Goethe often depicts the one person as several, as for example in *Tasso*: Antonio and Tasso. In this way Goethe manages to supply the autobiographical background without it being obvious, and at the same time to create a story full of tension. At various points in his life he gives hints of this tendency. In a letter to Knebel on 21 November 1782 in which Goethe tells his friend that a copy of 'the first three books of the *Theatralische Sendung* has been made', he speaks of a division of his person into several:

> ... I have separated my political and social life completely from my moral and poetic life (outwardly, of course) ... I now leave the Privy Councillor separate from my other self, without which a Privy Councillor can very well survive. Only in my innermost plans, resolutions, and ventures do I remain secretly true to myself and in this way tie my social, political, moral, and poetical life together in a hidden bond.

Five decades later Goethe mentions this technique again in a letter of 27 September 1827 to his writer-colleague Iken (1789-1841):

> Also, with regard to other obscure passages in earlier and later poems I would like to put forward the following considerations: since much in our experience cannot be fully revealed and directly communicated, I have for a long time now resorted to juxtaposing forms which, as it were, mirror one another, and in this way I have revealed to the observant reader the deeper, more secret meaning. Since everything I have communicated is based on experience of life I am allowed to give hints and hope that people are prepared to – and will – relive my writings.

The four protagonists of the novella stand for Goethe and Anna Amalia: the beautiful widow represents Anna Amalia in her public function as Princess, while Hilarie is the woman behind the mask of the Princess; Flavio is the stormy young Goethe, and the Major the respected statesman and world-famous poet. The choice of names of the figures in the novella confirms this, because only Flavio and Hilarie receive real names, while the Major and the widow have no personal names. Flavio, bewitched by the beautiful widow, describes her (*Wanderjahre* II, 3):

> She is a young widow, heiress of an old husband who died recently; she is independent, and deserves to be; she has many people around her, is loved by just as many, and is wooed by just as many, but if I am not deceiving myself her heart belongs to me.

When the Major becomes acquainted with the widow through Flavio so that he can give his blessing to their union, he is treated by her as the centre of the company present at the time. She is working on a magnificent and tasteful wallet which is further remarkable for its fairly large size; it will be significant for her relationship to the Major. When Flavio asks her what she thinks of his father, she answers with a smile (*Wanderjahre* II, 3): 'I think you could follow his example. Just see how nicely he dresses. See whether his demeanour and bearing are not better than his dear son's.' Flavio wants to marry her:

> ... I don't know how I could be so bold, in the middle of an indifferent conversation, as to take her hand suddenly, to kiss this tender hand, and to press it to my heart. She was not led away from me ... She did not go away herself, she did not resist, she did not answer. I dared to take her in my arms, to ask her if she wanted to be mine. I kissed her impetuously; she pushed me back. – Yes, but yes! or something like that she said indistinctly and as if confused. I moved away and called to her: 'I'll send my father and have him speak for me!' 'Don't say a word to him', she said, following me a few steps. 'Go, and forget what has happened.'

When the Major visits the widow she gives him the 'magnificent and tasteful wallet' (*Wanderjahre* II, 4):

> Take this wallet. It is somewhat similar to your hunting poem. Many memories are linked to it; much time passed while I worked on it. Now it is finished at last. Use it as a messenger to bring us your dear work.

The Major returns to his lodgings to look for the hunting poem, but his first task is to attend to the administration of the family's properties and possessions, which, through the marriage of Flavio and Hilarie are to remain undivided. To achieve this, the agreement of another brother, the Chief Marshall, is required. He agrees to the plans but wants to keep back something (*Wanderjahre* II, 4):

> ... also the fruits on the trellises are to be guaranteed to him ... but especially a certain sort of small grey apple, with which for many years he was accustomed to honour the widowed Princess, was to be faithfully delivered to him ... he had what was available of the little grey golden apples carefully packed and drove off with this treasure to the widow's residence, intending to make this welcome presentation to the Princess. When there, he was given a gracious and friendly welcome.

As a seemingly unimportant detail a widowed Princess appears here, a description which fits Anna Amalia. What is important is the reference to the strange apples, first described as 'grey', then as 'grey gold apples'. In the conversation with Eckermann on 25 December 1825 in which Goethe speaks of 'the seemingly insignificant details' of *Wilhelm Meister* which 'are always based on something higher', he then says: 'Shakespeare [Goethe said] gives us golden apples in silver bowls'. With the Chief Marshall who brings golden apples to the widowed Princess in her residence, Goethe is referring to himself bringing his writings as offerings to Anna Amalia. On 22 October 1828, shortly before Anna Amalia's birthday, in conversation with Eckermann Goethe added to the image of the golden apples: 'Women', he said, 'are the silver bowls in which we lay golden apples.' He immediately adds ironically: 'My idea of women is not abstracted from what I have experienced in reality; it was innate in me, or came to being in me God knows how.' Goethe explains in the *Lehrjahre* (V, 4) what the golden apples mean in the context of his whole work. He does this in relation to preparing plays for performance. You have to separate the grain from the chaff. You don't put 'the whole stalk on the table. The artist must offer his guests golden apples in silver bowls.' Goethe, who as theatre director was a master of cutting texts, is saying that the golden apples of his complete works are those which he has laid before Anna Amalia. In *Tasso* the Princess says (ll. 177ff.):

> The beautiful songs, ...
> Which, like golden apples, ...
> ...Don't you know they are all fruits of a true love?

The Major now looks for the hunting poem he has promised the beautiful widow. We are not told the text of it. It is written

> in a careful fair copy in Latin script as he had done it years ago, in large octavo. The superb wallet, of considerable size, received the work quite comfortably, and rarely has an author seen his work contained between such glorious covers.

He thinks about prefacing it with a few lines from Ovid's (BC 43-c. 17 AD) *Metamorphoses*:

> I saw it in the hands of a master.
> How gladly I think of that beautiful time!
> I saw it develop, reach completion
> More gloriously than anything seen before.
> True, I still possess it
> But if I would only admit it
> I would prefer it not to be finished.
> The doing was just so nice.

But the Major realizes that it would be risky to send the widow these particular verses, because

> they are said about Arachne, a weaver who is as clever as she is pretty and dainty. She was transformed into a spider by the envious Minerva, and so it was dangerous to see a woman as a spider – no matter how remote the comparison – hovering at the centre of an extended net.

This is an appropriate image for the Duchess Anna Amalia, who, as former Regent in the small duchy has spread out her net to protect the secret of her love for Goethe. The ageing Goethe says about his first decade in Weimar: 'I am not sure how to describe this time. I would have to do it in the form of a fairytale in which Amalia, as an all-powerful fairy, creates and brings everything to life.'[754] Arachne is a woman from Lydia, which today is West Anatolia in Turkey. On 1 June 1781 Goethe introduced the name 'Lydia' into his poems for Anna Amalia ('Frau von Stein') – 'the woman originating from Lydia[755] – which he subsequently changed to 'Lida'.

Goethe himself made a fair copy, like the one described regarding the hunting poem, of his Marienbad *Elegie*.[756] Three days after Anna Amalia's birthday, on 27 October 1823, he showed the *Elegie* to Eckermann:

> He had written the verses himself in Latin script on strong vellum and fixed it with a silken cord in a cover of red marocain, and so even the outward appearance showed that this manuscript had special value for him above all the others.

A little later in the conversation Goethe says that he 'sees the *Elegie* as a kind of shrine'. Goethe, who had written a copy of his poem in his own hand, is described by Eckermann two days previously, on 25 October, as follows:

> I was with Goethe for half an hour in the twilight. He was sitting on a wooden armchair in front of his work-table. I found him in a

> wonderfully gentle mood, like someone who is completely filled with heavenly peace or like someone who is contemplating the sweet happiness he has enjoyed and which is now in all fullness before his mind.

On Anna Amalia's birthday, 24 October 1823, Goethe commemorated her with a piano concert given by Marie Szymanowska who had arrived on the same day. The Princes' tutor Soret noted on this day: '... Madame Szymanowska's fantasies on the piano. Goethe, lost in listening, sometimes seemed enthralled and moved'.

In the *Elegie*, written when he was seventy-four, the Princess appears to him as a figure of light: 'No further doubt! She comes to the gate of heaven,/She raises you up into her arms.' With regard to the hunting poem for the beautiful widow the Major describes the individual hunting scenes as 'well observed, clearly captured, passionately followed, lightly and playfully, often ironically described.' Then: 'That elegiac theme resounded through the whole. It was written more like a leave-taking from these joys of life.' When he refers to the 'elegiac theme' – 'elegiac' meaning a poem with a melancholy and plaintive content – he means his hunting for Anna Amalia's heart in the land of poetry. The hunting poem that Goethe will present to the beautiful widow is therefore the Marienbad *Elegie*, another 'golden apple', which Goethe, now an old man, lays in the silver bowl, which is Anna Amalia.

The widow's wallet is a symbol for her relationship to the Major. Anna Amalia's whole striving is to transform the young, loving, aimless *Stürmer und Dränger* Goethe (Flavio) into a respected statesman and world-famous poet (Major); because she succeeded in this Goethe is able to write: 'It is rare for an author to find his work so superbly bound' (ill. 40). Johanna Schopenhauer describes Goethe in a letter to her son on 28 November 1806:

> He is the most perfect being I know, also in his exterior; a tall handsome figure who holds himself very erect; he dresses very carefully, always in black or dark blue, his hair tastefully cut and powdered as becomes his age, and a glorious face with two clear brown eyes which are at the same time gentle and penetrating (ill. 33).[757]

The condition in which Goethe came to Weimar as a *Stürmer und Dränger* was like that of Werther, the hero of his novel: he was always in danger of throwing himself into the abyss. Flavio embodies this condition and is therefore compared to the Orestes of antiquity (*Wanderjahre* II, 5): Hilarie and her mother 'were stunned. They had seen Orestes hounded by the Furies, not ennobled by art but in dreadful, repulsive reality'. The young Goethe was like Orestes, a restless hero, half crazed, on the brink of destruction. In Goethe's *Iphigenie auf Tauris* (1779/1787) Orestes is rescued from the threat of insanity by Iphigenie. Anna Amalia worked at the transformation from Flavio to the Major. She influenced the young poet even in his patterns of behaviour. In a letter to Goethe's mother on 21 April 1779 the Princess writes about his reaction to an unpleasant piece of news from their circle of friends: 'I have passed on your letter to Dr Wolf [Goethe]: but since court life has made him better behaved he didn't grind his teeth, let alone did he curse, but shrugged his shoulders about the wretched adventure.'[758] On 13 March 1781 Goethe wrote to Anna Amalia ('Frau von Stein'): 'I want to surrender to you my life and myself, in order to receive myself back from your hands.' This and similar utterances do not refer to his development into a courtier, which he never really became. Wieland wrote on 5 July 1776 to Merck:

> He [Goethe] has, despite all the apparent and real wildness in his nature, more manners in his little finger and more savoir-faire than all the court flunkies, creeps, and political manipulators, taken together, have in their body and soul.[759]

The experienced Regent Anna Amalia taught the young Minister and lover how a self-assured statesman behaves and what he has to do to be successful. In a letter to Anna Amalia ('Frau von Stein') of 31 March 1782 Goethe writes:

> I am contented because , aided by my love for you I can thread my way through the many strangers quietly and securely. Just as mussels swim when their bodies develop out of the shell, so I learn to live by gently unfolding what lies enclosed in me. I try everything that we have dealt with recently regarding behaviour, savoir-faire, propriety and refinement, I relax and am always composed.

In the novella the wallet is referred to as Penelope's work of procrastination. In Homer's *Odyssey* Penelope is the wife of the hero who is believed dead. Only when she has finished making the winding sheet for her father-in-law will she declare herself ready to marry again. But to delay this as long as possible she resorts to a ruse (*Odyssey* XIX, ll. 149f.): 'And by day I worked at weaving the big fabric/But at night I always undid it again by torch-light.'[760] While Anna Amalia worked during the day at transforming Goethe from Flavio into a Major, at night she is the beloved of Flavio. However, through this nocturnal love Goethe's position at the Weimar court is endangered, for discovery of their secret would mean separation for the lovers. When the wallet on which the widow is working – the transformation of Goethe into a respected statesman and world-famous poet – is finished, this means that their nocturnal love must end, because the wallet is at the same time a winding sheet for their physical love.

The rapprochement between Flavio and Hilarie, the young passionate Goethe and Anna Amalia behind her mask as Princess, stands for their nocturnal love, which is represented as sinful. Hilarie is with her mother when Flavio joins them (*Wanderjahre* II, 5):

> Flavio rushed in in total disarray, totally dishevelled, some of his hair standing on end and the rest hanging down, drenched with rain. His clothes were torn as if he had stormed through thorn and thicket, dreadfully dirty as if he had waded through muddy swamps.

The widow had rebuffed Flavio when he impetuously pressed her to marry him. He wandered 'through the night, through the storm and rain, to his aunt's residence' because he thought he would find his father there and wanted to tell him his woe. Now he approaches Hilarie and a slow transition takes place as he glides into the identity of his father. They bring Flavio into the remote guest room 'that his father was accustomed to use'. Then later:

> The son appeared fully dressed in his father's clothes, for since his own clothes were no longer of any use, they used clothes worn by the Major for outdoors and for the house and which he left at his sister's house for comfortable wear at the hunt and with the family.

Flavio's cousin visits him in his room:

> With longing Hilarie took the light and shone it on the sleeping figure ... Breathing lightly herself, she thought she could hear his light breathing. She brought the candle closer, like Psyche, in danger of disturbing the most salutary repose.

As we have seen, Apuleius' fairytale of *Amor and Psyche* was a leitmotif of Goethe's love for Princess Anna Amalia.

Now the motif crops up in the novella. The next day, when Flavio sees Hilarie, he says: 'Greetings, dear sister' – that cut her to the quick. He did not pull back, they looked at one another, a most glorious pair in the finest contrast to one another. Here we have another key word for Goethe's love relationship to Anna Amalia. At the end of October 1776, with great rapidity he dictated the short sixty-minute play *Die Geschwister*, in which it turns out that 'siblings' can marry because the supposed sister is really the daughter of the deceased beloved, a widow named Charlotte. In *Die Geschwister* as in Flavio's words there is a question of a possible incest. Goethe cannot compare the socially dictated prohibition of his marriage to the widowed Princess Anna Amalia with anything else but the prohibition of incest. When writing *Die Geschwister* he is still hoping that he can soon marry Anna Amalia and do away with the deception carried on with the help of Frau von Stein. Siblings are also the main characters in his *Iphigenie auf Tauris* (1779/1787), showing the fundamental importance Anna Amalia had for the direction his life would take, even though officially she could be nothing to him. Love between siblings is also a central motif in the *Lehrjahre*, for Mignon, one of the most mysterious characters in the novel, is the product of such an unaware union. When Flavio calls Hilarie his sister it is made clear that their love is prohibited.

At first Flavio is able to 'enjoy Hilarie's presence' after his prospects with the beautiful widow through his peremptory demand of her hand [in marriage] had vanished forever'. Goethe realizes that he cannot marry Anna Amalia. Flavio finds solace in writing and in music (*Wanderjahre* II, 5): 'Here the noble art of poetry could again show its healing powers. Intimately united with music, it is a radical cure for all the soul's sufferings.' Unofficially Goethe can escape the prohibited private love for Anna Amalia/Hilarie, as long as there is no threat of discovery, but the relationship between Hilarie and Flavio is seen as sinful.

Further on in the story there is a flood, a recurring motif in Goethe's work, as, for example, in *Werther* (1774). It stands for a 'chaotic mental landscape flooded with feeling and passion'.[761] Extremely cold weather freezes the water to ice and after coping with the work caused by the flood, Flavio and Hilarie find great enjoyment in ice-skating. Goethe had introduced ice-skating in Weimar and had aroused the enthusiasm of the whole court. Skating festivals were held in delightful surroundings. Carl von Stein recalls:

> At Goethe's instigation a pond ... was chosen. A small transportable house made of boards with an oven [Windoven] for heating was built at the edge; several chairs like sleighs were made for ladies to ride on the ice. The Duchesses came along with their ladies-in-waiting.[762]

On 15 February 1778 the violinist Johann Friedrich Kranz (1754-1810) writes to Goethe's mother that her son

> now and then goes skating in the evening with their lordships, and indeed *en masque*. The Duchesses, noble ladies, and Fräuleins are pushed along on sleighs. The pond, which is not small, is lit up all around with torches, lamps, and cauldrons of burning pitch. The spectacle is enhanced on the one hand by oboes and Janissary music and on the other by firewheels, rockets, cannons and artillery fire.[763]

Three days earlier Goethe had written in his diary: 'At night to (⊙) [Anna Amalia] walking with her again in the moonlight'.

> While Flavio and Hilarie are skating at night, suddenly the Major appears: Hilarie, coming to a stop, lost her balance because of the surprise and fell to the ground. Flavio went down on one knee at the same time and took her head in his lap. She hid her face. She didn't know what was wrong with her ... 'Let us flee,' she cried, 'I can't stand it'.

Here the moment has arrived when the woman behind the Princess's mask is thinking of flight with her lover so that they can at last live together without deceit. Goethe constructs this scene as a parallel to Odysseus' journey to the underworld. The clue to this is the mention of trees like the willow, the poplar, and the alder, which are, on the one hand, found on the island of the goddess and magician Circe, who gives Odysseus advice about his trip to the underworld, and, on the other hand, will indicate to him the place where he is to descend into it.[764] Hence the link between Flavio and Hilarie is under this very negative sign.

After this scene they all go into the residence, where music and dancing are in full swing. 'The young couple go separately, not daring to touch one another or to come close.' The Major is puzzled to find that in his room, though not unexpectedly occupied, his own clothes, underclothes and effects [were] lying around in a state of disorder he was not used to'. At first he is not aware that Hilarie's affection is taking a different turn. But the Major, deep down, is prepared for such an eventuality. A short time ago 'one of his front teeth had fallen out and he was afraid he might lose a second one'. This happened to Goethe in 1809, the year in which he turned sixty.[765] The Major realizes that he is too old for the young Hilarie, who, however, unexpectedly still sees him as her future husband. In talking to her mother, Hilarie justifies herself by stressing energetically and sincerely the unsuitable and even criminal nature of such a relationship [with Flavio]. Since Flavio is the son of the Major, the terms 'unsuitable' and 'criminal' cannot refer to their relationship. It is a reference to Goethe's forbidden love for a Princess.

At the end of the novel the widow asks the Major to meet her at an inn:

> I know everything', she continued, 'there is nothing we have to explain; you and Hilarie, Hilarie and Flavio'. Weeping bitterly, the widow admits responsibility for the calamity: 'Forgive me, have pity on me. You see how I am punished.'

Goethe, in the person of the Major, accepts his beloved's reasons for not deciding in favour of young Flavio's love. At the same time he shows in the depiction of the contrite widow that he exalts her:

> She was more beautiful than ever; ... she answered with a heavenly smile; ... from this remarkable woman, who was usually very reserved, emerged a modest, beautiful, attentive, and communicative person; ...She ... was ... more than charming ... her divine inner self appears and begins to transfigure her outer self.

Goethe once said in a maxim: 'You are not in love if you don't see the faults of the beloved as virtues.'[766] The beautiful widow describes to the Major what she felt when Flavio importuned her:

> I was not unhappy, but uneasy ... I was not quite myself, and I suppose that means not being happy. I didn't like myself anymore. No matter how I tried to compose myself in the mirror, I always felt I was making myself up for a masked ball.

Goethe's flight to Italy finally saw an end to the masquerade with Frau von Stein. Anna Amalia's plan to transform Flavio into a Major, a respected statesman and world-famous poet, proves prudent and far-seeing. At the end of the *Wanderjahre* (III, 14) Goethe has Flavio united with Hilarie and the Major with the widow, and thereby indicates that Anna Amalia has been the woman in his life: as Hilarie she is the nocturnal beloved of Flavio, and as the beautiful widow she is the beloved, in renunciation, of the Major.

Through this renunciation, dictated by reason, Goethe's and Anna Amalia's physical love was indeed sacrificed, but also raised to an exalted level. The *Lehrjahre* novel provides the details. The scene at Lake Maggiore (*Wanderjahre* II, 7) that follows the novella *Der Mann von Fünfzig Jahren* establishes an important connection between the two parts of the autobiographical novel *Wilhelm Meister*. In this scene Hilarie and the widow appear travelling with Wilhelm, together with a painter and singer who appears only in this scene in the novel. They are on a pilgrimage to the homeland of Mignon, this mysterious figure who dies at the end of the *Lehrjahre*. Through the figures of Mignon and Wilhelm, the beautiful widow (the Princess Anna Amalia) and Hilarie (the woman behind the mask of the Princess) are situated in the context of the whole *Wilhelm Meister* novel. Mignon stands for what Goethe and Anna Amalia have lost through their separation. That is the meaning of their pilgrimage to her. Wilhelm is accompanied by a singer characterized as a new Orpheus, singing and playing a lute, although he is introduced as a painter. Because of his bewitching song the mythological Orpheus was allowed by the gods to bring back his young deceased wife, Eurydice, from the underworld. Before he emerged from the underworld he ignored the command that he was not to look back at her. The result was that Eurydike had to remain there.

Not until the last evening of the pilgrimage does the link with Mignon become clear:

> A premonition of parting descended on everyone; a gradual lapsing into silence made them all uneasy. The singer took heart and decided to begin playing his instrument loudly, disregarding his earlier well-advised considerateness. He had in mind the image of the charming Mignon singing her first delicate song. Passionately transgressing the limits, he brought the strings to life with his longing touch and began to sing: 'Do you know the land/Where the lemon trees bloom,/In the dark foliage ...' Hilarie stood up, deeply moved, and walked away, covering her face; our beautiful widow made a sign with one hand for the singer to stop and with the other hand she gripped Wilhelm's arm. The completely confused young man followed Hilarie, and Wilhelm took the more composed widow and followed them. Then, when all four of them faced one another in the light of the moon the emotion they shared could no longer be hidden. The women threw their arms around one another, the men embraced, and Luna was witness to the most chaste tears. Gradually, calm was restored. They drew back in silence, experiencing strange feelings and wishes, for which, however, all hope had been cut off. Now our artist, whom his friend dragged off with him, felt, under the glorious sky at this lovely, sober hour of the night, that he was initiated into the first degree sufferings of the renunciants. They had already undergone them but they now saw themselves in danger of having to undergo them again.

With their separation Goethe and Anna Amalia had undergone the first degree of renunciation, but the singer still had to survive the experience of renunciation. But the possibility of failure is implied. The two women, who stand for Anna Amalia, are in Italy, where the singer David Heinrich Grave (1752-1789) committed suicide because of unrequited love. By 'passionately transgressing the limits' in singing Mignon's song, he is trying to find his way to Hilarie's heart – to declare his love to the woman behind the mask of the widowed Princess Anna Amalia. The song reminds Hilarie of Mignon, who is the personification of Goethe's and Anna Amalia's physical love. 'Hilarie' becomes sad because even after the forced separation there is only room for Goethe in her heart. The widow, the Princess Anna Amalia, remains in control of herself – she made a sign for the singer to stop. The confused young man, Grave, lost his inner equilibrium in Naples, and, like a new Orpheus, fell victim to the dangers involved in having to renounce his love.

The third novella, mentioned by Goethe in an entry for 1807 in the *Tag- und Jahreshefte*, is 'The Neue Melusine' (*Wanderjahre* III, 6). It is a free reworking of older models. The first part seems to have been conceived from 1782 onwards, the second part in 1807.[767] In the novella the hero is led into the realm of the gnomes. (Interestingly, the word 'gno-mi-n' can be formed out of the name 'Mi-gno-n'.) The hero of the novella becomes acquainted one day with a beautiful woman who has a mysterious little casket. As a reward for his carrying the casket for her, she becomes close to him for a while. One day, in the darkness he notices that light is emanating from the casket. He looks into it through a slit:

> How great was my astonishment when I found myself looking into a well-lit, tastefully and expensively furnished room, just as if I had looked down from above into a regal salon ... from the other side of the room came a woman holding a book in her hands. I recognized her immediately as my woman, although the image of her was contracted to the tiniest dimensions.

Later the woman comes to him in her completely normal form. Since he knows about her transformation she asks him:

> Think carefully whether this discovery has done harm to your love, whether you can forget that I am with you in two different forms and whether when I am reduced in size your affection for me is not also reduced.

Here Goethe is ironically comparing the official Anna Amalia with the unofficial. The Princess is for him nothing but a lessening of the woman Anna Amalia:

> I looked at her. She was more beautiful than ever, and I thought to myself: Is it such a bad thing to have a woman who from time to time becomes a dwarf – so small that she can be carried around in a casket?

Here the realm of the dwarfs stands for court society which Goethe caricatures in the myth of the creation of the dwarfs which he has his Princess narrate. The dwarfs, the oldest and noblest work of God's creation, are confronted with the problem that they are becoming ever smaller, 'but, more than all others, the royal family'.

To inject new blood into the dwarf race, the beautiful woman was:

> sent into the land ... to marry an honourable knight. They would perhaps have been slower to send out a Princess again if my younger brother had not turned out to be so small that the nursemaids lost him out of his baby's napkin and we don't know what became of him.

With the aid of a golden ring which makes him smaller the hero follows the Princess into the realm of the gnomes. But the hero, now the husband of the Princess, is unhappy amongst the gnomes – court society:

> Unfortunately, I had not forgotten my earlier condition. I found I was measuring by the standard of my previous size, which made me restless. For the first time I understood what the philosophers meant by their ideals which are supposed to be a torture for human beings. I had my own ideal for myself, and sometimes I dreamed I was a giant.

By filing through the ring he is transformed back into his original size: 'There I was again, much larger, but, as I felt, more foolish and more awkward ... and so I came, by a fairly circuitous route, back to the cook in the kitchen.'

It is important for the interpretation of the *Lehrjahre* to examine the comparison Goethe made between this novella and his fairytale 'Der Neue Paris'. He said he told this fairytale to his playmates when he was a boy, but it dates, in fact, from 1811.[768] Right at the beginning of *Dichtung und Wahrheit* (Book 10) we read: '"Die Neue Melusine" stands in relation to 'Der Neue Paris' more or less as the youth to the boy.' In the fairytale the messenger god Mercury appears to the boy Goethe on the night before Whit Sunday and hands him three apples: one red, one yellow, and one green:

> Then I held them up in the air towards the light and found they were completely transparent; but very soon they became elongated and turned into three beautiful, beautiful little women the size of normal dolls. Their clothes were the colour of the original apples.

After these disappeared, another one appeared to him: 'Suddenly I saw on my fingertips the loveliest girl dancing around, smaller than the previous ones, but dainty and cheerful.' She remains on his fingertips, but when he tries to take hold of her he feels 'a blow on the head that made me fall down stunned'.

Goethe, an untiring student of colour, made important scientific contributions to the subject, culminating in the sentence: 'Colours are acts of light, active and passive' [Taten und Leiden].[769] On the high desk at the east end of his study Goethe placed a small pyramid. He painted the four triangular surfaces in different colours and wrote on them the qualities belonging to each: yellow with the designation reason, red with fantasy, green with sensuousness, and blue with intellect (ill. 22).[770] He assigned three of these colours with their qualities to the three female figures, making them personifications of reason, fantasy, and sensuousness. This is crucial for interpreting the *Lehrjahre*. When the boy in the fairytale goes out on Whit Sunday morning, he finds to his surprise the entrance to a fairytale garden in which he encounters the three women and Alerte again. But as he is on his way to them a starling calls to him, 'Paris, Paris', and another,

'Narcissus, Narcissus'. Goethe does not become a new Paris because he is also a Narcissus. The starlings are predicting his future. Paris abducted the beautiful Helen and thereby brought about the Trojan War and finally the downfall of Troy. Goethe might well have fled with his 'Helen' – Anna Amalia – to America and could well have caused the downfall of the Duchy of Sachsen-Weimar-Eisenach. Through the prophecy that he would be the new Paris, in the fairytale Goethe is comparing Weimar with Troy, as he had also compared it with Bethlehem and Rome. If he is the new Paris, Anna Amalia is his Helen. This is a significant reference to the Faust play (c. 1772-1831), which, however, was still to be subjected to extensive development. Narcissus, the beautiful son of the River God Cephisos, spurned the love of the mountain nymph, Echo, and was punished by the goddess Aphrodite: bent over the water of a spring he fell in love with his own image. Here Goethe is referring to his self-centred, narcissistic insistence that his love relationship with Anna Amalia be made known, since he could not stand being allowed to love his Princess only in secret. As is shown in *Tasso*, the result is that the poet destroys his own happiness, and only renunciation is left.

In the enchanted garden the young boy Goethe meets the women, 'dressed in three different colours, one in red, one in yellow, and one in green', and along with them Alerte. The woman in red (Fantasy) is 'a dignified figure with strong facial features and majestic bearing'. The woman in yellow (Reason) is 'light, charming, and cheerful'. The one in green (Sensuousness)

> was the one who took most notice of me and seemed to play up to me; only I did not know what to think of her. She was at different times delicate, strange, open, self-willed, depending on how she changed her expression and her game. I would feel moved by her, and then teased. But no matter what she did, she didn't get far with me.

The boy Goethe is taken with Alerte: 'I would have preferred to take hold of the lovely little one if I had not remembered the blow she gave me in my dream.' Alerte leads Goethe into her room and puts oranges, figs, peaches, and grapes in front of him which ... are used as symbols of sex.[771] The boy and Alerte then play with toy soldiers. The game becomes increasingly grim and in a strange way seems to have real consequences, until – an ever recurring motif with Goethe – a kiss breaks the spell:

> My fiercest wish was to destroy her whole army; she, for her part, was not passive. She attacked and gave me a box on the ear that had my head ringing. Since I had always heard that a box on the ear warranted a good kiss, I took her by the ears and kissed her

> repeatedly. She let out such a penetrating scream that I myself got a fright and let go of her.

At the end of the adventure Goethe concludes for the boy that Alerte has to be his. Thus Alerte is a name for Anna Amalia. It means 'the cheerful one', and in a dangerous situation it means 'alarm'.[772]

Against the backdrop of the fairytale 'Der Neue Paris', three central female figures in the *Lehrjahre* can be interpreted as Fantasy, Sensuousness, and Reason. Because of the many women around Wilhelm (Goethe) this novel of rearing and education was exposed to vigorous criticism. It was even publicly burnt. Herder wrote: ' ... the Marianes and Philines, I hate them all'. Goethe's brother-in-law Schlosser saw the *Lehrjahre* as a depiction of a whore house.[773] But as personifications many of the women in the novel have no biographical reference. The first woman in the novel whom Wilhelm loves is called Mariane and stands for Fantasy (red). Wilhelm has met her first as an actress in the theatre (*Lehrjahre* I, 3):

> ... after a short time he had won her affection. He found that he had in her a person he really loved and even honoured, for she appeared to him first in the favourable light of theatrical performance, and his passion for the theatre became united with his first love for a woman.

Goethe, who from his early days wanted to become a writer, describes the feeling that took hold of him when he saw he belonged to the special band of people who were able to throw in their lot with Fantasy (*Lehrjahre* I, 10):

> When he awoke from the first transports of love and looked back on his life and his situation, everything seemed new to him: his duties seemed holier, his interests more alive, his knowledge clearer, his talents stronger, his resolutions more decisive.

Thanks to Fantasy Goethe can break away from the path mapped out for him:

> He [Wilhelm] thought he saw a clear sign from fate, helping him, through Mariane, to tear himself away from the stagnant, plodding middle-class life from which he had for a long time wished to be rescued.

In the poem 'Meine Göttin' sent to Anna Amalia ('Frau von Stein') on 15 September 1780, Goethe celebrates Fantasy. As a mortal he expresses his gratitude that he has been given 'a beautiful,/Unfading spouse' who is faithful; and he assigns colours to her: 'Crowned with roses,/Bearing lilies, she may walk/The flowered valleys.' The lily and the rose stand for white and red. They are the colours of love. White, for Goethe, stands for abstraction and purity,[774] and red, above all, for

Fantasy. When Mariane is introduced she is associated with red and white (*Lehrjahre* I, 2): 'With what liveliness she flew towards him [Wilhelm]. With what ecstasy he embraced the red uniform and pressed the white satin waist-coat to his bosom!'

Goethe does not necessarily presuppose knowledge of the fairytale 'Der Neue Paris' for understanding that many figures in the *Lehrjahre* are symbols. With regard to Marianne, Goethe explains quite openly in the text that she is the personification of Fantasy. He will treat other figures similarly later in the novel. From the beginning, Mariane appears accompanied by a certain Barbara, her 'old servant, confidante, advisor, agent, and house-keeper' (*Lehrjahre* I, 1). That both are personifications is clear from Wilhelm's stories (*Lehrjahre* I, 8). One evening he is telling Mariane about his life while Barbara sits at the table. In the middle of his story he says:

> I remember a poem, which has to be somewhere amongst my papers, in which the muse of tragedy [Melpomene] and another female figure through which I personified commerce were quarrelling vehemently about my good self. It was a wretched idea, and I don't remember if the verses were any good; but you should see it, just for the sake of the fear, the disgust, the love, and the passion it is full of.

Goethe has Wilhelm say: 'You should see it.' But this does not happen. So the poem is none other than the novel now being read. The muse is Mariane and the personification of commerce is Barbara. The narration continues in a manner which characterizes the development of Goethe's novel itself:

> How uneasily I had depicted the old woman with a distaff and key in her belt, spectacles on her nose, always busy, never at rest, quarrelsome, concerned with the house-keeping, petty, and difficult! ... How different was she! [Mariane]. What an apparition for the troubled heart. A glorious figure, in her attitude and bearing she looked like a daughter of freedom. Her self-awareness gave her dignity without pride ... What a contrast! ... The rivalry was vigorous, the speech of both was in fitting contrast ... The old woman spoke as you would expect of a person who picks up a thumb tack, and the other one spoke like someone who gives away kingdoms. The warnings and threats of the old woman were spurned. I saw myself turning away from the wealth that was promised me: disinherited and naked, I surrendered to the muse who threw me her golden veil to cover my nakedness. Had I imagined, O my beloved, he exclaimed as he clasped Mariane firmly to his breast, that a quite different, a lovelier goddess would come and strengthen my resolve and accompany me on my way, what a different turn my poem would have taken, how interesting the conclusion of it would have been. But

> it is not a poem. What I have in my arms is truth and life. Let us consciously enjoy the sweet happiness!

Goethe merges the level of a supposed poem with the level of the novel, which for the writer is 'truth and life'. 'Everything that moves him, be it in joy or in suffering, has to be released by finding expression [in his creative writing]', says Boisserée in an entry in his diary on 6 October 1815.[775] Goethe characterizes Mariane as Melpomene, the muse of tragedy – the dramatic genre in which the heroes are inevitably destroyed –, for Mariane, for dramaturgical reasons, has to die young. But she has awakened in Wilhelm a longing for the theatre and has born him a son: Felix, 'the happy one'.

The next female figure who can be interpreted as a personification is Philine, who stands for Sensuousness (green). There is constant talk about Philine's charms, which she knows how to use, as witnessed by her conquests. After the theatre troupe which Wilhelm has joined is attacked by bandits, those who have been robbed of their possessions are looking with displeasure at Philine (*Lehrjahre* IV, 7), because they

> wanted to see as a crime the way she rescued her case. From all kinds of innuendos and taunts one could conclude that during the pillaging she concentrated on winning the favour of the chief bandit and was able to persuade him, by who knows what artful attentions, to leave her case alone. She seemed to have gone missing for a while.

When Philine is to play the role of a Duchess in a comedy, she is absolutely delighted (*Lehrjahre* V, 5):

> I will do that just as naturally, she exclaimed, as one marries a second husband after having loved the first one to distraction. I hope to receive enormous applause, and every man will want to be number three.

For Friedrich Schlegel (1772-1829 she was 'the seductive symbol of frivolous sensuousness',[776] but she is also nothing more than the personification of Sensuousness: there is nothing biographical behind her.

Finally, Theresa is the personification of Reason (yellow). She tells Wilhelm about her youth and how little she understood it (*Lehrjahre* VII, 6)

> when the people I knew well disguised themselves, stood up there [on the stage] and pretended to be something other than they were ... So I rarely stayed in the audience. To have something to do I cleaned the lights, looked after the evening meal, and the next day, when they were all still sleeping, I put some order into their costumes which usually on the previous evening they left lying in a heap.

For Theresa lack of order is unbearable, for:

> What is our greatest happiness but to carry out what we consider right and good? That we are really master of the means to our ends. And where should and can our proximate ends lie except in the house. All our recurring, inescapable needs – where do we expect them, want them to be other than where we get up and lie down, where kitchen and cellar and everything needed by us and ours should always be ready?

Her small house is correspondingly described. There is hardly room for Wilhelm to turn around in her garden, for

> the paths were so narrow and there were so many plants. He had to smile as he returned across the yard, for the firewood was so accurately sawn, split, and stacked that it might have been part of the building and would remain there as such. All vessels were neatly in their proper place.

The text continues, caricaturing Reason, with the description of Theresa saying about herself: 'I had never loved, and still did not love' (*Lehrjahre* VII, 5). Theresa will finally admit (*Lehrjahre* VIII, 4): 'Insight, order, discipline, commands – those are my thing.'

The personifications of Fantasy, Sensuousness and Reason provide the framework in which Goethe unfolds his biography with many other symbolic figures. In a conversation with Chancellor von Müller on 22 January 1821 Goethe speaks of 'fronting persons' and says that 'the whole novel is completely symbolic'. Again on 8 June 1821 he says to von Müller: 'The whole thing is to be understood symbolically. Everywhere [you look] there is something else at the back of things.'[777]

The next figure in the novel that can be interpreted symbolically is Felix, the child of Wilhelm and Mariane (Fantasy). In the *Lehrjahre* Wilhelm will lose all that is dear to him to become the renunciant of the *Wanderjahre*. But Felix will remain with him (*Lehrjahre* VIII, 7): Come, dear boy! ... Occupy my mind with your beauty, your loveliness, your curiosity, and your talents.' At the end of the *Lehrjahre*, when Wilhelm receives from the members of the Tower Society his apprentice's indenture – a collection of aphorisms in the old tradition – he asks the question (VII, 9): 'Fine, you strange and wise men whose gaze penetrates so many secrets, can you tell me if Felix is really my son?' They confirm this for him. Felix suddenly appears. Wilhelm takes him in his arms and 'pressed him to his bosom. Yes, I feel it, he exclaimed. You are mine. How indebted I am to my friends for this gift from heaven!' Felix, a gift from heaven, the fruit of a union with Fantasy, stands for Goethe's poetic gift, for his artistic genius.

At the beginning of the *Wanderjahre* Wilhelm and Felix are led into a trap by the cunning boy Fitz – who stands for Fritz von Stein. In an underground passage 'there is suddenly a shot ... and at the same time two hidden iron gratings fall closed'. Wilhelm and Felix are trapped, while Fitz runs off laughing (I, 4). It is only a false alarm, like Fritz's anonymous confession that he knew Goethe's and Anna Amalia's secret. This, too, was a false alarm because it was never made public. The end of his first decade in Weimar is the point where Goethe goes back to the beginning of the story of how he (Wilhelm) and his poetic gift (Felix) become involved with the cover-up. Wilhelm and Felix are freed from the trap by armed men and immediately brought to an inn. There they are briefly deprived of their freedom until the matter is cleared up and both are asked to go to a castle. Within this framework Goethe is able to show how his poetic gift was affected by the need for deception:

> On entering, Wilhelm immediately sat down and thought through the situation; Felix, on the other hand, after recovering from his initial astonishment, gave vent to an unbelievable rage. These high walls, the high windows, the secure doors, being locked up – all this confinement was new to him. He looked around, ran backwards and forwards, stamped his feet, wept, shook the doors, pounded them with his fists, and he would have run at them head-on if Wilhelm had not taken hold of him and forcefully restrained him. 'Just look at it quite calmly, son', the father began. 'Impatience and violence will be no help in this situation.'

Felix now falls into a deep sleep and is not aware that an official enters, clarifies the situation with Wilhelm and then wants to bring them both out of the room. 'Felix could not be awakened. Servants carried him on a good mattress, like Ulysses of old, into the open air.' In Homer's *Odyssey*, the hero Ulysses (Odysseus), after wandering lost for a long time, finally finds his way back to his kingdom of Ithaca (*Odyssey* XIII, 115ff.):

> Oarsmen ...
> Climbed ashore from a well constructed ship
> First lifting Odysseus out of the hollow vessel,
> In the linen cloth and the shining blanket,
> Laid him down in the sand
> As he was, overcome by sleep.[778]

When Goethe found in Anna Amalia the woman of his life, he had to manage a plan of deception. It was still crucial for him to produce works with a ring of truth. To do this he resorted to encoding them – hence the image of the sleeping Felix, who after a traumatic experience suddenly finds himself in beautiful surroundings but is innocent of the deception that makes this possible. In his poem 'Zueignung' (1784) which Goethe wanted placed at the beginning of his Collected Works, there are the lines: 'Woven from the scent of morning air and clear sunlight,/The veil of poetry from the hand of truth'. For Goethe there is no poetry without truth. According to Riemer, Goethe's collaborator: 'Truth is the body, poetry is only the cloak, the frame which surrounded and limited an image of the real [ein wirkliches Bild].'[779]

Two further women competing for Wilhelm's love can now be identified as the official (the beautiful Countess) and the unofficial (the Amazon, Natalie) Anna Amalia. With the Countess there are direct links to the Princess, for example, her beautiful feet, much vaunted in Weimar. As an old man, a former page of Anna Amalia, recalled the feet of his Princess:

> Her small feet were admired by all, and since she put on a new pair of shoes every day which she then passed on to her chamber maids, the shoes were often up for sale and every lady was proud of being able to fit her foot into the Duchess's shoes. Court cavaliers and other cavaliers gallantly wore little golden shoes on ornamental chains.[780]

The beautiful foot is also mentioned in *Tasso* where it is said about the poet (ll. 190f.): 'When the revered lady leaves he treats as holy/The path which her lovely foot so lightly treads.' In the *Lehrjahre* (V, 5) it is now said about a pair of dainty gloves: 'They were made in Paris. Philine had received them as a present from the Countess, a lady whose beautiful feet were famous.' Philine is also the one who, when the Countess arrived, 'with a pious expression and humble demeanour bowed and kissed the lady's dress' (*Lehrjahre* III, 1). Kissing the dress was again an expression of honour to a Princess. Whole key scenes of the *Lehrjahre* are only comprehensible when the personifications are identified as such. Philine as the personification of Sensuousness is therefore the one present when Wilhelm is invited to meet the Countess (*Lehrjahre* III, 12):

> Philine grasped the right hand of the Countess and kissed it fervently. Wilhelm fell onto his knees, took her left hand and pressed it to his lips. The Countess seemed embarrassed but was not resisting ... But, Philine continued, laying her hand on the Countess's heart, 'it is not possible, is it, that the image of another man [other than that of her husband] has slipped into this hidden capsule?'

After Philine had gone, Wilhelm held

> the most beautiful hand in his hands ... He kissed her hand and wanted to stand up, but just as in a dream the strangest things surprise us by developing out of other strange things, Wilhelm,

> without knowing how it happened, held the Countess in his arms, her lips rested on his, and the passionate kisses they exchanged gave them the happiness we can only drink with the first sips from the bubbling cup of love. ... How Wilhelm was terrified, how he was stunned and started up out of this dream as the Countess tore herself away from him with a scream, and clasped her breast ... 'Leave me', she cried, and taking her hand away from her eyes she looked at him with an indescribable gaze and added with the loveliest voice: 'Flee from me, if you love me' ... Unlucky ones! What strange warning of chance or fate tore them from one another?

When Wilhelm is lying in Philine's lap after the attack by the bandits, a lady comes on the scene who is referred to as the beautiful Amazon (*Lehrjahre* IV, 6). Later we find out that she is called Natalie. This name could easily be seen as referring to Frau von Stein, who was born on 25 December, for Natalie means 'born at Christmas'. But Goethe used the two names 'Amazone' and 'Natalie' to encode the name of his beloved: AMA(zone Nata)LIE. The encounter with the Amazon is a key experience for Wilhelm and never leaves him (*Lehrjahre* IV, 10):

> All the dreams of his youth became tied to this image. He now believed he had seen with his own eyes the noble, heroic Chlorinde; he recalled the ailing King's son whose sickbed the beautiful, sympathetic Princess approached.

Here, as with the image of the Amazon, Goethe is linking up with images taken from Tasso's crusade poem *Jerusalem Delivered* (1581) and in this way is referring to the Princess in *Tasso*, and therefore to Anna Amalia.

Natalie, the beautiful Amazon, is the sister of the beautiful Countess. There is a striking similarity between them, right down to their handwriting (*Lehrjahre* IV, 11): 'They resembled one another as sisters can when one cannot be said to be younger or older than the other, for they seemed to be twins.' When Wilhelm sees Natalie again, we read (*Lehrjahre* VIII, 2):

> It was the Amazon! Wilhelm could not contain himself. He fell on his knees and exclaimed: 'It's you!' He clasped her hand and kissed it with infinite delight. The child [Felix] lay between both of them on the carpet in a gentle sleep.

The Countess expresses symbolically that she, the Princess Anna Amalia, and her sister Natalie, the unofficial Anna Amalia, are forming a bond with Wilhelm (Goethe) (*Lehrjahre* VIII, 10): 'As she was taking her leave the beautiful Countess took Wilhelm's hand before she let her sister's hand go, pressed all four hands together, turned around quickly and climbed into the carriage.' At the end of the *Lehrjahre*, when Wilhelm has found in Natalie the woman of his life and all hindrances to their union are removed, he is

> constrained to flee! Why does an insuperable need for possessing [her] go hand in hand with these feelings, this awareness? And why, where there is no possession, do these feelings and convictions destroy every other kind of happiness? Will I in future be able to enjoy the sun and the world, company, or any other good thing? Will you always have to say to yourself: Natalie is not there! – and yet, unfortunately, Natalie will always be present to you.

In a letter to Anna Amalia ('Frau von Stein') from Italy on 21 February 1787 the impossibility for Goethe of openly declaring his love is given as the reason for renunciation:

> Dear Lotte, you don't know what it has cost me, and still costs me, and that the thought of not possessing you, no matter how I look at it and from what angle I see it, upsets and consumes me.

Against this backdrop the figures of Mignon and her father, Augustin the harpist, are likewise to be understood as personifications. Wilhelm makes the acquaintance of Mignon as a small girl in boy's clothing and a member of a rope-dancing troupe (*Lehrjahre* II, 4):

> He looked on, appalled, as he pushed his way through the crowd and saw the head of the troupe dragging the interesting child out of the house by the hairs of her head and unmercifully striking the little body with blows from a whip-handle.

Wilhelm buys her free and keeps her with him. In a note-book dated 1793 Goethe refers to Mignon as 'insanity of a disproportionate relationship' [Mißverhältnis].[781] There is a clear parallel here to his characterizing of Tasso: 'It is a disproportion between talent and life.'[782] The Mignon story does not explain why Wilhelm, who has bought Mignon her freedom, is supposed to be indebted to her (*Lehrjahre* III, 2):

> Mignon had just approached. He took her in his arms and exclaimed: 'No, nothing is to separate us, you good little one! What seems to be worldly prudence is not an excuse for me to leave you or to forget what I owe you.'

This only becomes comprehensible if Mignon is understood as a personification of Goethe's and Anna Amalia's physical love, its heart. Seen in this way, all her utterances as well as her death take on a meaning. For this reason Goethe confesses in a conversation with

Chancellor von Müller on 29 May 1814 that 'the whole work [*Wilhelm Meister*] was written for the sake of this character [Mignon]'.

But in the course of the novel Wilhelm does have to be separated from Mignon, the personification of his love for Anna Amalia. She has to go into the country to Therese (Reason), where she could possibly be cured (*Lehrjahre* VII, 8):

> He [Wilhelm] thought of Mignon and Felix and how happy the children could be under such supervision [Therese's]; then he thought of himself and felt what a joy it must be to live in the company of someone so clear-headed (*Lehrjahre* VII, 6).

Mignon is crushed by this idea: 'You don't want me with you?' she said. 'Perhaps it is better if you send me to the old harpist. The poor man is so alone.' Wilhelm replied that he had not noticed this affection when the harpist was living with them, to which Mignon replied:

> I was afraid of him when he was awake. I couldn't look at his eyes. But when he was asleep I liked to sit down beside him ... He stood by me in some terrible moments. No one knows how much I owe him.

When Wilhelm sticks to his plan, Mignon says (*Lehrjahre* VII, 8): 'Reason [Therese] is cruel ... The heart [Mignon] is better. I will go where you want, but leave your Felix [poetic gift] with me.' For Felix, Mignon is his 'nurse, mother, sister, and friend'.[783] When Mignon is close to death, she is already seen in the form of an angel. Children stand around her and she is clothed in a white garment (*Lehrjahre*, VIII, 2): 'Are you an angel?' asked one of the children. 'I wish I were', replied Mignon. 'Why are you carrying a lily?' 'If my heart were as pure and open I would be happy.' Goethe's and Anna Amalia's heart, Mignon, the little gnome, has to put off all that is earthly, while Felix, the poetic gift, can live on (*Lehrjahre* VIII, 3):

> Mignon, dressed in long white woman's clothing, her rich brown hair partly curled, and partly pinned up, sat there with Felix on her lap, pressing him to her heart. While she looked completely like a departed spirit, the boy looked like life itself. It seemed as if heaven and earth were in an embrace.

When she races with Felix to open the door for a guest she is totally exhausted (*Lehrjahre* VIII, 5):

> Mignon lay in Natalie's arms, her heart pounding. 'Naughty child!', said Natalie. 'Weren't you told not to do anything strenuous? Look how your heart is beating.' 'Let it break', said Mignon with a deep sigh. 'It has been beating too long already.'

Therese (Reason) enters and says to Wilhelm, who, before finding Natalie again, has offered Therese his hand in marriage:

> 'My friend! My beloved! My husband, yes, [I am] eternally yours', she exclaimed amid passionate kisses ... Mignon suddenly put her left hand on her heart and, violently stretching out her right arm, with a scream she fell at Natalie's feet as if dead.

Mignon, the personification of Goethe's and Anna Amalia's physical love, dies because of Therese (Reason), but she turns into an angel. She is transported to a realm beyond the sense-world, as is Goethe's love for Anna Amalia.

Through the figure of Mignon, Goethe describes how he suffered in his early Weimar years by having to deny his love for Anna Amalia and maintain, for the public eye, an indefinable relationship to the married Frau von Stein. 'I see no noble man who has suffered more than I ever did' he writes in *Tasso* (ll. 3423f.). Mignon's subtle egg-dance stands for the deceptions daily required in that period. This began with the meeting in Ilmenau in 1776, where Goethe and Frau von Stein pretended to Carl August and his court that they had a special feeling for one another. Interestingly, the courthouse in Ilmenau is identified as the place where Goethe situates the scene in which Wilhelm observes Mignon's egg-dance.[784]

With the extremely complex egg-dance Goethe finds a comparison for the series of unbelievable tricks used, from 1776 until his flight to Italy in 1786, to make their nocturnal love possible. Out of love for Anna Amalia, Goethe performed with her, and with the co-operation of Frau von Stein, a veritable egg-dance. In November 1776 Countess Görtz reported 'Frau von Stein's sheer admiration for the game played by her friend' [Goethe][785] during a performance of *Die Geschwister* in Anna Amalia's amateur theatre. The Baltic writer Sophie Becker notes in her diary on 30 December 1784:

> I must not forget that we dined with Frau von Stein yesterday and at the end of the meal we saw Privy Councillor Goethe come in. He is a very familiar figure in the house of Herr von Stein. There is something dreadfully stiff in his demeanour and he says very little.[786]

From such descriptions it is clear that Goethe finally only felt disgust at his dissimulation. He had continually to perform an egg-dance.

Augustin, the harpist, is also one of Wilhelm's companions. He radiates sadness and is living with the fear that he must soon die. 'His greatest delusion is that he brings unhappiness everywhere with him and that death awaits him through an innocent boy' (*Lehrjahre* VII, 4). When Wilhelm goes to visit him he hears him singing a song (*Lehrjahre* II, 13):

> He who never ate his bread in tears,
> Who never sat weeping through

> The troubled nights,
> Knows you not, you heavenly powers.
>
> You lead us into life,
> You let a poor man become guilty
> Then you leave him to his pain:
> For all guilt is revenged on earth.

He will sing more sad songs about pain, torment, and guilt. In his youth Augustin had been a monk. Later he had committed an horrendous sin. Without knowing it he had been the lover of his sister Sperata ('hoping'). Mignon was the product of this union (*Lehrjahre* VIII, 9). When Mignon was abducted by the rope-dancers, Sperata thought her daughter was dead. Later she became a highly esteemed woman who after her death was thought to be a saint. The Harpist, as father of Mignon – who is Goethe's personification of Goethe's and Anna Amalia's physical love – can himself only be a personification: he stands for deception. Goethe chooses the name Augustin to refer to Anna Amalia's son Carl August, because to avoid endangering his position as ruler a deception had to be used. Mignon is born as daughter of hope and deception, both of which were necessary for Goethe's love for Anna Amalia. The innocent boy who brings death to the Harpist is Fritz von Stein, the 'traitor', who discovered Goethe's and Anna Amalia's secret and made the flight to Italy necessary.

When Augustin found out that Sperata, his beloved, was his sister, he justified himself by saying that Nature would not let anything survive if there was a curse on it. But he was told:

> He should bear in mind that he was not living in the free world of his thoughts and imagination but within a constitution whose laws and circumstances had become just as compelling as natural law.

For Goethe and Anna Amalia the social boundaries were just as fixed as laws based on nature. When Wilhelm tries to prevent the Harpist from leaving him, Augustin says (*Lehrjahre* IV, 1): 'Leave me my horrible secret and let me go. The vengeance that pursues me is not that of an earthly judge. My fate is inexorable ... My presence chases happiness away, and a good deed is robbed of its force when I come along.'

> The morning sun lights up for him
> With flames the pure horizon
> And the beautiful world collapses
> Above his guilty head.

Augustin says what the horrible secret is (*Lehrjahre* II, 13):

> O leave me to my torment
> And if I am left to myself
> Then I am not alone.
>
> A lover slips softly by
> Listening: is his beloved alone?
> So day and night creeps over me
> The pain of loneliness
> The torment of loneliness.
> Once I am alone in the grave
> It will leave me alone.

Goethe, the lover, visits his beloved Anna Amalia in the evenings in stealth and suffers pain and torment from the need for deception. For a long time Mignon and the Harpist are Wilhelm's travelling companions (*Lehrjahre* IV, 12). Later the Harpist tries to kill Felix, Goethe's poetic gift: 'Then he put Felix down [on burning straw], put his hands on the child's head with strange gestures and drew a knife as if he intended to sacrifice him.' Mignon prevents him. The continual deception was threatening to undermine Goethe's poetic genius, but the strength given him by his love for Anna Amalia prevented the worst. The Harpist, tortured by the fear of death is able to bear his ravaged moral and physical condition by keeping in his possession a glass of liquid opium, 'the strangest antidote'. The knowledge that he can end his existence at any time helps him to continue living (*Lehrjahre* VIII, 10):

> The feeling that it was desirable to see an end to the sufferings of this earth at first put me [Augustin] on the road to recovery; ... the possibility of ridding myself forever of the great suffering gave me the strength to bear the pain, and so, ever since I have had this talisman, I have forced myself, through the proximity of death, back into life.

Through the knowledge that he could end it at any time, Goethe was able to carry on this deception and to fool the world around him. But the plans for emigrating to America foundered. Instead, through an unfortunate set of circumstances Goethe was forced to beat a hasty retreat to Italy. Through the antidote, the glass of opium, Goethe explains why the existence of poetry and deceit side by side does not have disastrous consequences. Felix, Goethe's poetic self, is in danger (*Lehrjahre* VIII, 10):

> One day, despite the pain, they [Wilhelm and Natalie] were in a more cheerful mood than usual, when Augustin tore open the door and rushed in in a terrible frenzy. His face was pale, he had a wild look in his eye. It seemed as if he wanted to speak, but the words would not

> come ... He stuttered, his speech was muffled, then he spoke vigorously, violently: 'Hurry! Help! Save the child! Felix is poisoned!'

Augustin believes that Felix has drunk out of the glass into which he has just poured the liquid opium, and Felix 'admits' it:

> 'Father', he says, 'I didn't drink out of the bottle, I drank out of the glass. I was so thirsty.' Augustin wrung his hands and exclaimed: 'He is lost, finished!' They found a glass of almond milk on the table and a small flask beside it, half empty. The doctor came, was told what had happened, was horrified to see the familiar little bottle which had contained the liquid opium empty on the table. He had vinegar brought and called on all the means available to him.

Everything was set in motion to help Felix:

> The child lay resting on the bed and seemed very sick. He asked his father not to pour anything else into him, not to torment him any further ... Natalie sat with the child, who took refuge in her lap. He pleaded with her to protect him, pleaded for a piece of sugar, because the vinegar was too sour! ... Wilhelm, who was sitting in an armchair inconsolable, jumped up, cast a despairing glance at Natalie, and went out the door.

Meanwhile the Harpist, who had by chance come to read a summary of his life history and wanted to put an end to his life by taking the opium, found another means: 'He was found on the floor above lying in his blood with a razor beside him. He had probably cut his throat with it (*Lehrjahre* VIII, 10).' And so Goethe's secret is out. Augustin, the personification of the hated deception, can at last die a horrible death. After he was found alive and was rescued, he removed a bandage during the night: 'The next morning Augustin was found dead in his bed. He had deceived his attendants by his apparent calmness, loosened the bandage, and bled to death.' Before he died he grasped Wilhelm's hand. 'Why', he said, 'did I not leave you long ago? I knew that I would kill the boy and that he would kill me.'

Felix, the personification of Goethe's poetic gift, is still showing no symptoms of poisoning:

> 'I don't understand', said the doctor, after pausing for a while, 'that there is not the slightest trace of a dangerous condition in the child. With even just one swallow he must have taken an enormous dose of opium.' During the whole night no one slept, all were worried. The child wanted Natalie to stay with him. Wilhelm sat in front of her on a stool. The boy's feet were on his lap and his head and chest were on her lap, so that they shared the pleasant burden and the painful worry.

The doctor's only explanation for this was that Felix

> ... luckily, had drunk out of the bottle! A good spirit had led his hand, so that he did not take hold of the death that was so near. 'No! No!' shouted Wilhelm, covering his eyes with his hands, 'What an awful thing to say! The child said expressly that he did not drink out of the bottle. He drank out of the glass. He only seems to be healthy. He is going to die before our eyes.' ... Nathalie took the child for a walk. He was as cheerful as on his very best days. 'You are kind', Felix said to her, 'you won't scold me, you won't hit me. I'll only say it to you: I drank out of the bottle.'

Although Felix would have been saved if he had drunk out of the bottle, Goethe still has Wilhelm exclaim, covering his eyes with his hands, 'What an awful thing to say!' Through this apparent contradiction, Goethe is mocking, with subtle irony the colourless theoreticians like Kant who, totally abstracted from practical life, create categorical laws forbidding any kind of lie. If Goethe had acted on such a categorical law he would have been prevented by the prevalent social system from being close to the love of his life, and so the world would have been deprived of his incomparable creative work. In one of his *Maximen und Reflexionen* Goethe says: 'If God had really been concerned that people should be truthful in their life and dealings he would have had to organize things differently.' Goethe's Felix (poetic gift) could only survive through the pretence that he had drunk out of the 'poisoned glass' given by clever encoding, in his creative writings. The *Wanderjahre* represent the climax of this process. They only *seem* to break all the bounds of novel theory, but in fact they form a narrative unity on a higher level. On 18 February 1830 Goethe admits to Chancellor von Müller that the *Wanderjahre* novel presents itself as an aggregate.[787] 'Aggregate' means a whole made up of several parts, a sum, originally something to be added to a herd.[788] In the *Wanderjahre* the action providing the framework of the novel, and the novellas included in the framework, tell the story from different angles – as the *Lehrjahre* had already done – of Goethe's forbidden love for Anna Amalia in his first ten years in Weimar. The writer uses a proliferation of stories which always deal with the same subject.

The *Lehrjahre* novel ends with the words: 'I don't know the value of a kingdom', said Wilhelm, 'but I know that I have found happiness [Natalie] that I don't deserve and that I wouldn't exchange for anything in the world.' Yet Wilhelm is separated from this AMA (zone Nata)LIE. Letters to her form the large framework in which the continuation of the autobiography, the *Wanderjahre*, is played out. But Natalie herself no longer appears directly in the work. Wilhelm writes to her in the beginning:

> We have now reached the heights, the heights of the mountain range that will make an even greater separation between us ... What could separate me from you? I am eternally yours, although a strange fate separates me from you and unexpectedly closes to me the heaven I seemed so close to. I had time to gather myself, and yet no time would have been enough to give me this composure if I had not received it from your own lips at the decisive moment. How could I have torn myself away if the continuous thread had not been spun that was to link us for all time and eternity? But I am not permitted to speak of all that. I will not transgress your gentle commands. Here on this peak let it be the last time I say the word 'separation' to you.

The mountain peak stands for Anna Amalia's death in 1807 – he immediately began dictating the *Wanderjahre* – as well as for the Alps, which separated him from Anna Amalia when he fled in 1786.

For Goethe, the *Wanderjahre* novel deals with the 'problem of my life'.[789] Through the figure of Hersilie, Goethe tells the story of the forbidden love from the point of view of Felix, his poetic gift, and Anna Amalia as his muse. Hersilie appears only a few times and briefly, but she creates unifying links within the whole novel. Felix has an undying love for Hersilie although he is much younger than she. Hersilie 'repeatedly takes up the pen to continue my confessions' (*Wanderjahre* II, 3) and confesses the love of an older woman to a younger man, for the difference in age between Goethe and Anna Amalia was ten years:

> The definite and continuing affection of a boy who was becoming a young man [Jüngling] was flattering, but it occurred to me that it was not unusual at this age to be interested in older women. It is indeed the case that there is a secret affection of younger men for older women.

Hersilie says of herself (*Wanderjahre* I, 7): 'It never worked out for me with admirers of my own age. It seems that the next generation is about to compensate me.' But Hersilie's attention shifts between Wilhelm and Felix. In her thoughts Hersilie sometimes has father and son together, sometimes each alternately, before her eyes ... I feel like an innocent Alcmene continually visited by two beings, each representing the other.' Hersilie is comparing herself to the Alcmene who, in Greek mythology, is the wife of the general, Amphitryon. While he is away, Zeus, the supreme god of Greek mythology, approaches her in the form of her husband. Through this ruse Alcmene becomes Zeus' beloved and out of the innocent/guilty adultery Heracles (the Latin Hercules), the bravest of all heroes, is born. 'A horse gallops into the court-yard and wakes me out of my day-dream', Hersilie writes in a letter to Wilhelm (*Wanderjahre* III,

17), 'the door is flung open and in walks Felix, in the full flush of youth, like a little god.' When Goethe [Wilhelm] presents his immortal works to Anna Amalia [Hersilie] he seems to her to be like a god. The poet compares these works to the heroic works of Herakles.

Immediately after the comparison with Alcmene, Hersilie says (*Wanderjahre* II, 10): 'I am just finishing a wallet, a very dainty one, without quite knowing who is to have it – father or son – but certainly one of them.' In this way Goethe is identifying Hersilie with the beautiful widow in the 'Der Mann von Fünfzig Jahren', who was working on a marvellous, tasteful wallet in large format, the symbol for Anna Amalia's transformation of the aimless *Stürmer und Dränger* Goethe (Flavio) into the classical poet and statesman (Major). Through the figures of Wilhelm and Felix, Goethe is only narrating his biography from a different angle. The last of the *Weissagungen des Bakis* (begun 1798) is the key to understanding the manifold personifications of Goethe in the figures of *Wilhelm Meister*:

> Eternally he will be to you the one, divided into many,
> And yet, divided, he remains the one, eternally unique.
> Discover in one the many, feel the many like one;
> There you have the beginning and end of art.

The same applies to Anna Amalia, who has numerous names like Hersilie, beautiful widow, AMA(zone)LIE, and Hilarie. As early as 'Der Mann von Fünfzig Jahren' (*Wanderjahre* II, 7) Goethe made the connection between all these female figures and Wilhelm (Goethe):

> The beautiful widow meanwhile was walking with Wilhelm between cypresses and pine trees, now past the terraced grape vines, now past orange trees, and finally could not resist fulfilling the wish gently hinted at by her new friend: she had to reveal to him the strange circumstances linking the two (the widow and Hilarie) which had them, separated from their early relationship but still inwardly united, sent out into the world. Wilhelm, not lacking in the gift of noting everything carefully, later wrote down the confidential story, and it is our intention to tell our readers later how he wrote it and sent it to Natalie through Hersilie.

This story is never expressly told in the novel but makes up one of the many ways Goethe uses to link his figures together.

Another such link is the image at the beginning of the *Wanderjahre* (I, 5) which Goethe uses to show that the pair Felix and Hersilie and the pair Wilhelm and Natalie are, 'in a higher sense', one and the same:

> Meantime Hersilie was quite aware of the direction in which the handsome Felix's fiery glances were aimed. She was surprised and flattered and sent him the best tidbits, which he took with joy and

> gratitude. But now, when at dessert he looked across at her over a plate full of apples, she thought she could see in the attractive pieces of fruit so many rivals. As quick as a thought, she took one and handed it across the table to this budding adventurer. He took it hastily, began to peel it immediately, but, looking steadily at his attractive neighbour he cut himself deeply in the thumb. Blood flowed freely. Hersilie jumped up, busied herself with him and, when the bleeding stopped, she applied a plaster from her medicine box. Meantime, the boy had taken hold of her and did not want to let go.

Through this passage Goethe is establishing a connection with Wilhelm's first encounter with AMA(zone Nata)LIE in the *Lehrjahre*.[790] Wilhelm had been hurt in the attack by robbers. AMA(zone Nata)LIE found him severely wounded (*Lehrjahre* IV, 6): 'Wilhelm had fixed his gaze on the gentle, lofty, reposed and sympathetic features ... he thought he had never seen anything nobler or more charming.' AMA(zone Nata)LIE immediately brings a surgeon to give medical attention.

Using the image of Felix, Goethe makes further connections – with the scene in the *Lehrjahre* (IV, 20) where Wilhelm makes his vow of fidelity:

> Receive my vow, which comes from the heart ... I will resist every fleeting affection and will keep even the most serious ones secret. No woman will hear a confession of love from my lips unless I can devote my whole life to her.

Aurelie, unhappily in love with Lothario, receives this vow in a special way:

> 'Do you know what you are promising?' 'I do', said Wilhelm, offering his hand. 'I accept it', she said, and made a quick movement with her right hand, making him think she was going to grasp his. But like a flash she took a dagger from her pocket and drew the point and the blade across his hand. He pulled it back quickly, but the blood was running from it already. The cut went from the ball under his thumb, through the life line in the direction of the little finger. She bandaged it quietly, inwardly preoccupied with the significance [of her deed].

Goethe's poetic gift is also truly dedicated to one unique person: Anna Amalia. The fact that this has to be achieved by taking recourse to deception is expressed by Goethe – who describes himself as the 'eternal maker of parables'[791] – in the image of the apple, which refers to the fall of Adam and Eve in the Garden of Eden[792] (Genesis 3): 'And she took of the fruit and ate it and gave of it to Adam who was with her, and he ate it.' The deception which makes their love possible at the same time darkens Goethe's poetic work. In the poem 'Zueignung'

(1784) with which Goethe prefaced his complete works, the poet speaks the verses:

> Am I to have my eyes open in vain?
> A joyful will lives in my blood,
> I know entirely the value of your gifts.
> What I possess grows in me for others
> I can not, will not, any longer bury the talent!
> Why did I seek out the road so longingly
> If I am not to show it to my brothers?
> ...
> Woven from the scent of morning air and clear sunlight,
> The veil of poetry from the hand of truth.

Goethe wants to deny his love for Anna Amalia no longer. In his writing, however, he has to cover it with a veil of 'a thousand folds'. In a conversation on 13 June 1825 Chancellor von Müller asked Goethe to sketch the circumstances in Tiefurt during the Dowager Duchess's time. 'It would not be too difficult', Goethe answered him, 'one would just have to describe them quite faithfully as they appeared to the poetic eye at the time; poetry and truth, without the element of pure poetry [Erdichtung]'.[793]

Goethe saw America as an escape from the hated deception concerning his true beloved. During his first ten years in Weimar America played a central role for Goethe and Anna Amalia. In the first place America was to serve as the model for organizing the small duchy and as an example for Germany. When it became clear to Goethe that this was impossible, he planned to emigrate to America, with Anna Amalia, as an entrepreneur. In the two *Wilhelm Meister* novels Goethe deals with these two phases: 'America is here or it is nowhere,' we read in the *Lehrjahre* (VII, 3). In a letter to Knebel on 21 November 1782 he said he had completely separated his 'political and social life from my moral and poetic life (externally, of course) ... I am separating the Privy Councillor and my other self – without which a Privy Councillor can function quite well.' With the figure of Lothario he depicts himself as the Privy Councillor, whereas Wilhelm is the other self, the other Goethe. In relation to work on the autobiographical novel he has begun, Goethe speaks of a *salto mortale*, a three-fold somersault at a great height. In a letter to Anna Amalia ('Frau von Stein') on 31 October 1777 he writes: 'Last evening I made a *salto mortale* over three awkward chapters of my novel.' The pair Lothario and Aurelie stand as a mirror image reflecting Wilhelm and Mariane (Fantasy). Just as Mariane died of a broken heart because Wilhelm left her, the actress Aurelie will die because Lothario (Goethe as Minister) leaves her. Aurelie represents what Fantasy can be to the Minister Goethe. Wilhelm and Mariane's son Felix appears with Aurelie, together with Barbara, who, as the personification of commerce, is Mariane's 'old servant, confidante, advisor, agent, and house-keeper' (*Lehrjahre* I, 1). At this point Wilhelm knows nothing about Felix (poetic gift), the son he has had by Mariane (Fantasy). He takes him to be Aurelie's son and sees him for the first time in her company. Felix is compared to the sun (*Lehrjahre* IV, 15): 'For the most beautiful golden curls surrounded his open brown eyes and full face; on a brilliantly white forehead one saw his dark gently arched eyebrows, and there was a lively glow of health in his cheeks.' When Wilhelm encounters Barbara he asks (*Lehrjahre* VII, 8):

> 'Is it you?' ... she turned her face towards him. He saw her in the clear light. Startled, he retreated a few paces. It was old Barbara. 'Where is Mariane?' he said. The old woman came to him and handed him a letter. 'Here are Mariane's last words', she said. 'She is dead!', he exclaimed. 'Dead', said the old woman. 'If this note ever reaches you, pity your unfortunate beloved. Your love killed her. The boy, whose birth I will survive only a few days, is yours. I die faithful to you. In losing you I lost everything that bound me to life.'

Aurelie, too, will give Wilhelm a letter for Lothario, through which, in the novel, contact is made between them (*Lehrjahre* V, 16): 'She called for Wilhelm and handed over a letter to him. This letter, she said, has waited a long time for this moment. I feel I am near the end of my life. Promise that you will give it to him personally.'

Lothario is introduced as someone 'who has just come back from America, where, in the company of some Frenchmen, he had served with some distinction under the flag of the United States' (*Lehrjahre* IV, 16). This is a reference to the American Revolution which began in 1776 and as a consequence of which the French Revolution (1789) was made possible. At last, in America, they set about changing fundamental rights and division of powers and establishing the common good as the main objective of the state, while in Europe the private interests of the monarchs were in stark contrast to the good of the people. Goethe believed that this contrast could be removed. Accordingly, Lothario represents the progressive nobility. His name means 'distinguished hero'.[794] Minister Goethe, raised to the ranks of the nobility in 1782, was unceasingly interested in far-reaching reforms. Aurelie says about Lothario (*Lehrjahre* IV, 16): 'Young as he was, he had an eye on the emerging young people in his country who were full of hope, on the quiet work of active men in various fields of endeavour.' Lothario wants to introduce agrarian and social reform. The farmer should be freed from serfdom (*Lehrjahre* VII, 3): 'I feel full well how foolishly we let time go by. How many things I have planned and thought through. How slow we are to act on our best resolutions!' The right to free ownership as the basis for the economic system should be introduced. At the same time the class divisions can be overcome if, as Lothario sees it, the State

> in return for a regular contribution [tax] would forego the feudal hocus pocus and let us use our properties as we see fit, so that we don't have to keep them together in such large tracts ... How much happier would men and women be, if they could gaze freely around and, without further ado, choose to improve the life of a worthy young woman or a fine young man (*Lehrjahre* VIII, 2).

For Lothario the way to a better future is through sensible reforms. State taxes should be reduced (*Lehrjahre* VII, 3): ' ... we could do without some of the capital if we handled the interest less arbitrarily.'

But Minister Goethe soon became aware that he could not carry out any far-reaching reforms. At least he could counteract laziness, routine, and corruption in the civil service. Carl August, without giving it a thought, wasted vital financial resources. The 32-year-old Minister Goethe complains about this in a letter to Knebel on 17 April 1782:

> I climb upwards through all the classes. I see the farmer take from the earth what is required to satisfy his needs, and it would be enough if he was only sweating on his own behalf. But you know how the aphids sit on the rose branch and have sucked themselves fat and green, and then come the ants and suck liquid out of their bodies. And so it goes on, and we have brought it to the point that, up above, more is consumed in one day than can be produced down below in one day.

Under the name of Odoardo, Goethe will say in the *Wanderjahre* (III, 12):

> For several years now, in the name of my Prince, I have been managing a province which, separated from his states, has not been used the way it might have been. A lot of good could be done, but only within limits. I was always prevented from doing any better, and what was really desirable seemed to belong to another world.

Once Goethe knows that the statement 'America is here or it is nowhere' was utopian (*Lehrjahre* VII, 3), he has recourse to the plan of emigration to America and pursues it energetically. Wilhelm and most of the *Wanderjahre* figures are preparing for emigration. A colonization project is forged and a band of emigrés prepares for imminent departure to America. In *Dichtung und Wahrheit* (1811-1831) Goethe reports that before 1775 he had entertained the idea of emigrating to America:

> Well-wishers had confided to me that Lili [Goethe's fiancée in Frankfurt] said, when all the obstacles to our union were explained to her: out of love for me she would undertake to leave behind all the

> circumstances [and advantages] she enjoyed and go with me to America. America was in those days, perhaps even more than now, the El Dorado of those who felt oppressed in their present situation (Book 19).

Goethe's choice of words [mit nach Amerika zu gehen] suggests that there is a group plan of the *Stürmer und Dränger* that Lili wanted be included in.[795] Klinger's play *Sturm und Drang* is set in America. Right at the beginning the hero says: 'Ha, let me feel what it's like to stand on American soil, where everything is new, everything makes sense.' In *Dichtung und Wahrheit* Goethe says that as a youth in Frankfurt he observed developments in America with great interest, 'we wished the Americans luck and the names Franklin and Washington began to shine and sparkle in the skies of politics and war'. The desire to emigrate was wide-spread. Friedrich Schiller had made up his mind to emigrate to America if independence from the English crown was achieved. He writes to Henriette von Wolzogen on 8 January 1783: 'When North America becomes free I have decided I will go there.'[796] Referring to the same period, 'in a noticeable undertone of regret'[797] Goethe said to Boisserée in a conversation of 2 August 1815: 'What would have happened if thirty years ago [1785] I had gone to America with some friends and had never heard of Kant etc.?'[798] Later in the conversation with Boisserée Goethe makes a link between the failure of the plans for emigration and the development of his talents. It is a kind of excuse for the fact that finally he did not emigrate:

> How many talents and geniuses remain undeveloped and are held back because of circumstances; how many dunces, on the other hand, are raised through circumstances, training, and artificiality to university positions.

Goethe was in the fortunate position that, with Anna Amalia as Princess, it had become possible for him to develop his genius as he wished. If he had emigrated to America the German-speaking poet would have had to give up these unique working conditions and face great uncertainty. This must have been the main argument Anna Amalia used for not going to America after all.

The Weimar Minister Goethe, busy with plans for emigration, tells Lenardo in the *Wanderjahre* the meaning of the phrase 'brave as a lion'.[799] Lenardo confesses to Wilhelm that he is

> irresistibly drawn to [live in] primitive conditions, that my journeys through all the highly cultivated lands with their highly cultivated people cannot blunt these feelings. My imagination is looking for its ease overseas. A family property in those unspoilt regions, neglected up to now, will allow me finally to carry out, according to my wishes, a plan which has been gradually developing within me. (I, 11).

Lenardo says the motto must be to 'act and not to talk'. He is most inclined to 'start right from the beginning' (II, 7). The woman Lenardo wants is a young widow of whom it is said that 'she will marry the manager,[800] sell her possessions and go overseas with all the money' (III, 5). The young widow trades in cotton and is a good business woman. The reader is now introduced to the art of spinning and weaving and to economic conditions of production and distribution against the background of the industrial revolution (from 1785), which was introducing machines to replace manual work. This documents Goethe's and Anna Amalia's plans to go to America as textile manufacturers. For this reason Goethe was especially interested, during his early years in Weimar, in the stocking and cloth manufacturers in Apolda, near Weimar, where a home-based industry involving 780 looms was concentrated, one of the most significant in the German Reich.[801] His servant Seidel, in 1778, tried his hand at linen spinning and the stocking trade. Goethe assisted with his little book on spinning for the Weimar spinning school. As Minister for War, Goethe for a time pursued plans for a spinning and knitting school for the children of poor soldiers.[802] When he made a short visit to Berlin in 1778, part of his busy programme included a visit to see Wegelin's wool manufacturing. With great interest he studied a factory in which about 400 looms were in operation. For standards of the time the output was extraordinary and the products were distributed throughout Europe.[803] Not only Goethe but also Anna Amalia as Princess busied herself with spinning. Goethe's mother writes to Anna Amalia in a letter of 30 November 1778: 'I am delighted that your Highness is spinning.'[804] To this end Goethe had had a two-spool spinning-wheel made for Anna Amalia according to his own specifications.[805] The young widow whom Lenardo desires will confess (*Wanderjahre* III, 13):

> My husband was determined to emigrate with me. He often spoke about ways of getting away from here. He looked around for good people to gather around him, people with whom you can make common cause, people you can attract and bring along with you. We longed, perhaps with too much youthful optimism, to go where they hold as duty and right what is here considered a crime.

If Goethe and Anna Amalia were in America it would be Goethe's duty and right to marry the woman he loved. But in the Holy Roman Empire it was a crime for him to love the Princess Anna Amalia.

The knowledge of the textile industry that Goethe acquired was comprehensive. He even introduces his reader to the technical details of the processes of spinning and weaving. In 1810 he asked his friend and collaborator Meyer to make a relevant study which, with slight modifications, he took over into the *Wanderjahre* (III, 5).[806]

Quite apart from his own plans, Goethe writes about the question of emigration to America as such, dealing with its highs and lows (*Wanderjahre* I, 7):

> At the beginning of the eighteenth century there was a strong impulse to go to America. Everyone who found life somewhat uncomfortable here hoped to find freedom over there. This impulse was nourished by attractive properties to be acquired.

Europe, on the other hand, is characterized as

> this priceless culture which originated several thousand years ago, grew, became widespread, was subdued, oppressed but never stamped out, found its second breath, regenerated itself, and, as always, distinguished itself with unceasing activity.

He has the returning offspring of emigrants say (*Wanderjahre* I, 7):

> No matter where they are, people have to be patient and considerate, and I prefer to come to terms with my king, persuading him to give me this or that privilege than to do battle with the Iroquois to drive them out or to cheat them with contracts to dislodge them from their swamps where one is tortured to death by mosquitoes.

The tragic aspects of an unprepared mass emigration did not escape Goethe. When reviewing Ludwig Gall's (1790-1863) report *Auswanderung nach den Vereinigten Staaten* (1822), in which the horrible misery of the crossing and of the arrival of penniless emigrants is described,[807] he sketches the history of America in a few words. If his literary colleagues were to work on the material presented in Gall's book

> they must try to get a clear picture of things overseas: from the earliest colonization, the time of the early battles the Europeans had – first with the native inhabitants and then amongst themselves – ; from the time of the full possession of the great empire the English had won for themselves to the time of the secession of the later united states; to the war of independence, with its outcome and consequences.[808]

Goethe had expert knowledge of American history. He owned a considerable number of books about America and took a lively interest in American authors.[809] When in the 1790s there was widespread fear of inflation in the wake of the French Revolution, Goethe advised Carl August to buy American Thaler and to participate in Bertuch's plan to acquire mining rights for Mexican silver mines.[810] Goethe kept himself informed about the many developments in the New World, largely through Americans who visited him – the famous poet.[811] He entertained his friends with conversation about America. Chancellor von Müller reports on 13 July 1818 that he met the daughters of Henriette von Egloffstein with Goethe: 'Goethe gave a very droll description of America and the colonizations there. Julie's desire to emigrate there was abomination for Line.'[812] Americans who visited Goethe in Weimar were astonished by his comprehensive knowledge of their country 'as if our country was for him in his advanced years one of the subjects that interested him most'.[813] Around 18 June 1827 Goethe wrote the poem 'Den Vereinigten Staaten' which began with the lines

> America, you are better off
> Than our old continent,
> You have no ruined castles.[814]

On 18 June 1788 Goethe had returned from his Italian journey, on 18 June 1790 Anna Amalia had returned from hers. On 18 June 1798 Goethe dedicated to her the didactic poem 'Die Metamorphose der Pflanze', and now, twenty years after her death, with melancholy he commemorates her through the poem 'Den Vereinigten Staaten'. By 'ruined castles' Goethe means the monarchy, a state form in decline.

The many preparations for emigration in the *Wanderjahre* are to find their climax in a speech by Lenardo (III, 9):

> The highly significant day had dawned. Today the first steps towards the general emigration were to be taken. Today it was to be decided who was really prepared to go out into the [new] world and who preferred to stay here in the established old world to seek his happiness. A merry song resounded in all the streets of the cheerful place. Masses of people gathered. Individual members of each trade joined one another and, singing in unison, they moved into the room in a formation ordained by lot.

Now Lenardo begins his speech, but he no longer speaks of emigration but merely of travel, a motif which is woven into the novel from the beginning. 'My life is to travel', Wilhelm writes in his first letter to Natalie (*Wanderjahre* I, 1):

> I have to carry out the duties of the traveller and pass my own tests ... I am not to stay for more than three days under one roof. I am not to leave one inn without travelling at least a mile to the next. These rules are clearly designed to guarantee that my years are years of travel and to prevent even the slightest temptation there might be for me to settle down.

Now Lenardo explains the meaning travel has for artists (III, 9): 'Does not the painter, with his easel and palette, move from face to face?'

Explorers of nature 'consciously confront every hardship and danger to open up the world to the world and to create a path and a track through the most inaccessible terrain'. The traveller acknowledges the dictum: '... my fatherland is where I am useful ... let each one strive everywhere to be of use to himself and others.' This would apply to the statesman who has to open up prospects for a better life, whereby 'the most capable must think of himself as the most flexible'. Goethe will not emigrate. He remains in the Old World, with the result that the American utopia remains indeterminate,[815] but, as Anna Amalia's renunciant poet, Goethe will travel, more deliberately than ever before, from one poetic work to another, in order to imprint in them his message of love and the human wisdom he has learned through careful study and inspiration: 'What I possess grows in me for others', as he says in 'Zueignung' (1784).

In the middle of his thoughts and preparations for emigration in 1786, the 'betrayal' by Fritz von Stein and the Prussian change of ruler occurred. What Fritz did is indicated by Hersilie. A cunning boy wearing a pedlar's display box suspended by a strap around his neck brings Hersilie a message (*Wanderjahre* II, 10):

> He produces a very small slate, framed in white, as they are made in the mountains for teaching children the first steps in writing; I [Hersilie] take it, see that there is writing on it, and read what is clearly written on it with a sharp slate-pencil:
>
> Felix [Goethe]
> loves
> Hersilie [Amalia]
> The horse-master
> Is coming soon.
>
> I am taken aback. I am astonished at what I have in my hand, what I see with my eyes, but mostly because fate is going to show itself stranger than I am myself. What does it mean?

These few anonymous lines were highly confusing for Goethe and Anna Amalia at the beginning of 1786. Goethe had taught Fritz to write in different types of script.[816] To establish contact with the anonymous writer, who apparently was making no demands, Goethe and Anna Amalia give him the following answer at the same place, perhaps at the entrance to a secret passage:

> Hersilie's [Amalia's]
> Greeting
> To Felix [Goethe].
> Let the horse-master
> Hold firm.

Hersilie puts this answer into the wallet she has made. This establishes the link to the wallet made by the beautiful widow in 'Der Mann von Fünfzig Jahren' (*Wanderjahre* II, 3). As we have seen, the widow's wallet was a symbol for Anna Amalia's work on the transformation of Goethe from Flavio to the Major, from an aimless *Stürmer und Dränger* to a classical poet who reaches for the stars. Here the same process is repeated from the point of view of Goethe's poetic gift. The 'betrayal' by Fritz von Stein and all connected with it amounted to the liberation of Felix from heavy chains. The anonymous writer did not identify himself and remained silent. In the *Wanderjahre* (II, 7) it is said about Lothario (Privy Councillor Goethe): 'He undertook a journey to the educators to ask for good artists, just a few, for himself. The arts are the salt of the earth.' From the time of his flight to Italy Goethe will work primarily as a creative writer and scientist. Since the secret lovers could not decide in favour of emigration or separation, Fritz's 'betrayal' was the final deciding factor in the transformation that Anna Amalia had wanted for Goethe and had worked at from the very beginning.

For Goethe the 'betrayal' by Fritz came about by divine intervention. That is why Hersilie says, when she reads the little slate, that 'fate will prove to be almost stranger'. Goethe has his poetic gift, Felix, write the reply on the slate, for in the Pedagogical Province Wilhelm sees Felix through the crowd 'eagerly dealing and bargaining over trifling things with a young pedlar' (II, 8). Goethe's poetic gift (Felix) is indebted to the family of Josias von Stein – whom Anna Amalia in her Regency had promoted to Equerry and who under Carl August became Chief Equerry – for being able to carry on his secret love for Anna Amalia. Josias von Stein was responsible for the horses in the Duchy. In the horse markets he had to identify horses with a good pedigree, and every year about a dozen foals were acquired.[817] The deception could not have succeeded without the cooperation of Frau von Stein and her husband.

In the end it was only thanks to the 'betrayal' by Fritz that the longed-for escape from the unworthy, nerve-racking situation could be found: in renunciation. Only through renunciation was Goethe's writing set free. From 1787 one masterpiece after another was produced. Since the *Wilhelm Meister* novel deals with Goethe's autobiography for the first decade in Weimar, the 'Meisterjahre' [the years of mastery] continue with the years following his escape to Italy in 1786. They include *Iphigenie*, *Tasso*, the *Römische Elegien*, the *Farbenlehre*, and many small and many large masterpieces up to and including the completion of the *Faust* tragedy in 1831. Hersilie puts the 'betrayal' in her wallet, which, exactly like that of the beautiful widow, is a symbol for Goethe's transformation into a classical poet.

From the perspective Goethe opens through Hersilie and Felix he develops the motif of a mysterious casket. Details of the beautiful casket and the key that belongs to it are scattered throughout the whole of the *Wanderjahre*. Felix finds it in a cave under a castle. 'It is ancient and splendid to behold; it seems to be made of gold and decorated with enamel. Take it and hide it, father [Wilhelm], and don't let anyone see it!' (I, 4). On the same day that Felix finds the casket, his love for Hersilie ignites. Eventually Hersilie takes the key from Fitz's clothing when he is being investigated. What is meant here is a criminal investigation carried out by Carl August and Anna Amalia which led to the unmasking of the 'traitor' Fritz von Stein. When Hersilie takes the key, she thinks (III, 3):

> I feel strangely unsettled, between guilt and curiosity. I'm inventing a hundred different ideas and fairytales about what could come of this: justice and judgement are not to be toyed with. Hersilie, the spontaneous, occasionally high-spirited person, involved in a criminal trial, for that's what it amounts to, and what is left for me to do except to think of the friend for whose sake I am going through it all!

Goethe and Anna Amalia, with the help of Carl August, discovered the 'traitor' Fritz von Stein, who turned out to be harmless. It never went as far as the feared 'criminal trial'.

Hersilie ends up possessing the casket and prevents it from being presented in court (III, 8):

> The idea was repugnant to me that the glorious casket destined by fate for the lovely Felix should be left in a rusty old iron deposit box in the courthouse.

Now, with the casket and the key beside her, Hersilie wishes (III, 7)

> an end to it, at least that there be an indication of what this finding, finding again, separating and uniting could mean; and if I am not to be saved from all embarrassment, at least I long to see it clarified, brought to a conclusion, even if, as I fear, there is something bad in store for me.

The revelation that Anna Amalia is Goethe's secret love is in conflict with the dynastic interests of her descendants. The distortion of Goethe's and Anna Amalia's biography shows clearly that the private interests of the monarchy take precedence over the common good. But Goethe's writings could not be surpressed, and to them he entrusted the secret of his forbidden love for Anna Amalia. Hersilie says to Wilhelm (III, 2):

> We'll decide for ourselves to what seat of judgement the secret belongs ...

> But here, my friend, what do you finally say to this representation of the riddle? Does it not recall a barbed arrow? God have mercy on us! But the casket has to remain unopened between you and me, and then, when opened, dictate what happens next.

Until now there has been no consensus whether the image, the only one of its kind Goethe ever included in a poetic work,[818] is the key to the whole novel.[819] Arrows with barbs stand for love darts. By shooting arrows, Amor made people fall in love with one another.[820] In *Tasso* this symbol appears straight after the Princess pushes Tasso away from her and hurries off – in front of everyone he had thrown his arms around her and held her in a firm embrace. The statesman Antonio is shattered by the sight of this confession of a forbidden love of the poet for the Princess (ll. 3289ff.):

> Unhappy man, I'm hardly able to recover!
> When something happens, totally unexpected
> When our gaze hits on something monstrous
> Our mind stops still a while.
> We know nothing to compare with it.
>
> **Tasso:** (*After a long pause*)
> Carry out your duty, I see it's you!
> You, indeed, deserve the Prince's trust.
> Carry out your duty, torture me to death,
> Now that I am condemned,
> Pull, pull on the arrow
> So that I feel the cruel barb
> That tears my flesh!

The key with the barb breaks off when Felix turns it in the lock – 'the outer half fell on the table' (III, 17). When a goldsmith and jeweller examines the break

> [he] shows, what had thus far been overlooked, that the break was not rough, but smooth. When they make contact, both ends grip one another. He pulls the key out whole. They are joined magnetically, hold tightly to one another, but open only to the initiated. The man steps back a bit, the casket springs open, and he immediately closes it again: 'It is not good to be involved with such secrets', he said (III, 17)

Anyone who knows of the importance of Anna Amalia for Goethe's life can read *Wilhelm Meister* as the manifold representation of his forbidden love for her. When the barbs, smoothly broken apart, are separated into an outer and an inner half, they form the initials of Anna Amalia.

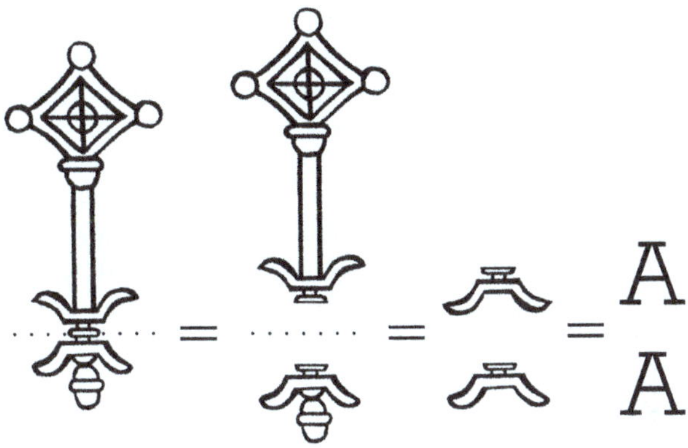

The key stands for Anna Amalia, who, in the figure of Hersilie, is the key to *Wilhelm Meister*, because Goethe uses her to create comparisons and allusions which are found throughout the whole work. The repetition of the wallet motif from 'Der Mann von Fünfzig Jahren' establishes the link with the widow and Hilarie and Flavio and the Major. The image of the apple and the deep cut on Felix's thumb points to Wilhelm's vow of fidelity and to the sin in the Garden of Eden as representing a temptation to fall away from the truth. Through the relationship with Felix (Goethe's poetic gift) Hersilie establishes the link with the von Stein family. As an older woman she confesses her love for a younger man.

Anna Amalia is, at the same time, the key to the interpretation of other works beside *Wilhelm Meister*. The embrace of the beloved, followed by an abrupt separation, is a variation of something found repeatedly in Goethe's work. Hersilie says (III, 17):

> I was more confused than one ... ought to be. He [Felix] took advantage of my distraction, came up to me and took me in his arms. I struggled in vain. His eyes came closer to mine, and it is beautiful to see one's own image in a loving eye. I saw it for the first time when he pressed his mouth against mine. I will admit, I answered his kisses. It is wonderful to make someone happy. I tore myself away. The gap dividing us was only too clear to me. Instead of controlling myself I went too far. I pushed him away reproachfully. My confusion gave me the courage and the words; I threatened, scolded, told him never to see me again. He took me at my word. 'Good', he said, 'I'll ride out into the world until I perish.'

Felix does not die, because Wilhelm will save him. At the end, Wilhelm and Felix are 'firmly entwined with one another, like Castor and Pollux, the twins who meet as they take their turn in going from Orkus to light'. In Greek mythology these are inseparable twin brothers, the gods of friendship, one of them mortal (Wilhelm, the human Goethe), the other immortal (Felix, his poetic gift). Pollux arranges it with his father, Zeus, that they be allowed, alternately, to spend one day in Olympus with the gods and the other day in the underworld. With regard to Felix we read further: '"You will always be created anew, glorious image of God!", he [Wilhelm] exclaimed, "and you will straight away be damaged again, hurt both inwardly and outwardly."'

The love scene between Hersilie and Felix is a variation of that in *Tasso*, *Der Grosskophta*, the *Lehrjahre*, 'Der Mann von Fünfzig Jahren' and 'Der Neue Paris'. This means that the casket is the symbol for Goethe's creative writing. Right at the beginning the splendid casket is referred to as a 'splendid little book' [büchlein] (*Wanderjahre* I, 4). The key to *Wilhelm Meister* and the other 'golden apples' of the poet Goethe, the Princess Anna Amalia, is at the same time the content of his work: in glorifying his beloved he raises her to the stars. Only when Anna Amalia is known to be Goethe's woman is it possible to find rational access to his works – symbolized as 'a hard rock'. This is Mignon's bequest (*Lehrjahre* V, 16):

> When the time is right, the light of day
> Will banish night, which must be illuminated;
> The hard rock will open its bosom
> And not begrudge the earth its deeply hidden springs.

15 | Epilogue: 'All for Love'

> If God was really concerned that people should be truthful in their life and dealings he would have had to organize things differently.
> *Maximen und Reflexionen*. From the bequest.

> If a person lives for a long time in significant circumstances he does not, of course, encounter everything possible for man to encounter; but at least something analogous, and perhaps something experienced before.
> From *Makariens Archiv, Wilhelm Meisters Wanderjahre* [Journeyman's Years] (1829)

Goethe and Anna Amalia could only realize the ambitious plan of inheriting Troy, Rome, and Bethlehem in Weimar if they worked together. Their key idea was the continual work of the individual to ennoble himself through science and art and to realize the divine in himself. At the end of the poem 'Das Göttliche', which Anna Amalia had printed in her *Tiefurter Journal* at the end of 1783, we read:

> Let the noble person
> Be helpful and good
> Untiringly let him do
> What is useful and right.'

In his creative work Goethe always kept to the truth, even though it was encoded. He left many clues to help the reader to see through the smoke-screen thrown up around Frau von Stein. Goethe always showed himself, in a higher sense, worthy of the gift of poetry as

> ... that which nature alone bestows,
> Something that remains out of reach of all effort and striving,
> Something that neither gold,

> Nor sword, nor cleverness, nor perseverance
> Can force to happen' (*Tasso* ll. 234ff.).

Involved in a princely court at the highest level, Goethe had the choice between, on the one hand, pretending to have an indefinable love relationship with the married Frau von Stein or, on the other hand, foregoing his basic happiness. He was able to live his love for the Princess Anna Amalia only by resorting to a deception. When the lovers put their letters under the motto 'All for Love' [see back cover] by using a seal with these words, they were indicating their noble motivation which justified the deceit. At the same time it was this very world that gave Goethe everything he needed and, within the limits of his social class, every conceivable honour and support. He had come to Weimar vague and without any plan for the future, and thanks to Anna Amalia, who was able to appreciate his achievements, he was able 'first to develop, then to perfect himself to a degree more glorious than was ever seen'. Riemer, who had collaborated with Goethe over a period of three decades, characterized him as follows (1841):

> In him the most superb and fruitful intellectual ideas are at work , as are the heart's noblest and most tender feelings, the finest and most varied perceptions of the senses, and the wisest prescriptions and maxims for attaining virtue and happiness.[821]

What the proud middle-class imperial city of Frankfurt would have had to offer soon became clear to the young Goethe. The author of *Götz* (1771/73), *Werther* (1774), and immortal poems would have found no space for his poetic genius in such a city. His father was insisting that he become a lawyer. His genius was to be forced into a corset. In the *Lehrjahre* Goethe said: ' ... disinherited and naked, I committed myself to the Muse who threw me her veil and covered my nakedness' (I, 8). Goethe wrote to Johanna Fahlmer in Frankfurt on 6 March 1776:

> Father may cook up what he likes ... I'm staying here ... but Father owes me my due inheritance. Mother will see to that in her own way. She is not to be like a child, since I am brother and everything else to a prince.

In Weimar as well Goethe had to deal with opposition. When at the Duke's behest he was to become a member of the State Council, Minister von Fritsch declared on 24 April 1776 'that I can no longer sit in a Council [Collegio] of which Dr Goethe is now to be a member'. In a letter of 12 May 1776 Carl August defended the appointment:

> Not I alone, but men of insight wish me well in possessing this man. His mind, his genius are known. You will realize yourself that this

> kind of man would not put up with the boring and mechanical work needed to work his way up from the bottom in a land commission. Not to place a man of genius where he can use his extraordinary talents is to abuse him.[822]

Goethe had no other alternative than to become an aristocrat and consequently a powerful supporter of the whole class system, because there was no future for him outside of it. Tasso says to the Princess and Duke Alfonse (ll. 402ff.):

> But if I look more closely at what gives this work
> Its inner value and dignity:
> I know very well I have it all from you.

Goethe is, however, critical of the monarchy. This is expressed by the fact that he chooses 23 October 1828, the day before Anna Amalia's birthday, for a conversation with Eckermann about Duke Carl August, who died on 14 June 1828. On the day in question he had already sent Marianne von Willemer the poem 'Dem Aufgehenden Vollmonde', the third part of the *Dornburger Trilogie*, which he had written on 25 August 1828 and which deals with a poetic meeting with Anna Amalia. This reference to Anna Amalia indicates that praise for Carl August's supposed promotion of the arts and sciences is in fact due to Anna Amalia. The decisive sentence about Carl August is an open criticism of birth as the exclusive criterion for ruling, because birth alone means nothing: 'When all is said and done, the Archduke was a great man by birth.' In the conversation, Goethe instructs Eckermann about the most important quality of a prince: 'And the most important point is that, when the purple is laid aside there remains much that is great, even what is best [in the prince].' After giving up the regency in 1775 Anna Amalia worked unceasingly on the idea of a Court of Muses which provided the model for a modern classicism: the continual ennoblement of the self through art and science. Since Napoleon's victories at Jena and Auerstedt on 14 October 1806, Goethe referred good-humouredly to all that preceded this epoch as 'antediluvian'.[823] When he was continuing his work on the novella *Die Neue Melusine* he compared the nobility to a race of dwarfs who become increasingly smaller. The younger brother of the Princess – Carl August was Anna Amalia's successor to the throne – was 'lost out of his baby's napkin'. This is an image for Carl August who looked in vain for the meaning of life in sexual excesses, hunting, and the military. In April 1817 Carl August sacked Goethe as theatre director after twenty-five years of service and after Goethe had been responsible for around 650 productions. The sole reason was that Goethe had come into conflict with Carl August's mistress, Caroline Jagemann. The Duke was prepared to accept that, as a result, 'the Weimar theatre would quickly sink to the level of provincial mediocrity'.[824]

With Napoleon, for a short while it seemed possible that in Germany the monarchy, which gave all-embracing power to one single person on the basis of birth, could be replaced by a system which also took real talents into account. Above all, Napoleonic law swept aside a thousand-year-long abuse of an impenetrable system of justice. Goethe recommended to his son the study of the *Code Napoléon*, the civil law book of France. Since the legislative work of Friedrich II of Sicily, such clarity in law had no longer been desirable. With a stroke of the pen Napoleon had wiped out class, feudal, and corporate laws as well as other privileges. Today's principles, such as the freedom of the person, the separation of Church and State, equality before the law, the right to property, and freedom of contract, had the force of law.[825]

But Goethe went a step further. Anna Amalia is for him the ideal of a princess, for she sought to promote culture and science. He juxtaposes her as an ideal with Napoleon, whom he admired as the 'greatest phenomenon possible in history'.[826] At the same time Anna Amalia was only representing her son while he was not yet of age, and she was not a ruler in her own right. In his *Unterredung with Napoleon 1808*, a sketch written in 1824 and not published until after his death, Goethe writes about his audience with the Emperor in Erfurt. He mentions Anna Amalia twice in it, the first time when Napoleon interrupted the interview and Goethe had the opportunity to take a look around in the salon: 'This is where a picture of Duchess Amalia used to hang, in masked-ball costume with a half mask in her hand.' Goethe speaks about her a second time because Napoleon is supposed to have asked him about 'the situation in the princely house, about Duchess Amalia'. This seems unlikely, since Anna Amalia was already dead over a year. Carl August, who had become a member of the Confederation of the Rhine (1806-1813), had informed Napoleon of the death of his mother and received his condolences.[827] Emperor Napoleon I had called thirty-four princes to Erfurt. He wanted this glittering backdrop of his vassals as he negotiated an alliance with Czar Alexander I (1777-1825). Napoleon's Foreign Minister Talleyrand (1754-1838) sarcastically referred to a 'parterre of kings' in the theatre.[828] Goethe managed only with difficulty to find a place in the theatre where the seating was arranged strictly according to dynastic and military criteria.[829]

Of all the rulers Goethe met and saw, the only one he mentions by name alongside Napoleon is Anna Amalia – and he mentions her twice. For Goethe, good politics as reflected in Napoleon's innovative lawgiving work has to provide the social conditions needed as a basis for art and science: 'The task of culture is the ennobling of mankind', according to Anna Amalia in her *Betrachtungen über Kultur*. 'Anything that does not have that as its goal is nothing.'[830] Goethe's mother once said about Anna Amalia: 'A real princess is one who has shown the world that she can rule, who understands great art, attracts all hearts, radiates love and joy around her, and who, in a word, is born as a blessing for mankind.'[831]

Goethe, the statesman, knew that enlightened absolutism was only a transitional phase, because no powerful man can check his own use of power. The main demand made by the American Revolution (1776) and the French Revolution (1789) was a genuine division of power on the basis of human rights. That Goethe, a 'prince's servant', was far superior to his critics, who, after the fall of Napoleon (1814/15) wanted a nation, is seen in *West-östlicher Divan* (from 1814), which begins with the poem 'Hegire'. Goethe uses this latter concept in the sense of 'flight'. In a letter of 14 October 1786 from Venice he writes to Carl August about his flight to Italy using the term 'Hegire'. In the *West-östlicher Divan* Goethe draws back from attempts to see a merely Germanified nation as an alternative to the current political system. On 8 February 1815 he writes to Knebel: 'I bless my decision to opt for this 'Hegire', for in this I am able to transcend time and lovely Central Europe.' Franz Grillparzer prophesied a development which would lead 'from humanity/via nationality/to bestiality'. In the *West-östlicher Divan* Goethe described the situation that lay beyond the insanity of nation, and in this he saw a long way into the future. By the beginning of the First World War (1914) the bookseller still had not sold most of the copies of the *Divan*.[832]

Goethe's illegitimate son August Vulpius became a serious problem for the renunciants. Illegitimacy brought with it social contempt. Goethe's mother cautiously touches on this problem with her son on the occasion of the birth of Karl Vulpius (born and died in 1795):

> It just irks me that I can't have a notice put in the paper about my little grandson and have a public celebration. But since there is nothing perfect under the sun I console myself in the knowledge that my favourite boy is content and happier than he would be in an unpleasant marriage. Give your little [bed-] treasure a kiss from me, also little August' (24 September 1795).

In the judgement of a contemporary: 'She [Goethe's mother] is happy with Goethe's relationship with Donna Vulpia because she has to be.'[833] In his wills of 1797 and 1800 Goethe made his son his heir, and Christiane was only to be provided for as his mother. Many people asked why Goethe did not marry Christiane with a view to making his son legitimate, for there were no apparent hindrances – not even social convention.[834] Like most people, Friedrich Schiller thought Goethe would soon marry Christiane. In a letter of 1 November 1790 he writes to Körner:

> It is very probable that he will marry her in a few years. He is supposed to be very fond of his son and he will tell himself that, if he marries the girl, it will be to the child's advantage and will at least lessen the ridiculous side of things.

Even for present-day biographers it remains

> difficult to understand that for nearly two decades he left his beloved and his child exposed to social discrimination ... No one knows the reasons for his attitude ... Why Goethe tolerated this under the prevailing circumstances and why he did it to her [Christiane] will always remain a puzzle.[835]

When Goethe was planning a third journey to Italy, which was ultimately abandoned because of the chaotic wartime conditions, Wieland confided to Böttiger on 26 March 1797: 'Goethe ought to take Vulpia to Italy with him as a page so that the Italians would get to see something. A sow wearing a string of pearls.'[836]

From the time he was a small child August Vulpius was made to feel his illegitimate origins. Henriette von Egloffstein reports that she was fondling him as a child when Duchess Luise entered the room:

> With her lorgnette before her eyes the Duchess stopped and asked me, as she looked at the child: 'And do you, too, know who the little one is?' Since I had to say I did not, she said, smiling strangely: 'It is Goethe's son.' Immediately I put the child down as if its proximity could sully me, for I knew that straight after his return from Italy Goethe had chosen a girl of very dubious repute (Mamsell Vulpius) as his beloved and, without being concerned with what people think, took her into his house.[837]

A letter from Charlotte von Schiller to Fritz von Stein shows how hostile people were to the Vulpius family: 'Vulpius's sister [Ernestine, 1779-1806] has died; the poor man [Goethe] has wept so! It pains me that his tears should have to flow for such objects.'[838] When in 1806 French plunderers raped the wife of Christian August Vulpius, the celebrated author of the robber novel *Rinaldo Rinaldini* (1797) could read about his misfortune in one of the most respected newspapers in Germany:

> Our splendid novel manufacturer V...s is having a hard life and his wife has suffered rape. But if it is sad to experience such things it is a delight to hear him describe the scene. In such moments, the womb of his mind, from which so many robbers and monsters have already emerged, must certainly have become pregnant again with a dozen

> such creations which, at the next fair, will be grunting around like little pigs.

Goethe protested about the 'vermin' that wrote such things because it was to do with his brother-in-law.[839]

In 1801 Goethe obtained from Carl August the legitimation document for his son August to give him the right to the name Goethe. This right was not effective, however, beyond the limits of the small duchy and even within the duchy the following sentence was required:

> that his illegitimate birth be used by no one to belittle him, to put him at a disadvantage, or [to cause him] any other hindrance under pain of investigation and inevitable severe punishment.[840]

The official state document of legitimation issued by the Duke was no real substitute for a Church marriage. When in the spring of 1806 August was planning a journey to visit Goethe's friend Zelter in Berlin, he was given to understand that it would be impossible for him to use the name Goethe while there. Plans for the journey had already been made but were dropped.[841]

Although Goethe had life-endangering illnesses on several occasions – in 1801 the doctors had given up all hope – it was a long time before he married Christiane. Goethe tells how, during his illness in 1801, he was unconscious. When he eventually recovered, his right eye was swollen. On the day on which

> the eye opened again, ... I felt I could hope to see the world freely and completely again. Next, as my sight healed I could respectfully acknowledge the presence of her highness the Duchess Amalia with her friendly and entertaining entourage (*Tag- und Jahreshefte*, entry 1801).

In one of the very few extant letters of Anna Amalia to Goethe, on 27 January 1801, the Princess expresses her joy at his recovery: '... and so I wish nothing more than to show you my joy myself. If it suits you I would like to come to you around 5.30 today.'[842]

The reason that, for a long time, Goethe did not want to marry Christiane was that he felt he was married to Anna Amalia. The oil-painting dating from 1806,[843] the last one Anna commissioned, depicts her as a bride and could for that reason be given the title *Anna Amalia as Bride* (ill. 32). Anna Amalia probably added some details of her own, for example the pen. One of her early biographers writes[844] that Anna Amalia had made excellent progress in painting, so that 'under Oeser's guidance the practised hand of the Duchess brought off oil-paintings closely resembling [their models]. In the painting, Anna Amalia is wearing a white veil and a white dress which, however, is almost completely covered by a reddish-brown coat. In her left hand she is holding a white glove and on a chain around her neck there is a medallion bearing the image of her son Carl August. Her left arm is resting on a table on which there are three books: by Goethe, Herder, and Wieland. These are on top of drawings, the uppermost of which depicts Homer. A laurel branch surrounds Goethe's book like a wreath, and beside it is a pen. In the middle of the front part of the table the profile of the goddess Athene can be discerned. Some references in the painting are easy to interpret, and, in addition, Anna Amalia is encoding her real relationship to Goethe. The medallion shows she is a Princess, the books stand for the Court of Muses that she founded in Weimar so that the small town became one of the leading cultural centres of Europe. She sees herself in the tradition of the goddess Athene, who, in Greek mythology was, amongst other things, the patroness of heroes, of science, and of the arts. In the eyes of her contemporaries Anna Amalia was seen as the 'foundress of Weimar, the benefactor of the whole land, the patroness of all arts and sciences.'[845] In a light-hearted poem 'An Luise von Göchhausen', written around 1778, Goethe compares Anna Amalia's lady-in-waiting to the owl on the shield of Minerva, the Roman equivalent of Athene and who therefore stands for Anna Amalia:

> The owl that sits on Minerva's shield
> Can be of use to gods and men
> The muses have so loyally protected you
> That now you can be of use to them.

The books are resting on the front part of a drawing with the profile of Homer, which seems to flow from the three books. Despite the achievements of Wieland and Herder, only Goethe is on the same level as Homer. Goethe is singled out, for his book is on top and is touching the laurel branch, which is the symbol of victory and fame. The laurel wreath is traditionally the highest distinction for a poet. The link between Anna Amalia and Goethe is reinforced by the pen. It is lying on the drawing of Homer as symbol for the greatest poet – here meaning Goethe -, while the tip of the pen points to the left wrist of Anna Amalia. In this left hand she is holding a white glove. This tells us to whom Goethe gave the white gloves he received on being admitted to the 'Freemasons Lodge Anna Amalia' on 23 July 1780. These gloves were to be given by the Freemason 'to the person with whom he is united in marriage or with whom he intends to be united'.[846] In a letter of 24 June 1780 Goethe had written to Anna Amalia ('Frau von Stein'): 'What is in appearance a small present awaits you on your return. The most remarkable thing about it is that I can give it only to one woman, only once in my life.' Anna Amalia is carrying a white glove in her left hand, which points to a 'left-handed' marriage – for the higher nobility, a marriage between people of unequal social rank. Furthermore, Anna Amalia is wearing a white veil and a white dress, which became in the nineteenth century a traditional bridal dress. Admittedly, she is wearing a reddish-brown coat over it. Goethe was, in a higher sense, already married to Anna Amalia, which is what the painting indicates. Already on 16 September 1776 Goethe wrote in his diary: 'Comedy the Secret Marriage!' There is only one other exclamation mark after a diary entry (up to 1782).[847] When this popular English comedy was formed by Cimarosa into the comic opera *Secret Marriage* it became one of Goethe's favourite operas. He corrected the libretti, time and again on fitting occasions quoted individual lines from them, such as: 'That's what gentlemen of high standing are like. I am like it myself sometimes.'[848]

On 14 October 1806, the day on which, not far from Weimar, the double battle of Jena and Auerstedt raged and the Prussian army was defeated, Anna Amalia fled at the last moment 'with a bleeding heart'.[849] She was to bring her granddaughter Caroline to safety. Five days later, on Sunday morning, 19 October 1806, Goethe married Christiane and thereby made his 17-year-old son August legitimate. August and Riemer were witnesses to the marriage.[850] Before the ceremony Goethe explained to the pastor:

> In these days and nights an old resolution has come to fruition in me. I want to acknowledge as mine, fully and in civil law, my little friend who has done so much for me and who has lived through these hours of trial with me.

He wrote to Carl August on 25 December 1806:

> While one often remembers the bad days, it is cheering also to think of the good ones ... so it occurred to me that seventeen years ago today my August delighted me with his arrival. He is still doing well, and I was able to count on your Highness's approval, when, in most uncertain times, I gave him the father and mother he has so long deserved.

Goethe wrote to Knebel on 21 October: 'You will be pleased that since the day before yesterday I am married to my good little one. Our wedding rings are dated from 14 October.' This was the day of Anna Amalia's departure from Weimar. Only in her absence could Goethe find the strength to marry Christiane. By the time Anna Amalia returned on 30 October Goethe's 'little friend' was now his wife.

Anna Amalia could not give Goethe the understanding he expected for the step he had taken, and for the first time she seems even to have criticized him[851] – for his supposed attitude of indifference while the war was on. From the time of Anna Amalia's return until the end of

November, in his diary alone he refers to thirteen visits to her. In December 1806 there are eight further visits which culminate in the poet's decision to stage a production of *Tasso*. On 13 February 1807 Goethe dictates for his diary: 'Evening rehearsal of Tasso in theatre. Then visit to Dowager Duchess.' Outwardly Anna Amalia showed composure, and when Goethe offered her the Co-Presidency of the Nature Research Society in Jena (from 1793) she accepted;[852] but in reality Anna Amalia was shattered by the 'total civil recognition' of Christiane as Goethe's wife. As a Princess she was from early childhood familiar with official state ceremonies and attributed the greatest importance to the bond of marriage. That is the reason why in the painting the Princess is holding only one Freemason glove in her hand. It is the answer to Goethe's marriage. In his novel *Die Wahlverwandtschaften* (1808/09) Goethe would make a passionate commitment to marriage, but it was not granted to him on earth to marry the woman he wanted, because she was a Princess. When the philosopher of aesthetics Carl Ernst Schubarth (1796-1861) wanted to marry his fiancée, he wrote to Goethe in October 1821:

> We Northerners see it as our duty to follow the maxims of higher morality, which require that we act in accordance with the laws. Only as an exception is it granted to a favoured Northern nature to deviate from this path and yet really live according to the highest possible meaning of the laws. The example your Excellency has given may give rise to astonishment and admiration, but one cannot aßspire to imitate it – because we are not you. For me the Römische Elegien are written in the same delicate, pure, true and moral spirit as the character of an Ottilie [in *Die Wahlverwandtschaften*].[853]

Goethe answers on 7 November 1821, the forty-second anniversary of his arrival in Weimar:

> I agree with everything you say about it, word for word. I might say that everything bad, even the worst thing we encounter within the law, whether it is something natural, civil, bodily, or economic, is not a thousandth part of what we have to battle through if, either outside the law, or parallel to it, or even cutting across law and custom, we find ourselves needing at the same time to remain in harmony with ourselves, with others, and with the general moral order.

Through his marriage which made his son legitimate Goethe had deeply wounded Anna Amalia, and so around this time he is very strict and irritated with his son, who is now called August von Goethe. Johanna Schopenhauer reports on 10 November 1806:

> I was with Adele visiting Goethe at midday. There were only a few people – myself, the Bertuchs, Major Knebel (a highly interesting

> man who has also made a name as a poet) and his wife from Jena, and a few strangers. I can't see enough of Goethe. Everything about him is in contrast to the usual and yet he is infinitely endearing. This time I saw him angry. His son, an awkward kind of boy, but not unlike his father in appearance, smashed a glass, which made a loud noise. Goethe was in the middle of telling a story and the noise gave him such a fright that he let out a roar. He gave August just one angry look, but I was surprised it did not make him fall under the table.[854]

The Duchy of Braunschweig from which Anna Amalia descended was wiped out by the words of Napoleon: 'The House of Braunschweig has ceased to exist.'[855] (On 14 October 1806 her brother Carl Wilhelm Ferdinand von Braunschweig, the Prussian general suffered a fatal wound in the head at the very beginning of the battle against the French at Auerstedt.) The Duchy of Weimar avoided a similar fate only because the wife of the Crown Prince, Maria Paulowna (1786-1859) was the sister of Czar Alexander I, whom Napoleon wanted to enter into an alliance with France.[856] Until the peace treaty of Posen at the end of 1806 Napoleon reserved the right to dissolve the Duchy of Sachsen-Weimar-Eisenach. In Posen he decided to accept Carl August – until recently a general of the Prussian avantgarde division – into the Confederation of the Rhine (1806-13) which had been formed only a few months previously. Goethe was enthusiastic about Napoleon and hoped for a better era in which the power to rule would depend on deserts rather than birth. Officers of outstanding bravery were billetted in his house, such as Marshall Jean Lannes (1769-1809), the son of a stable hand, and Marshall Pierre François Charles Augereau (1757-1816), the son of a fruit merchant. Both had been given princely status by Napoleon.[857] On the Prussian side the highest ranking generals were indeed Princes – 'great men by birth' – but often they had no military capabilities. This was said of Carl August, whom highly placed officers considered incapable.[858] During the annihilating double battle of Jena and Auerstedt Carl August was involved in a militarily meaningless side issue in Franconia. Anna Amalia's brother, the Prussian general Carl Wilhelm Ferdinand von Braunschweig, was equally incompetent. In 1792, he had already had to assume responsibility for the catastrophic first Coalition War against France. Beforehand the Brandenburg Gate (1788-91) had been built in his honour for his overrated military accomplishments in Holland (1787).[859]

Through Napoleon's victories Anna Amalia was forced to see that the Duchies existing by the grace of God were of only relative importance. She must have asked herself whether her concern for the monarchy, which had led her to renounce the chance of a life shared with Goethe in America, had involved an unnecessary sacrifice. Abuse of privilege and the corruption of a parasitic aristocratic ruling class characterized the monarchy. In Weimar there was also a rigid separation of classes, although the most famous figures were from the middle class: Wieland, Herder, Schiller, and Goethe. Wieland confided to Böttiger in a conversation of 22 April 1804: 'For the Dowager Duchess [Anna Amalia] he is always good enough to fill a gap, but for the rest one must never trust the honey-tongued words of Princes to people of the middle class.[860]' In the Weimar theatre, nobility and citizens were strictly separated. The former sat on the right-hand balcony and the latter on the left.[861] Only in 1848, the year of European revolutions, was this custom abandoned when for a moment in Germany the abolition of the monarchy seemed a possibility. Duchess Luise felt deeply insulted when Goethe, though now a nobleman, formed a liaison with Christiane Vulpius in 1788.[862] She was bitterly disappointed that the aristocrat Charlotte von Lengefeld married the middle-class Schiller in 1790,[863] and she viewed the marriage of the aristocrat Knebel to Luise Rudorff with intense animosity.[864] When her son became Grandduke in 1828 he forbade the nobility to invite middle-class people to social functions, which for Johanna Schopenhauer, the mother of the philosopher Arthur Schopenhauer (1788-1860), had obvious consequences:

> She [Johanna] was accustomed to taking part in all the social gatherings of the nobility. Now the Grandduke had formed the habit of frequenting them and since his deeply-rooted hatred of the middle-class rabble is well known, no one dared to invite them anymore. Now the poor woman finds herself banned from many social gatherings where she used to be received with open arms.[865]

Johanna Schopenhauer, Goethe's friend – for more than twenty years she had been the centre of a famous tea salon in Weimar – then left Weimar. She wrote to a friend: 'Next summer I am leaving Weimar – probably for ever! ... I'm moving to Bonn on the Rhine where I will again find almost everything I am leaving behind here – but not the court, thank God.'[866]

The wife of Carl August's successor, Maria Paulowna, also had a deeply-rooted hatred of the middle-class rabble. When her lady-in-waiting Henriette von Stein-Nordheim (1807-1869) showed she was determined to marry the middle-class Ludwig Schorn (1793-1842), Maria made violent attempts to dissuade her and even thirty years later this conflict caused her to have nightmares. When the Grandduke was told of the lady-in-waiting's engagement, 'in dismay he ran both hands through his hair'.[867] Yet it was the new Grandduke who, on the day of Goethe's death, decreed that he be buried beside Carl August in the Princes' vault and not, as Goethe had expressed the wish in 'Der Bräutigam' (1828), beside Anna Amalia:

> At midnight the shining stars lead me
> In a lovely dream to the threshhold where she sleeps
> O may it be possible for me to rest there too.

Though looking on the middle classes as 'rabble',[868] the new Grandduke began, without a second thought, to take over Goethe and exploit him for the monarchy. Since the papers which would document Goethe's forbidden love for Anna Amalia were suppressed, it looked as if the young Goethe had remained in Weimar because he was convinced about the value of the monarchy. In fact, he was its victim and he only tolerated it so that he could remain in Anna Amalia's presence as her lover, and later, as an old man, use all his strength to celebrate her in the land of poetry in the highest possible tones.

For the uninitiated, like his great admirer Johanna Schopenhauer, Goethe looked back, 'on a life which he himself had to a certain extent bungled'.[869] When in 1788 Goethe took Christiane as his partner with a view to remaining close to Anna Amalia as a renunciant, he did not realize all that would be involved in this step. For the poet there was never any doubt about his love for the Princess in this 'higher, inner sense'. Both of the white Freemason gloves belonged to her. In 1806 Goethe painted for Anna Amalia an aqueduct formed with the letters AMALIE (ill. 28) as well as, in a mountainous landscape, a lake with a large 'A' in front of it (ill. 29). At the same time he painted in front of an Italian coastal landscape a large 'C', standing for Princess Caroline, Anna Amalia's granddaughter, who for Goethe was 'the lovely little Princess'.[870] With the reference to her granddaughter, Goethe was trying to make his marriage comprehensible to Anna Amalia, for, just as she had joy in her legitimate grandchild and, to protect her, fled on 14 October, he, too, wanted to protect his son from further disadvantages and give him his name. In this situation, which was difficult for both of them, Goethe decided on the premiere of *Tasso*, the memorial of his love for Anna Amalia. In February 1807 he is supposed to have been influenced by his favourite pupil to do a production[871] which would require a long rehearsal period. The production was for Anna Amalia. She was meant to see it as the assurance of his undying love. He was begging her to understand that responsibility for his son dictated that the marriage with Christiane could no longer be postponed. But to no avail. The entry in the *Tag- und Jahreshefte* for 1807 reads:

> Very soon after the performance of *Tasso*, such a pure depiction of tender, cultured [geistvoll], loving scenes of the court and beyond,

> Duchess Amalia left her fatherland, which she saw as shaken to the foundations, even destroyed.

Shattered, Goethe dictated for his diary on 10 April: 'The Dowager Duchess died.' Anna Amalia died without any external signs of ill-health. Her loyal lady-in-waiting Charlotte von Stein was at her side to the very last moment.[872] At the beginning of Goethe's first decade in Weimar, Anna Amalia had the words of the Anacreontic poet Johann Georg Jacobi (1740-1814) engraved in the park of her forest residence Ettersburg:

> O may we go smiling through this life
> With the sound of sweet songs
> And when the last day descends on us
> With this same smile stand still.[873]

In his official obituary Goethe said: 'Her death, her loss should only cause pain as something necessary and inevitable, not because of any secondary circumstances involving chance, anxiety, and fear.' Her 'death was beautiful, gentle, and noble. She died in full consciousness', wrote Caroline von Egloffstein on 23 April 1807.[874] Goethe wrote the official memorial speech and composed an inscription for her tomb:[875]

Anna Amalia
of Saxony
Born in Braunschweig
honouring the sublime
enjoying the beautiful
doing good
she promoted all
that honours, adorns, and confirms
mankind
Mortal
1739-1807
now immortally
continuing her work
for
Eternity

Johanna Schopenhauer reports in a letter of 13 April 1807 that she attended the lying-in-state of Anna Amalia in the Wittumspalais:

> I saw and didn't see the front of the house draped in black; the stairs covered in black cloth; the night lit up artificially with a thousand candles; the long black gallery, on the walls of which the lights looked like stars and yet hardly shone because the surrounding black

> absorbed nearly every beam of light. All of this put me in a wonderful mood of celebration. ... Now I walked into the room. It was full of people, but not a sound was to be heard. I was pushed forward as far as the railing that separated the crowd from the raised funeral platform. There she lay in the coffin with her Princess's cloak. In the eerie light I could not distinguish her face. Beside her lay the Princess's hat and sceptre, on which the jewels sparkled marvellously in the semi-darkness. At her head stood two women veiled in crepe and on either side stood many men in mourning coats, with hats pulled down tight and decorated with long black strips of silk. They stood motionless and silent like ghosts.[876]

With Anna Amalia's death Goethe lived only to give his beloved further immortal works of love. Anna Amalia's depiction of the Neapolitan night sky could be used to describe Goethe's enormous life work. It is 'the sparkling Milky Way with a million stars, which like Venus's girdle, seem to surround the whole orb of the earth with love'.[877] The inexhaustible source of inspiration for Goethe's creative work was his first decade in Weimar, during which he was consumed with passionate love for Anna Amalia. During this time they happily 'set sail', if only with the help of deception. In *Tasso* the Princess says, when confronted with the poet's departure for Rome: (ll. 1875ff.):

> Worry fell silent, as did premonition
> And happily on board we were carried by the stream
> On gentle waves without a rudder:
> And now the gloomy present, terror
> About what the future holds,
> Secretly attacks my breast.

Renunciation of Anna Amalia meant the raising of their forbidden love to a higher level, but at the same time it meant unspeakable pain for both. Only the knowledge of Goethe's tragic love in those early years reveals to us the devastating meaning of the poem published in 1797. The gaping wound cannot close because Goethe's ship is not allowed to arrive in port: Goethe cannot have Anna Amalia as his wife:

> **'To Mignon'**
>
> Carried over vale and river
> The sun's chariot travels its pure course.
> On its journey, every morning
> It stirs up, deep in our hearts,
> Your pain and mine anew.
>
> Night brings no ease.
> Even dreams come now

In gloomy shapes
And I feel the force of these pains
Secretly at work in my heart.

For many lovely years now
I see the ships below.
Each comes into port.
For me, the constant pain,
Rooted in my heart
Does not flow away.

Beautifully dressed I must appear,
The clothes are taken from the closet
Because today there is a celebration.
No one suspects that
Deep in my heart of hearts
I am ravaged by cruellest pain.

My tears must be in secret,
My appearance can seem friendly,
Healthy even, and red-cheeked.
If this pain had been lethal
For my heart
I would long since be dead.

Like the oyster which cloaks a wound with concentric layers of mother of pearl to form a pearl, as a renunciant Goethe has continually to cloak the pain of his love with works of love. Like a torch in the darkness Goethe's love writings are to shed light that shines a thousand times more brightly when it is known that they were written for Anna Amalia. Without realizing the importance of this 'unusual woman and even more unusual Princess'[878] for Goethe's life, we cannot interpret his creative work: 'Do you not feel in my songs/That I am single and double?', Goethe wrote in 'Gingo Biloba'.

In an undated fairytale, only three pages in length,[879] Anna Amalia describes the discovery of her secret. The fairytale is about two 'extraordinarily beautiful diamonds in a town in Nubia, where people are proud of their intellectual prowess' – an ironic reference to Weimar. The larger diamond 'is half as big as an egg' and is thought by its owner to be the more valuable. A wise man has the diamonds shown to him and says about the bigger one: 'The stone [Der Stein] is not genuine.' Here Anna Amalia is going as close to a revelation as possible. If the masculine article 'Der' is replaced by the feminine article 'Die' the sentence would mean that Charlotte von Stein is not genuine. To prove his contention the wise man has a pan of charcoal brought to him.

He took both stones and threw them into the flames. The big one immediately went up in smoke, the genuine one remained what it was. A deep silence befell the whole company. The wise man spoke up and said: 'Permit me, ladies and gentlemen: from this you can see, one and all, the way of the world. What is false is often held to be the truth and preferred to it. The fool lets himself be convinced by shining colours, the wise man judges a thing by its intrinsic worth.' All shouted, acclaiming him a wise man, a reputation he retained until the end of his life.

Bibliography

The bibliography includes editions of Goethe's texts and any secondary literature which is of central importance for the study. Other literature is referenced in full in the endnotes.

Editions

Goethe, Johann Wolfgang v.: *Goethes Werke*, Weimarer Ausgabe, Weimar 1887–1919, facsimile edition, München 1987.

---: *Torquato Tasso – Ein Schauspiel*, Stuttgart (^{1}1969) 1999. The text is based on the: *Goethes Werke*, Festausgabe, Robert Petsch (ed.), VII, *Dramen III*, Leipzig 1926.

---: *Poetische Werke*, Berliner Ausgabe, XIV, *Italienische Reise*, Berlin ^{3}1978; XV, *Briefe aus der Schweiz 1779*, Berlin ^{2}1972; XVI, *Tag- und Jahreshefte – Als Ergänzung meiner sonstigen Bekenntnisse*, Berlin ^{2}1973.

---: *West-östlicher Divan*, Ernst Beutler (ed.), Leipzig 1943.

---: *Sämtliche Werke*, Frankfurter Ausgabe, I 9, Wilhelm Voßkamp/Herbert Jaumann (eds), *Wilhelm Meisters Theatralische Sendung, Wilhelm Meisters Lehrjahre, Unterhaltungen deutscher Ausgewanderten*, Frankfurt 1992; X, Gerhard Neumann/Hans-Georg Dewitz (eds.), *Wilhelm Meisters Wanderjahre*, Frankfurt 1989; II 2, Hartmut Reinhardt (ed.), *Das erste Weimarer Jahrzehnt, Briefe, Tagebücher und Gespräche vom 7. November 1775 bis zum 2. September 1786*, Frankfurt 1997; VI, Rose Unterberger (ed.), *Napoleonische Zeit, Briefe, Tagebücher und Gespräche vom 10. Mai 1805 bis 6. Juni 1816*, Frankfurt 1993.

---: *Dichtung und Wahrheit*, Walter Hettche (ed.), Stuttgart 1998.

---: *Briefe an Charlotte von Stein*, Julius Petersen (ed.), I, II/1, II/2, Leipzig 1923.

---: *Gedichte in zeitlicher Folge*, Heinz Nicolai (ed.), Frankfurt am Main/Leipzig ^{11}1999.

---: *Römische Elegien*, Dominik Jost (ed.), *Deutsche Klassik*, München ^{2}1978.

Secondary Literature

Andreas, Willy: *Carl August von Weimar, Ein Leben mit Goethe 1757 – 1783*, Stuttgart 1953.

Anna Amalia: *Briefe über Italien*, Heide Hollmer (ed.), St. Ingbert 1999.

---: *Meine Gedanken*, repr. in Volker Wahl (ed), *Wolfenbütteler Beiträge* IX, Wiesbaden 1994, pp.102 ff.

---: 'Märchen', repr. in: Goethe-Museum Frankfurt (ed.), *Goethe-Kalender auf das Jahr 1932*, Leipzig 1931, pp.101ff.

Beaulieu-Marconnay, Carl F. v.: *Anna Amalia, Carl August und der Minister von Fritsch*, Weimar 1874.

Berger, Joachim: *Anna Amalia von Sachsen-Weimar-Eisenach (1739–1807), Denk- und Handlungsräume einer 'aufgeklärten' Herzogin*, Jena 2002 (Manuscript); Heidelberg 2003.

Biedermann Flodoard F. v./ Herwig, Wolfgang (eds.): *Goethes Gespräche, Eine Sammlung zeitgenössischer Berichte aus seinem Umgang*, vol.1, 1749–1805, München 1998.

Biedrzynski, Effi: *Goethes Weimar – Das Lexikon der Personen und Schauplätze*, Zürich ²1993.

Bode, Wilhelm: *Amalie Herzogin von Weimar*, I: *Das vorgoethische Weimar*; II: *Der Musenhof der Herzogin Amalie*; III: *Ein Lebensabend im Künstlerkreise*, Berlin 1908.

---: *Charlotte von Stein*, Berlin ⁵1920.

Boisserée, Sulpiz: *Tagebücher 1808–1854*, H.-J. Weitz (ed.), Darmstadt 1978.

Bojanowski, Eleonore v.: *Louise Großherzogin von Sachsen-Weimar und ihre Beziehungen zu den Zeitgenossen*, Stuttgart 1903.

Böttiger, Karl August: *Literarische Zustände und Zeitgenossen. Begegnungen und Gespräche im klassischen Weimar*, 1838 (incomplete), K. Gerlach/R. Sternke (eds), Berlin ²1998.

Bornhak, F.: *Anna Amalia, Herzogin von Sachsen-Weimar-Eisenach*, Berlin 1892.

Boyle, Nicholas: *Goethe – The Poet and the Age*. Vol.1: *The Poetry of Desire* (1749-1790), Oxford 1991; vol.2: *Revolution and Renunciation* (1790-1803), Oxford 2000.

Bürgin, Hans: *Der Minister Goethe vor der römischen Reise. Seine Tätigkeit in der Wegebau- und Kriegskommission*, Weimar 1933.

Carl August, Duke of Sachsen-Weimar-Eisenach: *Briefe des Herzogs Carl August von Sachsen-Weimar an seine Mutter, die Herzogin Anna Amalia*, Alfred Bergmann (ed.), Jena 1938.

Conrady, Karl Otto: *Goethe – Leben und Werk*, München/Zürich 1994.

Damm, Sigrid: *Christiane und Goethe – Eine Recherche*, Frankfurt am Main/Leipzig 1998.

Eckermann, Johann Peter: *Goethes Gespräche mit Eckermann*.

---: *Friedrich Sorets Gespräche mit Goethe in Eckermanns Bearbeitung*, with an introduction by Edith Zenker, Berlin 1955.

Egloffstein, Hermann F. v. (ed.): *Alt Weimars Abend. Briefe und Aufzeichnungen aus dem Nachlasse der Gräfinnen Egloffstein*, München 1923.

Esenwein, Jürgen v./Gerlach, Harald (eds): *Johann Wolfgang von Goethe: Zeit – Leben – Werk*, CD-ROM, Berlin u. a. 1999.

Friedenthal, Richard: *Goethe. Sein Leben und seine Zeit*, 1963, München 1999.

Geese, Walter: *Gottlieb Martin Klauer – Der Bildhauer Goethes*, Leipzig 1935.

Göchhausen, Luise v.: *Die Göchhausen – Briefe einer Hofdame aus dem klassischen Weimar*, Werner Deetjen (ed.), Berlin 1923.

Goethe, Catharina Elisabeth: *Die Briefe von Goethes Mutter*, Albert Köster, M. Leis, K. Riha, C. Zelle, (eds), Frankfurt am Main/Leipzig 1996.

Grawe, Christian: *Johann Wolfgang Goethe, Torquato Tasso, Erläuterungen und Dokumente*, Stuttgart 1981

Grumach, Ernst/Grumach, Renate (eds): *Goethe. Begegnungen und Gespräche*, I, 1749-1776, Berlin 1965; II, 1777-1785, Berlin 1966.

Grumach, Renate (ed.): *Goethe. Begegnungen und Gespräche*, III, 1786-1792, Berlin and elsewhere 1977.

Harnack, Otto: *Zur Nachgeschichte der italienischen Reise – Goethes Briefwechsel mit Freunden und Kunstgenossen in Italien 1788–1790*, Weimar 1890.

Herwig, Henriette: *'Wilhelm Meisters Wanderjahre': Geschlechterdifferenz, sozialer Wandel, historische Anthropologie*, Tübingen/Basel ²2002.

Heuschele, Otto: *Herzogin Anna Amalia. Die Begründerin des Weimarischen Musenhofes*, München 1947.

Houben, H.H. (ed.): *Damals in Weimar, Erinnerungen und Briefe von und an Johanna Schopenhauer*, Berlin ²1929.

Keil, Robert: *Vor hundert Jahren, Mitteilungen über Weimar, Goethe und Corona Schröter aus den Tagen der Genie-Periode*, vol.2, Leipzig 1875.

Klauß, Jochen: *Charlotte von Stein. Die Frau in Goethes Nähe*, Zürich 1995.

Kleßmann, Eckart (Hrsg.): *Goethe aus der Nähe, Berichte von Zeitgenossen*, München/Zürich 1994.

Knebel, Carl Ludwig v.: *K.L. von Knebel's Literarischer Nachlaß und Briefwechsel*, K.A. Varnhagen v. Ense/Th. Mundt (eds), Leipzig ²1840.

Lyncker, Karl v.: *Am Weimarischen Hofe unter Amalien und Karl August*, Berlin 1912.

Merck, Johann Heinrich: *Johann Heinrich Mercks Briefe an die Herzogin-Mutter Anna Amalia und an den Herzog Carl August von Sachsen-Weimar*, Hans Gerhard Gräf (ed.), Leipzig 1911.

Müller, Friedrich v.: *Unterhaltungen mit Goethe*, Ernst Grumach (ed.), 1870, Weimar 1956, ²1982.

Pleticha, H. (ed.): *Das Klassische Weimar*, München 1983.

Riemer, Friedrich Wilhelm: *Mitteilungen über Goethe*, 1841, A. Pollmer (ed.), Leipzig 1921.

Scheidemantel, E. (ed.): *Erinnerungen von Charlotte Krackow*, Weimar 1917.

Schmidt, Peter: *Goethes Farbensymbolik*, Berlin 1965.

Schopenhauer, Johanna: *Im Wechsel der Zeiten, im Gedränge der Welt. Jugenderinnerungen, Tagebücher, Briefe*, München 1986.

Schulz, Karlheinz: *Goethes und Goldonis Torquato Tasso*, Frankfurt am Main 1986.
Schwanke, Martina: *Name und Namengebung bei Goethe, Computergestützte Studien zu epischen Werken*, Heidelberg 1992.
Sengle, Friedrich: *Das Genie und sein Fürst, Die Geschichte der Lebensgemeinschaft Goethes mit dem Herzog Carl August*, Stuttgart/Weimar 1993.
Steiger, Robert: *Goethes Leben von Tag zu Tag*, vol.1, 1749–1775, München 1982.
Stein, Charlotte v.: *Dramen* (Complete edition), Susanne Kord (ed.), Hildesheim 1998.
Tümmler, Hans: *Politischer Briefwechsel des Herzogs und Großherzogs Carl August von Weimar*, vol.1, 1778-1790, Stuttgart 1954.
Wahl, Hans (Hrsg.): *Briefwechsel des Herzogs-Großherzogs Carl August mit Goethe*, vol.1, 1775–1806, vol.2, 1807–1820, (1915), repr. Bern 1971.
Werner, Charlotte Marlo: *Goethes Herzogin Anna Amalia*, Düsseldorf 1996.
Wilpert, Gero v.: *Goethe-Lexikon*, Stuttgart 1998.
Zeitler, Julius (ed.): *Goethe-Handbuch*, Stuttgart, I/1916, II/1917, III/1918.

Abbreviations for Endnotes

BA	Berliner Ausgabe
FA	Frankfurter Ausgabe
FA/WMW	Frankfurter Ausgabe/*Wilhelm Meisters Wanderjahre*
WA	Weimarer Ausgabe
Andreas	Willy Andreas: *Carl August von Weimar, Ein Leben mit Goethe 1757–1783*
Beaulieu-Marconnay	Carl F. v. Beaulieu-Marconnay: *Anna Amalia, Carl August und der Minister von Fritsch*
Berger	Joachim Berger: *Anna Amalia von Sachsen-Weimar-Eisenach (1739–1807)*
Biedermann	Flodoard F. v. Biedermann/ Wolfgang Herwig (eds): *Goethes Gespräche*
Biedrzynski	Effi Biedrzynski: *Goethes Weimar–Das Lexikon der Personen und Schauplätze*
Bode/Amalia	Wilhelm Bode: *Amalie Herzogin von Weimar*
Bode/von Stein	Wilhelm Bode: *Charlotte von Stein*
Boisserée	Sulpiz Boisserée: *Tagebücher 1808–1854*
Bojanowski	Eleonore v. Bojanowski: *Louise Großherzogin von Sachsen-Weimar und ihre Beziehungen zu den Zeitgenossen*
Böttiger	Karl August Böttiger: *Literarische Zustände und Zeitgenossen. Begegnungen und Gespräche im klassischen Weimar*
Bornhak	F. Bornhak: *Anna Amalia, Herzogin von Sachsen-Weimar-Eisenach*
Boyle 1	Nicholas Boyle: *Goethe – The Poet and the Age*, vol.1
Boyle 2	Nicholas Boyle: *Goethe – The Poet and the Age*, vol.2
Bürgin	Hans Bürgin: *Der Minister Goethe vor der römischen Reise*
Conrady	Karl Otto Conrady: *Goethe – Leben und Werk*

Damm	Sigrid Damm: *Christiane und Goethe – Eine Recherche*
Damm/Lenz	Sigrid Damm (ed.): J.M.R. Lenz: *Briefe und Gedichte, Werke und Briefe III*
Dobenecker	Georg Mentz: 'Aus den Papieren des Grafen Görtz, des Erziehers Karl Augusts', in *Festschrift für Otto Dobenecker*
Eckermann	Johann Peter Eckermann: *Goethes Gespräche mit Eckermann.*
Egloffstein	Hermann F. v. Egloffstein (ed.): *Alt Weimars Abend. Briefe und Aufzeichnungen aus dem Nachlasse der Gräfinnen Egloffstein*
Ernst Grumach/ Renate Grumach	Ernst Grumach/ Renate Grumach (eds): *Goethe. Begegnungen und Gespräche*
Friedenthal	Richard Friedenthal: *Goethe. Sein Leben und seine Zeit*
Geese	Walter Geese: *Gottlieb Martin Klauer – Der Bildhauer Goethes*
Grawe	Christian Grawe: *Johann Wolfgang Goethe, Torquato Tasso*
Herwig	Henriette Herwig: 'Wilhelm Meisters Wanderjahre': *Geschlechterdifferenz, sozialer Wandel, historische Anthropologie*
Heuschele	Otto Heuschele: *Herzogin Anna Amalia. Die Begründerin des Weimarischen Musenhofes*
Houben	H.H. Houben. (ed.): *Damals in Weimar, Erinnerungen und Briefe von und an Johanna Schopenhauer.*
Keil	Robert Keil: *Vor hundert Jahren, Mitteilungen über Weimar, Goethe und Corona Schröter aus den Tagen der Genie-Periode*
Klauß	Jochen Klauß: *Charlotte von Stein. Die Frau in Goethes Nähe*
Kleßmann	Eckart Kleßmann (ed.): *Goethe aus der Nähe, Berichte von Zeitgenossen*
Knebel	Carl Ludwig v. Knebel: *K.L. von Knebel's Literarischer Nachlaß und Briefwechsel*
Kord	Susanne Kord (ed.): Charlotte v.Stein: *Dramen* (Complete edition)
Lyncker	Karl v. Lyncker: *Am Weimarischen Hofe bei Anna Amalia und Karl August*
Marlo Werner	Charlotte Marlo Werner: *Goethes Herzogin Anna Amalia*
Müller	Friedrich v. Müller: *Unterhaltungen mit Goethe*
Petersen	Julius Petersen (ed.):J.W. v. Goethe: *Briefe an Charlotte von Stein*
Renate Grumach	Renate Grumach (ed.): *Goethe. Begegnungen und Gespräche*

Riemer	Friedrich Wilhelm Riemer: *Mitteilungen über Goethe*
Scheidemantel	E. Scheidemantel (ed.): *Erinnerungen von Charlotte Krackow*
Schopenhauer	Johanna Schopenhauer: *Im Wechsel der Zeiten, im Gedränge der Welt. Jugenderinnerungen, Tagebücher, Briefe*
Schulz	Karlheinz Schulz: *Goethes und Goldonis Torquato Tasso*
Schwanke	Martina Schwanke: *Name und Namengebung bei Goethe*
Sengle	Friedrich Sengle: *Das Genie und sein Fürst, Die Geschichte der Lebensgemeinschaft Goethes mit dem Herzog Carl August*
Steiger	Robert Steiger: *Goethes Leben von Tag zu Tag*
Tümmler	Hans Tümmler: *Politischer Briefwechsel des Herzogs und Großherzogs Carl August von Weimar*
Urzidil	Johannes Urzidil: *Das Glück der Gegenwart, Goethes Amerikabild*
Wahl	Hans Wahl (ed.): *Briefwechsel des Herzogs-Großherzogs Carl August mit Goethe*
Wilpert	Gero v. Wilpert: *Goethe-Lexikon*

Endnotes

Introduction

[1] Marlis Helene Mehra, *Die Bedeutung der Formel 'offenbares Geheimnis' in Goethes Spätwerk,* Austin 1976, p.iv (quotation), pp.231f.

[2] At the Leipzig Book Fair in March 2003, the author's attention was drawn to a Faust interpretation in which the thesis of a secret liaison between Goethe and Anna Amalia was posed: 'Anna Amalia and Goethe were, in my opinion, a couple.' See Manfred Dimde, *Goethes geheimes Vermächtnis. Die Botschaften im 'Faust' entschlüsselt,* Essen 1995, pp.44f., pp.52ff.

[3] Ibid., p.152.

[4] See Regine Otto/Christa Rudnik, 'Karl Ludwig von Knebel Goethes „alter Weimarischer Urfreund"', in J. Golz (ed.), *Das Goethe- und Schiller-Archiv 1896-1996,* Weimar 1996, p.311.

[5] Hermann F. v. Egloffstein (ed.), *Alt-Weimars Abend, Briefe und Aufzeichnungen aus dem Nachlasse der Gräfinnen Egloffstein,* München 1923, p.261. (Hereafter: Egloffstein)

[6] See Joachim Berger, *Anna Amalia von Sachsen Denk - und Handlungsräume einer 'aufgeklärten' Herzogin,* Heidelberg 2003, p.39. (Hereafter: Berger)

[7] Wolfgang Vulpius, *Walther Wolfgang von Goethe und der Nachlass seines Großvaters,* Weimar 1963, p.196.

[8] Carl Alexander, quoted in *Wolfgang Vulpius, Walther Wolfgang von Goethe und der Nachlass seines Großvaters,* Weimar 1963, p.205.

[9] See Jutta Hecker (1904-2002), the daughter of Max Hecker, the archivist at the Goethe- und Schiller-Archiv, in *Rudolf Steiner in Weimar,* Dornach [2]1999, p.24.

[10] Höfer, p.7.

[11] Ibid.

[12] See Hans Wahl (ed.), who makes explicit mention of the catalogue. See Wahl's note on Anna Amalia: 'Amalia, Herzogin zu Sachsen. Briefe über Ischia und Apulien', in *Goethe. Viermonatsschrift der Goethe-Gesellschaft 1939,* p.127.

13 When a biographer of Carl August was examining the correspondence he did mention that he had read of a liaison between Goethe and Anna Amalia but had considered it of no particular importance. See Willy Andreas, 'Sturm und Drang im Spiegel der Weimarer Hofkreise', in *Goethe, Viermonatsschrift der Goethe-Gesellschaft, Neue Folge des Jahrbuchs*, 8 (1943), p.243. A biographer of Anna Amalia quotes a passage from a letter of Countess Görtz referring to the love relationship [die Liebschaft] between Anna Amalia and Goethe, but does not pursue this clue. See Joachim Berger, *Anna Amalia von Sachsen-Weimar-Eisenach (1739-1807), Denk- und Handlungsräume einer 'aufgeklärten' Herzogin*, Heidelberg 2003, pp.285f.; p.157, fn.250; pp.38ff. (Hereafter: Berger)

The State Secret

14 Quoted in Friedrich v. Müller, *Unterhaltungen mit Goethe*, E. Grumach (ed.), 1870, Weimar 1956, p.281. (Hereafter: Müller)
15 Her first names are not consistently written. See Wilhelm Bode, *Charlotte von Stein*, Berlin [5]1920, p.7. (Hereafter: Bode/von Stein)
16 See Friedrich Wilhelm Riemer, *Mitteilungen über Goethe*, 1841, A. Pollmer (ed.), Leipzig 1921, p.396, entry: 'Liebe'. (Hereafter: Riemer)
17 See Bode/von Stein, p.v; Bodenstedt is quoted in K. Heinemann, *Goethes Briefe an Frau von Stein*, vol.1, Stuttgart 1894, p.3.
18 See Robert Keil, *Vor hundert Jahren, Mitteilungen über Weimar, Goethe und Corona Schröter aus den Tagen der Genie-Periode,* vol.2, Leipzig 1875, pp.78ff. (Hereafter: Keil)
19 According to Klauß, *Charlotte von Stein. Die Frau in Goethes Nähe*, Zürich 1995, p.136, 'a film script writer could not have invented this love relationship'.
20 Fritz Liebeskind, *Der große Hermannstein bei Ilmenau*, Ilmenau [2]1928, p.37.
21 Angelika Fischer/Bernd Erhard Fischer, *Schloss Kochberg Goethe bei Frau von Stein*, Berlin-Brandenburg 1999, p.76, p.30, p.14.
22 Nicholas Boyle, *Goethe – Der Dichter in seiner Zeit*, vol.1, 1749-1790, H. Fliessbach (translation), München 1995, p.261. (Hereafter: Boyle 1)
23 Susanne Kord (ed.), 'Einleitung zu Charlotte von Stein', *Dramen* (Gesamtausgabe), Hildesheim 1998, p.v. (Hereafter: Kord)
24 Ingelore M. Winter, *Goethes Charlotte von Stein. Die Geschichte einer Liebe*, 1992; repr. Düsseldorf 2003, p.157.
25 Helmut Koopmann, *Goethe und Frau von Stein*, München 2002, p.278.
26 Höfer, p.71.
27 See Bode/von Stein, p.267.
28 Quoted in Doris Maurer, *Charlotte von Stein*, Frankfurt am Main 1997, p.290.
29 Letter to Carl v. Holtei of 26 September 1828, quoted in *Frauen der Goethezeit in ihren Briefen*, G. Jäckel (ed.), Berlin [2]1969, p.392.
30 Wilhelm Bode, 'Lotte Kestner in Weimar', in Bode (ed.), *Stunden mit Goethe, Für die Freunde seiner Kunst und Weisheit*, vol.10, Berlin 1913, p.314.

[31] Richard Friedenthal, *Goethe. Sein Leben und seine Zeit*, 1963, München 1999, p.223.
[32] See Adolf Stahr, quoted in Keil, vol.2, p.74.
[33] Höfer, p.9.
[34] *Dichtung und Wahrhei*, Book 7.
[35] Riemer, p.47.
[36] Quoted in Keil, vol.2, p.64.

Anna Amalia and Charlotte von Stein

[37] Quoted in Ursula Salentin, *Anna Amalia. Wegbereiterin der Weimarer Klassik*, Köln [3]2001, p.121.
[38] See Christian Graf zu Stolberg, quoted in Bode/von Stein, p.87.
[39] See Karl Otto Conrady, *Goethe – Leben und Werk*, München 1994, pp.280f., p.287. (Hereafter: Conrady)
[40] Egloffstein, p.350.
[41] The lady's maid Spormann, quoted in E. Scheidemantel (ed.), *Erinnerungen von Charlotte Krackow*, Weimar 1917, p.1. (Hereafter: Scheidemantel)
[42] Ibid., p.1.
[43] See in detail Carl F. v. Beaulieu-Marconnay, *Anna Amalia, Carl August und der Minister von Fritsch*, Weimar 1874, pp.18f. (Hereafter: Beaulieu-Marconnay)
[44] See Wilhelm Bode, *Amalie Herzogin von Weimar – Das vorgoethische Weimar*, vol.1, Berlin 1908, p.53, pp.94f. (Hereafter: Bode/Amalia)
[45] Keil, vol.2, p.69.
[46] See Voigt-Ludecus, quoted in Gisela Sichardt, *Das Weimarer Liebhabertheater unter Goethes Leitung*, Weimar 1957, p.124.
[47] Quoted in Hellmuth F. v. Maltzahn, *Karl Ludwig von Knebel*, Jena 1929, p.39.
[48] Quoted in Karl August Böttiger, *Literarische Zustände und Zeitgenossen. Begegnungen und Gespräche im klassischen Weimar*, 1838 (incomplete), K. Gerlach/R. Sternke (eds), Berlin [2]1998, p.240. (Hereafter: Böttiger)
[49] Quoted in Bode/Amalia, p.125; see also pp.124ff.
[50] Wilhelm Bode, *Karl August von Weimar, Jugendjahre*, Berlin 1913, p.127.
[51] Willy Andreas, 'Aus der Kindheit Carl August von Weimar, Tagebuchaufzeichnungen und Berichte seines Erziehers', in *Archiv für Kulturgeschichte 1941*, pp.282f. (Hereafter: Andreas)
[52] See A. Schöll, *Carl August Büchlein*, Weimar 1857, pp.28ff.
[53] J.W. Goethe, Weimarer Ausgabe (1887-1919), I 36, pp.311ff.: *Zu brüderlichem Andenken Wielands*, 1813. (Hereafter: *WA*)
[54] See Keil, vol.2, p.68; see also Andreas, *Carl August von Weimar, Ein Leben mit Goethe 1757-1783*, Stuttgart 1953, pp.56ff.
[55] *Thüringisches Hauptstaatsarchiv Weimar*, HA AXVIII, no. 110. Original in French: 'Une princesse, qui par les grandes qualités de Son esprit et de Son coeur fait le bonheur de Son peuple, l'admiration des étrangers et l'ornament de son siècle.'
[56] See Gerhart v. Westerman/Karl Schumann, *Knaurs Opernführer*, München 1969, p.57.

[57] Keil, p.69.
[58] See Gisela Sichardt, *Das Weimarer Liebhabertheater unter Goethes Leitung*, Weimar 1957, pp.69ff.
[59] Michael Wenzel, *Adam Friedrich Oeser und Weimar*, Heidelberg 1994, pp.48ff.
[60] See Bode/von Stein, pp.13ff.
[61] Sigmund v. Seckendorff, *Weimarische Briefe*, Leipzig 1865, p.6; see also Bode/von Stein, p.108.
[62] See Bode/von Stein, pp.26ff.
[63] Jochen Klauß, *Charlotte von Stein. Die Frau in Goethes Nähe*, Zürich 1995, p.203. (Hereafter: Klauß)
[64] Bode/von Stein, p.28.
[65] Klauß, p.203; she was also seen as such. See Johanna Schopenhauer's letter to her son on 22 December 1806; repr. H.H. Houben (ed.), *Damals in Weimar, Erinnerungen und Briefe von und an Johanna Schopenhauer*, Berlin [2]1929, p.62. (Hereafter: Houben)
[66] See the Gesamtkatalog-Auszug des Goethe-Nationalmuseums in Weimar, no. 330.713.
[67] A pastel drawing of Goethe's, 1777, showing a woman in profile, was originally thought to represent Duchess Luise or Goethe's sister Cornelia. In the meantime it has, unconvincingly, been held to be an image of Charlotte von Stein. See Helmut Koopmann, *Goethe und Frau von Stein*, München 2002, p.101; for Ludwig Münz, *Goethes Zeichnungen und Radierungen*, Wien 1949, picture no. 63, it is 'probably Charlotte von Stein'; for Friedrich August Hohenstein, *Weimar und Goethe – Ereignisse und Erlebnisse*, Berlin 1931, p.112, it is Duchess Luise; similarly for Bode/Amalia, p.4, the identification of the woman as Frau von Stein began in 1932, when with no hesitation Hans Wahl rejected the claim that it was Luise. He referred, amongst other things, to Goethe's diary entry of 15 March 1777, according to which he had painted Frau von Stein; see Gerhard Femmel (ed.), *Corpus der Goethezeichnungen*, vol.1, *Von den Anfängen bis zur italienischen Reise 1786*, Leipzig [3]1983, p.102, for the opinion that it was a representation of Goethe's sister Cornelia; see Gerhard Schuster/Caroline Gille (eds), *Wiederholte Spiegelungen, Weimarer Klassik*, München/Wien 1999, p.249; see also Klauß, p.53, 'in all probability' Frau von Stein.
[68] Klauß, p.59.
[69] Quoted in Eleonore v. Bojanowski, *Louise Großherzogin von Sachsen-Weimar und ihre Beziehungen zu den Zeitgenossen*, Stuttgart 1903, p.238. (Hereafter: Bojanowski)
[70] See Walter Geese, *Gottlieb Martin Klauer – Der Bildhauer Goethes*, Leipzig 1935, illustration no.30. (Hereafter: Geese)
[71] See Gabriele Oswald, 'Personen des Geschehens', no.5, in C. Juranek, *Abenteuer Natur Spekulation, Goethe und der Harz*, Halle an der Saale 1999, pp.16f.
[72] See Andreas, p.337; Klauß, pp.92f.
[73] Carola Sedlacek, 'Hochzeitskniekissen von Charlotte von Stein', in *Bestandhalten, Sechzig Neuerwerbungen des Goethe-Nationalmuseums*

Weimar, München 1996, p.19.

[74] See Ingelore M. Winter, *Goethes Charlotte von Stein. Die Geschichte einer Liebe*, 1992; repr. Düsseldorf 2003, p.22.

[75] Quoted in Flodoard F. v. Biedermann/Wolfgang Herwig (eds), *Goethes Gespräche, Eine Sammlung zeitgenössischer Berichte aus seinem Umgang*, vol.1, 1749-1805, München 1998, p.361, letter 727. (Hereafter: Biedermann); see also Klauß, p.32.

[76] Bode/von Stein, pp.240ff., p.245 (quotation).

[77] Quoted in Georg Mentz, 'Aus den Papieren des Grafen Görtz, des Erziehers Karl Augusts', in *Festschrift für Otto Dobenecker*, Jena 1929, p.414. Original in French: '... *la Stein devient de jour en jour plus grande favorite ... dans peu elle aura effacé toutes les autres*'. (Hereafter: Dobenecker)

[78] Ibid., p.415. Original in French: 'La Stein continue à être fort bien avec la D.[uchesse] ... elle devient poète, on m'a dit qu'elle fait de très jolis vers.' (Hereafter: Dobenecker)

[79] See Olga G. Taxis-Bordogna, *Frauen von Weimar*, München 1948, p.51.

[80] Heinrich Düntzer, *Charlotte von Stein, Goethes Freundin*, vol.1, 1742-1793, Stuttgart 1874, p.36.

Beginnings

[81] Julius Zeitler (ed.), in *Goethe-Handbuch*, vol.2, Stuttgart 1917, entry: 'Die Halsbandgeschichte', p.115.

[82] Riemer, p.234.

[83] Helmut Mathy, *Die Halsbandaffäre*, Mainz 1989, p.106.

[84] For the number references see Klauß, p.206.

[85] See K. Heinemann, *Goethes Briefe an Frau von Stein*, vol.1, Stuttgart 1894, pp.8f.

[86] Karl v. Lyncker, *Am Weimarischen Hofe unter Amalien und Karl August*, Berlin 1912, p.23; F. Bornhak, *Anna Amalia, Herzogin von Sachsen-Weimar-Eisenach*, Berlin 1892, p.104. (Hereafter: Bornhak)

[87] See the coin in the Goethe-Nationalmuseums Weimar collection, NE-No. 375/1959.

[88] Quoted in Conrady, p.290.

[89] Quoted in *Weimarische Wöchentliche Anzeigen*, 65, 12 August 1772, p.257.

[90] See Fritz Liebeskind, *Der große Hermannstein bei Ilmenau*, Ilmenau [2]1928, pp.40f., who provides a history of the carvings in the cave. For a catalogue of the astronomic symbols inserted by Goethe see J.W. Goethe, *WA*, III 1, p.346; *FA*, II 2; Hartmut Reinhardt (ed.), *Das erste Weimarer Jahrzehnt*, Frankfurt am Main 1997, p.1268.

[91] Bode/Amalia, p.137.

[92] F. Arndt, *Mütter berühmter Männer, Anna Amalia, Herzogin von Sachsen-Weimar, die Mutter Carl Augusts*, Berlin 1872, pp.60f.

[93] *Italienische Reise*, 22 September 1787; see also Hellmuth F. v. Maltzahn, *Karl Ludwig von Knebel*, Jena 1929, p.140

[94] Quoted in Bode/Amalia, vol.2, p.207.

[95] Bornhak, p.168.

[96] Boyle 1, p.307.

97 Böttiger, p.289f.
98 For the three examples see Wilhelm Bode/Valerian Tornius, *Goethes Leben 1790-1794*, Berlin 1926, p.122.

Rise and Fall of a State Minister

99 Boyle 1, p.241.
100 See Karl-Heinz Hahn, 'Die Regentin und ihr Minister. Herzogin Anna Amalia von Sachsen-Weimar und Eisenach und der Minister Jakob Friedrich Freiherr von Fritsch', in *Wolfenbütteler Beiträge*, IX, Wiesbaden 1994, pp.76ff. (quotation p.77); especially Beaulieu-Marconnay, pp.55ff.
101 Bode/Amalia, p.21.
102 Andreas, 'Aus der Kindheit Carl Augusts von Weimar, Tagebuchaufzeichnungen und Berichte seines Erziehers', in *Archiv für Kulturgeschichte 1941*, p.295.
103 See Andreas, 'Kämpfe und Intrigen um den Regierungsantritt Carl Augusts von Weimar', in *Historische Zeitschrift*, München 1949, pp.514ff.
104 Ibid., p.551.
105 Dobenecker, p.417. Original in French: '... et alors [1771] déjà la D.[uchesse] me haïssoit autant qu'à présent.'
106 See Andreas, p.287.
107 See Andreas, 'Kämpfe und Intrigen um den Regierungsantritt Carl Augusts von Weimar', in *Historische Zeitschrift*, München 1949, pp.554ff.; see also Andreas, 'Die Kavaliersreise Carl Augusts von Weimar nach Paris', in *Archiv für Kulturgeschichte* 1952, pp.180ff.
108 Conrady, p.291.
109 Andreas, p.299.
110 See Felix Freiherr von Stein-Kochberg, in *Kochberg, dem Reiche von Charlotte von Stein*, Leipzig 1936, p.46.
111 Quoted in Andreas, 'Kämpfe und Intrigen um den Regierungsantritt Carl Augusts von Weimar', in *Historische Zeitschrift*, München 1949, p.555.
112 Quoted in Kleßmann (ed.), *Goethe aus der Nähe, Berichte von Zeitgenossen*, München/Zürich 1994, p.33. (Hereafter: Kleßmann)
113 H. Guenther Nerjes, *Ein Unbekannter Schiller – Kritiker des Weimarer Musenhofes*, Berlin 1965, p.84.
114 Quoted in Hellmuth F. v. Maltzahn, *Karl Ludwig von Knebel,* Jena 1929, p.122.
115 Bojanowski, p.132, p.217.
116 *WA,* I 36, p.233.
117 Böttiger, p.217.
118 Quoted in Julius Petersen (ed.), *Goethes Briefe an Charlotte von Stein,* vol.1, Leipzig 1923, p.530. (Hereafter: Petersen)
119 Sigmund v. Seckendorff, *Weimarische Briefe*, Leipzig 1865, p.5; see also Berger, p.470.
120 See Wilhelm Bode (ed.), *Goethe in Vertraulichen Briefen seiner Zeitgenossen 1749-1793*, vol.1, Berlin 1999, p.191.
121 Quoted in Müller, p.283.
122 See the balanced description by Bode/Amalia, vol.2, pp.6ff., p.82.

123 Höfer, p.42.
124 Wilhelm Bode, *Karl August von Weimar, Jugendjahre*, Berlin 1913, p.343.
125 Quoted in Bode/Amalia, vol.2, pp.197f.
126 See Renate Müller-Krumbach, 'Nachlaß Johann Wolfgang von Goethe', in *Stiftung Weimarer Klassik, Verlassenschaften – Der Nachlaß Vulpius*, Weimar 1995, pp.22ff.
127 Sometimes thought to be Frau von Stein. See Rollet, p.54. (Hereafter: Rollet)
128 Bornhak, p.117.
129 Conrady, p.291.
130 Alfred Bergmann (ed.), *Briefe des Herzogs Carl August von Sachsen-Weimar an seine Mutter die Herzogin Anna Amalia,* Jena 1938, p.viii.
131 Ibid., p.137.
132 Quoted in Biedermann, vol.1, letter 398; Conrady, p.305.
133 Conrady, p.305.
134 Art. 131 of the *Peinlichen Gerichtsordnung*.
135 See Sigrid Damm, *Christiane und Goethe – Eine Recherche*, Frankfurt am Main/Leipzig 1998, pp.81ff.
136 Quoted in Ernst Grumach/Renate Grumach, vol.2, p.311.
137 Quoted in Bode/Amalia, vol.2, p.219.
138 See the account by Kurt Steenbuck, *Silber und Kupfer aus Ilmenau. Ein Bergwerk unter Goethes Leitung, Hintergründe, Erwartungen, Enttäuschungen*, Weimar 1995, pp.19ff.
139 Ibid., p.333.
140 See Hans Bürgin, *Der Minister Goethe vor der römischen Reise. Seine Tätigkeit in der Wegebau - und Kriegskommission*, Weimar 1933, pp.1ff.
141 Ibid., pp.32ff.
142 Ibid., p.76.
143 Ibid., pp.107ff.
144 Ibid., p.175.
145 Ibid., pp.147f.
146 For the Hauptmann see Denis Loch, *Die Jagd in Goethes Leben*, Gehren 2002, pp.123f.
147 Gisela Sichardt, *Das Weimarer Liebhabertheater unter Goethes Leitung*, Weimar 1957, pp.13ff. See Andreas, *Carl August von Weimar, Ein Leben mit Goethe 1757-1783*, Stuttgart 1953, p.346.
148 J.W. Goethe, *WA*, I 38, p.496, fn.39.
149 Klaus Seehafer, *Johann Wolfgang Goethe. Mein Leben ein einzig Abenteuer*, Berlin [2]2002, p.178.
150 Gero v. Wilpert, *Goethe-Lexikon*, Stuttgart 1998, p.1062. (Hereafter: Wilpert); see also Hans Knudsen, *Goethes Welt des Theaters, Ein Vierteljahrhundert Weimarer Bühnenleitung*, Berlin 1949, p.90.
151 See Gisela Sichardt, *Das Weimarer Liebhabertheater unter Goethes Leitung*, Weimar 1957, pp.30ff., p.1, p.116 and *passim*.
152 Ibid., p.87.
153 Böttiger, p.42.
154 Werner Deetjen, *Auf Höhen Ettersburgs*, 1924; repr. Weimar 1993, p.24.
155 Christian Friedrich Koch, quoted in Werner Deetjen, *Auf Höhen*

Ettersburgs, pp.22ff.

[156] Quoted in Andreas, 'Sturm und Drang im Spiegel der Weimarer Hofkreise', in *Goethe, Viermonatsschrift der Goethe-Gesellschaft, Neue Folge des Jahrbuchs*, vol.8 (1943), p.243.

[157] Ernst Grumach/Renate Grumach, vol.2, p.73. Original in French: 'Les nouvelles de la journée d'hier, sont une partie de plaisir à Jena, pour voir une comedie d'étudians, Mad. la D.[uchesse] M[ère] y est allé avec son cher ami Goethe'.

[157] F. Arndt, *Mütter berühmter Männer, Anna Amalia, Herzogin von Sachsen-Weimar, die Mutter Carl Augusts*, Berlin 1872, p.30.

[159] Quoted in Ernst Grumach/Renate Grumach, vol.2, p.93.

[160] Quoted in Biedermann, vol.1, p.304, letter 588.

[161] See Willi Ehrlich, *Das Wittumspalais in Weimar*, Weimar 1984, pp.11f., p.36.

[162] Quoted in Biedermann, pp.298f., letter 568.

[163] Caroline Herder, quoted in Biedermann, p.324, letter 638.

[164] Heinrich Düntzer, *Charlotte von Stein, Goethes Freundin*, vol.1, 1742-1793, Stuttgart 1874, p.33.

[165] Effi Biedrzynski, *Goethes Weimar – Das Lexikon der Personen und Schauplätze*, entry: 'Die Egloffsteins', Zürich [2]1993, p.354. (Hereafter: Biedrzynski)

[166] For Goethe's career as a Mason, see Joachim Bauer/Gerhard Müller, *'Des Maurers Wandeln, es gleicht dem Leben' – Tempelmaurerei, Aufklärung und Politik im klassischen Weimar*, Rudolstadt/Jena 2000, pp.107ff.

[167] See Hermann Schüttler, 'Freimaurerei in Weimar zum 200. Todestag von Johann Joachim Christoph Bode', in *Ettersburger Hefte* 3, Weimar 1995, pp.10ff.

[168] For 'Strikte Observanz' see Joachim Bauer/Gerhard Müller, 'Des Maurers Wandeln, es gleicht dem Leben' – Tempelmaurerei, Aufklärung und Politik im klassischen Weimar, Rudolstadt/Jena 2000, pp.24ff., pp.50ff.; for the closure of the lodge in 1782, see ibid., pp.117ff.; see also Hermann Schüttler, 'Freimaurerei in Weimar zum 200. Todestag von Johann Joachim Christoph Bode', in *Ettersburger Hefte* 3, Weimar 1995, pp.12ff.

[169] See Hermann Schüttler in *Ettersburger Hefte* 3, Weimar 1995, pp.17f., p.29; Hartwig Kloevekorn, 'Anna Amalia zu den Drei Rosen', in *Zeitschrift für Gesellschaft, Kultur und Geistesleben 1999*, vol.25, 5, p.20.

[170] Similarly Eberhard Schmitt, 'Elemente einer Theorie der politischen Konspiration im 18. Jahrhundert', in Peter Christian Ludz (ed.), *Geheime Gesellschaften*, Heidelberg 1979, pp.65ff.

[171] Quoted in Biedermann, vol.1, p.238, letter 446.

[172] Ibid., p.344, letter 685.

[173] Quoted in Woldemar F. v. Biedermann, *Goethes Gespräche, Eine Sammlung zeitgenössischer Berichte aus seinem Umgang*, vol.3: 1811-1818, Leipzig 1889, p.185.

Flight to Italy: 'Oh, What an Error!'

[174] Boyle 1, p.304.

175 H.-J. Weitz (ed.), *Gespräch vom 7. Oktober 1815 mit Sulpiz Boisserée, Tagebücher 1808-1854*, Darmstadt 1978, p.283. (Hereafter: Boisserée)
176 Hellmuth F. v. Maltzahn, *Karl Ludwig von Knebel*, Jena 1929, p.16.
177 See Konrad Scheurmann, 'Goethes Schatten in Rom', in *animo italo-tedesco 2000*, p.162.
178 Quoted in Klauß, p.113.
179 See Johann Eustachius G. v. Görtz, *Historische und politische Denkwürdigkeiten*, vol.2, Stuttgart/Tübingen 1828, pp.43ff.; see also Hans Wahl (ed.), *Briefwechsel des Herzogs-Großherzogs Carl August mit Goethe*, vol.1, 1775-1806, (1915); repr. Bern 1971, pp.378f., marginal no.53. (Hereafter: Wahl)
180 See Andreas, 'Kämpfe und Intrigen um den Regierungsantritt Carl Augusts von Weimar', in *Historische Zeitschrift*, München 1949, pp.514ff.
181 Quoted in Beaulieu-Marconnay, p.103.
182 Thüringisches Hauptstaatsarchiv Weimar, HA AXVIII, no. 23, Blatt 10. Original in French: '... *il a tord de conseiller à Monseigneur le Duc de commencer par faire des changements*'.
183 Quoted in *Dobenecker*, p.416. Original in French: 'A quoi bon faire des changements subits; deja partout le bruit se répand que C. A. n'est pas bien avec sa mère et plus d'une fois j'ai entendu de mes oreilles ...: Il a bien tord, car sa mère a bien administré. Quel mal y a til après tous que C. A. ne fasse aucun changement dans le premiers mois? Il ne m'a jamais paru, je l'avoue, que le conseil privé de la Duchesse fut mauvais ou ridicule au point d'exiger une réforme subite qui serait réellement un outrage pour la mère ... Je vous en prie, tranquilisez vous: tout ira bien.'
184 Quoted in Beaulieu-Marconnay, p.98, p.250.
185 Quoted in Dobenecker, p.416. Original in French: 'Si Wieland a dit au Duc que je l'avois chargé de parler contre Frankenberg il en a menti. Si c'est lui qui a trahi à la Duchesse le plan de Ch.[ales] Au.[guste], qui lui avoit été confié, si vous en êtes bien sur, je le méprise à jamais.'
186 Ibid., p.417. Original in French: 'Le Stadthalter m'a dit l'avoir reçu froidement, j'ai cru que Wieland voudroit se justifier, mais il l'évite. ... La D.[uchesse] a assuré au Stadthalter que le coup qu'elle vous a porté, partoit uniquement de sa tête.'
187 Böttiger, p.217.
188 Quoted in Dobenecker, p.417. Original in French: 'Je suis sûre que le Stadthalter fera tout pour vous raccommoder avec la D.[uchesse], mais cela ne se fera, je crains, jamais. Mon ami, vous êtes trop confiant, on vous a trahi. ... je désire de ne pas rester ici.'
189 Ibid., p.421. Original in French: '... *l'auteur de nos peines*'.
190 Quoted in Biedermann, p.217, letter 403.
191 Ibid., p.218, letter 405.
192 See Hans Tümmler, 'Zum Weggange des Grafen Görtz aus Weimar', in *Zeitschrift des Vereins für Thüringische Geschichte und Altertumskunde*, Jena 1941, p.185.
193 Graf Görtz, *Mémoire historique de la négociation en 1778 pour la succession de la Baviere. Confieé par le Roi de Prusse Fréderic le Grand au Comte Eustache de Goertz*, Frankfurt am Main 1812, p.9.

194 Letter to 'Frau von Stein' of 5 May 1780.

195 Graf Görtz, *Mémoire historique*, p.8 ; see also Andreas, 'Aus der Kindheit Carl Augusts von Weimar, Tagebuchaufzeichnungen und Berichte seines Erziehers', in *Archiv für Kulturgeschichte* 1941, p.299.

196 See the account by G.P. Gooch, *Friedrich der Große. Herrscher – Schriftsteller – Mensch*, München [6]1984, pp.95ff.

197 Quoted in G.P. Gooch, p.98.

198 Quoted in Hans Tümmler, 'Zum Weggange des Grafen Görtz aus Weimar', in *Zeitschrift des Vereins für Thüringische Geschichte und Altertumskunde*, Jena 1941, p.188.

199 Quoted in Hans Tümmler, p.189.

200 'W.[eimar] le 14 de Mars 1778 – ...'Maman est mieux que jamais avec le genie par Excellence, et malgré ses froideurs en publie la médisance en parle, il est des presque tous les soupers fuis[t], ... mon ami, notre train de vie devient plus insoutenable de jour en jour. ... il faut que je vous avertise d'une chose. Klinck.[owström] est venu ches moi ce matin me faire part d'une confidence que Fr.[itsch] lui a fait ... Le D[uc] lui a dit qu'il lui feroit part en conseil d'une lettre qu'il avoit eu de vous. On à trové moyen de le rendre furieux de ce que vous etes parti sans lui en faire la confidence, c'est sans doute la liaison de maman et G.[oethe] qui se sont reunis pour vous jouer un tour. Fr.[itsch] pretend avoir pris votre parti, mais le D.[uc] à assuré qu'il vous écriroit pour vous en faire des reproches. Je né'espere pas que jamais il aura le courage de le faire, mais je vous supplie que si cela arrive vous le tractés comme un fou, ou un enfant, et que vous ne vous fassiés point emporter par un mouvement de vivacité. Je vois fort bien ou tout cela méne, on en veut à votre pension mais le Roi [Friedrich II], soutiendra vos droit, et je voudrois qu'on pousser jusqué là l'ingratitude. Il a été décide dans ce conseil qu'on ne pouvoit donner la place de Ratisbonne a un Homme qui avoit rendu de si muovais services à l'Emp[ereur], et j'espere que votre refus arrivera d'ailleurs au premier jour. La Maman n'a pas la consience nette, je le vois a la façon d'être avec moi. Je me mocque de tout cela et me trouve fort heureuse de pouvoir m'en mocquer, mais au fond je donnerais tout au monde pour être loin de ses hames, de ces indignités, et de ces coquinèries ... Huffland [Arzt] vient de me quitter, il ne peut rien me dire de positif sur mon état, mais il est sure qu'il me reste bien peu d'espoir. Mes coliques continuent ... Je suis dans le plus grand embaras. Tous vos arrangemens sont pour une longue absence, et je reçois encore dans ce moment une lettre de M. votre frere [Prussian General] qui ne me parle que de votre très prochain voyage à Berlin, et de toutes les honetetes possibles qu'on y aura pour vous. Que faire dans cet embarras? ... Mon ami pourvu que je ne fasse rien qui vous déplaise. Les embaras en tout genre s'accumul j'avois écrit á M. votre frere au nom des plusieurs officier d'ici, pour le Bataileon de Stein. Il me repond dans ce moment qu'il les voudroit tous pour un régiment de dragons qu'il doit ériger. Mon dieu que faire? on trouvera fort mal si je les enleve, nouvelle raison pour se gendarm contre vous, pour vouloir vous prendre ce que vous aves. D'un autre coté dois-je empêcher la fortune de ces pauvres gens. Je tacherai de tirer mon épingle du jeu, affin que cela ne retombe n'y sur

vous, n'y sur moi. Ah si j'etois hors de cette galere! ... Weimar est pour moi l'enfer. ... Adieu meilleur des Maris, recevés les assurances de ma plus vive tendresse et de celle de vos enfants.'

201 The designation 'Maman' refers to Anna Amalia. See also Andreas, 'Sturm und Drang im Spiegel der Weimarer Hofkreise', in *Goethe, Viermonatsschrift der Goethe-Gesellschaft, Neue Folge des Jahrbuchs*, vol.8 (1943), p.243, who sorted the correspondence of Countess and supplied some commentary; see his comment that Countess Görtz is supposed to have written 'that malicious tongues treat the rapports between Goethe and Anna Amalias – despite the outward indications of coldness – almost as if there was a little liaison [kleine Liaison] between the two'.

202 Letter of 17 March 1778, quoted in Ernst Grumach/Renate Grumach, p.68. Original in French: *'La seule chose que je crains, c'est une missive de Mr. G. signée par le D[uc]'*

203 Quoted in G.P. Gooch, *Friedrich der Große. Herrscher – Schriftsteller – Mensch*, München [6]1984, p.101.

204 Quoted in Hans Tümmler, 'Zum Weggange des Grafen Görtz aus Weimar', in *Zeitschrift des Vereins für Thüringische Geschichte und Altertumskunde*, Jena 1941, p.190.

205 Quoted in Biedermann, p.253, letter 475.

206 Quoted in Ernst Grumach/Renate Grumach, p.242. Original in French: 'Goethe file toujours le parfait amour, et la pauvre Stein plus bête qu'il n'a été reçoit en patience les mauvais propos du public, et de Mr. Goethe, et les humeurs de sa femme. Vous voyés que tout cela reste sur l'ancien pied.'

297 Quoted in Biedermann, p.305, letter 589. Original in French: 'Madame de Stein s'affiche plus que jamais avec son ami, enfin la plupart des choses sont telles que nous les avons laissées.'

208 Quoted in Ernst Grumach/Renate Grumach, p.317. Original in French: 'Cette derniere [Anna Amalia] vient de faire encore une jolie folie, Elle a célébrée hier à Diefurth le jour de Naissance de Göthe par une Comedie d'Hombres chinoisés, et un pétit feu d'artifice, comment cela vous plait il?'

209 Quoted in Biedermann, p.324, letter 640. Original in French: 'Nos nouvelles d'ici ne vous le seront pas tant, et attendant, le renvoi de Kalb vous aura pourtant étonnée davantage au moins que la nouvelle noblesse de Goethe, les amours de ce dernier avec sa vieille haridelle vont toujours grand train, et le pouvoir de cette clique auprès du Duc et de la Duchesse est plus grande que jamais. Ma maladie et mon absence leur a fait gagner du terrain, de façon qu'il y en a pour dégobiller, mais j'en suis fort tranquille, s'ils en font trop, je sais où aller et être reçue à bras ouverts.'

210 See Biedrzynski, entry: 'Kalb auf Kalbsrieth', Zürich [2]1993, pp.222ff.; that Goethe did not use the title 'Kammerpräsident', as Herder – who was convinced of von Kalb's innocence – mentions in a letter (Biedermann, p.321, letter 633), is accounted for by the fact that Goethe, as a Minister, had no use for the subordinate title; see Alfons Pausch/Jutta Pausch, *Goethe im Finanzdienst*, Berlin 2003, p.94.

211 Repr.: in Biedermann, vol.1, p.326, letter 646; also repr. in Ernst Grumach/Renate Grumach (eds), p.387. Original in French: 'J'ai passe

hier ma journée à la cour ... Le Baron Goethe est venu à moi très cordialment me demandant avec beaucoup d'intérêt des nouvelles de votre santé et continuant la conversation jusqu'au moment qu'on me rappela pour le jeu. Madame de Stein m'a étouffée de tendresse. 12. Oktober] Pour le Sieur Baron de Goethe, il est devenu très gentil et parlant et a un peu adopté les façons de gentilhomme, il conserve toujours le même empire et sur mari et sur femme [Carl August und Luise], ainsi que madame de Stein qui joue toujours son rôle le mieux qu'elle peut, mangeant des pommes de terre presque tous les soirs dans sa maison avec G.[oethe] et la D[uche]sse. Le mari Stein, s'étant mis audessus de tout plus que jamais, est redevenu gros et gras, est aussi insipide et faux que jamais.'

212 See Andreas, pp.348f.

213 Quoted in Helene Matthies, *Lottine – Lebensbild der Philippine Charlotte, Schwester Friedrichs des Großen, Gemahlin Karls I. von Braunschweig*, Braunschweig 1958, p.90; further references on pp.89ff., p.104, p.175 and *passim*.

214 See Charlotte Marlo Werner, *Goethes Herzogin Anna Amalia*, Düsseldorf 1996, p.96. (Hereafter: Marlo Werner)

215 See Bornhak, pp.220 ff; see also 'Anna Amalias Briefe an Friedrich II' in *Thüringisches Hauptstaatsarchiv Weimar*, Collection F 1532 III, Blatt 182ff.

216 Quoted in Helmut Probst, 'Prinz Louis Ferdinand von Preußen. Seine Beziehungen zu Goethe und Carl August', in *Weimarbrief* 2/2000, p.99.

217 Quoted in Hans Tümmler, *Politischer Briefwechsel des Herzogs und Großherzogs Carl August von Weimar*, vol.1, 1778-1790, Stuttgart 1954, p.253.

218 Ibid., p.256.

219 Ibid., p.258.

220 Ibid., p.259.

221 Ibid., pp.277f.

222 Ibid., p.493.

223 Quoted in Wilhelm Bode, *Amalie Herzogin von Weimar – Der Musenhof der Herzogin Amalie*, vol.2, Berlin 1908, p.223.

224 *WA*, II 6, p.131.

225 See Hans Wahl (ed.), *Briefwechsel des Herzogs-Großherzogs Carl August mit Goethe*, vol.1, 1775-1806, (1915); repr. Bern 1971, p.387, marginal no.97 and p.388, marginal no.101.

226 Ibid., p.399, marginal no.109, with precise references to Austrian surveillance.

227 Quoted in Hans Tümmler, *Politischer Briefwechsel des Herzogs und Großherzogs Carl August von Weimar*, vol. 1, 1778-1790, Stuttgart 1954, pp.303f.

228 Zurückhaltend Konrad Scheurmann, 'Goethes Schatten in Rom', in *animo italo-tedesco* 2000, p.174.

229 For Tischbein's moving letters of petition sent to Weimar by Goethe's friend Merck to promote his career as a a painter see Hans Gerhard Gräf (ed.), *Johann Heinrich Mercks Briefe*, Leipzig 1911, pp.142ff., which include expressions like: '... when I look at what I am smearing on canvas

these days I think of my father and I see his ghost threatening and saying to me: "Be ashamed, useless boy; I did not rate you so low"" (p.145).

230 Klauß, p.108.

231 See Bode/von Stein, pp.249ff.

232 Quoted in Robert Steiger, *Goethes Leben von Tag zu Tag*, vol.1, 1749-1775, München 1982, p.671. (Hereafter: Steiger)

233 Martina Schwanke, *Name und Namengebung bei Goethe, Computergestützte Studien zu epischen Werken,* Heidelberg 1992, p.426. (Hereafter: Schwanke)

234 See Bode/von Stein, p.590, p.660.

235 Ibid., pp.362ff., pp.392ff., pp.436ff. and *passim*; Klauß, pp.113ff.

236 See Bode/von Stein, pp.520ff.

Italy: 'The Turning Point'

237 See commentary in *WA*, III 1, pp.143ff., p.363; I 30, p.284.

238 See commentary of Wilhelm Bode, who first published the letter in his (ed.), *Stunden mit Goethe, Für die Freunde seiner Kunst und Weisheit,* vol.9, Berlin 1913, p.307: '... so mußte es sie [Frau von Stein] seltsam berühren, daß er [Goethe] ihr nicht den ersten Abdruck brachte.'

239 See Paul Kühn, *Die Frauen um Goethe*, introduced and revised by G. Biermann, Salzburg 1949, p.348. (Hereafter: Kühn)

240 Wilhelm Bode, *Amalie Herzogin von Weimar – Das vorgoethische Weimar*, vol.1, Berlin 1908, p.137; for the year 1772, see *Weimarische Wöchentliche Anzeigen*, No. 89 of 4 November 1772, p.373.

241 See Bode/Amalia, vol.2, Berlin 1908, pp.54f.

242 For detailed account of her Italian language skills see Berger, *Anna Amalia von Sachsen-Weimar-Eisenach (1739-1807) – Denk- und Handlungsräume einer 'aufgeklärten' Herzogin*, Jena 2002, pp.260ff. (Hereafter: Berger)

243 Quoted in Joachim Berger, 'Herzogin Anna Amalia als Vermittlerin italienischer Kultur', in J. Rees, et al., (ed.), *Europareisen politisch-sozialer Eliten im 18. Jahrhundert*, Berlin 2002, p.278, fn.11.

244 Thüringisches Hauptstaatsarchiv Weimar, HA AXVIII, No. 62, Blatt 1: 'Se la vostra filosofia vi ha fatto prendere la risoluzione di menare una vita solitaria, ne sono contenta, e avete ragione che il mondo non è più fatto per un uomo che pensa e che è pieno di meriti come voi ... Per tutto l'amicizia mia vi seguirà financo nell'inferno!'

245 Böttiger, p.47.

246 Bärbel Raschke, 'Anna Amalia von Sachsen-Weimar-Eisenach – Buchbesitz, Lektüre und Geselligkeit', in J. Berger (ed.), *Der Musenhof Anna Amalias*, Köln 2001, p.87.

247 Quoted in Gertrud Bäumer, *Goethes Freundinnen, Briefe zu ihrer Charakteristik*, Leipzig/Berlin 1909, p.146.

248 Repr.: in Wilhelm Bode (ed.), *Stunden mit Goethe, Für die Freunde seiner Kunst und Weisheit*, vol.6, Berlin 1910, p.189.

249 See J.M.R. Lenz, *Briefe und Gedichte, Werke und Briefe III*, Sigrid Damm (ed.), Frankfurt am Main 1992, p.507.

[250] See Bode/von Stein, p.155.
[251] Quoted in Biedermann, p.305, letter 589. Original in French: 'Madame de Stein s'affiche plus que jamais avec son ami, enfin la plupart des choses sont telles que nous les avons laissées.'
[252] Repr.: in Biedermann, p.326, letter 646; also in Ernst Grumach/Renate Grumach, p.387. Original in French: '... madame de Stein qui joue toujours son rôle le mieux qu'elle peut, mangeant des pommes de terre presque tous les soirs dans sa maison avec G.[oethe] et la D[uche]sse.'
[253] M. Hecker (ed.), *Briefwechsel zwischen Goethe und Zelter 1799-1832*, vol.1, 1799-1818, Frankfurt am Main 1987, p.633; Höfer, p.142.
[254] For establishing dates, see Heide Hollmer (ed.), epilogue, *Anna Amalia von Sachsen-Weimar-Eisenach, Briefe über Italien,* St. Ingbert 1999, p.92.
[255] Letter of 19 February 1787.
[256] See Jochen Klauß, 'Johann Wolfgang von Goethe, Italienische Landschaft mit Grotte, "hier ist der Schlüssel zu allem"', in *Aus dem Goethe Nationalmuseum*, Faltblatt no. 15/1999.
[257] See the coin in the *Bestand des Goethe-Nationalmuseums Weimar*, NE-No. 331/1959.
[258] Letter of 13 May 1779; see the commentary to *WA*, IV 4, p.384, no.815.
[259] Quoted in Werner Deetjen, *Auf Höhen Ettersburgs*, 1924, here repr. Weimar 1993, p.40.
[260] Quoted in Wilhelm Bode/Amalia, p.224.
[261] See Paul Weizsäcker, *Anna Amalia, Herzogin von Sachsen-Weimar-Eisenach, die Begründerin des Weimarischen Musenhofes*, in: *Sammlung gemeinverständlicher wissenschaftlicher Vorträge*, 161, Hamburg 1892, p.45. (Hereafter: Weizsäcker)
[262] See Christian Lenz, *Tischbein – Goethe in der Campagna di Roma*, Frankfurt am Main 1979, pp.41f.
[263] Damm, p.114.
[264] Klauß, p.171.
[265] Boyle 1, p.535.
[266] Quoted in Berger, p.527.
[267] Quoted in Biedermann, p.431, letter 861.
[268] Ibid., p.432, letter 864.
[269] Quoted in Tümmler, pp.287f.
[270] Boyle 1, p.537.
[271] Ibid., p.658.
[272] See Biedrzynski, entry: 'Die Egloffsteins', pp.68ff.
[273] Egloffstein, p.357.
[274] Ibid., p.82 (2nd quotation).
[275] Ibid., pp.358f.
[276] Ibid., p.357.
[277] Ibid., pp.354f.
[278] Riemer, p.164.
[279] Damm, p.101, according to whom Christiane's father had died on 29 March 1786.
[280] René Sternke (ed.), preface to Böttiger, p.vi, Böttiger, p.77.
[281] Böttiger, p.77.

282 See Ernst Grumach/Renate Grumach, p.342, p.475.
283 Quoted in Renate Grumach, p.40
284 See *WA*, I 55, Register, p.384.
285 Quoted in Renate Grumach, p.218.
286 Ibid., p.60.
287 See Volkmar Braunbehrens, *Goethes 'Egmont', Text – Geschichte – Interpretation*, Freiburg/Br. 1982, pp.75ff.
288 Boyle 1, p.571.
289 Repr.: *Die Italienische Reise, Zweiter Römischer Aufenthalt*, 3 November 1787, *WA*, I 32, pp.136f.
290 Friedrich Kluge, *Etymologisches Wörterbuch der deutschen Sprache*, Berlin/New York [23]1999, entry: 'Nuance', p.593. (Hereafter: Kluge)
291 *WA*, IV 9, pp.21f.
292 Klauß, p.266.
293 Conrady, p.282.
294 Here with reference to Amelie v. Seebach, the fiancée of Carl von Stein, Bode/von Stein, p.445.
295 Friedenthal, p.184.
296 Andreas, p.185; Wolfgang Huschke, 'Unebenbürtige Sprosse Carl Augusts von Weimar', in *Familie und Volk*, 6 (1957), p.258.
297 Quoted in Dobenecker, p.419. Original in French: 'Hier il a été jusqu'à une heure chez la Werther boire du Punch, chanter et baiser avec la Bechtolsheim et la Kauffberg; c'étoit à qui baiseroit le mieux.'
298 Quoted in Alfred Bergmann (ed.), *Briefe des Herzogs Carl August von Sachsen-Weimar an seine Mutter die Herzogin Anna Amalia*, Jena 1938, p.179. Note to p.73: 'Cherchez ... une demoiselle nommée Enkchen, qui m'a donnée la chaude pisse, dites-lui que je suis guéri, et que je souhaite qu'elle le soit aussi, l'assurant de mon attachement.'
299 See Bojanowski, p.233.
300 Boyle 1, p.538.
301 See Biedrzynski, entry: 'Die Egloffsteins', p.124.
302 Quoted in Petersen, vol 2/2, p.715, note 1653.
303 Boyle 1, p.360.
304 But see Boyle 1, p.581; see also Wilpert, p.401.
305 See also Damm, p.134, pp.158f.
306 Conrady, p.547.
307 Karoline Jagemann, quoted from: *Das Klassische Weimar*, H. Pleticha (ed.), München 1983, p.287. (Hereafter: Pleticha)
308 Christine Reinhard in a letter to her mother of 5 July 1807, repr.: *FA*, II 6, Rose Unterberger (ed.), *Napoleonische Zeit*, Frankfurt am Main 1993, p.200.
309 Karoline Jagemann, quoted from Pleticha, p.287.
310 Quoted in Heuschele, p.245.
311 See Johanna Schopenhauer, quoted in Damm, p.351.
312 Ibid., p.196 and *passim*.
313 B. Maurach (ed.), *Briefe an Carl August Böttiger*, Bern 1987, p.96.
314 Quoted in Biedermann, p.700, letter 1449.
315 See Frau Augusti, quoted from Pleticha, p.289.

[316] Damm, pp.310f.
[317] Ibid., pp.512f.
[318] Quoted in Müller, p.60.
[319] See Knebel, quoted in Bode/von Stein, p.70.
[320] Bode/Amalia, vol.3, pp.115f.
[321] Quoted in Biedermann, p.502, letter 1034.
[322] Rollet, pp.100ff.
[323] Quoted in Biedrzynski, p.70.
[324] Quoted in Kleßmann, p.55.
[325] C. v. Kalb, *Gedenkblätter von Charlotte v. Kalb*, Emil Palleske (ed.), Stuttgart 1879, pp.193f. (Hereafter: Palleske)
[326] Introduction to Johann Gottfried v. Herder, *Ausgewählte Werke in einem Bande*, Stuttgart/Tübingen 1844, p.27.
[327] For the following, see Böttiger, pp.47ff.
[328] See Conrady, pp.729ff.
[329] Bode/Amalia, vol.3, p.58.
[330] Quoted in Biedermann, p.319, letter 630.
[331] Quoted in Houben, p.58.
[332] Quoted in Heuschele, p.289.
[333] See Boyle 2, p.135.
[334] Eberhard Zahn, *Die Igeler Säule bei Trier*, Neuß 1968, p.6.
[335] Ibid., p.36.
[336] See also the commentary to *BA*, 10, p.705, marginal no.170: 'ihr Leben... zurückzurufen' is in 1792 an anachronism.
[337] See Berger, pp.324f.
[338] See Anna Amalia's letter to Goethe's mother of 4 November 1778: 'Das Gemälde vom Bänkelsänger hat Wolf [Goethe], Kraus und ich gemalt'. Quoted in Bode/Amalia, vol 2, p.201.
[339] Similarly Angela Borchert, 'Die Entstehung der Musenhofvorstellung aus den Angedenken an Anna Amalia von Sachsen-Weimar-Eisenach', in J. Berger (ed.), *Der Musenhof Anna Amalias*, Köln 2001, p.166, fn.3.
[340] Quoted in Bode/Amalia, p.203.
[341] Böttiger, p.96; Bojanowski, pp.217ff.; John Hennig, 'A note on Goethe and Charles Gore', in *Monatshefte*, Madison, Wisconsin, 1951, pp.28f.; see also Biedrzynski, entry: 'Die Egloffsteins', pp.170f.

Tasso: 'A Dangerous Undertaking'

[342] See Karlheinz Schulz, *Goethes und Goldonis Torquato Tasso*, Frankfurt am Main 1986, pp.120ff. (Hereafter: Schulz)
[343] See W. Gaede (1929) quoted in Schulz, p.7.
[344] Conrady, p.484.
[345] See Christian Grawe, *Johann Wolfgang Goethe, Torquato Tasso, Erläuterungen und Dokumente*, Stuttgart 1981, pp.124f. (Hereafter: Grawe)
[346] Egloffstein, pp.352f.
[347] Ibid., p.353, fn.1.
[348] 20 March 1789; repr. Wilhelm Bode (ed.), *Goethe in Vertraulichen Briefen*

seiner Zeitgenossen 1749-1793, vol.1, Berlin 1999, p.393; see also Boyle 1, p.555.
349 Scheidemantel, p.12.
350 Müller, p.183.
351 Quoted in Bojanowski, p.303. Original in French: 'C'est un beau morçeau et on voit avec étonnement, qu'elle jouit encore après sa mort du privilège, dont elle jouissait pendant sa vie, c'est à dire de celuici d'une grande réputation.'
352 Ibid., p.303.
353 See Herman Grimm, *Goethe-Vorlesungen*, 1877, quoted in Grawe, p.223.
354 Ibid., pp.201f.
355 See Marlo Werner, p.134; see also Joachim Berger, 'Anna Amalias Rückzug auf ihren "Musensitz"', in Berger, p.153.
356 Quoted in Gerhard Bott, *Herzogin Anna Amalia von Sachsen-Weimar und ihre Freunde im Park der Villa D'Este in Tivoli*, München 1961, p.490.
357 Quoted in Bode/Amalia,vol.3, p.183.
358 See also Kühn, p.12; Bornhak, p.6.
359 Grawe, pp.5f.
360 Ibid., p.54.
361 See Schulz, p.34
362 See Grawe, pp.49ff.
363 Letter to Knebel, 7 July 1783.
364 See also Schulz, pp.110f.
365 Quoted from Pleticha, p.44.
366 See Kühn, pp.347f.
367 Weizsäcker, p.9.
368 See also Marlo Werner, p.69.
369 Quoted in Volker Wahl, 'Anna Amalia und die Wissenschaft in Weimar und Jena', in *Wolfenbütteler Beiträge*, vol. 9, Wiesbaden 1994, p.95.
370 E. Scheidemantel (ed.), *Erinnerungen von Charlotte Krackow*, Weimar 1917, p.10. (Hereafter: Scheidemantel)
371 Boyle 1, p.508.

Anna Amalia: An Outstanding Woman

372 Quoted in Gotthard Frühsorge, 'Der Abt Jerusalem als Erzieher und Berater Anna Amalias', in *Wolfenbütteler Beiträge*, vol.9, Wiesbaden 1994, p.63.
373 Quoted in Bode/Amalia, p.29.
374 Karl v. Lyncker, *Am Weimarischen Hofe unter Amalien und Karl August*, Berlin 1912, p.21. (Hereafter: Lynker)
375 Scheidemantel, p.9.
376 Egloffstein, p.354.
377 Johanna Schopenhauer, *Im Wechsel der Zeiten, im Gedränge der Welt. Jugenderinnerungen, Tagebücher, Briefe*, München 1986, p.371. (Hereafter: Schopenhauer); see Houben, pp.92f.
378 Lyncker, quoted in Renate Grumach, p.397.
379 Weizsäcker, p.3.

380 Heuschele, p.324.
381 Letter to H.A.O. Reichard, 13 December 1808, in Schopenhauer, p.384.
382 See her letter to F.A. Brockhaus vom 24. February 1817; repr. Schopenhauer, p.402.
383 Egloffstein, p.261.
384 Quoted in Müller,p.177.
385 Henriette v. Egloffstein, married name v. Beaulieu-Marconnay, quoted from Bode/Amalia vol.3, p.73.
386 Karoline Jagemann, quoted from: Pleticha, p.44; Scheidemantel, p.4; see also Hans Wahl, *Tiefurt*, Leipzig 1929, p.83.
387 Quoted in Bode/Amalia, p.214.
388 Quoted in Biedermann, pp.320f., letter 632.
389 Quoted in Ernst Grumach/Renate Grumach, p.366.
390 Ibid., p.390.
391 Quoted in Biedermann, p.327, letter 650.
392 Thüringisches Hauptstaatsarchiv Weimar, Rechnungsbuch 1782, A 949 Blatt 1058.
393 Quoted in Biedermann, p.351, letter 702.
394 See Böttiger, p.36, pp.73f.
395 See Andreas, pp.332ff.
396 Böttiger, pp.73ff.
397 See Bode/Amalia, pp.85f., p.138.
398 Ibid., p.201.
399 Jakob Michael Reinhold Lenz, *Werke*, München 1992, epilogue by G. Sauder, p.590.
400 Quoted in Bode/von Stein, p.127.
401 Quoted in Petersen, p.533.
402 See Andreas, p.327.
403 J.M.R. Lenz, *Briefe und Gedichte, Werke und Briefe III*, Sigrid Damm (ed.), Frankfurt am Main 1992, p.478. (Hereafter: Damm/Lenz)
404 Friedenthal, p.192.
405 Andreas, p.591.
406 Damm/Lenz, p.439.
407 Ibid., pp.188f.
408 Ibid., pp.189f.
409 Christoph Weiss, 'Zu den Vorbereitungen einer Lenz-Gesamtausgabe: Wiederentdeckte und unbekannte Handschriften', in I. Stephan/H.-G. Winter (eds), *'Die Wunde Lenz', J.M.R. Lenz Leben, Werk und Rezeption*, Bern 2003, p.20.
410 J.M.R. Lenz, *Gesammelte Schriften*, Ludwig Tieck (ed.), vol.3, Berlin 1828, p.285 (1st quotation), p.286 (2/3 quotations), p.290 (4th quotation).
411 Ibid., p.507.
412 Ibid.
413 See M. Rieger, *Klinger in der Sturm- und Drangperiode*, Darmstadt 1880, pp.144f., pp.25ff.; Andreas, pp.330f.
414 Quoted in Sigrid Damm, *Vögel, die verkünden Land, Das Leben des Jakob Michael Reinhold Lenz*, Frankfurt am Main 1992, p.274.
415 Quoted in Biedermann, p.217, letter 403.

416 See Andreas, p.333.
417 Bode/von Stein, p.137; for a critical appraisal of previous explanations see the commentary to *FA*, II 2, Hartmut Reinhardt (ed.), *Das erste Weimarer Jahrzehnt*, Frankfurt am Main 1997, pp.770f.
418 Böttiger, p.73.
419 Damm/Lenz, p.517.
420 Quoted in Sigrid Damm, *Vögel, die verkünden Land, Das Leben des Jakob Michael Reinhold Lenz* Frankfurt am Main 1992, p.288.
421 Ibid., p.325.
422 Ibid., pp.324ff.
423 Ibid., p.325.
424 Quoted in Bode/Amalia, p.208.
425 Quoted in Sigrid Damm, *Vögel, die verkünden Land, Das Leben des Jakob Michael Reinhold Lenz*, Frankfurt am Main 1992, pp.337f.
426 M. Rieger, *Klinger in der Sturm - und Drangperiode*, Darmstadt 1880, p.154.
427 Ibid., pp.396f.
428 Ibid., p.155; Jörg-Ulrich Fechner, epilogue to Friedrich Maximilian Klinger, *Sturm und Drang, 1776*, Stuttgart 1998, pp.152f.
429 Quoted in M. Rieger, *Klinger in der Sturm- und Drangperiode*, Darmstadt 1880, p.398.
430 Böttiger, p.46.
431 Quoted in Ernst Grumach/Renate Grumach, vol.1, p.458.
432 Sigrid Damm, *Vögel, die verkünden Land, Das Leben des Jakob Michael Reinhold Lenz,* Frankfurt am Main 1992, pp.292f.; in Ernst Grumach/Renate Grumach, it is supposed that Goethe visited Kaufmann in Switzerland: see Ernst Grumach/Renate Grumach, p.204; according to another opinion this was not true: see Wilpert, p.555; Carl August writes to his wife on 3 December 1779: '... we haven't met him'.
433 Quoted in M. Rieger, *Klinger in der Sturm- und Drangperiode*, Darmstadt 1880, p.401.
434 Ibid., p.177.
435 Quoted in Ernst Grumach/Renate Grumach, vol.1, p.458.
436 Bode/Amalia, p.56.
437 See Olga G. Taxis-Bordogna, *Frauen von Weimar*, München 1948, p.19.
438 Quoted in Bode/Amalia, vol.2, p.210.
439 Ibid., p.220.
440 *WA*, I 16, p.440.
441 Quoted in Bode/Amalia, vol.2, p.150.
442 See Andreas, pp.55ff.
443 For a balanced judgement see Wolfram Huschke, 'Anna Amalia und die Musik ihrer Zeit', in *Wolfenbütteler Beiträge*, IX, Wiesbaden 1994, pp.143f.; see also Sandra Dreise-Beckmann, 'Anna Amalia und das Musikleben am Weimarer Hof', in J. Berger (ed.), *Der Musenhof Anna Amalias*, Köln 2001, p.63, pp.66ff.; Heide Hollmer, 'Herzogin Anna Amalias Kunstwahrnehmung und Kunstförderung', ibid., p.117.
444 With reference to the singer and occasional composer Corona Schröter see Sandra Dreise-Beckmann, 'Anna Amalia und das Musikleben am

Weimarer Hof', in J. Berger (ed.), pp.281ff.

445 Quoted in K.A. Varnhagen von Ense/Th. Mundt, *K.L. von Knebels Literarischer Nachlaß und Briefwechsel*, Leipzig ²1840, p.190; see also Carl Georg Jacob, *Erinnerungen aus dem Leben der Herzogin Amalia von Weimar*, Jena 1838, p.45; Berger, p.316, fn.112.

446 Quoted in Ernst Lieberkühn, *Die Herzogin Anna Amalia von Sachsen-Weimar und ihr Einfluß auf Deutschlands Literaturzustände, Eine Vorlesung*, Weimar 1847, pp.464f.

447 Quoted in Bode/Amalia, vol.2, p.224.

448 Eckermann, 3 May 1827.

449 Quoted in Heuschele, p.223.

450 Ibid., p.290.

451 Quoted in K.A. Varnhagen von Ense/Th. Mundt, *K.L. von Knebels Literarischer Nachlaß und Briefwechsel*, Leipzig ²1840, pp.198f.

452 Quoted in Gertrud Bäumer, *Goethes Freundinnen, Briefe zu ihrer Charakteristik*, Leipzig/Berlin 1909, pp.196f.

453 Goethe- und Schiller-Archiv Weimar, Bestand: Göchhausen, Signatur 24/II, 1; Steiger, p.671; see also Marlo Werner, p.229.

454 See Damm, p.514.

455 *WA*, II 6, p.132.

456 Ibid, p.143.

457 Goethe- und Schiller-Archiv Weimar, Bestand: Anna Amalia, Signatur 28/767, Blatt V.

458 See the introductory note to the 'Lesarten und Paralipomena der Morphologie' in *WA*, II 6, pp.367ff.; see Rudolf Steiner, *Goethes Weltanschauung*, Weimar 1897.

459 Goethe- und Schiller-Archiv Weimar, Bestand: Anna Amalia, Signatur 28/767, Blatt X.

460 *WA*, I 13.1, pp.167f.; see for datings, 13.2, p.230.

461 Dated around 1800 by Erich Trunz (ed.), *Goethe – Faust, Der Tragödie erster und zweiter Teil, Urfaust*, München ¹⁴1989 p.507.

462 See Bode/Amalia, vol.1, Berlin 1908, p.145; for the text with an image of the original, see Anna Amalia, 'Meine Gedanken', Volker Wahl (ed.), in *Wolfenbütteler Beiträge*, vol.9, Wiesbaden 1994, pp.102ff.; for a dating at 1774 – no reasons given – see Berger, p.107, p.111 and *passim*.

463 See Wilpert, p.66.

464 See Wahl, p.xiii.

465 Hans Gerhard Gräf (ed.), *Johann Heinrich Mercks Briefe*, Leipzig 1911, p.vii.

466 See Kord, p.vi.

467 Rollet, pp.3f.; similarly Edmund Hoefer, 'Goethe's Stellung zu Weimar's Fürstenhause', Stuttgart 1872, p.5.

468 For the date, see Steiger, p.544.

469 Marlo Werner, p.93; Berger, pp.127f.

470 Thüringisches Hauptstaatsarchiv Weimar, *Fourier-Buch für das Jahr 1772*, pp.246ff.

471 Robert Keil, *Vor hundert Jahren, Mitteilungen über Weimar, Goethe und Corona Schröter aus den Tagen der Genie-Periode*, vol.2, Leipzig 1875,

p.74. (Hereafter: Keil)

472 See the letter of Countess Görtz to her husband of 28 March 1775; repr. Dobenecker, p.415.

473 *Dichtung und Wahrheit*, Book 15.

474 Repr.: in Wilhelm Bode (ed.), *Stunden mit Goethe, Für die Freunde seiner Kunst und Weisheit*, vol.9, Berlin 1913, p.303.

475 See Böttiger, pp.241f.; see also Sandra Dreise-Beckmann, 'Anna Amalia und das Musikleben am Weimarer Hof', in J. Berger (ed.), *Der Musenhof Anna Amalias*, Köln 2001, pp.60f.

476 See Wolfram Huschke, 'Anna Amalia und die Musik ihrer Zeit', in *Wolfenbütteler Beiträge*, IX, Wiesbaden 1994, pp.128f.; see also Bode/Amalia, vol.2, pp.171f.; Friedrich August Hohenstein, *Weimar und Goethe – Ereignisse und Erlebnisse*, Berlin 1931, pp.102ff.

477 See Böttiger, p.424.

478 *Antje Vanhoefen*, 'Zum Oßmannstädter Porträt der Herzogin Anna Amalia von Georg Melchior Kraus', in *Die Pforte* 6/2002, p.34.

479 See Hans Gerhard Gräf (ed.), *Johann Heinrich Mercks Briefe*, Leipzig 1911, pp.xf.

480 Klauß, p.261.

481 Quoted in Beaulieu-Marconnay, p.133, p.252; see also Bornhak, pp.89f.

482 Quoted in Ernst Hallbauer, 'Graf Görtz und Goethe', in Wilhelm Bode (ed.), *Stunden mit Goethe, Für die Freunde seiner Kunst und Weisheit*, vol.8, Berlin 1912, pp.86f.

483 Ibid., p.87 (1st quotation), p.88 (2nd quotation).

484 Andreas, p.185.

485 Wilhelm Bode, *Karl August von Weimar, Jugendjahre*, Berlin 1913, p.212.

486 Quoted in Ernst Hallbauer, 'Graf Görtz und Goethe', in Wilhelm Bode (ed.), *Stunden mit Goethe, Für die Freunde seiner Kunst und Weisheit*, vol.8, Berlin 1912, p.88.

487 Wilpert, p.164.

488 Böttiger, p.214; see also Bode/Amalia, vol.2, Berlin 1908, p.85.

489 Böttiger, p.213.

490 Ibid., p.217.

491 Wilpert, p.1025.

492 Quoted from Pleticha, pp.44f.

David Heinrich Grave: A Human Catastrophe

493 Quoted in Eduard Bamberg, *Die Erinnerungen der Karoline Jagemann*, vol.1, Dresden 1926, p.174. (Hereafter: Bamberg)

494 Egloffstein, p.354.

495 Quoted in Bode/Amalia, vol.2, Berlin 1908, p.32.

496 Quoted in Bamberg, p.42.

497 Ibid., p.174.

498 See 14, 15 and 18 from the year 1789.

499 Quoted in Johann Gottfried Herder, *Italienische Reise, Briefe und Tagebuchaufzeichnungen 1788-1789*, A. Meier/H. Hollmer (eds), München 1988, p.173.

500 Ibid., p.225.
501 Ibid., p.420.
502 Ibid., p.482.
503 Quoted in Bamberg, p.180.
504 Ibid., p.42; Anna Amalia took care of the child, who died, however, as early as 1791. See the letter of Grave's wife, Louise, to Einsiedel, Goethe- und Schiller-Archiv Weimar, Bestand: F. H. v. Einsiedel, Signatur 14/76; Berger, p.412.
505 Friedenthal, p.194.
506 Palleske, pp.180f.
507 Olga G. Taxis-Bordogna, *Frauen von Weimar*, München 1948, p.26, pp.90f.
508 Goethe- und Schiller-Archiv Weimar, Bestand: F.H. v. Einsiedel, Signatur 14/76, Blatt 2 und 6. The author is indebted to Prof. Dr. Detlev Forst and Hans Zürn for deciphering the Gothic script.
509 Bode/Amalia, vol.3, Berlin 1908, p.34.
510 Quoted in Bamberg, p.180.
511 Quoted in Heide Hollmer, 'Herzogin Anna Amalias Kunstwahrnehmung und Kunstförderung', in J. Berger (ed.), *Der Musenhof Anna Amalias*, Köln 2001, p.113, fn.22.
512 Quoted in Bamberg, p.181.
513 Quoted in Otto Harnack, *Zur Nachgeschichte der italienischen Reise*, Weimar 1890, pp.203f.
514 See Goethe's letter to Carl August of 28 February 1790.
515 See Horst Rüdiger, *Goethe und Europa*, Berlin 1990, p.62.
516 Quoted in Marlo Werner, p.227.
517 Boyle 1, p.665.

Deception: Letters to Frau von Stein

518 About a third are undated. For the history of the edition, see Jonas Fränkel, *Marginalien zu Goethes Briefen an Charlotte von Stein*, Jena 1909, pp.2ff.
519 It is presumed that the addressee destroyed them. This is based on three letters from Goethe, in which he says, 8 December 1786: 'The boxes in the archive belong to you. If you still love me a little, please don't open them until you have news of my death. While I am still alive, give me the hope of opening them in your presence'. The contents of two boxes are written on an extant folio page. According to this, box 1 contains, amongst other things, 'Letters from ⊙'. In front of the letters [Briefe] there is a hook-like sign. See the commentary to *WA*, IV 7, p.335. In Goethe's diaries the sun symbol (⊙) officially refers to 'Frau von Stein'. There is no mention of destroying the letters, but rather of giving them back. See the justifiably critical view of Susanne Kord (ed.), 'Einleitung zu Charlotte von Stein', *Dramen* (Complete edition), Hildesheim 1998, p.vi and fn.35.
520 Goethe - und Schiller-Archiv Weimar, Bestand: Luise v. Göchhausen, Signatur 54/274,2 Blatt 3b.

521 Quoted in Doris Maurer, *Charlotte von Stein*, Frankfurt am Main 1997, p.77.
522 Quoted in Bode/von Stein, p.154.
523 See the commentary to *WA*, IV 3, p.276.
524 Henriette v. Egloffstein, married name v. Beaulieu-Marconnay, quoted from Bode/Amalia, vol.3, p.73.
525 Willmar Hager, *Brieftauben, ihre Geschichte und ihre Leistungen*, Berlin 1938, p.10.
526 See http://www.brieftaubenring.de/geschichte.htm
527 Hager, *Brieftauben*, p.13.
528 See the commentary to *WA*, IV 3, p.311; IV 5, p.382, letter 1393 and *passim*.
529 See the letter of 12 December 1781.
530 See Bode/von Stein, pp.86f.
531 See in detail Bojanowski, pp.121ff. and *passim*.
532 Introduction to Johann Gottfried v. Herder, *Ausgewählte Werke in einem Bande*, Stuttgart/Tübingen 1844, p.27.
533 Similarly Bojanowski, p.132, p.136 and *passim*.
534 Quoted in Bode/von Stein, p.146; see also Bojanowski, p.105
535 Quoted in Bode/von Stein, p.146.
536 Quoted in Bojanowski, p.151.
537 Letter of 22 July 1782 to Duke Carl August, in Hans Gerhard Gräf (ed.), *Johann Heinrich Mercks Briefe*, Leipzig 1911, pp.151f.
538 Quoted in Bode/Amalia, vol.2, p.200.
539 Bornhak, p.187.
540 Quoted in Bode/Amalia, vol.2, p.215.
541 Ibid., p.217.
542 Michael Wenzel, *Adam Friedrich Oeser und Weimar*, Heidelberg 1994, p.51.
543 For the image and a description see Bode/von Stein, p.179.
544 Quoted in Ernst Grumach/Renate Grumach, p.242. Original in French: 'Goethe file toujours le parfait amour, et la pauvre Stein plus bête qu'il n'a été reçoit en patience les mauvais propos du public, et de Mr. Goethe, et les humeurs de sa femme.'
545 See Bode/von Stein, p.191, p.267.
546 See Petersen, vol.1, p.593, note 335.
547 Kluge, entry: 'Omen', p.601.
548 See his bust from the summer 1780, in Geese, illustration 49f.
549 See the commentary in *BA*, 19, pp.777ff., quoted in Jürgen von Esenwein/Harald Gerlach (eds) *Johann Wolfgang von Goethe: Zeit – Leben – Werk*, CD-ROM, Berlin 1999.
550 *WA*, I 47, p.107.
551 Quoted in Geese, p.27.
552 Quoted in Bode/Amalia, vol.2, p.214.
553 See Geese, pp.25ff.
554 See the list in Geese, p.218, pp.212ff.
555 See Hans Wahl, *Tiefurt*, Leipzig 1929, p.144.
556 See the Gesamtkatalog-Auszug des Goethe-Nationalmuseum in Weimar,

No. 20.663 and *passim*: 'Eventuell Geschenk d. Herzogin Anna Amalia an Goethe im August 1778. Diese besaß die Serie selbst.'

557 See also Marlo Werner, p.137.

558 See the commentary to *BA*, vol.2, p.708, quoted in Jürgen von Esenwein/Harald Gerlach (eds): *Johann Wolfgang von Goethe: Zeit – Leben – Werk,* CD-ROM, Berlin 1999.

559 For the list of Anna Amalia's courtiers in 1777, see Marlo Werner, pp.140f.

560 Max Hecker, 'Anna Amalia, Herzogin von Sachsen-Weimar und Eisenach', in *Deutsches Mädchenbuch 1892*, p.236.

561 Lyncker, p.86.

562 Repr.: Wilhelm Bode (ed.), *Goethe in Vertraulichen Briefen seiner Zeitgenossen 1749-1793*, vol.1, Berlin 1999, p.287.

563 See Boyle 1, p.239.

564 Also 1811 and 1813. See Steiger.

565 See Conrady, p.319.

566 Quoted in H. Bräuning-Oktavio in Julius Zeitler (ed.), *Goethe-Handbuch*, vol.2, Stuttgart 1917, entry: 'Lavater', p.424.

567 See Wilpert, p.2, pp.610f.

568 Johann Kaspar Lavater, *Pontius Pilatus oder die Bibel im Kleinen und der Mensch im Großen*, vol.1, 1782; repr. Zürich 2001, p.3.

569 *WA*, IV 8, p.415.

570 Quoted in Kühn, p.103.

571 Repr.: *FA*, II 2, Hartmut Reinhardt (ed.), *Das erste Weimarer Jahrzehnt*, Frankfurt am Main 1997, p.349.

572 Petersen, p.630, note 726.

573 Quoted in Steiger, vol.1, p.540.

574 The boy was Karl v. Lyncker; see Lyncker, p.48.

575 Boyle 1, p.341.

576 For the dates see the letter of Anna Amalia to Merck, 3 March 1783, printed in Bode/Amalia, vol.2, pp.217f.

577 Wilhelm Bode, *Karl August von Weimar, Jugendjahre*, Berlin 1913, p.222.

578 Andreas, p.188.

579 Lyncker, pp.96f.

580 Böttiger, p.38.

581 Repr.: in Biedermann, p.326, letter 646; simultaneously printed in Ernst Grumach/Renate Grumach, vol.2, p.387. Original in French: '... *madame de Stein qui joue toujours son rôle le mieux qu'elle peut, mangeant des pommes de terre presque tous les soirs dans sa maison avec G.[oethe] et la D[uche]sse. Le mari Stein, s'étant mis audessus de tout plus que jamais* ...'

582 Letter of 2 April 1776, quoted in Dobenecker, p.421. Original in French: '... *l'auteur de nos peines*'.

583 Original in French: 'Nous faisons si bien notre devoir ma chere Lotte qu'a la fin on pourroit douter de notre amour.'

584 From the French translated in *FA*, II 2, Hartmut Reinhardt (ed.), *Das erste Weimarer Jahrzehnt*, Frankfurt am Main 1997, pp.1059f.

585 See Heinz Nicolai, 'Nachwort zu Friedrich H. Jacobi', *Woldemar*, 1779; repr. Stuttgart 1969, pp.6f.

[586] See Regine Otto/Christa Rudnik, 'Karl Ludwig von Knebel – Goethes "alter Weimarischer Urfreund"', in J. Golz (ed.), *Das Goethe- und Schiller-Archiv 1896–1996*, Weimar 1996, p.299. For Anna Amalia's participation, see her letter of 1 January 1780 to Knebel; repr. in K.A. Varnhagen von Ense/Th. Mundt, *K.L. von Knebels Literarischer Nachlaß und Briefwechsel*, Leipzig ²1840, p.185; see also Marlo Werner, p.147, pp.161f., letter of Jacobi to Heinse, 20-24 October 1780; repr. Wilhelm Bode (ed.), *Goethe in Vertraulichen Briefen seiner Zeitgenossen 1749-1793*, vol.1, Berlin 1999, p.262.
[587] See Wilpert, p.528.
[588] Commentary to *WA*, IV 7, pp.313f., letter 2180.
[589] See also Steiger, p.456.
[590] Quoted in Petersen, pp.541f.
[591] Marlo Werner, p.202.
[592] See Bode/von Stein, pp.232ff.
[593] Letter to Charlotte Schiller, quoted in Marlo Werner, p.263; see also Alfons Nobel, *Charlotte von Stein*, München 1985, p.98.
[594] Quoted in Woldemar F. v. Biedermann, *Goethes Gespräche, Eine Sammlung zeitgenössischer Berichte aus seinem Umgang*, III: 1811-1818, Leipzig 1889, p.185.
[595] Alfons Nobel, *Charlotte von Stein*, München 1985, p.168.
[596] Letter of Frau von Stein to Zimmermann on 10 May 1776.
[597] See Damm, p.126.
[598] Klauß, p.174.
[599] Boyle 1, p.541.
[600] Quoted in Biedermann, vol.1, letter 1010.
[601] Quoted in Doris Maurer, *Charlotte von Stein*, Frankfurt am Main 1997, p.261.
[602] Palleske, p.164; see also Marlo Werner, p.204.
[603] Palleske, p.164; see the sketch of a letter from Goethe to Wieland 10 April 1776.
[604] See Boyle 1, p.555.
[605] Egloffstein, p.353 (both quotations).
[606] Quoted in Kleßmann, pp.45f.
[607] Repr.: in Wilhelm Bode (ed.), *Goethe in Vertraulichen Briefen seiner Zeitgenossen 1794-1816*, vol.2, Berlin 1999, pp.550ff.
[608] Ibid., p.355.
[609] Goethe - und Schiller-Archiv Weimar, Bestand: Anna Amalia, Signatur 28/767, Blatt I.
[610] Ibid., Blatt IX.
[611] Ibid., Blatt XIII.
[612] Ibid., Blatt VII.
[613] See Olga G. Taxis-Bordogna, *Frauen von Weimar*, München 1948, p.209.
[614] See also Bode/von Stein, p.672.
[615] Quoted in Müller, p.177; see also Renate Seydel, *Charlotte von Stein und Johann Wolfgang von Goethe, Die Geschichte einer großen Liebe*, München 1993, p.14.

Frau von Stein's Literary Works

616 Quoted in Biedermann, p.307, letter 598.

617 For a comparison with Virgil's version, see Susanne Kord (ed.), 'Einleitung zu Charlotte von Stein', *Dramen* (complete edition), Hildesheim 1998, pp.viiif.

618 Ibid., p.viii.

619 Ibid., p.508.

620 Quoted in K.A. Varnhagen von Ense/Th. Mundt, *K.L. von Knebe's Literarischer Nachlaß und Briefwechsel*, Leipzig ²1840, p.198.

621 Kord, p.501, p.511.

622 See Wolfgang Huschke, 'Unebenbürtige Sprosse Carl Augusts von Weimar', in *Familie und Volk*, 6 (1957), pp.257ff. A newly discovered daughter of 'Carl August' seems indisputably to be Goethe's child. See Walter E. Ehrhardt, 'Goethes Clausthaler Tochter? – Auguste Böhmer starb vor 200 Jahren', in *Unser Harz*, 2000, pp.183ff. On 10 August 1784 Goethe did arrive in Clausthal-Zellerfeld, but with him was the libertine Carl August. In a letter to his mother, Anna Amalia, 17 August 1784, from Braunschweig Carl August writes: '... but I couldn't leave the Harz so quickly; I had to add in two days.' This daughter was called Auguste (1785-1800), although her mother, Caroline Böhmer (1763-1809), later v. Schlegel and v. Schelling, was not a subject of Duke Carl August. The writer of the article shows (p.187) that Auguste must have been born a princess, for the monument meant for her grave depicted two snakes, which in mythology indicated a princely birth. Since Goethe, though a poet-'prince', in reality only had a title of nobility of the lowest rank, the mythological reference does not apply to him.

623 See Scheidemantel, pp.6f.

624 J.M.R. Lenz, *Gesammelte Schriften*, Ludwig Tieck (ed.), III, Berlin 1828, p.288 (1st quotation), p.289 (2nd quotation); for the interpretation of the Pandolfo figure using Knebel, see Christoph Weiss, 'Zu den Vorbereitungen einer Lenz-Gesamtausgabe: Wiederentdeckte und unbekannte Handschriften', in I. Stephan/H.-G. Winter (eds), *'Die Wunde Lenz', J.M.R. Lenz Leben, Werk und Rezeption*, Bern 2003, p.20.

625 Boyle 2, p.204.

626 Boyle 2, p.603.

627 See Hellmuth F. v. Maltzahn, *Karl Ludwig von Knebel*, Jena 1929, pp.171ff.; Klauß, p.267.

628 See Olga G. Taxis-Bordogna, *Frauen von Weimar*, München 1948, pp.283ff.; see also Bode/Amalia, vol.3, p.140.

629 See Bamberg, vol.2, pp.283ff.

630 Repr.: in Ludwig Rohmann, *Briefe an Fritz von Stein*, Leipzig 1907, p.195.

631 Kord, p.49 (both quotations).

632 Ibid., p.50.

633 Ibid., pp.46f.

634 Ibid., p.59.

635 See Werner Schäfer/Erwin Böhm, *Agnes Bernauer, Geschichte, Dichtung,*

Bild, Straubing 1995.

636 See Helene Matthies, *Lottine – Lebensbild der Philippine Charlotte, Schwester Friedrichs des Großen, Gemahlin Karls I. von Braunschweig*, Braunschweig 1958, pp.114f.

637 August Wilhelm Heffter, *Beiträge zum deutschen Staats- und Fürstenrecht, I., Ueber Ebenbürtigkeit, Standesgleichheit und Standesungleichheit in den deutschen souveränen und ersten standesherrlichen Häusern*, Berlin 1829, pp.26f.

638 See für die folgenden Angaben Rudolf Reiser, *Adliges Stadtleben im Barockzeitalter – Internationales Gesandtenleben auf dem Immerwährenden Reichstag zu Regensburg*, München 1969, pp.127ff.

639 Ibid., pp.120ff.

640 Ibid., p.157.

641 Olga G. Taxis-Bordogna, *Frauen von Weimar*, München 1948, p.296.

642 See See Bode/von Stein, pp.215f, p.360.

643 See Bode/von Stein, p.265.

644 Ibid., p.564.

645 Wilhelm Bode, Bode/Amalia, vol.1, Berlin 1908, p.108.

646 Marlo Werner, p.16.

647 Boyle 2, p.90.

648 Bode/von Stein, p.260.

649 Ibid., p.449.

650 Quoted in Kühn, p.360.

651 Felix Freiherr von Stein-Kochberg, *In Kochberg, dem Reiche von Charlotte von Stein*, Leipzig 1936, p.50.

652 Bode/von Stein, p.560.

653 Quoted in Klauß, p.126.

654 Kord, p.57.

655 Ibid., p.142.

656 Ibid., pp.xviiif.

657 Ibid., pp.46f.

658 Ibid., p.13.

659 See Winfried Schröder, 'Goethes 'Groß-Cophta' – Cagliostro und die Vorgeschichte der Frenchen Revolution', in *Goethe Jahrbuch* 1988, p.200, p.202, pp.204ff., p.208.

660 See Liselotte Blumenthal, 'Goethes Großkophta', in *Weimarer Beiträge*, 1961, p.25.

Love Poetry: Belonging to One Alone

661 Horst Rüdiger, epilogue to *Goethes Römische Elegien*, Frankfurt am Main [4]1993, p.125.

662 Conrady, pp.496f.

663 See the documents in Thüringisches Hauptstaatsarchiv Weimar, *HA* AXVIII, No. 142a, No. 141 (fair copy); see also Bode/Amalia, vol.2, p.54; Bornhak, p.121.

664 Bode/von Stein, p.421.

665 Karl A. Böttiger, letter to Friedrich Schulz, 27 July 1795, quoted in Dominik

Jost, *Deutsche Klassik: Goethes 'Römische Elegien'*, München ²1978, p.86.
666 Ibid., letter to Charlotte Schiller, 7 November 1794, p.85.
667 See Falk's report; repr. Heinz Amelung, *Goethe als Persönlichkeit, Berichte und Briefe von Zeitgenossen*, vol.1: 1749-1797, Berlin 1925, pp.189f.
668 Bornhak, p.163.
669 Christoph Martin Wieland, *Briefwechsel*, vol.7.1, W. Hagen (ed.), Berlin 1992, pp.113f.
670 Quoted in Bode/Amalia, vol.2, p.200.
671 Quoted in Dominik Jost, *Deutsche Klassik: Goethes 'Römische Elegien'*, München ²1978, p.86.
672 See the poet Domenico Gnoli, *Gli amori di Volfango Goethe*, Livorno 1875, p.205, fn.1.
673 See Dominik Jost, pp.168f.
674 See Sandra Dreise-Beckmann, 'Anna Amalia's musikalische Reise. Eine deutsche Fürstin in Italien 1788-1790', in S. Düll/W. Pass, *Frau und Musik im Zeitalter der Aufklärung*, Sankt Augustin 1998, pp.164f. (quotation), p.167, p.162, p.157.
675 See the commentary to *WA*, I 53, pp.468ff.
676 'Nihil contra Deum, nisi Deus ipse', see Riemer, p.272, p.315; *FA*, II 6, Rose Unterberger (ed.), *Napoleonische Zeit*, Frankfurt am Main 1993, p.183, p.886.
677 As also Napoleon, Paganini, Byron, Czar Peter the Great and Christ; see the commentary to *J.W. Goethe: Dichtung und Wahrheit*, Walter Hettche (ed.), Stuttgart 1998, p.1189.
678 This could only refer to Weißer's studio, for after Klauer died in 1801 his two sons carried on the business only until 1806. See Walter Steiner/Uta Kühn-Stillmark, *Friedrich Justin Bertuch, Ein Leben im klassischen Weimar zwischen Kultur und Kommerz*, Köln 2001, p.68; see also Marlo Werner, p.321.
679 See Michael Hertl, 'Gedenken in Totenmasken', note 82, Goethe-Museum Düsseldorf 2000/2001, Faltblattseite 2; a second mask (1816) by Schadow is based on a cast of Weißer's face mask of 1807. See Biedrzynski, entry: 'Die Egloffsteins', p.473; Wilpert, p.929; in other cases the sculptors modelled Goethe live. See Geese, pp.53ff.
680 See also Steiger, vol.5, pp.130f.
681 See the comments of Adolf Stahr (1805-1876); repr. in Kleßmann, p.207.
682 Weißer had been Tieck's assistant in the creation of a large number of statues for the new residence in Weimar. Later he organizedthe sale of his casts in Germany. They were in constant contact. See Bernhard Maaz, *Friedrich Tieck, Briefwechsel mit Goethe*, Berlin 1997, p.112, fn.67, fn.69; p.11, fn.51; p.132, fn.543; p.94, p.87.
683 This bust seems to be wrongly attributed to Weißer. Gabriele Oswald, probably the only expert on Weißer's work, attributes it to Tieck. See Gabriele Oswald, 'Die Plastiksammlung der Herzogin Anna Amalia Bibliothek in Weimar', Diploma thesis, Weimar 1995, p.42; see also pp.37ff.; see also the Gesamtkatalog-Auszug des Goethe-Nationalmuseum in Weimar, no.1.719, in which Weißer 'or Tieck' is named as the artist. It is known that sometimes Tieck's models were only completed by Weißer. See

Bernhard Maaz, *Friedrich Tieck, Briefwechsel mit Goethe*, Berlin 1997, pp.129f., fn.456; p.132, fn.543.

684 Biedrzynski, p.473.

685 See Angela Borchert, 'Die Entstehung der Musenhofvorstellung aus den Angedenken an Anna Amalia von Sachsen-Weimar-Eisenach', in J. Berger (ed.), *Der Musenhof Anna Amalias*, Köln 2001, pp.165ff.

686 Friedenthal, p.422.

687 See Ilse-Marie Barton, *Auf den Spuren von Goethes Minchen*, Oldenburg 1995, p.42.

688 Ibid., pp.12f.

689 Ibid., p.16.

690 Ibid., p.25, p.13, p.31 (quotation).

691 See Ernst Beutler, preface to *Johann Wolfgang Goethe, West-östlicher Divan*, Leipzig 1943, pp.xf.

692 Theodor Creizenach, quoted in Dagmar von Gersdorff, *Marianne von Willemer und Goethe. Geschichte einer Liebe*, Frankfurt am Main/Leipzig 2003, p.59.

693 Conversation on 3 October 1815 quoted in Boisserée, p.276.

694 Herman Grimm, *Goethe und Suleika. Zur Erinnerung an Marianne von Willemer*, 1869; repr. Berlin 1999/2000, pp.5ff.

695 For the preceding time see Hans-J. Weitz (ed.), *Goethe. Sollst mir ewig Suleika heißen, Goethes Briefwechsel mit Marianne und Johann Jakob Willemer*, Frankfurt am Main 1995, p.xi; Heinrich Düntzer, 'Goethe und Marianne von Willemer', in *Illustrierte Deutsche Monatshefte*, 1870, p.639.

696 Quoted in Hans-J. Weitz (ed.), *Marianne und Johann Jakob Willemer, Briefwechsel mit Goethe, Dokumente, Lebens-Chronik, Erläuterungen*, Frankfurt am Main 1965, p.214.

697 Boisserée, p.271.

698 See Hans-J. Weitz (ed.), *Goethe. Sollst mir ewig Suleika heißen, Goethes Briefwechsel mit Marianne und Johann Jakob Willemer*, Frankfurt am Main 1995, p.319.

699 Ibid., p.ix.

700 Quoted in Kühn, p.505.

701 Riemer, p.47.

702 Quoted in Dagmar von Gersdorff, *Marianne von Willemer und Goethe. Geschichte einer Liebe*, Frankfurt am Main/Leipzig 2003, p.220.

703 Riemer, p.49.

704 Quoted in Egloffstein, p.150.

705 See Hans-J. Weitz (ed.), *Marianne und Johann Jakob Willemer, Briefwechsel mit Goethe, Dokumente, Lebens-Chronik, Erläuterungen*, Frankfurt am Main 1965, p.882; Herman Grimm, *Goethe und Suleika. Zur Erinnerung an Marianne von Willemer*, 1869; repr. Berlin 1999/2000, pp.20ff.

706 Hans-J. Weitz (ed.), *Marianne und Johann Jakob Willemer*, pp.877ff.

707 Herman Grimm, *Goethe und Suleika. Zur Erinnerung an Marianne von Willemer*, 1869, undated; repr. Darmstadt, p.13. (Hereafter: Grimm)

708 Letter of 23 February 1832 to Marianne and Johann Jakob v. Willemer.

709 Grimm, pp.15f.; see also Heinrich Düntzer, 'Goethe und Marianne von Willemer', in *Illustrierte Deutsche Monatshefte 1870*, p.650; commentary to *WA*, I 6, p.425.

710 See Dagmar von Gersdorff, *Marianne von Willemer und Goethe. Geschichte einer Liebe*, Frankfurt am Main/Leipzig 2003, pp.65f.; Hans-J. Weitz (ed.), *Marianne und Johann Jakob Willemer, Briefwechsel mit Goethe, Dokumente, Lebens-Chronik, Erläuterungen*, Frankfurt am Main 1965, p.551f.

711 See Dagmar von Gersdorff, pp.185ff.; Hans-J. Weitz (ed.), *Goethe. Sollst mir ewig Suleika heißen, Goethes Briefwechsel mit Marianne und Johann Jakob Willemer*, Frankfurt am Main 1995, p.xxiii.

712 See Dagmar von Gersdorff, pp.174ff.

713 Grimm, p.20.

714 Ibid., p.12.

715 Riemer, p.49.

716 Friedenthal, p.512.

717 Hans-J. Weitz (ed.), *Goethe. Sollst mir ewig Suleika heißen, Goethes Briefwechsel mit Marianne und Johann Jakob Willemer*, Frankfurt am Main 1995, pp.xxiiif.

718 See Ernst Beutler, *Erläuterungen zu Johann Wolfgang Goethe, West-östlicher Divan*, Leipzig 1943, p.580, p.590.

719 *WA*, I 41.1, p.88.

720 Buch Suleika, poem 43. See *WA*, I 6, p.429, pp.343f.; see also Hans-J. Weitz (ed.), *Marianne und Johann Jakob Willemer, Briefwechsel mit Goethe, Dokumente, Lebens-Chronik, Erläuterungen*, Frankfurt am Main 1965, pp.32f. and p.349.

721 A recent attempt to deal with the meeting between Goethe and Marianne as lovers has Anna Amalia (1749-1807), at the beginning of 1816, listening to Goethe's reading from the *Divan*: Dagmar v. Gersdorff, *Marianne von Willemer und Goethe. Geschichte einer Liebe*, Frankfurt am Main/Leipzig 2003, p.153; for further carefree handling of dates, see p.115, pp.134f., p.157, p.253.

722 Gert Ueding, 'Verborgen glühende Bedeutung', in *J.W. Goethe – Verweile doch, 111 Gedichte mit Interpretationen*, M. Reich-Ranicki (ed.), Frankfurt am Main [2]1992, p.355.

723 See Petersen, Introduction to *Goethes Briefe an Charlotte von Stein*, vol.1, Leipzig 1923, p.xli.

724 Quoted in Wilhelm Bode (ed.), *Goethe in Vertraulichen Briefen seiner Zeitgenossen 1794-1816*, vol.2, Berlin 1999, p.645.

725 Similarly Friedrich Sengle, *Das Genie und sein Fürst, Die Geschichte der Lebensgemeinschaft Goethes mit dem Herzog Carl August*, Stuttgart/Weimar 1993, p.469. (Hereafter: Sengle)

726 See her memoirs, repr. Jochen Klauss, '*... keine Liebschaft war es nicht*': *eine Textsammlung. Johann Wolfgang v. Goethe/Ulrike von Levetzow*, Zürich 1997, pp.16-18 (quotation p.17).

727 Conrady, p.547.

728 Quoted in Jochen Klauss, '*... keine Liebschaft war es nicht*', p.34.

729 Therefore the offer of marriage cannot be dated around the end of August,

but see Jochen Klauss, '... *keine Liebschaft war es nicht*', p.108, because after the completion of his treatment [Kur] the Grandduke left for Berlin on 9 August. See Goethe's letter to his daughter-in-law, Ottilie, 14 August 1823, and his letter to Schultz, 9 August 1823.

730 Quoted in Kleßmann, p.250.

731 Sandra Dreise-Beckmann, 'Anna Amalia und das Musikleben am Weimarer Hof', in J. Berger (ed.), *Der Musenhof Anna Amalias*, Köln 2001, p.63.

732 Friedenthal, p.547.

733 See the account by W. v. Humboldt; repr. Kleßmann, pp.252ff.

734 Conversation on 1 December 1831.

735 See Regine Ziller, *Goethes Beziehung zur Musik*, Goethe Museum Düsseldorf 1992, note 68, last page of fold.

736 See Karl Eberwein, 'Goethes Hausmusik', in Wilhelm Bode (ed.), *Stunden mit Goethe, Für die Freunde seiner Kunst und Weisheit*, vol.7, Berlin 1911, pp.270ff.; the same in Pleticha, pp.303f. and in Kleßmann, pp.89ff., p.111. See also Ulrike Müller-Harang, 'Geselligkeit', in K.-H. Hahn, *Goethe in Weimar*, Leipzig 1986, pp.246f.

737 Quoted in the commentary to *WA*, III 9, p.384.

738Quoted in Egloffstein, pp.198f.

739 Quoted in Geese, p.130; see also Berger, p.295, fn.274.

740 Quoted in Heuschele, p.290.

741 '... le paradis est pour les âmes tendres, et condamnés sonst ceux qui n'aiment rien.' Quoted in Biedermann, vol.1, p.378, letter 766.

742 Eckermann, 1 December 1831.

743 Quoted in Woldemar F. v. Biedermann, *Goethes Gespräche, Eine Sammlung zeitgenössischer Berichte aus seinem Umgang*, vol.10, Addenda 1755-1832, Leipzig 1896, pp.196f.

Wilhelm Meister: 'There is Life in It'

744 Kluge, entry: 'pseudo-', p.653.

745 See *FA*, I 10, Gerhard Neumann/Hans-Georg Dewitz (eds), *Wilhelm Meisters Wanderjahre*, Frankfurt am Main 1989, pp.778f.

746 Henriette Herwig, *'Wilhelm Meisters Wanderjahre': Geschlechterdifferenz, sozialer Wandel, historische Anthropologie*, Tübingen/Basel ²2002, p.11. (Hereafter: Herwig)

747 Regarding the *Wanderjahre*, see Wilhelm Emrich, 'Das Problem der Symbolinterpretation im Hinblick auf Goethes "Wanderjahre"', in *Protest und Verheißung*, Bonn ³1968, p.57.

748 Quoted in Wilhelm Bode, Bode/Amalia, vol.2, p.219.

749 Quoted in *FA* I, 6, Gerhard Neumann/Hans-Georg Dewitz (ed.), *Wilhelm Meisters Wanderjahre*, Frankfurt am Main 1989, p.894. (Hereafter: *FA/WMW*)

750 Herwig, p.6.

751 *FA/WMW*, p.855.

752 Riemer, p.130.

753 *FA*, I 9, Wilhelm Voßkamp/Herbert Jaumann (eds), *Wilhelm Meisters*

Theatralische Sendung, Wilhelm Meisters Lehrjahre, Unterhaltungen deutscher Ausgewanderten, Frankfurt am Main 1992, p.1058.

[754] Quoted in Keil, vol.2, Leipzig 1875, p.64.

[755] See also Schwanke, p.352.

[756] See the commentary in *FA/WMW*, p.1117.

[757] Quoted in Houben, p.53.

[758] Quoted in Bode/Amalia, vol.2, p.203.

[759] Quoted in Biedermann, vol. 1, letter 403.

[760] Homer, *Odyssee*, quoted in Roland Hampe's translation, Stuttgart 1988, p.317.

[761] See the commentary in *FA/WMW*, p.1120.

[762] Quoted in Biedermann, p.177, letter 344; see also Carl Diem, 'Goethe und der Eislauf', in *Olympische Rundschau*, Berlin 1943, pp.12ff.

[763] Quoted in Biedermann, vol.1, p.252, letter 472.

[764] See Claus Sommerhage, 'Familie Tantalos, Über Mythos und Psychologie in Goethes Novelle Der Mann von Fünfzig Jahren', in *Beihefte zur Zeitschrift für deutsche Philologie*, 1984, pp.95ff.

[765] *FA/WMW*, p.1121.

[766] *Maximen und Reflexionen.*

[767] See *FA/WMW*, pp.1204ff.; see also Monika Schmitz-Emans, 'Vom Spiel mit dem Mythos, Zu Goethes Märchen "Die neue Melusine"', in *Goethe Jahrbuch 1988*, pp.317f.

[768] See Wilpert, pp.760f.

[769] *WA*, II 1, p.ix, preface to the *Farbenlehre.*

[770] See Rupprecht Matthaei, *Die Farbenlehre im Goethe-Nationalmuseum*, Jena 1941, p.69, p.135; also Peter Schmidt, *Goethes Farbensymbolik*, Berlin 1965, pp.7ff.

[771] See the commentary to J.W. Goethe: *Dichtung und Wahrheit*, Walter Hettche (ed.), Stuttgart 1998, p.886.

[772] Ibid., p.886.

[773] See the commentary to Johann Wolfgang Goethe, *Poetische Werke*, Berliner Ausgabe, vol.10, Berlin, p.662, quoted in Jürgen von Esenwein/Harald Gerlach (eds): *Johann Wolfgang von Goethe: Zeit – Leben – Werk*, CD-ROM, Berlin 1999.

[774] See Peter Schmidt, *Goethes Farbensymbolik*, Berlin 1965, pp.143f., pp.213ff.

[775] Boisserée, pp.237f.

[776] Quoted in *FA*, I 9, Wilhelm Voßkamp/Herbert Jaumann (eds), *Wilhelm Meisters Theatralische Sendung, Wilhelm Meisters Lehrjahre, Unterhaltungen deutscher Ausgewanderten*, Frankfurt am Main 1992, p.1403.

[777] Müller, p.61.

[778] Homer, *Odyssee*, quoted in Roland Hampe's translation, p.212.

[779] Riemer, p.47.

[780] Lyncker, p.21.

[781] *FA*, I 9, Wilhelm Voßkamp/Herbert Jaumann (eds), *Wilhelm Meisters Theatralische Sendung, Wilhelm Meisters Lehrjahre, Unterhaltungen deutscher Ausgewanderten*, Frankfurt am Main 1992, p.1402.

782 Quoted in Grawe, p.91.
783 Herwig, p.356.
784 See Paul Pasing, *Goethe und Ilmenau*, Weimar 1902, p.11.
785 Quoted in Andreas, 'Sturm und Drang im Spiegel der Weimarer Hofkreise', in *Goethe, Viermonatsschrift der Goethe-Gesellschaft, Neue Folge des Jahrbuchs*, vol.8 (1943), p.239.
786 Quoted in Biedermann, vol.1, p.358, letter 722.
787 Quoted in Müller, p.184.
788 See Kluge, entry: 'Aggregat', p.18.
789 Quoted in *FA/WMW*, p.855.
790 See also Herwig, p.352.
791 Letter to Anna Amalia ('Frau von Stein') 8 March 1781.
792 This is Goethe's variation of a motif, which is scarcely known in the West, from the twelfth sura of the *Koran*. Western readers will naturally be reminded of the original sin in the Garden of Eden, but see Herwig, pp.354f.
793 Müller, pp.148f.
794 Schwanke, pp.368f.
795 Johannes Urzidil, *Das Glück der Gegenwart, Goethes Amerikabild*, Stuttgart 1958, p.11. (Hereafter: Urzidil)
796 Friedrich Schiller, *Werke*, vol.23, W. Müller-Seidel (ed.), Weimar 1956, p.60.
797 Urzidil, p.12.
798 Quoted in Woldemar F. v. Biedermann, *Goethes Gespräche, Eine Sammlung zeitgenössischer Berichte aus seinem Umgang*, III: 1811-1818, Leipzig 1889, p.185.
799 Schwanke, p.433.
800 For Faktor Daniel, see Schwanke, pp.467ff.
801 Klaus Seehafer, *Johann Wolfgang Goethe. Mein Leben ein einzig Abenteuer*, Berlin ^{2}2002, p.154.
802 Conrady, p.368.
803 Hans-Hellmut Allers, *Goethe und Berlin*, Berlin 1999, p.52.
804 Quoted in Biedermann, vol.1, p.262, letter 490.
805 Commentary in *FA/WMW*, p.1202.
806 See for Meyer's technical description *WA*, I 25.2, pp.262ff.
807 See Herwig, pp.173ff.
808 *WA*, I 41.2, p.296.
809 Urzidil, p.16.
810 Ibid.; see Walter Steiner/Uta Kühn-Stillmark, *Friedrich Justin Bertuch, Ein Leben im klassischen Weimar zwischen Kultur und Kommerz*, Köln 2001, pp.138f.
811 For further proofs, see Herwig, p.164, fn.1.
812 Müller, p.35.
813 George Bancroft (1800-1891), quoted in Urzidil, p.27.
814 On 21 June 1827, Goethe wrote: 'Vor einigen Tagen erging ich mich in folgenden Zeilen: Amerika, du ...', *WA*, IV 42, p.378.
815 Herwig, p.192.
816 Bode/von Stein, pp.249ff.

817 See Andreas, p.337; Klauß, pp.92f.
818 So also the commentary in *FA/WMW*, p.599.
819 See Herwig, pp.369f.
820 Ibid., p.362; commentary in *FA/WMW*, p.1189.

Epilogue: 'All for Love'

821 Riemer, p.36.
822 Quoted in Beaulieu-Marconnay, pp.155ff., p.160; see also Wilhelm Bode, *Karl August von Weimar, Jugendjahre*, Berlin 1913, pp.338ff.
823 Riemer, p.174.
824 Wilpert, p.1062, p.526.
825 See Franco Zizzo, *Die Unikative: Vereinfachung als Motor für die Vereinheitlichung von Rechtsnormensystemen*, Weimar 2003, pp.26ff. and *passim*.
826 Letter to Knebel, 3 January 1807.
827 Sengle, p.235.
828 Quoted in Gonthier-Louis Fink, 'Goethe und Napoleon', in *Goethe Jahrbuch 1990*, p.83.
829 Friedenthal, p.450.
830 Quoted in Heuschele, p.288.
831 Quoted in Keil, p.65.
832 So Ernst Beutler, preface to Johann Wolfgang Goethe, *West-östlicher Divan*, Leipzig 1943, p.xii.
833 Böttiger, p.92.
834 See Alfons Nobel, *Charlotte von Stein*, München 1985, p.222, p.208.
835 Conrady, p.467, pp.807f.
836 Böttiger, p.221.
837 Quoted in Egloffstein, p.82.
838 Quoted in Kleßmann, p.77.
839 Quoted in Friedenthal, p.438.
840 Quoted in Damm, pp.267ff.
841 See Conrady, p.808.
842 Goethe- und Schiller-Archiv Weimar, Bestand: Anna Amalia, Signatur 28/767, Blatt VI.
843 The artist's signature is found on a drawing of Homer within the painting and next to it is the date 1806; a different dating, without reference to the one just referred to, is given by Antje Vanhoefen, 'Zum Oßmannstädter Porträt der Herzogin Anna Amalia von Georg Melchior Kraus', in *Die Pforte* 6/2002, p.43.
844 Ernst Lieberkühn, *Die Herzogin Anna Amalia von Sachsen Weimar und ihr Einfluß auf Deutschlands Literaturzustände, Eine Vorlesung*, Weimar 1847, p.463.
845 See Egloffstein, p.352.
846 So Johann C. Gädicke (ed.), *Freimaurer-Lexicon*, Berlin 1818, entry: 'Handschuh'.
847 See the entries 5-7 February 1777.
848 Riemer, p.343.

849 See her lady-in-waiting Luise v. Göchhausen in a letter to a friend, quoted in Gabriele Henkel/Wulf Otte, *Herzogin Anna Amalia – Braunschweig und Weimar*, Braunschweig 1995, p.107.
850 Riemer, p.177.
851 See Bode/Amalia, vol.3, p.166; Frances Gerard, *A Grand Duchess, The life of Anna Amalia*, vol.2, London 1902, p.559.
852 Frances Gerard, p.549.
853 Quoted in the commentary to *WA*, IV 35, p.357.
854 Quoted in Houben, p.50.
855 Quoted in Bode/Amalia, vol.3, p.163.
856 See also Bojanowski, pp.296ff.
857 See Friedenthal, p.436.
858 Ibid.
859 Ibid., pp.436ff.; Conrady, pp.809f.
860 Böttiger, p.283.
861 Adelheid v. Schorn (ed.), *Zwei Menschenalter, Erinnerungen und Briefe*, Berlin 1901, p.12.
862 Quoted in Egloffstein, p.82.
863 Biedrzynski, entry: 'Die Egloffsteins', p.354.
864 See Boyle 2, p.603.
865 See her friend the poet and translator Johann Diederich Gries in a letter to Heinrich Abeken 12 June 1829, quoted in Houben, p.408.
866 Schopenhauer, p.441.
867 See the daughter's account, Adelheid v. Schorn (ed.), *Zwei Menschenalter, Erinnerungen und Briefe*, Berlin 1901, pp.11f. (quotation).
868 Kluge, entry: 'Kanaille', p.421.
869 Letter to Carl v. Holtei, 26 September 1828, quoted in *Frauen der Goethezeit in ihren Briefen*, G. Jäckel (ed.), Berlin [2]1969, p.392.
870 For an illustration, see Gerhard Femmel (ed.), *Corpus der Goethezeichnungen*, vol.IVa, Leipzig 1966, No. 77.
871 Lieselotte Blumenthal, 'Goethes Bühnenbearbeitung des Tasso', in E. Grumach (ed.), *Beiträge zur Goetheforschung*, Berlin 1959, p.184.
872 Egloffstein, p.14.
873 Quoted in Werner Deetjen, *Auf Höhen Ettersburgs*, 1924, here repr. Weimar 1993, p.14.
874 Egloffstein, p.14.
875 *WA*, I 36, p.449.
876 Quoted in Houben, pp.93f.
877 Letter to Knebel, 13 September 1789, quoted in Heuschele, p.223.
878 J. Schopenhauer, quoted in Houben, p.92.
879 Anna Amalia, Goethe-Museum Frankfurt, (ed.), *Goethe-Kalender auf das Jahr 1932*, Leipzig 1931, pp.101ff.

Index of Persons and Places

Gluck, Christoph Willibald v. (1714–1787, 1756 ennobled), 119

Index of Goethe's Works

Index of Other Works